THE RISE OF THE SOCIAL GOSPEL IN AMERICAN PROTESTANTISM
1865–1915

AMS PRESS

NEW YORK

The Rise of the Social Gospel
in American Protestantism
1865-1915

BY

CHARLES HOWARD HOPKINS

New Haven : Yale University Press
London : Humphrey Milford : Oxford University Press
1940

Library of Congress Cataloging in Publication Data

Hopkins, Charles Howard, 1905-
  The rise of the social gospel in American Protestantism, 1865–1915.

  Reprint. Originally published: New Haven: Yale
University Press, 1940. (Yale studies in religious
education; 14)
  Includes index.
  1. Social gospel—History—19th century. 2. Social
gospel—History—20th century. 3. Theology, Doctrinal—
United States—History—19th century. 4. Theology,
Doctrinal—United States—History—20th century. 5. Uni-
ted States—Church history—19th century. 6. United
States—Church history—19th century. I. Title.
II. Series: Yale studies in religious education; 14.
BT738.H666   1982   261.8'0973   75-41141
ISBN 0-404-14771-2   AACR2

MANUFACTURED
IN THE UNITED STATES OF AMERICA

TO NORMAN W. TAYLOR

*This volume is published under the joint sponsorship of
The Samuel B. Sneath Memorial Publication Fund
of the Yale University Divinity School
and
The Rauschenbusch Memorial Lectureship Foundation
of the Colgate-Rochester Divinity School.*

PREFACE

THERE are not a few interpretations of the uniquely American movement toward the socializing and ethicizing of Protestantism known as the "social gospel," but heretofore no adequate history has been available. Consequently many have assumed that social Christianity was the accomplishment of a handful of clergymen who at the opening of the twentieth century challenged religious conservatism by the proclamation of the social content of their faith. Study of an extensive and varied literature indicates, however, not only that the social gospel originated in the early years of the gilded age but also that its prophets were legion and their message an integral part of the broad sweep of social and humanitarian efforts that concerned America during the half century between the Civil War and the World War.

So plentiful are the records of the rise of social Christianity that a supplementary bibliography is planned in which the more than 1,500 items utilized in this research will be classified.

The number and quality of the writer's obligations to those who have aided in the making of this book are evidence that such a project is a coöperative enterprise. My appreciation is due first to Professor H. Richard Niebuhr for the inspiration that launched the study and for a multitude of aids during its progress. My largest measure of gratitude is to Professor Ralph H. Gabriel, who directed its development in the form in which it was presented for the degree of doctor of philosophy at Yale University. I am also profoundly indebted to the National Council on Religion in Higher Education and to the administrators of the Hooker-Dwight Fellowship of the Yale Divinity School for the stipends that made possible the completion of the study. I have received many and varied courtesies from the several members of the Rauschenbusch Lectureship Committee of the Colgate-Rochester Divinity School. A large and intangible debt is that to Dean Luther A. Weigle for his long sustained interest and encouragement.

I wish to acknowledge my debt to Dr. Vernon P. Bodein, Dr. D. R. Sharpe, Professors F. W. C. Meyer and Conrad H.

Moehlmann of the Colgate-Rochester Divinity School, and to Mrs. Rauschenbusch for personal data concerning Walter Rauschenbusch; to Dr. and Mrs. Nathaniel M. Pratt for material concerning Josiah Strong; to Professor Vida D. Scudder for help in reconstructing the story of the Society of Christian Socialists; to Mrs. Leighton Williams for personal favors as well as materials relevant to the career of Dr. Williams; to Mrs. Williams, the Reverend Mitchell Bronk, Professor Nathaniel M. Schmidt, and the Reverend E. Tallmadge Root for assistance in understanding the Brotherhood of the Kingdom; to Professors Rufus Jones and Thomas E. Drake for their judgment concerning the place of Quakers in the rise of the social gospel; to the Reverend Edmund B. Chaffee for information respecting the early history of Labor Temple; to Dr. R. H. Martin for data on the National Reform Association; to Dr. Worth M. Tippy for materials relevant to the beginnings of the Federal Council of the Churches of Christ in America and for personal data concerning George D. Herron; to Mr. John S. Ellsworth, Jr., for some sidelights on the career of William S. Rainsford; to Mr. Francis C. Willey for materials on the Labor Church of Lynn, Massachusetts; to Dr. Noel J. Breed for aid in understanding George D. Herron; and to Professors John R. Commons, Richard T. Ely, and Graham Taylor for personal materials and reminiscences. My data concerning the development of curricula in social ethics in the theological schools have been enriched through the kindness of Professor Francis G. Peabody of Harvard, Professor Emeritus Curtis M. Geer, official historian of Hartford Theological Seminary, Professor Charles Lyttle of Meadville, the Reverend W. B. Snedden, Librarian of Princeton Theological Seminary, Professor G. Walter Fiske of Oberlin, Professor Edgar J. Goodspeed of the University of Chicago, and Professor Norman B. Nash of Cambridge.

I am indebted to Mr. Richard H. Edwards for materials and for his critical reading of the section on his "Social Problems Group"; to Mr. Edwards and Professor Clarence P. Shedd for information and reading of the section dealing with the beginnings of social interest in the Student Christian Movement; to Dr. Robert C. Dexter for advice and materials on the formation of the Unitarian Department of Social and Public Service;

to Professor Harry F. Ward for data concerning the Methodist Federation for Social Service; to Dr. Charles S. Macfarland for reading the chapter on the formation of the Federal Council of Churches; to Dr. James Dombrowski for the use of certain materials from his *Early Days of Christian Socialism in America* and for reading the section dealing with the Christian Commonwealth Colony and the origin of the term, "social gospel"; and to Professor George P. Murdock for a critical reading of the chapter, "Sociology in the Service of Religion."

I am especially appreciative of the facilities provided by the Sterling Memorial Library of Yale University. Privileges were likewise accorded me by the Public Library of the City of Boston, the New York Public Library, the John Crerar Library, and the McCartney Library of Geneva College. Professor Reuben E. E. Harkness of the American Baptist Historical Society provided me with certain valuable materials, and I am conscious of many favors at the hands of Dr. William W. Rockwell, Librarian of Union Theological Seminary, and from Professor Theodore L. Trost, Librarian of the Colgate-Rochester Divinity School.

My thanks are due also to Professor George R. Geiger for helpful materials from his book *The Philosophy of Henry George;* to the Reverend Arthur C. Lichtenberger for data from his thesis *The Relation of the Episcopal Church to Social Problems in America;* to Professor Paul F. Laubenstein for references to his S.T.M. thesis *A History of Christian Socialism in America;* to Professor Kenneth E. Barnhart for the use of his Ph.D. dissertation *The Evolution of the Social Consciousness in Methodism;* and to Professor Harvey J. Locke for citations used in his Ph.D. dissertation *A History and Critical Interpretation of the Social Gospel of Northern Baptists in the United States.*

For copyright permissions I am grateful to the Misses Strong for quotations from *The New Era* by Josiah Strong; to the Columbus School for Girls for the generous use I have been allowed of the works of Washington Gladden; to The Macmillan Company for the wide latitude given me to quote certain books by Walter Rauschenbusch; to the Reverend Maxwell Savage for the use of the hymn "How Shall Come the Kingdom Holy?" by Minot J. Savage; to Mr. Eric M. North for the words of the hymn "Where Cross the Crowded Ways of Life," by Frank Mason North; and to Houghton, Mifflin Company for the use of the poem "O Pure Reformers," by John Greenleaf Whittier.

Among the many friendly critics who have read manuscript or proof my obligations are largest to Dr. Wilfred M. Mitchell, Professor Raymond P. Morris, the Reverend and Mrs. Harold B. Ingalls, Mr. George Pohlmann, Miss E. Winifred Hawes, and Professor Emery Fast. For painstaking and arduous service in the preparation of the manuscript I am particularly indebted to Miss Florence G. MacDonald.

C. H. H.

Stockton Junior College,
Stockton, California,
September, 1940

CONTENTS

PART IV: 1900–1915

Maturity and Recognition

O pure reformers! not in vain
Your trust in human kind;
The good which bloodshed could not gain,
Your peaceful zeal shall find.

The truths ye urge are borne abroad
By every wind and tide;
The voice of nature and of God
Speaks out upon your side.

The weapons which your hands have found
Are those which heaven hath wrought,
Light, truth, and love; your battleground,
The free, broad field of thought.

O may no selfish purpose break
The beauty of your plan,
No lie from throne or altar shake
Your steady faith in man.

Press on! and, if we may not share
The glory of your fight,
We'll ask at least, in earnest prayer,
God's blessing on the right.

John Greenleaf Whittier, 1843

THE RISE OF THE SOCIAL GOSPEL
IN AMERICAN PROTESTANTISM
1865–1915

INTRODUCTION

AMERICA'S most unique contribution to the great ongoing stream of Christianity is the "social gospel." This indigenous and typically American movement, initiated in the "gilded age," was called into being by the impact of modern industrial society and scientific thought upon the Protestantism of the United States during the half century following the Civil War. Defined by one of its leaders as "the application of the teaching of Jesus and the total message of the Christian salvation to society, the economic life, and social institutions . . . as well as to individuals,"[1] social Christianity involved a criticism of conventional Protestantism, a progressive theology and social philosophy, and an active program of propagandism and reform. It reached its climax in the optimistic prewar years of the twentieth century.

The social element in the Christian religion is at least as old as the gospel.[2] Jesus inherited the high moral aspirations of the Hebrew prophets, who were in a sense themselves social reformers. The followers of Christ have endeavored to apply his teachings in every age. The apostolic church experimented with a form of voluntary communism; the Christian ethic wrought a decided change in the mores of the Roman world. The Middle Ages, the Reformation, and modern times have all produced their quota of attempts to establish the kingdom of God. The American social gospel is but one of the latest adjustments of the Christian ethic to the exigencies of history.

When Puritan emigrants looked across the Atlantic to a place where the Lord would "create a new Heaven, and a new Earth in new Churches, and a new Common-wealth together," they were expressing the hope for a perfected society that came to be a vital part of "the American dream." With the rise of the

---

1. Shailer Mathews, "Social Gospel," in Shailer Mathews and G. B. Smith, *A Dictionary of Religion and Ethics* (New York, 1921), pp. 416–417. By permission of The Macmillan Company, publishers.
2. See Chester C. McCown, *The Genesis of the Social Gospel* (New York and London, 1929).

young republic and the equalitarian aspirations of the early nineteenth century, the democratic ideal and the kingdom hope blended in a climate of opinion highly favorable to the germination of the modern social gospel.[3]

The seedbed in which the ideological roots of social Christianity found themselves most at home was Unitarianism, which liberal faith was fundamentally ethical and intended to influence the conduct of life.[4] It stressed the dignity and divine possibilities of man, the achievement of salvation through character culture, the unity and immanence of God, and the importance of the present life, and itself exerted a germinal influence upon other schools of American theology.[5] The generous faith of Unitarianism in human nature, with its insistence upon humanitarian service, was illustrated by the inauguration in Boston in 1826 of a Unitarian "ministry at large" to the unchurched classes. This pioneer work, initiated and carried on for a number of years by the Reverend Joseph Tuckerman, was not only the first example of religious social service in America but was also the first serious effort on the part of a religious body to cope with the social and religious problems of the submerged population of a sizable city. Tuckerman "initiated a new sphere" of Protestant philanthropy by his development of most of the principles of scientific charity.[6] A similar spirit characterized later Unitarianism as represented by Theodore Parker, Edward Everett Hale, Orville Dewey, and Frederic Dan Huntington.[7] Transcendentalism, an offshoot from Uni-

3. See H. R. Niebuhr, *The Kingdom of God in America* (Chicago and New York, 1937), pp. 150 ff.

4. See Joseph H. Allen, *Our Liberal Movement in Theology* (Boston, 1882), p. 149, and George Willis Cooke, *Unitarianism in America* (Boston, 1902), chap. xvi.

5. See, for example, William Ellery Channing, "Unitarian Christianity: Discourse at the Ordination of the Reverend Jared Sparks," in *Works* (17th ed. Boston, 1862), III, 59–103.

6. Cooke, *op. cit.,* chap. x, and Christopher R. Eliot, "Joseph Tuckerman, Pioneer in Scientific Philanthropy," Unitarian Historical Society *Proceedings,* IV (1935), 1–32. Tuckerman's best statement is *The Principles and Results of the Ministry at Large in Boston* (Boston, 1838). For further titles see the writer's forthcoming *Bibliography of Social Christianity.*

7. Huntington's most significant early utterance touching social religion was the final lecture of his Lowell Lectures of 1857–58, *Divine Aspects of Human Society,* reprinted in New York in 1891 as *Human Society: its providential structure, relations, and offices.* Huntington later became an Episcopalian and as bishop of Central New York exerted a strong influence for the social gospel.

tarianism, enthusiastically faced Christian orthodoxy with the humanitarian challenge of moral idealism, while as early as 1848 left-wing Unitarian "religion of humanity" was distinctly hospitable to socialism.

These currents that appear to have flowed directly from the emphases upon the goodness of God and the perfectibility of man were not confined to the rationalistic streams of Unitarianism. There were strongly ethical impulses radiating from evangelicalism,[8] while "the rights and duties of the Christian pulpit in relation to politics" had been asserted since the first election sermon preached in colonial New England.[9]

However, the great liberalizer of mid-nineteenth century American theology was Horace Bushnell, from whom the social gospel of Washington Gladden and others was to stem directly. Bushnell's *Christian Nurture* did more than any single factor to break down the extreme individualism of the old Puritanism.[10] He insisted upon experience in theology, leveled the dividing wall between nature and the supernatural, and set Christ in the center of the Christian system.[11] The "new theology" that later built upon these premises provided the religious background for a social gospel movement that was rapidly nearing maturity as the century drew to its close.

About 1850 there began to impinge upon these schools of thought some of the social issues that were later to produce the social gospel. A few liberal clergymen, attracted to the utopian socialism of the period, saw the literal fulfillment of Christ's promise of heaven on earth in a collectivistic society, the principles, ends, and methods of which appeared to them as definitely Christian.[12] An alarm similar to that which was to call

8. See, for example, Gilbert H. Barnes, *The Anti-Slavery Impulse,* 1830–44 (New York and London, 1933). Niebuhr, *loc. cit.,* discusses this.

9. As examples, see Lyman Beecher, "Lectures on Political Atheism and Kindred Subjects . . .," in *Works* (Boston, 1852), I; Caleb Cushing, *A Discourse on the Social Influence of Christianity* . . . (Andover, 1839); R. H. Tyler, *The Bible and Social Reform* (Philadelphia, 1860); Samuel Harris, "Politics and the Pulpit," *New Englander,* XII (1854), 254–275. Others are to be found in the writer's *Bibliography.*

10. Arthur Cushman McGiffert, *The Rise of Modern Religious Ideas* (New York, 1915), p. 277.

11. See John Wright Buckham, *Progressive Religious Thought in America* (Boston and New York, 1919), pp. 3–32.

12. William Henry Channing, *The Christian Church and Social Reform* (Boston, 1848). Also Henry James, *Moralism and Christianity* (New York, 1850),

forth the "institutional" church and the religious social settlement was sounded in 1848 by a New England minister concerned about the religious life of industrial cities,[13] while certain types of expanded church work were begun by the Reverend William A. Muhlenberg prior to the Civil War.[14]

The earliest statement of a social gospel in the modern sense was that of Stephen Colwell, a Philadelphia iron merchant and student of economics who startled religious circles in 1851 with his book, *New Themes for the Protestant Clergy*. Colwell blamed the slow progress of Christianity upon its preoccupation with creeds and doctrine rather than with true charity. The Christian religion, he asserted, "embraces humanity as well as divinity in its range." The charitable spirit of Christianity should be extended to "the whole mass of humanity"— the poor, prisoners, laborers, infidels, socialists, and all men. Socialism, from which Colwell "totally" dissented, nevertheless had "rendered a great service to social science by demonstrating the justice and necessity of reform." As to social problems, this pioneer wrote: "What has so long been neglected remains to be done; the social economy which will resolve the most difficult questions yet proposed, must be developed by Christians from the teachings of Christ and his apostles."[15]

Certain British influences aided in the germination of the American social gospel. The writings of the Scotch divine Thomas Chalmers were widely read in the United States. His *Christian and Civic Economy of Large Towns* (1821) was afterward considered of such value to the institutional church movement that an abridgment was edited in 1900 by Professor Charles R. Henderson of the University of Chicago. Chalmers' other important work, *The Application of Christianity to the Commercial and Ordinary Affairs of Life*, had numerous Ameri-

---

p. 52, and C. Hartley Grattan, *The Three Jameses: A Family of Minds* (New York, 1932).

13. Henry M. Dexter, *The Moral Influence of Manufacturing Towns* (Andover, 1848).

14. Anne Ayres, *Life and Work of W. A. Muhlenberg* (New York, 1880), pp. 199–208.

15. Stephen Colwell, *New Themes for the Protestant Clergy* (Philadelphia, 1851), p. 244. Colwell's later works were *Politics for American Christians* (Philadelphia, 1852), the Preface and Notes to *The Race for Riches* (Philadelphia, 1853), by William Arnot, and *The Position of Christianity in the United States* (Philadelphia, 1854).

can printings during the first half of the century.[16] A more pervasive influence was the English "Christian Socialism" of 1848–54, of which Frederick Denison Maurice and Charles Kingsley were the leaders to exert the most effect in this country. Mediated to Americans chiefly through the Protestant Episcopal communion, both the social protest of Kingsley—as expressed in his novels, *Yeast* and *Alton Locke*—and the social theology of Maurice were widely influential in this country for decades.[17]

These stirrings were given added impetus by the popular interest in reform that characterized the middle decades of the century. Stress upon the ethical aspects of religion and zeal for prohibition, women's rights, peace, and the antislavery crusade were inextricably interwoven. However, when the slavery controversy began to absorb attention, other causes were pushed into the background and all efforts concentrated upon abolition. The religious conscience was completely engaged in the ensuing civil struggle, while all lesser reforms waited. But with emancipation and the gradual return of the American mind to its normal interests after the war, the social impulse of Christianity was freed to concern itself with the ills of the new industrial civilization that the conflict had helped bring to birth.

16. These were at Hartford and Boston in 1821; Lexington, Kentucky in 1822; and New York in 1855.

17. Maurice's books read in America were *The Gospel of the Kingdom of Heaven* (London and Cambridge, 1864), *The Commandments considered as Instruments of National Reformation* (London, 1866), *Social Morality* (London and Cambridge, 1869), and *Faith and Action* (Boston, 1886), the last a compilation from Maurice's writings, with the Preface by Phillips Brooks.

PART I: 1865–1880
THE BIRTH OF SOCIAL CHRISTIANITY

Now that God has smitten slavery unto death, he has opened the way for the redemption and sanctification of our whole social system.

EDWARD BEECHER

O Master, let me walk with thee
In lowly paths of service free;
Tell me thy secret; help me bear
The strain of toil, the fret of care.

Help me the slow of heart to move
By some clear, winning word of love;
Teach me the wayward feet to stay,
And guide me in the homeward way.

Teach me thy patience; still with thee
In closer, dearer company.
In work that keeps faith sweet and strong,
In trust that triumphs over wrong;

In hope that sends a shining ray
Far down the future's broadening way;
In peace that only thou canst give,—
With thee, O Master, let me live!

WASHINGTON GLADDEN, 1879

INTRODUCTION

THE years immediately following the Civil War opened a new era in American life. During the period of "reconstruction" the forces of industrial revolution, stimulated by the demands of the great conflict, swept triumphantly to victory over the agricultural economy that remained from the nation's youth. By 1880 a vigorous capitalism had laid the foundations of modern America in an industrial order that was rapidly transforming the rural United States of Lincoln and Lee into a closely knit nation of swarming cities.

Mark Twain satirized the unique society that emerged from the crucible of war and from the new iron furnaces of Pittsburgh as the "gilded age." A "welter of crude new energy," this "chromo civilization" satisfied its elemental desires by raping a virgin continent and ignoring its illegitimate offspring. The scramble for possession of the country's boundless resources was nothing less than the "Great Barbecue" at which the common man was handed a farm, while the "Iron Buccaneers" of railroad, industry, and finance carved for themselves empires whose vastness and power—and whose rulers' methods—Caesar might have envied.

The postwar moral reaction severely strained certain traditional ethical and social standards. Corruption in local, state, and national government was widespread and in many places unashamed, and business ethics suffered a similar decline. In an atmosphere of optimism and moral laxity speculation flourished until the panic of 1873 brought the sobering realization that progress could not be built on watered stocks or blueprints. The lesson was made painfully clear to the working classes by unprecedented unemployment and desperate poverty. Bread lines appeared in the city streets of a nation rapidly becoming the richest country in the world. But the kings of industry and finance paid little heed and an exaggerated individualism continued to ride roughshod over human rights. Even the volcanic eruption of working-class discontent in 1877 hardly checked them.

This violent birth of a new world called forth heroic efforts on the part of a minority of Protestant leaders who saw the very genius of Christianity contradicted by the assumptions of the new capitalism. Their attempts to reorient the historic faith of America to an industrial society comprised the social gospel. But the forces that gradually effected the new social viewpoint in American Christianity did not all come from without. Inside the religious community itself liberalizing ferments had long been at work, as has been noted. About the middle of the century a noticeable change in the religious climate had definitely fostered this-worldly interests, and as these subtle factors slowly permeated the religious mind, its reaction to the stimulus of a new industrial, urban, and scientific environment produced what has come to be known as the social gospel.

Social Christianity was not an unnatural child of the American religious heritage. The most austere conservatism had produced missionary zeal of heroic caliber, and works of charity and benevolence had always been looked upon as natural and quite necessary fruits of the Christian life. Most of the social crusades of the nineteenth century had derived their dynamic from Christianity.

The first expressions of the new social viewpoint were attempts to reorient the philanthropic urges of the historic faith to the needs of the modern world without seriously modifying the old doctrines. Social reform was approached by way of the traditional conception of a stewardship that was to be applied by individuals to business and industry, and the few radicals of the 1870's who demanded that the church enter the class struggle on the side of the workers were completely ignored, if they were at all understood.

That the evolution of social Christianity was comparatively slow during the years that saw the bitterest industrial struggles and the most glaring gaps in social condition between classes in the nation's history was due as much to the preoccupation of the churches with interests that had consumed their social, missionary, or charitable energies for decades, as it was to their theology. All other social interests had been submerged in the slavery crusade, and now that emancipation was an accomplished fact the religious conscience naturally concerned itself with the further well-being of the freedmen through widespread programs of educational, missionary, and welfare activity in the South. The great task of following the moving frontier with missionaries was still urgent in the postwar years when the process of western exploitation had been given added impetus by technical advance. The Indian situation, which during the mid-nineteenth century inspired some of the noblest missionary efforts in the annals of American religious history, continued to be a live issue among the religious bodies as well as in the nation at large. In dealing with these historic problems the church had developed a technique well suited to them, and her social inertia during the 'seventies and the 'eighties must be attributed in part to reluctance to exchange her time-tested methodology for the untried modern schemes proposed to meet the new needs of the day.

Social Christianity, therefore, was forced to concern itself with practical as well as theoretical changes. Habits as well as theology needed to be redirected. When the attention of Protestant leaders began to turn toward the "whole social system," as Edward Beecher declared it must, it was with but slowly clarifying ideas and techniques that the prophets of a kingdom of God on earth took up their task.

CHAPTER I

PROTESTANTISM IN THE GILDED AGE

In so far as individual men are concerned, religion aims first and mainly at the production of character. Although Christianity has respect to the outward life, to society, to the most minute acts, it is only as results, not as the primal ends. It seeks to produce a state of mind of great purity and power, and from that state it derives the influences which shall control all the details of human life.

HENRY WARD BEECHER

A HISTORY of the social gospel must begin with the theological climate that sheltered its birth and nourished its early growth. The religious atmosphere of the gilded age comprised at least four distinct winds of doctrine that affected the development of American social Christianity. Conventional, institutionalized, orthodox Protestantism provided the frozen foundation of complacency, whose stubborn refusal to warm to the social gospel was to constitute a perennial problem. At the same time, the new movement probably obtained its greatest impetus from those enlightened conservatives who strove to reconcile the truths of Christianity with the new science, and to reorient Protestant ethics to the needs of a newly industrialized society. Further, the social gospel was the heir of that evangelical hope and fervor that had provided the religious motivation of an earlier generation's crusade against slavery and intemperance, and that had energized its heroic devotion to missions. Lastly, to the left of these more or less middle-of-the-road currents, there moved a coolly rational but nevertheless determined and influential Unitarian school that frankly challenged both the presuppositions and the ethics of conservatism.

The characteristic religion of mid-nineteenth-century America comprised a well-articulated body of doctrines and doctrinaires, effectively insulated against the corrosive forces of the new science and of social unrest by an otherworldly dualism that resulted in a smug preoccupation with the salvation and perfection of the individual. More and more on the defensive as the nineteenth century drew to a close, orthodoxy later precipitated the "fundamentalist-modernist" controversy of the early twentieth century and lives on today in the "Bible belt" and other geographically or intellectually sheltered areas. Held in the gilded age by most denominations except Unitarians and some Congregationalists, conservative Christianity willingly contributed little to the social gospel. In such attacks as it made upon the perplexing problems of the new urban and mechanical age, orthodoxy depended upon individual regeneration and the bolstering of the old sanctions rather than what it called the "spurious reforms" of more liberal groups.

The prevailing institutionalized faith of American Protestantism was the supernaturalistic religion of the Bible, a book regarded as "a repertory of facts, a revelation of doctrines, and a standard of appeal upon all questions to which it bears any relation." Robert Ingersoll once declared that American Christians held the Bible to be "the only light that God has given for the guidance of his children . . . the foundation of all morality, of all law, of all order, and of all individual and national progress." They looked upon the Scriptures as the only means of ascertaining "the will of God, the origin of man, and the destiny of the soul."[1]

Equally characteristic was orthodoxy's pietistic view of life and its almost medieval belief in the present existence as a period of testing, as well as its conception of heaven as a reward for individual virtue or suffering. A leading religious editor could write in 1868 that if the working classes received unfair treatment on earth they should "first lay up treasures in heaven" where they would find their real reward.[2] Insistent upon conversion as proof of religious experience, conservatism was still bound by the habits of morbid introspection inherited from a decadent Calvinism; nor was it yet sufficiently colored by Bushnellism and other liberal ferments to sublimate its belief in a literal hell and the concomitant doctrine of substitutionary atonement.

1. Robert G. Ingersoll, "The Christian Religion," *North American Review,* 1884; quoted from p. 4 of reprint.
2. Lyman H. Atwater, *Presbyterian Quarterly and Princeton Review,* nsv 4 (1875), 529.

But when orthodoxy faced the skepticism of the rising scientific movement and the social confusion attendant upon the industrial revolution, its strongest bulwarks of doctrine and institutionalism became at once inhibiting factors. Biblical literalism with its attitude of almost fatalistic reverence for the Scriptures effectively sealed the conservative mind against intrusion by the questions of the day. In fact, it went out of its way to criticize liberalism at this very point. "The advocates of spiritualism, of woman's rights, of social changes of nearly every kind, have nearly all of them been touched with a liberalism amounting to deism, and are inclined to reject as authoritative the Old and New Testament writers," declared the editor of the *Biblical Repertory and Princeton Review* in 1868.[3] When it likewise refused to modify a high Christology conventional Protestantism rendered itself impervious to the new social impulses that in other religious circles were finding sanction in the humanity of Jesus.

However, conservatism was not deaf to the social outcry. Its response was simply that of tradition. It devoted itself to the reformation of the individual, leaving social consequences to take care of themselves. Its characteristic stress upon stewardship and charity contained the germs of humanitarianism, but orthodoxy's influence upon the social gospel was nevertheless small and indirect. The editor quoted above went on to state that Christianity need not be abandoned as "the only agency that has any influence of worth on the affairs of men"; it will work out "the true solution of the problem of this world, if aught can." And it will do so through "the power of God in Jesus Christ to develop and ennoble the whole character of man."[4] This attitude was perhaps the greatest single obstacle to a developing social conscience in the churches. Not until the last decade of the century did preachers of a social gospel label the ideal of personal regeneration as socially ineffective unless conversion be to a social religion. When, thirty years after the period we are describing, a great denomination first attacked the industrial problem, its methods were distinctly evangelistic, while in 1936 no formal course in social ethics had yet found its

3. *Biblical Repertory and Princeton Review*, 40 (1868), 126–127.
4. *Op. cit.*, p. 128.

way into the leading Presbyterian theological school of the nation.

To supplement this ethic of individualism, orthodoxy strongly supported the traditional mores and institutions of an "ascetic Protestantism" whose forms it regarded as the foundation of all morality and social order. Although it set the good man or the Word of God over against the sin of the world, conservatism did not hesitate to utilize repressive means if its traditions were threatened. The crusade against alcohol, for example, proceeded upon both of these assumptions. The churches, viewing the individual drinker, considered temperance "the center of all social reform." But when temperance failed, prohibition was enlisted to support an essentially Puritan ethic.

The crystallization of orthodoxy's attitude into an actual program is vividly illustrated in the long career of the National Reform Association. This organization of "Christian citizens," still active in 1936, came into being at Allegheny, Pennsylvania, in 1864, when representatives of eleven denominations united for the purpose of amending the Constitution of the United States to "acknowledge Almighty God as the source of all authority and power in civil government . . . and his Will, revealed in the Holy Scriptures, as of supreme authority, in order to constitute a Christian government."[5] The reformers proposed to "defend and maintain whatever is distinctly Christian in our national life, and to resist all unchristian influences which may seek to affect the action of our government." For more than seventy years the National Reform Association has, in its own words, labored "to secure all needed legal safeguards, both constitutional and statutory, for our Christian institutions."[6] In 1867 the Association dedicated its journal, the *Christian Statesman*, not only to the support of the proposed constitutional amendment, but also to the aid of "the Christian Law of Marriage, the Sabbath and legislation for its observance, the Temperance question in all its aspects, the Limitations of the Franchise, the Prevention and Punishment of Crime, and the fundamental question of all—the Inspiration of the Word of God."[7] To this list might well have been added the use of the

5. *The Christian Statesman*, I, No. 1, 4.
6. National Reform Association, *Annual Report for 1904*.
7. *Christian Statesman, loc. cit.*, p. 8.

Bible in the public schools, a concern that was to absorb much of the Association's activity. After years of effort in behalf of these causes, an apologist could assert in 1890 that the Association "never failed to stand in the breach when any of the Christian institutions of our government were assailed and needed sturdy defense."

Standing in the breach against the downfall of tradition was conservatism's defense against the threats of modern civilization. Despite noble achievements in missions, children's aid, and education of the freedmen, the ethic of orthodoxy had become a sterile union of individualism and formalism. Conservative Christianity, wrote William Jewett Tucker, while a religion of charity and experience that sent the religious man out into the byways and hedges as well as to his closet in prayer, nevertheless failed to send him into the shop or the factory:

It was not a type of religion fitted to understand or to meet the problems involved in the rise of industrialism. It virtually accepted the prohibition written over the doors of the new workshops,— "No admittance." It was bold to the highest degree of sacrificial courage in its missionary zeal, but it shrank from contact with the growing material power of the modern world. It saw the religious peril of materialism, but not the religious opportunity for the humanizing of material forces.[8]

The social gospel owes probably its greatest intellectual debt to those enlightened conservatives who faced with open minds both the new science and the new industrial order of the later half of the nineteenth century. Aware that the content of Christianity was of more import than its currently accepted forms, these leaders embraced a progressive attitude that was to lead far from the sentimental piety of the gilded age. Their views were later to be carefully if somewhat inconsistently formulated in the "new theology" of the 1880's, while the movement was destined to ripen into the "modernism" of the twentieth century.

In the years following the Civil War the acclimatization of Christianity to the optimistic America of the "century of progress" was proceeding apace under the leadership of such pulpit

8. William Jewett Tucker, *My Generation* (Boston and New York, 1919), p. 97. By permission of copyright owner.

giants as Henry Ward Beecher. Stressing the love of God rather than the more somber attributes of justice or majesty, this sentimentalized Protestantism tended to emphasize heaven and the rewards of religion while overlooking other equally historic doctrines. Divine judgment was now tempered by a romantic optimism; the basic Christian conception of crisis was smoothed over by the softer idea of progress. The sympathizing Jesus gradually replaced the Christ of Calvary. Pioneered by Horace Bushnell, this emasculated Calvinism was preached by Beecher, Phillips Brooks, Washington Gladden, and other progressive ministers of the time. In spite of its sentimentality, it retained a strong supernaturalism and insisted upon the primacy of individual character. Men were shown the human Jesus (who was also the superhuman Christ) as their supreme example and as the epitome of a loving God at work in the world. This trend away from the older high Christology was later to bring the realization that Jesus was a man among men whose words could be taken as literal truth applicable to human affairs. At the end of the century when New Testament scholarship discovered "the Jesus of history," a maturing social gospel enthusiastically embraced his social teachings as its reasoned intellectual foundation.

Progressive orthodoxy rendered specific service to the rising social conscience of the gilded age not only in its humanistic leanings but in its conception of the kingdom of God as an actuality realizable on earth. Although definitions of the kingdom were always to lack concreteness, the belief that the ideal preached by Christ was a terrestrial, social kingdom as well as a heavenly or spiritual one was a matter of vast import to a nascent social gospel. Denied the consistency of orthodoxy or naturalism, and unaware as yet of the techniques of social science, enlightened conservatism groped uncertainly toward a sound theological foundation for its social aspirations, thus far unable to free itself from most of the theological and institutional presuppositions of the age.

The Reverend Edward Beecher, writing in 1865, took issue with the traditional view that the kingdom of God is purely spiritual. The church, he declared, was ordained for the purpose of ultimately bringing "civil government, the state, commerce, political economy, the arts and sciences, and the schools, under the influence of God."[9] While such a result will be obtained through the universal indwelling of God in individuals, the reign of God, the kingdom of God, in all phases of human society is not merely the visible church: it is "a Christian organization of society, in all nations and in all parts, effected, sustained, and animated by God, acting in regenerated men." The gospel has not completed its task until it has leavened the whole lump. Therefore the full meaning of the kingdom of God should be studied and its realization seriously attempted.

Although his reasoning bore the unmistakable stamp of an older evangelicalism, Beecher would have found himself at home thirty years later with Walter Rauschenbusch and his comrades of the Brotherhood of the Kingdom, who sought the kingdom as the inclusive social, and therefore to them, complete, gospel. Although the heir of an earlier ethical hope, the kingdom idea stood, even in this first dawn of a socialized Christianity, for the distinctly Christian social ideal whose naturalistic equivalent was then being expressed in a "religion of humanity." When, fifty years after Beecher's statement, Rauschenbusch declared that the doctrine of the kingdom of God "is itself the social gospel,"[10] he expressed not only the religious conviction of social Christianity but indicated by inference the fundamental distinction between the social gospel and secular reform.

A third stratum in the theological atmosphere of the gilded age was the heritage from an evangelicalism that had seen the element of crisis in human life and looked to the divine initiative to accomplish the necessary revolutionary change. This attitude sought the realization of the kingdom of God in the world as the needed resolution of that unfortunate dualism between heaven and earth, present and future, that had followed in the wake of revival movements from Jonathan Edwards to Charles G. Finney. Conventional piety had separated the other world from the present one, and the historic Christian element of dynamic hope had become attached to a remote ideal no longer valid in a skeptical world. But in the idea of the kingdom of

9. Edward Beecher, "The Scriptural Philosophy of Congregationalism and Councils," *Bibliotheca Sacra,* 22 (1865), 287.

10. Walter Rauschenbusch, *A Theology for the Social Gospel* (New York, Macmillan, 1917), p. 131.

God on earth a form of the hope was closely related to the present.[11]

The evangelical viewpoint was well stated in a series of lectures entitled *The Kingdom of Christ on Earth*, given in 1870 to the students of Andover Theological Seminary by Samuel Harris, then president of Bowdoin College and later professor of Systematic Theology at Yale. Harris regarded contemporary movements for social justice, the expectation of human progress, and the current practical interest in the person of Jesus as of divine origin. The kingdom of God, he declared, is not an abstraction, but "the universal reign of justice and love" under Christ, the Messianic king. Such a kingdom will come not by any natural process "but by the divine grace in Christ coming down upon humanity from above."[12] The distinctive and essential characteristic of the kingdom is redemption as a historical act of God. While the kingdom will progress toward a universal reign of justice and love, it "is not originated and advanced by the spontaneous development of humanity." Rather, "a redeeming power comes down upon humanity from God," quickening men to spiritual life and transforming society. Although such a conception is repugnant to a rationalistic age, it is nevertheless distinctive and essential in Christianity, asserted Harris, who then moved on to a discussion of the social ethics of the kingdom, declaring that the evils of present civilization could be removed "only by obedience to the Christian law of service."[13]

It may well be contended that evangelicalism had prophesied an earthly kingdom of justice and righteousness since the days of Jonathan Edwards.[14] There was likewise a close relationship between the ideologies expressed by Harris and by Edward Beecher. What is significant to the present context is that in the confusion of a transitional era the evangelical note of dynamic hope with its ethical overtones was being sounded even by those whose heritage and outlook fitted them better to understand a

---

11. The writer is indebted to Professor H. Richard Niebuhr for this view.

12. Samuel Harris, *The Kingdom of Christ on Earth* (Andover, 1888), p. 3. These lectures were originally published in *Bibliotheca Sacra*, beginning in April, 1871.

13. *Op. cit.*, pp. 165–166.

14. H. Richard Niebuhr, *The Kingdom of God in America* (Chicago, 1937), chap. iv.

bygone era than to cope with the complexities of modernity. But the dynamic element was to play a large part in later views of the kingdom—notably in the thought of Rauschenbusch.

The fourth stream of mid-nineteenth-century thought to influence the social gospel was Unitarianism and certain radical eddies to the left of it. Although these will be discussed later, Unitarian liberalism was, in the period now under consideration, much farther along the road of social concern than were its contemporaries. Leading Unitarians were pointing out the ethical character of the kingdom, that Jesus had had definitely social purposes in view in the establishment of the church,[15] and that an ideal church should symbolize the brotherhood of man. The Unitarian emphasis upon the ethical character of true religion is well known and need not be examined here.[16] Christianity was defined as belief in the life and teachings of Jesus and in the fatherhood of God. Although it made free use of the Christian tradition, this optimistic and rationalistic strain was actually far to the left of conservative Protestantism. For it the coming of the kingdom meant social progress. Unitarian leaders occupied the front line among pioneers of the social gospel, while, as we shall see later, the leaven of their ethical faith unquestionably aided the slowly rising social conscience of Protestantism.

An important and pervasive expression of the liberal and humanitarian religious viewpoint, and one of considerable significance for American thought, came from the able pen of Sir John Robert Seeley in 1866. Entitled *Ecce Homo: A Survey of the Life and Work of Jesus Christ*, this British book at once "surprised and somewhat shocked" religious people on both sides of the Atlantic. Seeley found the meaning of the person and message of Jesus in his purpose for the church, which Seeley declared was the improvement of morality: the ethics of Jesus are therefore social. A "strictly social and civic" life is enjoined upon members of the church, while Christianity's morality is shown by its "enthusiasm of humanity"—a phrase immediately accepted into the American social-gospel vocabulary.

15. See James Freeman Clarke, *Orthodoxy: Its Truths and Errors* (Boston, 1866), p. 402.

16. Andrew Preston Peabody, "The Relations of Ethics and Theology," in *Christianity and Modern Thought* (Boston, 1872), p. 154.

The kingdom of God is at once present and future, and it waits upon the Christian's supreme and only law—the enthusiasm of humanity—which moves every member of the divine society "to do as much good as possible to every other member." As practical applications of his ideal Seeley suggested medical research, investigation of the causes of physical evil, and study of the relations of education, labor, and trade to health; he then proposed the reorganization of life in accordance with the findings obtained. The wide popularity of *Ecce Homo* in the United States suggests not only the growing interest of Americans in a more ethical religion, but provides an excellent example of the occasional and imponderable influence of significant British thought upon the movement we are tracing.

Such were the chief components of the spiritual climate in which the American social gospel was born. Outside the religious fold, however, the storms created by a virile industrial revolution were exuberantly battering the traditions of a civilization still rural in its customs and ideology. Christianity could not long remain immune to influences that challenged its conceptions of man and of social organization and that threatened to replace traditional American culture with a materialistic civilization whose very genius was both a contradiction of and a threat to the Christian ethic. Protestantism's measured response was the social gospel.

CHAPTER II

CHRISTIANITY AND THE MORALS
OF SOCIETY

Now that slavery is out of the way, the questions that concern our free laborers are coming forward; and no intelligent man needs to be admonished of their urgency. They are not only questions of economy, they are in a large sense moral questions; nay, they touch the very marrow of that religion of good-will of which Christ was the founder. It is plain that the pulpit must have something to say about them.

WASHINGTON GLADDEN[1]

IN the preceding chapter we have described certain currents within American Protestantism that were gradually preparing the way for the development of a social conscience. This movement was tremendously accelerated by the social unrest that broke in upon the naïve complacency of an agricultural nation still unaware of the industrial revolution already seething within it. Although to the people at large it was the railroad strike of 1877 that seemed to have "partially uncapped the crater of a social volcano," many alert ministers had detected rumblings a decade earlier. Their reactions were in general along the lines a more fully developed social Christianity was to follow later.

These pioneers of the social gospel saw clearly four types of problems. They questioned the prevalent rationalization of unrestricted competition by classical economics; they regarded the conflict between labor and capital as the crux of the maladjustments attendant upon the industrial revolution; they condemned the business ethics of the "Great Barbecue"; and they began an attack upon the problems of urban life, notably the relation of the church to the masses.

Early efforts to apply Christian ethics to the solution of these questions were for the most part utopian. Although social Christianity came to be the response of religious leaders to real needs as they faced them in their own parishes, clergymen of

1. Washington Gladden, *Working People and their Employers* (New York, 1885 [1st ed., 1876]), p. 3.

the gilded age were theologically rather than sociologically minded. Children of their age and unaware of the titanic forces that were rapidly remodeling the very structure of society, these pioneers must be regarded as religious men weighing social standards in the scales of Christian ethics. Their findings do not compare with the documented reports of social conditions that the development of sociology was later to make possible. Nevertheless many of them bravely challenged the current ideology. These early years were "a time of lonesomeness," the first prophets were few, and as Walter Rauschenbusch said later of the period before 1900, they "shouted in the wilderness." But that is the lot—and the joy—of prophets.

The first advocates of social Christianity subjected the presuppositions of classical economic theory to searching criticism. They regarded unrestricted competition as an arrogant contradiction of Christian ethics and the inhuman treatment accorded the laborer as a violation of fundamental Protestant conceptions of the nature of man. One reformer told a Massachusetts Methodist Convention that apologists for *laissez faire* had substituted Adam Smith for the Bible and that political economy was not really a science but only an "ingenious and plausible theory of business details."[2]

In one of the most searching utterances of its kind in this period, the Reverend George N. Boardman of Binghamton, New York, writing in 1866, pointed out the absurdity of expecting a combination of individualism and selfishness to produce beneficent results. If self-seeking is the highest social good, he argued with thinly veiled irony, then "enlarged, comprehensive self-seeking is public benevolence." By such a test social progress is sheer accident, he concluded.[3] Professor John Bascom of Williams College, while admitting certain beneficial results of self-interest, declared it inadequate to sustain progress, on the ground that it tends to create an irresponsible ruling class incapable of understanding or providing for the needs of the masses.[4] To Washington Gladden, who may well be called "the

2. Edward H. Rogers, *The Relations of Christianity to Labor and Capital* (Boston, 1870), p. 5.
3. George N. Boardman, "Political Economy and the Christian Ministry," *Bibliotheca Sacra*, 25 (1866), 98.
4. John Bascom, "Labor and Capital," one article in a series on "The Natural Theology of Social Science," *Bibliotheca Sacra*, 25 (1868), 686.

father of the social gospel," it seemed "profoundly untrue" that economic questions should be considered outside the realm of morals, economic forces beyond the reach of moral causes, and all this past human control. He contrasted the law of love with the economic law of supply and demand and invoked Christian principles as a check upon the inhuman tendencies of economic forces.[5]

Boardman proposed a curb on the evils of competition that was unusual for the times. He held that governments exist for more than the mere execution of cold justice: they should protect the weaker members of society by acting as referees in the competitive struggle. In the war of all against all, is there success for every man? Must there not be some superintending power protecting the weak and suppressing violence? Is infinite war the same as peace? When the minister of Christ looks upon the impoverished laborer's family with its misshapen children at work in the mills, will he not ask whether protection is possible for this class of the human race? Are these to be left to themselves "and to the 'tender mercies' of their employers"? Must not governments, and all social institutions, be based on "positive virtue, on morality, not on selfishness, not on each man's ability to take care of himself"? This viewpoint led Boardman to recommend poor laws and compulsory support of free schools as society's payment of family wages in addition to those earned by the individual worker.

Such criticism of *laissez faire* unquestionably rested upon the historic Christian recognition of the spiritual worth of the individual. In fact, it is exactly at this point that the clergyman may render a real service to economics, asserted Boardman. Even Calvinistic theology, he declared, is "altogether tame in its depreciation of human dignity" as compared to the contemptible position in which man has been placed by the social economists who judge him solely in terms of what he is worth in this world. Washington Gladden, whose career we shall examine shortly, reviewed the classical doctrine of wages before his Sunday-evening congregation in 1876. They tell us, he said, that the whole question is a matter of supply and demand, determined by fixed laws unalterable by either employer or laborer. This may be true, Gladden challenged, but only "if men are not

5. Gladden, *op. cit.*, pp. 24–25.

moral beings, if the doctrines of materialism or of high Calvinism are true, and if the actions of men are determined by forces outside of themselves." But he would assume that the wills of men are free and that social and economic questions are in part moral questions.[6]

Criticism of unrestricted competition and of classical economics have remained basic planks in the platform of social Christianity. Although its proponents did not recognize the fact, this position involved an implicit critique of one of the foundations of capitalism. Other presuppositions of the *status quo* were not included in their strictures; explicit criticism of capitalism came later under the stimulus of socialism. The attack upon classical economics was to attain the prestige of academic sanction during the 1880's; it afterward became a perennial contention of the Christian Socialists, and it occupied a significant place in the thought of Walter Rauschenbusch, social Christianity's greatest prophet.

During the 1870's America became painfully aware that the sorest spot beneath the gilded surface of an age of industrial expansion and exploitation was the condition of the wage earner. Leaders of religious social thought were impressed by the "magnitude and universality" of the conflict between capital and labor, which a prominent editor regarded as "one of the portents of the time." In 1872 Charles Loring Brace wrote to a friend that "in general, the laboring classes do not receive their fair share" and that strikes are to be understood as their means of getting more. The great problem of the future, he asserted, "is the equal distribution of wealth or of the profits of labor."[7] The most important discussion of this issue prior to 1880 was that of Washington Gladden, then pastor of the North (Congregational) Church of Springfield, Massachusetts, who in the autumn of 1875 began in his church a series of Sunday-evening lectures on the labor question. These were published the next year as *Working People and their Employers*—a book that became one of the first mileposts set by American social Christianity.

Gladden (1836–1918) was a farmer boy educated at Williams College, where he wrote the college song and came under

6. *Ibid.,* pp. 36–37.
7. Charles Loring Brace, *Life* (New York, 1894), p. 355.

the tutelage of Mark and Albert Hopkins and John Bascom. Prior to his call to Springfield in 1875, Gladden had taught school, contributed to the Springfield *Republican* and to *Scribner's Magazine,* and ministered to churches in Brooklyn and Morrisania, New York, and in North Adams, Massachusetts. His induction sermon at North Adams had been preached by Horace Bushnell, who had stayed in Gladden's home for a week at the time, and whose influence upon Gladden was notable.

Between 1871 and 1875 Gladden served on the editorial staff of the New York *Independent,* from which he resigned in protest against the paper's advertising policy. On one occasion, while acting editor, Gladden had attacked the Tweed ring. To Tweed's misunderstood query—"What are you going to do about it?"—he had written:

We are going to turn you and all your creatures out of your offices. . . . We are going to get back as much as we can of the booty you have stolen. . . . We are going to . . . send you to your own place, the penitentiary. . . . We are going to make the city and the whole country too hot for you. . . . God may have mercy on you; but as for us, we promise you that your ill-gotten booty shall be but a poor compensation for the inheritance of shame which shall be yours forever.[8]

Attracted to the ministry by a religion "that laid hold upon life with both hands, and proposed, first and foremost, to realize the Kingdom of God in this world," Gladden stood directly in the liberal tradition championed by Bushnell. Influenced also by Frederick Robertson and John Ruskin,[9] Gladden, forced to deal with the labor situation in his own parish, was convinced that "the Christian church must have a large concern" in its solution.

8. Gladden, *Recollections* (Boston and New York, 1909), p. 206.
9. Ruskin's influence upon Gladden is a good case of the effect of British thought upon the American social gospel. See Appendix B of *Working People,* the Preface to Gladden's *The Lord's Prayer* (Boston, 1880), his *Witnesses of the Light* (Boston and New York, 1903), chapter on Ruskin. For evaluations of this influence see Gaius Glenn Atkins, *Religion in Our Times* (New York, 1932), pp. 48–49; Vida D. Scudder, *Social Ideals in English Letters* (Boston and New York, 1898) and *On Journey* (New York, 1937), index; W. D. P. Bliss, "John Ruskin," in *Encyclopedia of Social Reform* (New York, 1897 and 1908). Ruskin's *The Crown of Wild Olive* and *Unto This Last* were both published in this country.

He regarded the struggle between capital and labor as "a question of conduct, a question concerning the relations of man to man"—relations that it is Christianity's duty to define and regulate. He believed that the application of "the Christian law" would solve the problem, and that the church should know how to apply that law. Observing that church members were making no effort to establish right relations in industry and that in fact many practiced injustice and cruelty on the assumption that the Christian rule of life had no application to business, Gladden declared that "the Christian law covers every relation of life" and should be applied to the common affairs of men.[10]

One of the most realistic notes of the social gospel and one that has remained a basic contention since it was sounded at the very beginning of the movement was the demand for fair play and simple justice for the worker. Gladden and other religious leaders believed that the mutual interests of labor and capital might be harmonized by the recognition of these rights. The industrialist who crushes the families of his workers sins against God, declared George N. Boardman, while Lyman Atwater wrote in the *Presbyterian Quarterly and Princeton Review* that regardless of civil law the capitalist is bound "by every moral and Christian obligation" to give the laborer "a fair and righteous share of the rewards of production." Gladden refused to take sides in the conflict. To employers he pointed out the obligations of stewardship, facing them with the responsibility for the well-being of their workers: provision for health and comfort, treatment with "polite consideration," intellectual improvement, and moral and religious welfare. Laborers are likewise under obligation to honest and conscientious service, he held.[11]

But although a "mutually dependent and auxiliary" relationship exists ideally between labor and capital, actual situations are productive of "deep and wide-spread dissatisfactions" that have brought into being labor combinations "assuming a portentous aspect" in the public eye. Gladden frankly accepted the unions, although he believed their tactics "often unwise and unprofitable." As long as workers' societies perform needed

10. Gladden, *Recollections,* p. 252.
11. Gladden, *Working People,* chap. viii.

services they are worthy of all commendation, he declared. Further:

They have a perfect right to deliberate together concerning the wages they are receiving, and to unite in refusing to work unless their wages are increased. The law gives to capital an immense advantage in permitting its consolidation in great centralized corporations; and neither law nor justice can forbid laborers to combine, in order to protect themselves against the encroachments of capital, so long as they abstain from the use of violence, and rely upon reason and moral influence.[12]

Gladden recognized the workers' right to strike but warned that this method of obtaining desired ends usually resulted "in more loss than gain to the laboring classes." But strikes are not always morally wrong. This is a free country; if one or one hundred laborers do not choose to work for a certain wage no one can compel them to do so, and if they prefer "to be idle for a season rather than to take less than the price demanded for their services, they have a right" to do so.[13] But workers should consider whether by combining for their own gain they may not be inflicting serious damage upon the community at large. The superficiality of this analysis led Gladden thirty years afterward to evaluate *Working People and their Employers* as "not an important book" and its discussion of labor unions as "not quite so sympathetic as it ought to have been." Nonetheless, that a leading clergyman should concern himself at all with this matter in 1876 was significant.

When these pioneers of a more socialized religion turned to remedies for the ills they had diagnosed, they were greatly impressed by the possibility of a practical realization of Christian ethics through profit sharing and other forms of industrial cooperation. Profit sharing as demonstrated in Fall River, wrote Lyman Atwater, "beautifully harmonizes the principles of economics with those of Christian ethics."[14] In 1877 Charles Loring Brace declared that "if industrial society ever rises to the Christian ideal, it will be under some form of coöperation between labor and capital . . . whereby the laborers shall have a

12. *Op. cit.,* pp. 137–138.   13. *Op. cit.,* pp. 40–41.
14. Lyman H. Atwater, "The Labor Question in its Economic and Christian Aspects," *Presbyterian Quarterly and Princeton Review,* nsv I (1872), 491.

pecuniary interest in the profits of production beyond their wages."[15] John Bascom believed that joint stock companies and copartnerships would utilize the "enterprise and talent" of individual laborers.[16] Joseph Cook, whose weekly "Boston Monday Lectures" were being followed by hundreds of thousands of readers, endorsed the Rochdale coöperative system and the German coöperative savings banks as practical aids in the solution of the labor problem.[17]

Gladden regarded coöperation as the ultimate system of economic organization, defining it as "the arrangement of the essential factors of industry according to the Christian rule."[18] Admitting that this ideal was hardly a present possibility, he looked to education to improve "the mental and moral qualities of working-people" so that they might be fitted to participate in such an economy. Gladden rejected both socialism and Ruskin's benevolent feudalism (which latter had strongly influenced him) and sought some system wherein the laborer might join the capitalist class. He believed that the workers' status would be raised by the preservation of private property "in all its sacredness" and the consequent stimulation of the virtues that aid in its accumulation,[19] for the man who owns a share in the business at which he works is by that fact made a better workman and a better citizen.

But the inclusive panacea for industrial ills was Christianity itself. "The power of Christian love" was declared to be strong enough to "smoothe and sweeten all the relations of capitalists and labor." There would be instant peace, said Gladden, if the capitalist would measure his profits and the workingman his wages by the golden rule.[20] Clergymen went on to point out Christianity's aid to the oppressed throughout its history; they emphasized Christ's concern for the poor, and identified the traditional interests of the church with those of the working classes. Gladden asserted that the church's right to speak on the problem rests upon Jesus' vocation as a carpenter, while the power that came into the world with Him has "stricken the shackles from the laborer . . . lightened his burdens . . .

15. Brace, *op. cit.*, pp. 355–356.   16. Bascom, *op. cit.*, p. 684.
17. Joseph Cook, *Socialism* (Boston, 1880), chaps. iv, v.
18. Gladden, *Working People,* p. 50.   19. *Op. cit.,* p. 206.
20. *Op. cit.,* p. 43.

lifted him up . . . and put into his hands the key of a great future." To the laborers in his congregation Gladden recommended the study and practice of "those principles of Christian prudence and morality" taught by the church.[21]

Preachers of the social gospel have always been concerned to awaken their fellow ministers and the churches to a sympathetic understanding of labor and other social problems. This began to be strongly urged in the gilded age. John Bascom wrote in 1872 that religious principles should be broadened so as to include "all useful social theories" lest Christianity be left behind in the onward march of society. He warned that both the natural and supernatural in religion would lose their power unless they should be related to "a life of Christian love."[22] Gladden pointed out that the church must recognize the practical bearings of Christian principles, while it is the duty of the minister to protest in the name of Jesus against the division of the church and of society into jealous and unsympathizing classes, and to show both and all classes that they are bound together in a community of interests.[23]

During the same winter that Washington Gladden delivered the above lectures, the Reverend Richard Heber Newton, foremost liberal minister in the Episcopal Church, was presenting a series of addresses on business ethics to his congregation at All Souls' (Anthon Memorial) Church of New York City. Like Gladden, Newton was influenced, but doubtless more directly so through the Anglican communion, by such leaders of British social Christian thought as Frederick Denison Maurice, F. W. Robertson, and the author of *Ecce Homo*, John R. Seeley. His lectures, published in 1876 as *The Morals of Trade*, were serious studies based on carefully organized data.

Because he regarded business as the basic factor in social organization Newton ignored warnings against "meddling with trade customs," holding that because society is founded on business its morality is of the greatest importance. Trade, in turn, said Newton, rests upon veracity. But in many typical businesses he found the most flagrant dishonesties commonly prac-

21. *Op. cit.,* pp. 51, 142.
22. John Bascom, "The Influence of the Pulpit," *Bibliotheca Sacra,* 29 (1872), 715, 719.
23. Gladden, *Working People,* p. 191.

ticed and accepted. In advertising—"one of the most curious moral studies" in his entire research—Newton found truth represented by "X, an unknown quantity." Dealing in turn with adulteration of foods, speculation, frauds, and a wide range of commercial practices, this reformer declared the worst feature of the situation to be that "these practices are allowed, unrebuked by the public opinion of the business world." Few condemn them, he said, and it is generally thought impossible or utopian to apply Christian ethical standards to business—business whose code of conduct is merely "non-criminality and whose standard of integrity is the truth and honesty which clear the hands of the law."[24] Decadence of honor is the characteristic sign of the times in the business world.

Rejecting *laissez faire* as a regulator of commercial morality, Newton proposed its restriction, a better distribution of trade, associations for price control and standardization of materials and workmanship, coöperation, a revival of craftsmanship, and improved business education.

However, the church is a factor of great importance in this situation, declared Newton; the fifty thousand businessmen who are members of New York's five hundred churches ought to have been taught honesty there. But, he complained, the church has emphasized spirituality rather than morality; the ethical "alphabet of religion" has not been well learned. Instead of the regeneration of the world the church has sought the deliverance of the few from its corruption. The church has failed to turn her energies into the realm of practical affairs; she has not been "the leaven working until the whole social mass, politics and business and pleasure, should be leavened," but has rather acted only as the salt "keeping the saved from the spread of putrefaction." She has forsworn her office of conscience-guide and left her honest-hearted but ill-instructed children to wander among the pitfalls of trade and to fall into dishonor and ruin. Calling the church to a revival of ethical religion, Newton challenged his congregation to "study greater personal scrupulousness" and to make religion truly vital. Buttressing his book with fifteen appendices ranging in content from evidence of the adulteration of milk to a plea for social science in the education of the clergy, and quoting Ruskin on trade guilds and cheap

24. R. H. Newton, *The Morals of Trade* (New York, 1876), p. 23.

purchases, this aggressive minister of the days of the Tweed ring holds a unique place among the pioneers of American social Christianity.[25]

Although individual wrongdoings of the robber barons provided "the theme for a thousand condemnatory sermons,"[26] the gilded age was not prone to self-criticism. Newton had considered titling his book *The Morals of Society*, but it was another Episcopalian, the Reverend Edward A. Washburn of New York, who issued a general indictment of the ethical pattern of the times. This preacher spoke of war, indifference to life, vice, tenements, unsafe factories, and child labor as "the murders that society does not love to know." He asked Christian businessmen to practice "social honesty" and pointed out that avarice and covetousness were imperiling private and national life. Observing the widespread corruption in government, this frank critic could believe in "no rhetoric about our glorious destiny or our immortal constitution" in view of his understanding from the study of history that "justice, honesty, and holiness are for man or nation, and nations live or die as they keep or scorn them." The morality of Christ, he declared, must rebuke the sins "of our own hearts, of the church and the social world in our own time."[27]

During the 1870's Protestant leaders were becoming aware of conditions in the rapidly growing cities. Naturally enough this interest first appeared in New York. Washburn regarded "the hideous statistics of the great city" as the "growing curse of civilization"—a plague center where "thousands are bred in the sunless dens of vice and seemingly doomed to moral death." He pointed out the effects of environment upon the individual, declaring it necessary to begin reform "with the cure of outward evils" before efforts for the training of moral or religious character could be effective.[28] In the late years of the 'seventies

25. Another statement similar to Newton's was *Creed and Greed* (Cincinnati, 1879) by the Rev. Dudley Warner Rhodes, rector of the Church of Our Saviour, Mount Auburn, Cincinnati, who castigated conditions among street-car operators, municipal maladministration, tenement conditions, and food adulterations.

26. Allan Nevins, *The Emergence of Modern America* (New York, 1932), p. 201.

27. E. A. Washburn, *The Social Law of God* (New York, 1875), pp. 121, 212.

28. *Christian Truth and Modern Opinion* (New York, 1874), pp. 89–90.

the sensitive social conscience of Henry Codman Potter, then rector of Grace Church and later Episcopal bishop of New York, was leading him to preach on the perils of wealth, indifference to social need, the duties of citizenship, children in the slums, the tenement problem, and kindred topics growing out of his parish work.[29] Potter believed that the church should face these problems squarely if it hoped to retain its hold on thoughtful people. As to the tenement problem, he asserted that the church's function as a moral teacher should justify its having "a good deal to say" about the management of real estate. As "the witness and messenger of an eternal moral Governor" the pulpit has a much more serious office to perform than the preaching of "comfortable sermons."[30] The church is on trial and must justify its exemption from taxation by rendering social service to the community, he declared.

Thus it was that prior to 1880 four of the basic concerns of social Christianity had been explored. Competition and its rationalization in classical economics, the labor question, business ethics, and the problems of the cities were receiving careful attention, not only at the hands of the few lone leaders we have mentioned but rather widely in the religious press and at some church conferences.

The first social problem to attract the interest of several denominational journals during the 'seventies was that of crime. While this question never became a major social-gospel interest in the half century covered by the present study, the implica-

29. Harriet A. Keyser, *Bishop Potter, the People's Friend* (New York, 1910), chap. i. Also Henry Codman Potter, *Sermons of the City* (New York, 1881).

30. *Ibid.*, pp. 58–59. Two remarkable discussions of the subject matter of this chapter have come to light since it was written. In 1876 Andrew A. Lipscomb declared that *The Social Spirit of Christianity* (Philadelphia, 1876) had never been adequately developed partly because the church's avoidance of the poorer classes had perverted its social interests with consequent loss of social power. John F. Bray of Pontiac, Michigan, wrote (*God and Man a Unity,* Chicago, 1879) that to make Christianity real requires "the recognition of the common rights of humanity to employment and an equitable reward"—meaning a living wage for workers. He declared that "the age needs and must have an expansion of its social and religious ideas and usages." To become Christian we must have Christian surroundings and proper social conditions for Christian growth. These can be secured only through an entire change in our industrial and social status and its replacement by "a Christian system of equity based on the recognition of the unity of God and man, and of man with man." The foundation of this would be an adequate supply of the necessities of life.

tions of their investigations frequently led early writers on criminology to conclusions that were significant for a nascent social Christianity.

The *Biblical Repertory and Princeton Review*, a typically conservative Presbyterian periodical, evinced a broad interest in social problems, publishing articles on prison reform, the unchurched masses in the cities, the Indian question, sociology, the panic of 1873, the currency, the railroad strike of 1877, and labor reform. While most of the writing reflected an individualistic and otherworldly ideology, one article at least took a realistic view of the "Responsibility of Society for the Causes of Crime." Under this title the Reverend J. B. Bittinger laid the blame for antisocial behavior squarely upon the social order that had created environments productive of delinquency. Revealing a wide knowledge of his subject, this minister proposed several remedies: improved relations between labor and capital, compulsory education, legislation controlling the idle, vagrant, and helpless, "prompt and rigid prosecution and punishment of the capitalists and caterers of crime," and a humanitarian reform of prison discipline.[31]

The *Methodist Quarterly Review* likewise indicated a social concern first in the matter of criminology. Several realistic articles and book reviews on the subject are to be found in its pages during the 'sixties and 'seventies, but the first well-articulated statement of social-gospel principles came from the pen of the Reverend Bostwick Hawley of Saratoga Springs, New York, who wrote in 1879 on the "Relations of Politics and Christianity." The latter, he declared, is concerned with all the relationships of men, including social and civil life as well as personal wrongs; its mission will not be complete until it has established righteousness, truth, and freedom in all the earth.[32]

The Baptist *Standard* had considerable to say about the strike of 1877. Although condemning violence the editors of this religious paper were on the whole friendly toward labor and its organization, asserting that the railroad system needed thoroughgoing reform and that the strikers' grievances were real and serious. Warnings were sounded that revolutions might

31. *Biblical Repertory and Princeton Review*, 43 (1871), 36.
32. Bostwick Hawley, "Relations of Politics and Christianity," *Methodist Quarterly Review*, 51 (1879), 78.

result from failure to control the autocratic practices of corporations. Aware of the distinction between the radical element and the laboring class as a whole, the *Standard* blamed an alien group for the bloodshed and destruction that had taken place and insisted that the socialistic faction be permanently crushed. A series of carefully analytical articles pointed out the disproportionate share of the profits of industry awarded to capital, and declared that "every principle of equity" would entitle labor to a fair portion of its own products and their benefits. Causes of industrial unrest were found in immigration, war, the panic of 1873, increase in urban population, development of labor-saving machinery, the power of capital, the spread of infidelity and "communism," increase of charitable institutions, and the liquor traffic.[33]

In 1878 Washington Gladden undertook the editorial responsibilities of *Sunday Afternoon, a Magazine for the Household,* in which he proposed to include "questions of social life and of national well-being" within an inclusive aim of providing "wholesome and entertaining" Sunday reading. Gladden's editorial manifesto is typical of his own broad interests:

Questions of practical philanthropy will . . . occupy the largest space in *Sunday Afternoon* [he wrote]. How to mix Christianity with human affairs; how to bring salvation to the people that need it most; how to make peace between the employer and the workman. . . .[34]

Gladden was as good as his word. Editorials on pauperism, competition, and similar topics were frequent, while contributed articles discussed poor relief, children's aid, bank failures, destitute and delinquent children, women in prison, the kingdom of heaven, tenements, and financial ethics. Contributors included Charles Loring Brace, William Graham Sumner, Borden P. Bowne, Charles Caverno, Alexander Hyde, E. A. Washburn, Edward Bellamy, Julia McNair Wright, and John Bascom.

33. This paragraph is condensed from Harvey James Locke: *A History and Critical Interpretation of the Social Gospel of Northern Baptists in the United States,* University of Chicago Ph.D. dissertation, 1930. References to the *Standard* include issues for July 26, August 8 and 16, 1877, and May 23, 1878; Locke, *op. cit.,* pp. 114–117. By permission.

34. *Sunday Afternoon,* 1 (1878), 85.

During the 'seventies the Protestant Episcopal Church began to show the deep concern in social problems that has characterized its significant contribution to the growth of American social Christianity. In the latter years of this decade its leading periodical, *The Living Church*, was insisting upon the importance of the church as a teacher of public virtue and discussing such problems as church and state, capital and labor, and children's aid.

Social issues first came to the semiofficial attention of a major American religious body in the early meetings of the Episcopal Church Congress, an annual joint session of clergy and laity that first met in New York in 1874. From the beginning social questions always held an important place in the deliberations of the Congress. At the New York gathering the Reverend W. D. Wilson of Cornell University read a paper on "The Mutual Relations of Capital and Labor," in which he took a purely spiritual view that certainly would have been challenged had not a confusion in the program prevented discussion.[35] When the Congress met in Philadelphia the next year a series of papers and extended discussion centered around the ministration of the church to the working classes. A progressive clergyman asserted that modern Christianity must arouse herself from her elegant ease and face the practical solution of this problem if she is to be trusted as a guide in present-day life. Several specific suggestions were made by laymen, among them free sittings and the training of friendly visitors.[36] The third Congress, meeting at Boston in 1876, devoted part of its program to the morals of politics, one speaker declaring that an "enlightened Christian conscience" should be applied to the study of political questions.[37] These early interests were to continue. In the latter part of the 'seventies the Congresses were addressed on such problems as civil-service reform, the tariff, charity organization, and social service, by Seth Low, William Graham Sumner, Everett P. Wheeler, Robert Treat Paine, and other prominent laymen.

Episcopalians took note of the labor problem officially once before 1880. Following a memorial to the House of Bishops in 1877 an official committee investigated the alienation of the la-

---

35. *Authorized Report of the Proceedings* (New York, 1875), First Congress.
36. *Op. cit.,* Second Congress, p. 70.   37. *Op. cit.,* Third Congress, p. 184.

boring classes from the church. Among the findings it was asserted that the church's ministry should be widened and that she should assert her prophetic function in a reminder to society that "property and culture, and social and official position, have no rights that do not impose equivalent obligations." One of this church's first attempts to actually expand its program was the development of workingmen's clubs, the first of which was begun at St. Mark's, Philadelphia, in 1870; fifteen years later thirty such clubs had been organized, with a total membership of five thousand. Some of these practiced coöperative buying, fifteen owned libraries, and five owned their meeting places.[38]

Indicative of a concern that was later to absorb the interest of its American branch, the Evangelical Alliance, holding a world meeting in New York in 1873, devoted an entire section of its program to "Christianity and Social Reforms." Among the eight speakers presented under this heading, three Americans dealt with a similar number of problems that were then exciting considerable interest in this country. The Reverend Henry A. Nelson of Lane Theological Seminary discussed the temperance question, the Reverend E. C. Wines dealt with the relation of Christianity to crime and criminals, and President William H. Allen of Girard College presented the various aspects of the labor question to the distinguished international gathering. Analyzing the causes of labor's unrest, this speaker lauded coöperation and industrial arbitration and begged his hearers to support an effective world-peace program that would lift the load of war from the worker's back.[39]

During these germinal years, one man probably did more than any other individual or group in bringing the social implications of Christianity to the attention of Americans. In the winter of 1870–71 there came to the interim pastorate of the First Congregational Church of Lynn, Massachusetts, the Reverend Joseph Cook. A recent graduate of Andover Theological Seminary, Cook was at once a fluent orator and a born reformer. Ample scope for the exercise of both these talents was shortly

38. This paragraph is based on Arthur C. Lichtenberger, *The Relation of the Episcopal Church to Social Problems in America* (typescript in Cambridge Episcopal Theological School Library), pp. 16–17, 24–25, 27. By permission.

39. Evangelical Alliance, *Sixth General Conference* (New York, 1874), p. 674.

provided when he undertook to reform the shoe factories of Lynn. Beginning a series of Sunday-evening lectures with a survey of the industrial revolution and its effects, he laid a firm foundation of historical and sociological facts upon which to base startling revelations of immoral conditions in the city's great industry. After analyzing the factory system of Lynn specifically, Cook demanded "in the name of the working class of the manufacturing centers of New England" that men and women be segregated in the workrooms and that good overseers be appointed. His dramatic presentation and the controversial character of the charges aroused such excitement that a thousand persons were reported turned away from the lecture hall, while a representative of the business interests of the city undertook to challenge Cook on his own platform. The debate raged for several months, with the working classes solidly supporting Cook who, in spite of some overstatement and lack of tact, was genuinely interested in their welfare. Reviewing the results of the campaign in his last lecture, Cook asserted that he had exposed "a subtle and large evil," he had suggested remedies for it, and public sentiment had been "carried overwhelmingly in favor of those remedies."[40] Before leaving Lynn for study in Europe, Cook admonished his church to "resist all the temptations incident to a crowded population."

This was only the beginning of Joseph Cook's career. After an interim abroad he was asked in 1873, while lecturing at Amherst, to conduct a series of noon meetings in Boston. Such was the oratory of this "Heaven-ordained man," as President McCosh of Princeton described Cook, that the largest auditorium in the city was soon too small for his audiences. Organized in 1875 as the "Boston Monday Lectures" and publicized as such throughout the English-speaking world, Cook's ex-cathedra utterances on the conservative side of the conflict between science and religion made his name a household word in orthodox circles, whether he dealt with biology, labor, transcendentalism, heredity, or socialism. In 1880 it was estimated that the lectures, published in newspapers both in America and in England, were reaching a million readers weekly. Cook also spoke outside of Boston, giving over one hundred and fifty addresses

40. Joseph Cook, *Outlines of Music Hall Lectures* (Boston, 1871).

that involved more than ten thousand miles of travel during the winter of 1877–78.[41]

The significance of all this for the social gospel was that Cook, a reformer by nature, prefaced every lecture with a "Prelude" in which he dealt with the ethical or religious aspects of some current issue. The preludes were frequently more widely quoted than the lectures. In them Cook often presented a vigorously social gospel. During the winter of 1878–79 the addresses themselves were devoted to the closely related problems of labor and socialism. Cook always retained the genuine interest in the working class that he had evidenced at Lynn and his analyses of social problems usually bespoke a real grasp of the factors involved. In 1888 he began the publication of *Our Day: A Record and Review of Current Reform*, which he edited until the end of his active career in 1896.

The preludes, packed with bristling facts, dealt vividly with "insurrections of hunger," "bachelor and family wages," free churches, "young men in politics," remedies for the evils of cities, saloons, civil-service reform, and countless other current situations. A good example of Cook's style was his reference to "Plymouth Rock as the cornerstone of a factory" when discussing industrial conditions in New England. Analysis of the tenement situation led him to say that "the way from Jerusalem to Jericho now lies through city slums."

The lectures of 1878–79 dealing with socialism and labor opened with an unbridled denunciation of the "brainless and blasphemous and bloodthirsty" speeches of Dennis Kearney at Faneuil Hall just previously. Cook rejected socialism or any sort of radicalism, as did most of his contemporaries, on practical grounds: it could not be actually realized, would lead to even worse governmental corruption than was then prevalent, and would tend to discourage individual initiative. But the Boston Monday Lecturer endorsed coöperation of the Rochdale type and the German coöperative savings banks on the ground that these institutions fostered "self-help" on the part of the poor.[42]

Cook analyzed the labor problem in words reminiscent of his

41. Cook, *Socialism,* unpaged addendum.
42. *Op. cit.,* p. 89, and chaps. iv, v.

attitude at Lynn. Showing how machinery had lowered wages and forced women and children into the factories, he described in detail the effects of child labor upon the working population. He demanded legislation against the evil, basing his plea upon statistics of the Massachusetts labor bureau, and declared that wages should be adequate to provide for the decent rearing of workers' families, the keeping of wives and children out of the factories, and provision for old age and for education up to fifteen years. He believed that employers would sooner or later recognize just wages as the only adequate protection against "insane communists and infuriated socialists." Cook was sympathetic toward labor unions, holding that no protest could be raised when either labor or capital combined for legitimate ends. But he warned that labor organizations composed of the ignorant classes provided a fertile field for "socialistic demagogues"—a view similar to that of Washington Gladden.[43]

Cook called upon the church to assert a democratic and theocratic standard over against the power of the plutocracy and the secularization of morals, for, he said, "only the Golden Rule can bring the golden age." The church must be "the sheet anchor of moral reform."[44]

Thus was a social gospel sandwiched in between orthodoxy and evolution.

The earliest-known American organization dedicated to the propagation of social-gospel principles was the "Christian Labor Union" of Boston, a small but diverse group of earnest reformers who set the first marker along the unpopular path of left-wing social Christian movements in the United States. The Union was the outgrowth of a meeting held by several reformers in the summer of 1872 for the purpose of considering the plight of labor in New England. This conference issued "an address from friends of the workingman, to the pulpit, the platform, and the press, in the United States of America." It asked the ministry in particular whether light on the labor problem could

43. Cook, *Labor* (Boston, 1880), chap. x. See also Gladden, *Working People,* pp. 138 ff.

44. Cook, *Transcendentalism* (Boston, 1878), p. 223. Other lectures were *Biology* (1877), *Heredity* (1879), *Marriage* (1879), and *Conscience* (1879). For a contemporary criticism of Cook, see an article by John Fiske in the *North American Review,* March, 1881, reprinted in his *Century of Science.*

be sought in the Bible, whether the "present business system is founded upon the teachings of the Bible," and what the Scriptures have to say about land ownership, interest, and profit. In answer to its own queries the "address" declared that the Bible contains abundant truth bearing on the labor question, and asserted that the wage earner would be an attentive listener to a gospel that could aid in lifting him from his wretched condition.[45]

Led by the brilliant but quixotic Congregational minister Jesse Henry Jones,[46] whom Joseph Cook had once described as "the most promising young man I know," the Christian Labor Union set out to reform the relations of labor and capital, conscious that its task presented "the most gigantic and complex problem which has ever challenged human society."[47] Perhaps the widest influence exerted by a member of the Union was exercised by Edward H. Rogers, a ship carpenter, Methodist lay preacher, and former member of the Massachusetts legislature and of the Eight-Hour Commission in 1865.[48] The third and perhaps most distinguished member of the group's nucleus, and its chief financial supporter, was a Roman Catholic, T. Wharton Collens, a lawyer, writer, and former New Orleans judge who had at one time taught in the University of Louisiana.[49] The Union's friends or membership roll included the names of George E. McNeill, "father of the American Federation of Labor,"[50] Henry T. Delano, and Gen. H. K. Oliver.[51]

These reformers described themselves as "persons who seek to obey Jesus Christ's command, 'Follow me,' and to secure obe-

45. A Conference of Labor Reformers, *Live to Help Live* (Boston, 1872), pamphlet.

46. The only biography of Jones known to the writer is in the Preface to his *Joshua Davidson, Christian* (New York, 1907), Halah H. Loud, ed.

47. Jesse H. Jones, *Shall We Have a New Labor Reform Paper?* (n.d., n.p.), broadside.

48. Rogers' picture, with a single sentence describing his contributions to the American labor movement, is in John R. Commons' *Documentary History of American Industrial Society,* IX, 143. Rogers contributed a chapter to George E. McNeill's *The Labor Movement* (Boston and New York, 1887), in which he included a brief sketch of the Christian Labor Union (p. 146).

49. See *DAB* article, "Thomas Wharton Collens."

50. McNeill was not a member of the Christian Labor Union.

51. Others were E. D. Linton, W. F. Mallalien, William Brown (of Montreal) ; James Dombrowski, *The Early Days of Christian Socialism in America* (New York, 1936), p. 77, lists others.

dience to it, in the conduct of every form of human labor." The Union claimed to adopt "the Bible principles of the Hebrew Church in its relations to Land, Labor, and Capital." Influenced by such diverse thinkers as Ruskin, Fourier, Robert Owen, and Josiah Warren, the Union's beliefs were a confused mixture of religious idealism, biblicism, utopian socialism, and the labor theory of value.

Attributing the alienation of the poor from the church largely to poverty and its resultant moral degradation, and convinced that current methods of evangelism were obsolete, Jones and his colleagues proposed "in the true spirit of Jesus" three practical measures by means of which they believed the churches could meet the needs of the working classes. They would create within the churches mutual-benefit societies for care during illness or financial distress; they would ask the support of the organized church for "all forms of industrial coöperation" and trades unions; and they called upon the churches to support an economic order based upon the labor theory of value—a plan to be carried out by patronizing only "dealers who adopt the cost system."[52]

Acting upon the belief that "the press ought to be the right arm of the Labor Reform Movement," and planning to offer "a calm, deep, reverent, thorough discussion of the Labor Problem from the Christian standpoint," the Union, with Collens' financial backing and Jones as editor, began the publication of *Equity: A Journal of Christian Labor Reform,* in April, 1874. The paper's first editorial announced its creed as

Bible righteousness, Christian equity, consecration in the name of Jesus to the material, equally as to the spiritual service of our fellows; and this *in the very processes through which wealth is produced.* . . . We seek to build upon earth that part of the holy city of God, wherein his will can be done here in the sphere of work, just as it is now done in Heaven. . . . *Even in the sphere of bodily toil.*[53]

52. Rogers, *"Like Unto Me"* (Chelsea, Mass., n.d.). Also in Evangelical Alliance of the United States, *National Perils and Opportunities* (New York, 1887), p. 236.
53. *Equity,* I, No. 1 (April, 1874), 1.

Some dozen-and-a-half issues of the brave but unpopular little paper appeared. Every edition was full of earnest religious conviction and confused economics. Specific reforms were endorsed, such as shorter hours of labor and the Union's three-point program for aiding the poor through the churches. On one occasion Rogers wrote that the kingdom of God would be practically realized on earth to the extent to which the truths of the Sermon on the Mount were incorporated in reforms. From time to time *Equity* urged the abolition of interest, profit, rent, and the wages system. The last of these was once described as the reverse of the Golden Rule, as born of injustice, and as entirely unchristian. The ethics of profit and the wages system were so consistently attacked that one historian has interpreted the Union's criticism of "the system" as an attack upon capitalism. Although the Union was cognizant of the class struggle, its practical proposals for social change were usually in the form of coöperation or partnership schemes and its criticism of the wages system can hardly be called socialistic.[54] There is no evidence that its members had read Marx, whose writings were not generally available in America, and their frequent appeals to the churches rule out at once any belief in such fundamentals of socialism as the economic interpretation of history. The Christian Labor Union's primary motive was a religious humanitarianism, for the support of which it invoked whatever economic theories it found convenient.[55]

Equity's criticism of Protestantism was directed at its social ineffectiveness. Jones maintained that the church had been so concerned with the "work in the heart of the individual that the coördinate and equally essential work of reorganizing society has first been lost sight of and then denied." The result is that "our business system is pagan in origin, selfish in nature, and the deadly foe of Christianity." Even so, Protestantism has no word against it. A prominent Boston clergyman was once quoted as having said that the religion of Christ must "go outside of its elegant sanctuaries, leave its padlocked pews, forsake its gentility and fastidiousness, and go forth to meet mankind. . . ." Henry Ward Beecher was sarcastically described as "the

54. *Op. cit.,* I, No. 9 (December, 1874), 65–66.
55. This is the writer's chief criticism of Dombrowski's account of the Union.

bright, consummate flower of American Christianity" who ex-emplified the attempt to unite the service of God and mammon. To a correspondent who asked why he did not preach "the good old gospel," Jones replied that what is usually meant by that phrase is only "half of Christianity"—the half known by a Protestantism that energetically denies the other half.[56] On one occasion the Union sent a strongly worded protest to the New York Y.M.C.A. in which it declared that that organization's action in supplying strikebreakers during a longshoreman's strike was "not only unchristian but anti-christian" and typical of the attitude of the Protestant church toward the working classes.

With the December issue of 1875 *Equity* came to the inevitable end of most radical reform papers. But in October, 1877, another journalistic venture was launched. The new quarterly sheet "devoted to the welfare of the working people" was called *The Labor-Balance.* Supported by Judge Collens until his death in 1878, *Equity's* successor advocated economic and religious doctrines that it claimed "no paper of the Protestant denominations would print." This was doubtless true, for the sponsors of *Labor-Balance* had moved decidedly to the left since the demise of *Equity.* Although *Labor-Balance* continued to assert the Union's belief in the labor theory of value, it now advocated political socialism and in 1878 printed the platform of the Socialistic Labor Party.[57] While their ideal was referred to as "communism," members of the Union had obviously been converted to one of the milder forms of socialism. Rogers wrote that the only hope for the survival of this republic lay in socializing "land and the instrumentalities for the production of wealth." The church must substitute a "broad and generous objective Christian communism" for its present "narrow and selfish individualism," subjective pietism, and dwarfed practice.[58] *Labor-Balance* was sympathetic toward the strikers of 1877, declaring that Christ would have sided with them had he been here, although he would have disapproved of their violence.[59]

During its life of some six years the Union held two "Bible

56. *Equity,* II, No. 6 (July, 1875), 24.
57. *The Labor-Balance,* I, No. 3 (April, 1878), 14.
58. *Op. cit.,* I, No. 4 (July, 1878), 14.
59. *Op. cit.,* I, No. 1 (October, 1877).

Labor Reform Conventions" in Boston, one in connection with the Eight-Hour League in which Rogers was particularly active. The purpose of these gatherings was "to present the Bible laws, and especially the principles expressed or involved in the teachings of Jesus Christ which apply to the getting and using of wealth." At the conference held in May, 1875, Jones told a meager audience that the Christian Labor Union's platform was founded upon the Bible as the "chief Labor Reform book of the world" and upon the complementary principles of regeneration and the kingdom. Decrying the church's preoccupation with individuals, he declared that the Union felt the responsibility for directing the attention of the Christian world toward "that other and equally essential work of Jesus, which was that he came to reshape society throughout, making it 'a new structure' just as he makes of the individual 'a new creature.' " The two aspects of the kingdom, according to Jones, were "regeneration for the individual, reorganization for the community."[60]

In their various other writings the members of the group presented a similar set of ideas. Jones, in a fantastic but in some ways remarkable book on *The Kingdom of Heaven,* located the divine society in the United States as "an actual, human, civil government upon the ϵ rth"—"a temporal system of human society perfectly developed from the germinal principle love,"[61] compatible with and based upon American institutions: brotherhood involved in democracy, public officers as public servants, public spirit the embodiment of the great commandment, and the emancipation of the slaves as actual fulfillment of Christ's proclamation of "release to the captives."[62] The purest form of American democracy is the "communism" we have seen above; this should be the rule in society at large, in industry, and with respect to the ownership of property. Also, said Jones, in the ideal society woman will hold an equal place with man. In spite of his scriptural literalism, Jones believed the millennium would be brought in through natural processes. In *The Bible Plan for the Abolition of Poverty* he presented a curious anticipation of Henry George, basing his

---

60. *Equity,* II, No. 5 (June, 1875), 17.
61. Jesse H. Jones, *The Kingdom of Heaven* (Cambridge, 1871), pp. 80, 122.
62. Jones, *Joshua Davidson,* p. 186.

argument for the socialization of land upon the Old Testament: land should never be sold; every human being has a free and inalienable birthright to its use; society should hold it in trust. Such a scheme, plus recognition of the labor theory of value, industrial democracy, self-sacrificing service, and the abolition of profit and interest would destroy the causes of poverty.

Rogers, whose influence was probably wider than that of Jones, frequently appeared before religious bodies to plead labor's cause. He once told a Methodist convention in the perhaps injudicious words of Channing that modern civilization stood "in direct hostility to the great ideas of Christianity." The church, he declared, ought to demand that wealth be managed for the common good of the people. He asserted that the fulfillment of God's will "on earth, as in heaven" involved the equitable distribution of the products of labor. He spoke before the great Washington Conference of the Evangelical Alliance in 1887, including in his address a brief résumé of the career of the Christian Labor Union, and describing its three-point program for bringing the church and labor closer together.[63] In a pamphlet entitled *"Like Unto Me"* Rogers asked the churches for "a candid and prayerful inquiry why the existing forms of Christianity are not more effective" in removing the evils contributing to the progressive degradation of the workers.[64] Dissenting from "the prevailing Protestant theory" of the spiritual character of the church, Rogers believed that "one-half of Christ's glad tidings has not been preached in modern times."

Collens contributed articles on social problems to papers in his home city, to *The Communist*, and to the Boston *Labor Standard*, and had been a disciple of Owen and Fourier in his youth. Influenced also by Josiah Warren, Collens declared in the Preface to his book, *The Eden of Labor; or, the Christian Utopia*, that "labor is the real measure of the exchangeable value of all commodities and services." This principle rests upon "the rights of God and the law of *neighborly love*" propounded by Christ. Anticipating a time when Christ's reign should be established on earth, Collens based his utopia upon religious faith and the "consequent recognition of human

63. Evangelical Alliance, *op. cit.*, pp. 236–237.
64. Edward H. Rogers, *"Like Unto Me,"* p. 2.

brotherhood, and of the Divine title to all national or inherent values."[65]

Such was the first radical chapter in the development of American social Christianity. Although an indifferent Boston ignored them, these pioneers were true prophets of the social gospel. Moved by religious zeal, they addressed themselves to that fundamental concern of social Christianity, the labor problem. And when the strictures of socialism provided new insights into the weaknesses of the civilization of which they considered the working classes the victims, their appeals to the church were prophetic of those to come from more respectable sources in later decades.

Jesse H. Jones considered his life a failure. But the seed thus sowed did not all fall upon stony ground, for a decade afterward when George E. McNeill became a pillar in W. D. P. Bliss's socialist Church of the Carpenter, the Union had not been forgotten and in 1897 Bliss described *Equity* in the *Encyclopedia of Social Reform* as "really a paper of Christian Socialism."

The American social gospel was to develop in the general directions proposed by these scattered prophets of a broader religion. We have surveyed their criticisms of classical economics, their analyses of the conflict between labor and capital, their condemnation of business ethics, and their first attacks upon the growing urban problem. Although their interests were to broaden with insight, these concerns, with the important addition of socialism, remained fundamental to social Christians throughout the years. While the social gospel has been utopian in much of its ideology and has usually been more critical than constructive in its attitude toward the *status quo*, its strongest claim to realism lies in the fact that it continued to regard the relations of labor and capital as the sore spot of modern machine civilization. Perhaps it was but natural that this characteristically American development of the religion of the Divine Laborer should concern itself with the relations between the owners and the tenders of the machines.

65. Thomas Wharton Collens, *The Eden of Labor; or, The Christian Utopia* (Philadelphia, 1876), p. 201.

PART II: 1880–1890

THE 'EIGHTIES: A YOUTHFUL MOVEMENT

The times call for an *applied Christianity* that can meet all the needs and relations of man to man. It cannot remain merely defensive, and must prove its adaptedness to all needs and all conditions. The full brotherhood of men under one Father and in one household must be its watchword, with a meaning never known before.

WILLIAM E. DODGE

Hail the glorious golden city,
Pictured by the seers of old:
Everlasting light shines o'er it,
Wondrous things of it are told.
Only righteous men and women
Dwell within its gleaming wall;
Wrong is banished from its borders,
Justice reigns supreme o'er all.

We are builders of that city.
All our joys and all our groans
Help to rear its shining ramparts;
All our lives are building stones.
Whether humble or exalted,
All are called to task divine;
All must aid alike to carry
Forward one sublime design.

And the work that we have builded
Oft with bleeding hands and tears,
Oft in error, oft in anguish,
Will not perish with our years:
It will live and shine transfigured
In the final reign of right:
It will pass into the splendors
Of the city of the light.

FELIX ADLER, 1878

INTRODUCTION

WE have seen that the pioneer period of social Christianity was a time of vague awakenings. Foreign influences were somewhat marked, while American discussions of problems were hazy, generalized, and based entirely on the ideology of an earlier era. However, the ideal of the kingdom of God as a terrestrial possibility was beginning to appeal to men's minds. But the social consciousness of the church reoriented itself slowly after a long and absorbing preoccupation with the slavery cause, and the few radicals born out of time in the indifferent 'seventies had almost as well not spoken.

With the coming of the 1880's the progress of the social gospel became more apparent. Liberal ferments within the religious community had commenced to make themselves felt, the "acids of modernity" had begun to eat through the surface of a hollow orthodoxy, and the increased intensity of the social struggle had aroused the nation to the realization that beneath the crust of the gilded age there lurked forces of destruction. This growing appreciation of the seriousness of the conflict tended to make the pronouncements of social Christianity more realistic in that it forced leaders of the new movement to formulate their own solutions in relation to actual situations they themselves encountered. It also broadened the sweep of the as yet youthful social gospel.

To clergymen as well as to other observers the most apparent of the threats to social stability, and the most obviously freighted with dire consequences, was the dissatisfaction of labor that, fed on starvation wages and to a certain extent a radical socialism, had rioted in 1877 on a national scale. Such discontent showed little sign of abating as the 'eighties came and went. In 1879 Henry George's *Progress and Poverty* had proclaimed that the rich were getting richer and the poor poorer—a thesis that in no way diminished the anger of a sullen proletariat already convinced that its share of the plunder of a continent was too small. To make matters worse, the working classes were listening eagerly to the propagandism of an aggressive socialism, the very foreign nature of which sufficed to make it anathema to the middle classes and so to intensify the social maladjustment. Thus it was that socialism and the labor problem first attracted the attention of socially minded clergymen to the point of dominating their interest so that other questions such as the problems of the rapidly growing cities received relatively little discussion in this period. The great concern of social Christianity in the industrial problem and socialism's solution of it remained throughout subsequent decades the most realistic aspect of the new movement.

In the absence of a well-developed sociology, the 'eighties became the period of discussion rather than practical application of social Christian principles. Ideas were spread abroad in the land but without great immediate effect. The demand for a new technique with which to deal with fresh problems in unique settings found the church off her guard and for the moment bewildered by the very novelty of the situation. As the decade wore on the demand for a foundation of social science beneath all reform became more and more insistent, and the quest for a Christian sociology proved itself a significant phase of the maturing movement in the last years of the century. Although sudden popularity ushered social Christianity into the national forum before the close of the 'eighties, it even then was but a minority movement, and was destined so to remain.

CHAPTER III

THE NEW THEOLOGY AND THE NEW ETHICS

[The new theology] holds that every man must live a life of his own . . . and give an account of himself to God: but it also . . . turns our attention to the corporate life of man here in the world. . . . Hence its ethical emphasis . . . holding that human society itself is to be redeemed.

THEODORE THORNTON MUNGER[1]

WE have seen in a previous chapter that during the gilded age there began to ferment within conventional Protestantism an enlightened conservatism that led inevitably to a more ethical religion. In the 1880's this still amorphous growth developed into a careful if inconsistent school of thought that referred to itself as "progressive orthodoxy" or the "new theology." Upon its theological and ethical foundation the social gospel could build securely.

To the left of this middle-of-the-road viewpoint the acids of modernity fomented liberal and even radical reactions against a placid Protestantism. Fully receptive to the confident new science, one group of Unitarians sought to purify its own liberal tradition. Another dissatisfied minority slipped all Christian moorings and radically declared for a religion of humanity. Still further to the left a group of religious outcasts sought a new spiritual home in Societies for Ethical Culture. Across this scene there moved such bizarre figures as Col. Robert G. Ingersoll and Henry George, demanding that a socially ineffective Protestantism show ethical cause for its continued existence.

While all such influences aided the growth of a socialized Christianity, its greatest stimuli nevertheless came from the inner liberalizing forces of progressivism, the ethical implications of which were immediately productive of social interests.

1. Theodore Thornton Munger, *The Freedom of Faith* (Boston and New York, 1883 [12th ed., 1885]), p. 25.

I. MORAL RELIGION

Unitarianism, that gadfly of the New England theology, was a mordant factor in liberalizing American religion throughout the nineteenth century. The dissatisfied schools that developed in this communion following the Civil War focused their criticism of the rationalistic Unitarian heritage chiefly upon the ethical aspects of Christianity. Confident of "the inevitable surrender of orthodoxy" these left-wing groups discarded supernaturalism, branded the traditional plan of salvation as immoral, buried Protestantism as an ethical failure, and turned to the construction of a scientific religion based upon ethics and psychology.[2]

Liberal Unitarians of the 1880's claimed to base their "liberal movement in theology" upon "the primary facts of human experience." Frankly humanistic, they rejected all speculative theology; they retained the term "Christian" only as a recognition of habit or inheritance that "meant much for the higher life of men"; and they phrased their religious purpose in terms of evolution—"the accepted scientific theory of our time." The great task of religion, wrote the Reverend Joseph Henry Allen, a leader of the movement, "is to aid in the unfolding of human nature, society, and life, toward the highest, noblest, fairest forms of which they are capable."[3] The Divine remained in this system "only to give lift to imagination"; its value was chiefly emotional. The final sanction for such a religion was ethical. Salvation, said Allen, has always been found by returning upon the deepest moral convictions of the soul; the foundations of the universe must be laid in equity. The true province of religion must be "experience and duty of the life that now is, not vain strivings to fathom the eternal and unknown."[4]

This school demanded that the Bible be judged by the same standards of literary and historical criticism used in evaluating other records. It would "gather and preserve whatever is good in the tradition to be found from every source"—a typical humanist interest in comparative religions. The practical appli-

2. See Minot J. Savage, "The Inevitable Surrender of Orthodoxy," *North American Review,* 148 (1889), 711–726.

3. Joseph Henry Allen, *Our Liberal Movement in Theology* (Boston, 1882), p. 171.

4. Allen, *Sequel to Our Liberal Movement* (Boston, 1897), p. 58.

cation of this moralistic religion was to be through the study of "history, politics, economy, social statics and dynamics, the laws of wealth, the laws of charity, the laws of character and heredity, the laws of population, the laws of crime."[5] These ethical and social interests would be realized through the Unitarian ideal of a free church—a natural human fellowship cemented by devotion to the highest good recognizable by each member.[6] Such a church would exist for the purpose of "developing the religious character of the community, of inspiring and regulating active efforts for the improvement of man"; it would apply the religious spirit to the solution of social problems; its clergy would be leaders in "every work of practical humanity."[7] When, at the end of the century, Joseph H. Allen summarized the course of the liberal movement, he regarded the study of social ethics as its most important trend.[8]

In 1867 a group of radical Unitarians avowing a "religion of humanity" broke with their denomination and organized a Free Religious Association. Deeply indebted to Theodore Parker, they denied the unique authority of Christ and of the Bible, and pushed the liberal doctrines of Unitarianism to their logical extremes.[9] They declared the intellect rather than the soul to be the first authority in a religion whose rationalistic ethics would be independent of Christianity. The magna charta of the Free Religionists came from the pen of the Reverend Octavius Brooks Frothingham in 1873. Entitled *The Religion of Humanity*, this manifesto rejected all forms of supernaturalism, located the Divine in human nature, defined salvation as "spiritual health and sanity," declared the Bible to be inadequate to the needs of humanity, and interpreted the incarnation in terms of a broad humanism. But since these radicals made little effort to apply their humanistic ideals to specific social situations, their influence was pervasive and intellectual rather than practical.

Another religious development that sprang from similar ra-

---

5. *Our Liberal Movement,* p. 173.
6. The accepted church was regarded as an anachronistic institution "for occupying the leisure hours of Sunday with what is now called religious services." See Charles Eliot Norton, "The Church and Religion," *North American Review,* 106 (1868), 376–396.
7. *Ibid.*   8. Allen, *Sequel,* p. 62.
9. George Willis Cooke, *Unitarianism in America* (Boston, 1902), p. 202.

tionalistic roots but that did not stagnate in a barren intellectualism was the ethical-culture movement. Rejecting the rationalistic emphasis of the Free Religionists, Felix Adler and his associates chose a platform of "natural ethics," holding that true religion is based upon the moral life and that the moral law "has an immediate authority, not contingent on the truth of religious beliefs or philosophical theories."[10]

This ethical faith did not confine its expression to criticism of the moral failures of Protestantism. It bore fruit almost immediately in significant social concerns. Taking seriously its motto, "Not the creed but the deed," the movement at once plunged into reform activity. In 1877 the New York Society completed its first model-tenement project.[11] Adler and other leaders frequently acted as arbitrators or impartial chairmen in industrial disputes. In 1887 Dr. Stanton Coit established the "Neighborhood Guild" in New York as the first social settlement in America. Societies in St. Louis, Chicago, and Philadelphia developed similar activities.[12] Walter L. Sheldon, leader of the St. Louis group, told his people on their fifth anniversary that lecturers of ethical societies "should be familiar with the labor problem, with the social and political agitation of the day. Their one purpose should be to bring the moral standard to bear on the practical issues in the sphere of commerce, social and personal life, or the state"; in order to be adequately equipped they should study economics and political science rather than comparative religion.[13] The societies' belief in moral education has been exemplified in the Ethical Culture Schools for children and the Schools of Applied Ethics for adults.

While criticism of Protestantism was a considerable part of the *raison d'être* of these radical religious bodies, formal Ameri-

10. M. W. Meyerhardt, "The Movement for Ethical Culture at Home and Abroad," *American Journal of Religious Psychology and Education,* 2 (1908), 76, 78.

11. "News from the Societies," *Ethical Record* (Philadelphia, April, 1888).

12. See *The Cause* and the *Ethical Record;* also John Lovejoy Elliott, "The Relation of the Ethical Ideal to Social Reform," in *Aspects of Ethical Religion,* Horace J. Bridges, ed. (New York, 1926).

13. Walter L. Sheldon, *The Meaning of the Ethical Movement. Fifth Anniversary Address* (St. Louis, 1891), p. 39. In this connection see also William M. Salter, *Ethical Religion* (Boston, 1890); Leo Jacobs, *Three Types of Practical Ethical Movements of the Past Half Century* (New York, 1922); and Felix Adler, *Creed and Deed* (New York, 1877).

can Christianity probably received its most severe castigation during the 'eighties from two individuals, both crusaders and incidentally prophets of a socialized religion—Col. Robert G. Ingersoll, apostle of the "liberty" of agnosticism, and Henry George, evangelist for the single tax. Both proclaimed the unethical character of an otherworldly religion unfit to meet the demands of the new age of industry and science.

Ingersoll had retired voluntarily from a political career that might well have taken him to the White House in order to devote his consummate oratorical skill to the liberation of the mind of his time from what he referred to as the "mistakes of Moses." In spite of much bombast Ingersoll frequently expressed belief in a fatherly God and a loving human Christ. Although he fulminated against a church that for a thousand years "extinguished the torch of progress in the blood of Christ," Ingersoll affirmed simply that

There is no religion except humanity. Religion comes from the heart of man. Human affection is the foundation of all that is holy in religion.

Human intelligence, applied to human conduct, is what we call morality; and you add to simple morality kindness, charity, love —and there can be no more perfect religion imagined by the brain of man.[14]

No Hebrew prophet rebuked wayward Israel more severely than Henry George attacked vested wrongs and a religion that "allies itself with injustice." Himself devoutly religious, George's mission bore the stamp of a crusade consecrated to social justice. This accounts for the zeal that filled converts to his panacea the single tax, among whom were many religious leaders.[15] His major work, *Progress and Poverty*, published in 1879, was the first critical analysis of the misery and desolation that hid in the shadows of the gilded age. George became a world figure and the single tax a national movement, although few concrete results came from the crusade. His vivid picture

14. Edward Garstin Smith, *Life and Reminiscences of Robert G. Ingersoll* (New York, 1904), p. 56.
15. See George R. Geiger, *The Philosophy of Henry George* (New York, 1933), p. 339.

of light and darkness in American life was an entering wedge in arousing the nation's social conscience.

In a true Christianity that attacks vested wrong, wrote George, there is power to regenerate the world. But it must not be that spurious thing that in ignoring its social responsibilities has really forgotten the teachings of Christ. "The religion which allies itself with injustice to preach down the natural aspirations of the masses is worse than atheism."[16] George proclaimed a militant Christianity that would crusade against economic injustice; he attacked religious institutions for their social failures; he held that the social question was at the bottom a religious question; he plead for justice, not charity or Christian socialism.[17]

These contentions profoundly influenced several men who were later to be outstanding leaders of American social Christianity. Walter Rauschenbusch, greatest prophet of the social gospel, owed his first awakening to the world of social problems to George.[18] William Dwight Porter Bliss, American pioneer of Christian socialism, was likewise aroused in part by the author of the single tax.[19] George D. Herron, who dominated the social-gospel stage during the 1890's, at one time advocated the single tax because it would provide the "elemental basis for the ideal society."[20] A Maine Congregational minister declared that George's argument concerning the concentration of wealth was impregnable, while the editor of the *Unitarian Review*, although rejecting the single tax, agreed that "nationalization" of wealth should begin with natural resources.[21] In 1889 the Reverend James B. Converse of Morristown, Tennessee, issued a Christian version of George's gospel, entitled *The Bible and Land*, in which he demanded the adoption of the single tax be-

16. Henry George, "The Land Question," in *Works,* III, 96; quoted by Geiger, *op. cit.,* p. 339. Used by permission.

17. Geiger, *op. cit.,* p. 365; also *Progress and Poverty,* pp. 546–547, quoted by Geiger, *op. cit.,* p. 380.

18. Walter Rauschenbusch, *Christianizing the Social Order* (New York, 1912), p. 394. See chap. xiii below.

19. "William Dwight Porter Bliss," *Encyclopedia of Social Reform* (New York, 1908). See chap. x below.

20. George D. Herron, *A Confession of Social Faith* (Chicago, 1899), p. 7. See chap. xi below.

21. *Unitarian Review,* 29 (1888), 440–451.

cause it is the only form of taxation "in accord with the Creator's plans."

From such a bizarre group of influences did the social gospel derive momentum during the 1880's. Georgism, the oratory of Ingersoll, the ethical church, and the religion of humanity suggest certain religious currents of the decade. But whatever the effect of these external factors, we must examine the internal dynamics of progressive Protestantism to discover the larger and genuinely fertile springs of the youthful social Christian movement.

II. Progressive Orthodoxy

The enlightened conservatism first stated by Horace Bushnell came to be of great moment for a nascent social gospel. In the 1880's this thought current was channeled into a fairly definite school by leading progressive theologians. Among these were the faculty of Andover Theological Seminary, whose "progressive orthodoxy" was widely circulated in the *Andover Review* founded in 1884. The outstanding prophet of the movement was the "New Haven seer," the Reverend Theodore Thornton Munger, pastor of United (Congregational) Church, biographer of Bushnell, and author of *The Freedom of Faith*, a book rated by the New York *Times* as "the most forcible and positive expression" of the new theology to appear in this country. Other leaders of the movement were the Reverend Newman Smyth, minister of Center Church, New Haven, whose *Christian Ethics*, written in 1892, was still in print in 1936; the Reverend Elisha Mulford, distinguished Episcopal clergyman, teacher, and author of *The Nation* and *The Republic of God;* and Washington Gladden, whose theology we shall examine in the introduction to our study of the 1890's. This deepening stream was later to blend into the "modernism" of the twentieth century.

A modified supernaturalism, the new theology pursued a careful though somewhat illogical course between the stern dualism of orthodoxy and the frank monism of the religion of humanity.[22] Progressivism stoutly maintained its belief in a

22. Munger, *op. cit.*, p. 26; see also Newman Smyth, *Old Faiths in New Light* (New York, 1879), p. 341.

personal God, accepted "the theory of physical evolution as the probable method of creation," insisted upon the freedom of the human will, and proposed to read the Bible as literature and as a revelation the full meaning of which is to be seen in history. The new theology criticized orthodoxy for its "hard, formal, unsympathetic, and unimaginative" attitude toward the Scriptures, and for its alienation from human life. Munger declared that the old theology stood on a structure of logic remote from actual life, and that its clergy were men apart from the world and out of practical sympathy with it. Against this, progressivism preached a living Incarnation active "in all the processes of human life."

The new theology made two proposals that were of particular importance to the social gospel. It sought to replace the excessive individualism of orthodoxy with "a truer view of the solidarity of the race"; it professed the "broad, healthy, social philosophy of human nature which is taken for granted in the Bible."[23] The individual life can express itself only in terms of the common life, said John Bascom, while Munger pointed out the impossibility of completely isolating the individual from society. But this was not to lose sight of persons, warned Munger: the state, the family, society, commerce, were regarded as areas in which God manifests himself. Progressivism therefore stood ready to "ally itself with all movements for bettering the condition of mankind."[24]

Rather than seeking its methodology in the formal logic of theology, progressivism sought "a wider study of man" in the "every-day processes of humanity." This practical criticism of orthodoxy led naturally to ethical interpretations of dogma. Progressivism would have a moral God, a truly moral divine government, a moral atonement, and a faith that involved moral action. Concerned more with the logic of life than of system, it accepted the charge of inconsistency with the statement that it had no interest in a logical scheme that stood "aside from the ordinary thought of men." One of its philosophers saw the kingdom of heaven coming along the lines of

23. Smyth, *op. cit.*, p. 141.
24. Munger, *op. cit.*, p. 25. For Munger's significance as a theologian, see John W. Buckham, *Progressive Religious Thought in America* (Boston and New York, 1919), chap. ii.

union between scientific research and religious insight; man and God, nature and the supernatural, working together for a perfect individual and social life, redeeming the present and by it marching victoriously into the future.[25]

"The process and end of the life of the spirit is the development of a perfect humanity," wrote Elisha Mulford, "the aim is the attainment and fulfillment of a perfect manhood."[26]

Professor William Jewett Tucker of Andover, later president of Dartmouth College, summarized the contribution of the new theology to the social gospel in his autobiography:

The distinctive characteristic of the progressive movement . . . was its humanistic impulse. It carried religion, and even theology, farther out into human relations. It took account of the individual in his human environment. It viewed him more definitely as a social being, a part of a vast but closely fitting social organization. It followed him into those classifications into which modern society had divided itself, chiefly as the result of the new economic conditions. It refused to obey the mandate of the old political economy, and leave the individual to the fortune of the market-place. It assumed the right to know the reason, for example, of the contentions of capital and labor, and the right no less to take part in the whole economic conflict according to its social significance. The movement early acquired the name of social Christianity.[27]

III. The Christian Ethic in History

A further significant step toward a social gospel was the appearance in the early 'eighties of a literature describing the influence of Christian ethics upon the social life and institutions of Western civilization. In general, this was not a new development, but its pragmatic attitude, which endeavored to establish the validity of Christianity on ethical grounds, is a suggestive barometer of the religious climate of the period.

Identification of Christianity with the forces making for

25. John Bascom, *The New Theology. A Baccalaureate Sermon* . . . (Milwaukee, 1884), p. 22 See also his *The New Theology* (New York and London, 1891).

26. Elisha Mulford, *The Republic of God* (Boston, 1881), p. 235.

27. William Jewett Tucker, *My Generation* (Boston and New York, 1919), p. 97. By permission of copyright owner.

progress was an integral article in nineteenth-century ideology. The author of one of the first books written as a defense of American democracy asserted that Christianity gave to our morals "a decided and continuous impulse toward improvement" and that it tended "directly to the institution of a democracy."[28] Most Americans would have agreed with a centennial orator who declared that democracy "sprang full-armed and perfect from Christianity."[29] A common apologetic was the statement that Christianity is the only religion that fosters education, philanthropy, and reform, and otherwise exerts itself "for the renovation of society."[30]

The theme of "the achievements of Christ" in history was most cogently stated during the 1880's by Charles Loring Brace, founder and superintendent of the Children's Aid Society of New York. Early in his thirty years' work among "the dangerous classes" of the metropolis Brace had been convinced that Christ was "the central figure in the world's charity." He believed with Lecky that humanitarianism in the West rooted in the Christian doctrine of the inestimable value of the human soul.[31] In 1882 Brace published his reasoned judgment based on years of study, as *Gesta Christi: or A History of Humane Progress under Christianity.* The book, an instant success, stated its author's case for believing Christianity to be "the *greatest* element in modern progress." Brace maintained that Christianity would remodel the world in spite of the fact that the organized church had frequently been reactionary and that Stoic ethics, Roman law, Arabic science, and other elements had contributed to Western civilization.

The author of *Gesta Christi* claimed that, although the teachings of Jesus were not unique, their presentation to mankind in his person did comprise "a new moral force in the world's history." Brace then outlined the influence of Christianity upon the ancient world, the Middle Ages, and modern times. Aware of

28. G. S. Camp, *Democracy* (New York, 1841), pp. 179–181.

29. From a collection of orations gathered by the Librarian of the Astor Library, New York, *Our Centennial Jubilee* (New York, 1877).

30. J. U. Parsons, *The Philanthropies* (Boston, n.d.). See also Peter Bayne, *The Christian Life, Social and Individual* (Boston, 1855).

31. Charles Loring Brace, *Short Sermons to Newsboys* (New York, 1866), p. 11; see also his *The Dangerous Classes of New York and Twenty Years Work among Them* (New York, 1872 [3d ed., 1880]), pp. 14–15.

the failures of the church, he sought to follow the pervasive influence of the belief and practices of the countless silent followers of Christ who "illustrated and transmitted the divine truths which they received from Him." The true and invisible church has been composed of those whose discipleship was attested by their lives of purity, human brotherhood, honesty, faithfulness, compassion, and true humanity. Living for Him, they have lived for the human race.

. . . Their spirit and their sacrifices have made it possible that ages hence some of the great evils of mankind should come to an end, that some tears should be forever wiped away, and a fair prospect held forth of a distant future of humanity, justice and righteousness. . . . The victories they have won in their silent struggles, and bequeathed to us, were really the *"Gesta Christi"*— the achievements of Christ.[32]

Such accomplishments may be seen at work in our civilization, continued Brace. Among the "practices, principles and ideals" that had been "either implanted or stimulated or supported by Christianity" Brace named respect for woman; regard for personality; humanitarian care for the child, the prisoner, the needy; "unceasing opposition to all forms of cruelty, oppression and slavery"; the duty of personal purity and the sacredness of marriage; and temperance. To these individualistic ideals were added several definitely social goals: "the obligation of a more equitable division of the profits of labor, and of greater co-operation between employers and employed"; the right of every individual to the fullest development of his personality, and of all to equal social and political privileges. Certain international ideals concluded the enumeration: "the principle that the injury of one nation is the injury of all"; "unrestricted trade and intercourse between all countries"; and, finally and principally, opposition to war—determination to limit its evils and to prevent its outbreak by means of arbitration.[33]

This identification of Christian ethics with the liberalisms of the day led Brace not only to the conclusion that Christianity is

32. Brace, *Gesta Christi* (New York, 1882 [4th ed., 1884]), p. 3.
33. *Op. cit.*, p. vi.

"the absolute and universal religion" but to a further apologetic for its supernatural origin. He was joined in this argument by the Reverend Richard S. Storrs of Brooklyn, whose Lowell Institute lectures were published in 1884 as *The Divine Origin of Christianity Indicated by Its Historical Effects.* Storrs's findings were similar to those of Brace, although he stood more definitely in the evangelical tradition. Taking the condition of woman in the Roman world as an example, Storrs declared that as soon as Christianity had gained a place in the empire woman's social and legal position "instantaneously improved"—"the effect of direct, immediate, constant pressure from the religion brought by Jesus."[34] Storrs similarly attributed the abolition of slavery to the influence of the Sermon on the Mount, the ideals of the fatherhood of God and the brotherhood of disciples, and the Christian conceptions of mutual duty and common immortality. Although Christianity had always attacked the problem of reform from within the individual it would nevertheless in time produce a perfect society that would be harmonious and free.

Such ethical apologetics marked a long step toward a social gospel. Prophets of a socialized Christianity who had themselves vaguely held similar views adopted Brace's statement with enthusiasm. Thus strengthened in their own preconceptions they faced the complex social questions of the day with new vigor. If Christianity had influenced the social institutions of antiquity, might it not prove a powerful agent in dealing with the problems of a newly industrialized America—socialism, labor, the growing power of wealth, crime, and the complexities of the great cities?

34. Richard S. Storrs, *The Divine Origin of Christianity* (New York, 1884), p. 151.

CHAPTER IV

THE CHURCH CHALLENGES SOCIALISM

The church's remedy for social discontent and dynamite bombs is
Christianity as taught in the New Testament.

RICHARD T. ELY

THE coming of the 1880's marked an era in the development
of American social Christianity. We have seen that for some
years a few alert ministers had been prying into the shadows of
the gilded age and had uncovered situations that they regarded
as not only unlovely and unethical, but unchristian. Clergymen
were among the leading diagnosticians of the industrial maladjustments of the late 'seventies. After 1880 this concern in social matters developed out of its pioneer phase into a well-de-
fined although minority movement that ten years later numbered its protagonists by the score and found its audience
across the nation.

Religious leaders focused their interest in social conditions
upon the labor problem, which, since the great strike of 1877,
had assumed dangerous proportions in the eyes of many observers. The menace was heightened by the red glare thrown
over an already serious situation by the rapid growth of socialism within the ranks of labor. The program of socialism at once
aroused the deep concern of Protestant clergymen. Before the
Civil War Henry James, senior, had equated the aims of socialism and Christianity.[1] Washington Gladden had discussed the
subject seriously if superficially in his lectures to *Working
People and their Employers* in 1876. However, the appearance
in 1879 of a book entitled *Socialism* by the "broadly and fearlessly progressive" Roswell D. Hitchcock of Union Theological
Seminary marked the beginning of a discussion that soon became one of the focal points of the social gospel.

The modern scientific socialism that was alarming Americans
in 1880 owed little or nothing to early idealistic communism of

1. Henry James, Sr., *Moralism and Christianity* (New York, 1850), p. 92.

the Fourieristic type.[2] Having begun to take definite form about 1872, it was still a comparatively new phenomenon largely of foreign origin.[3] Torn between two basically antagonistic philosophies, American socialism had struggled through the 'seventies in a constant state of internal dissension until the arrival in 1882 of the firebrand John Most, whose violent utterances drove the two factions of the party to definite separation the next year.

The platform of the radical, anarchistic wing, known as the "International Working People's Association," called for "destruction of the existing class rule" by whatever means necessary. It demanded the establishment of "a free society based upon coöperative organization of production," free exchange without profit, complete equality of the sexes, and entire freedom of contract. Professor Richard T. Ely, youthful economist of the Johns Hopkins University and outstanding protagonist of the social gospel in this decade, branded these doctrines as nihilism and declared that they exaggerated the influence of environment on character. He held that anarchism attacked religion and the family, while threatening the foundations of law and order with its threat of revolution backed by the terrorism of the Black Hand.[4] When, in 1886, the Haymarket bombing occurred in Chicago, the accumulated suspicion and hatred of the nation descended upon these radicals, and although its adherents disclaimed all responsibility, anarchism never recovered from the effects of this demonstration of its tenets.

The "far more decent" right wing of socialism, the "Socialistic Labor Party," was, however, the dominant force in the socialist movement. It based its beliefs upon the labor theory of value and asserted that "a just and equitable distribution of the fruits of labor is utterly impossible under the present system of society." Competition, declared its platform, results in monopoly. To abolish existing conditions the party held that "land, the means of production, public transportation and exchange" must be socialized.[5] The Socialistic Labor Party pro-

2. Morris Hillquit, *History of Socialism in the United States* (New York, 1903), p. 149.

3. Hillquit, *op. cit.*, pp. 155, 171–172, 241; Richard T. Ely, "Recent American Socialism," in *Johns Hopkins University Studies in Historical and Political Science,* 3d ser. (April, 1885), 255.

4. Ely, *op. cit.*, pp. 257–258, 270.   5. *Op. cit.*, p. 277.

posed to accomplish these aims by means of the ballot; it substituted evolution for revolution, and peaceful agitation for violence. Seeking industrial as well as political democracy these socialists looked for a universal system of coöperation that would hold the means of production as the property of the whole people. They believed in their principles as leaven preparing the way for the revolution. Professor Ely held that the party's attitude toward religion and the family was less extreme than that of the radical group. It stood for reforms such as the reduction of the hours of labor, abolition of child labor, compulsory education, and cash payment of wages.

Although the organized socialism of the 'eighties was a minority of almost negligible power, the fears aroused by it are understandable when it is realized that the growing labor movement was honeycombed with it. The Knights of Labor, whose membership passed the half-million mark in 1886, bore a definitely socialistic tinge although it was far from being a socialistic organization. The American Federation of Labor, only an infant in the 1880's, harbored a strong minority of socialists and even its president, Samuel Gompers, was at that time friendly to socialism. Serious students such as Professor Ely thought that socialism's steady growth boded ill for the country. Ely went as far as to enumerate reports of armed companies in training for the revolution, although he could give no definite figures. He regarded industrial discontent as fuel for social conflagration, fearing "large loss of life, estrangement of classes, incalculable destruction of property and a shock to the social body" that would hamper economic development for years.[6] Distrust of socialism was unquestionably based also upon its foreign character and the fact that it came to America with the great German migration, in whose language much of its propaganda was carried on.[7] The nation was wary of another eruption of the social volcano whose outburst in 1877 had so set its nerves on edge.

When clergymen analyzed socialism they unanimously rejected it as an economic and social philosophy. The more pro-

6. *Op. cit.*, pp. 293–294.
7. Allan Nevins, *The Emergence of Modern America* (New York, 1927), p. 382.

gressive regarded it as a symptom of social illness. Many accepted the challenge of its criticisms, but none embraced it prior to 1890. Those who saw it as a spur to the socializing of Christianity sometimes referred to their views as "Christian Socialism," by which they meant essentially a social gospel.

Religious leaders frankly recognized the justice of many of the strictures of socialism, but they refused to admit the validity of its constructive program. President David Jayne Hill of Lewisburg University told the Baptist Congress of 1885 that however inadequate socialism might be as a cure, it could not be denied that "there are evils that need to be remedied in the present order of things."[8] Washington Gladden asserted that socialism's indictment of modern society described "the natural issues of an industrial system whose sole motive power is self-interest, and whose sole regulative principle is competition."[9] A lecturer on "Christian Socialism" told the American Institute of Christian Philosophy in 1885 that nothing was "more painfully apparent" than the "sickness, disorganization, and pain in human society." The characteristic social-gospel note of urgency was not lacking in this discussion. The need of the hour, wrote the Reverend A. J. F. Behrends of Brooklyn in his book, *Socialism and Christianity*, is for Christianity to meet the socialists' indictment of the reigning economic policy of modern life; socialism is no side issue. Gladden declared in *Applied Christianity* that the time had passed when socialism could be dismissed.

Many clergymen regarded socialism as the immediate fruitage of American social and industrial conditions in the gilded age. The fundamental cause of this situation was held to be the enormous increase of wealth brought about by the industrial revolution, a process that, goaded by an exaggerated individualism careless of natural resources, had resulted not only in overproduction of goods[10] but in the division of society into antagonistic classes separated by an ever-widening gulf.[11] This

---

8. David J. Hill, "Socialism: False and True," *Proceedings* of the fourth annual session of the Baptist Congress . . . (New York, 1886), pp. 27–28.

9. Washington Gladden, *Applied Christianity* (Boston and New York, 1886), pp. 69–70.

10. Minot J. Savage, *Social Problems* (New York and London, 1887), p. 102.

11. Josiah Strong, *Our Country* (New York, 1885), p. 94; Edward S. Parsons, "A Christian Critique of Socialism," *Andover Review*, 11 (1889), 599–600.

logic of events was inevitably concentrating industrial ownership and power in fewer and fewer hands—"the growth of the
plutocracy, into whose hands is falling the power of the state,
as well as the direction of commerce." Worse still, such concentration was followed by "selfish, conscienceless use," waste, ex-
travagance, luxury, and utter lack of regard for public welfare, while the malefactors of wealth treated "this whole business as if the money belonged simply to them." Across the gulf
both clergy and socialists saw the workers' share of the wealth
increasing less rapidly than that of the owning class, and in
time of depression sinking to alarmingly low levels at the cost
of widespread distress not only in immediate suffering but in
moral degradation.[12] The laborer's position was regarded as
additionally insecure as a result of recurring periods of business stagnation due to the overproduction that was thought to
be an inevitable issue of the system of competition.[13]

At least one minister saw the socialism of his time as a first
step toward a coöperative society. The Reverend R. Heber
Newton, whom we met in the previous decade, believed that the
social commonwealth would develop out of the social revolution
of the nineteenth century, quite as democracy had been born
out of the political revolutions of the eighteenth century.[14]

The reactions of these and many other clergymen to the socialistic criticism of capitalism may be seen at once as a powerful stimulus to the growing social gospel. For example, Behrends, whose *Socialism and Christianity* was perhaps the best
book on its subject published during the 1880's, declared that
Christianity could not remain blind to the evils pointed out by
socialism. A Cincinnati minister held that the church could have
nothing to do with political socialism as such, but its social influence and responsibility were nevertheless great.[15] The Reverend C. O. Brown of Dubuque, Iowa, proposed to listen to the
pleas of the socialists and to demonstrate in practical ways that
the churches were the friends of the laboring classes,[16] while

12. Roswell D. Hitchcock, *Socialism* (New York, 1879), p. 79; Savage, *op. cit.*, p. 105.
13. Gladden, *op. cit.*, p. 65.
14. R. H. Newton, "Communism," *Unitarian Review*, 16 (1881), 485–533.
15. F. C. Monfort, *Socialism and City Evangelization* (Cincinnati, 1887), p. 52.
16. C. O. Brown, *Talks on Labor Troubles* (Chicago, 1886), pp. 19–20.

Gladden said that if Christianity possessed any vitality it would remedy the ills complained of by the socialists through "the application by individuals of Christian principles and methods to the solution of the social problem."[17]

As clergymen analyzed the ideology of socialism they inclined to view it on the one hand as an economic and political panacea and on the other as a moral or religious philosophy. The Reverend Edward S. Parsons of Greeley, Colorado, defined socialism as "a theory, based upon a claim of justice for the laboring classes, which aims at the transformation of the state into a cooperative commonwealth, and inaugurating and carrying on all industry."[18] Behrends reduced socialism to five points: the labor theory of value, capital a species of theft, the true function of government the solution of the economic problem, common ownership of the means of production and resources, and the fundamental and international nature of the political issue involved.[19] Other analyses mentioned such socialistic dogmas as the abolition of the family and of religion, the curtailment of individualism, the socialization of land (an example of the influence of Henry George), the seizure of the government by the proletariat after the revolution, and the socialization of capital. The essentially practical mind of Washington Gladden was absorbed by the political and economic aspects of socialism. It aims, he said, "fundamentally at the reconstruction of the industrial order; and it need not concern itself with questions of morality or religion."

But for other socially minded leaders the moral and religious aspects of socialism were its greatest fascination. Parsons declared that its claim to regenerate society brought it into the same sphere with Christianity: there is a kingdom of socialism similar to the kingdom of God and the two may be contrasted. The Reverend Edwin B. Webb of Boston told the American Home Missionary Society in 1885 that both Christianity and socialism aimed at a better future and recognized wrongs to be removed.[20] R. H. Newton saw in socialistic striving an ethical

17. Gladden, *op. cit.*, p. 100.   18. Parsons, *op. cit.*, p. 598.
19. A. J. F. Behrends, *Socialism and Christianity* (New York, 1886), pp. 52–53.
20. Edwin B. Webb, *Socialism and the Christian Church* (New York, 1885), p. 17.

idealism similar to that of the Hebrew prophets, and he anticipated later Christian Socialists in asserting that Jesus and the early church practiced a simple communism.[21] Another writer declared that Jesus' attempt to establish a kingdom contemplated a practical communism with the aim of humbling the upper classes and elevating the lower.[22] It was further pointed out that both Christianity and socialism protested an extreme individualism, condemned industrial autocracy, urged the ideals of brotherhood and coöperation, and hoped "for a future society in which there shall be justice to all, coöperation, peace, plenty, intellectual and moral growth and attainment."[23]

When Protestant ministers of the 1880's rejected socialism they did so on grounds that may be roughly classified as economic, political, practical, individualistic, and religious. Their fundamental economic objection was directed against the labor theory of value, which they regarded as the cornerstone of socialism. Gladden declared flatly that regardless of who was the author of the doctrine, it was unsound; for this reason he held that socialism could never survive a thorough discussion of its economic basis, for value is comprised of additional elements beyond labor[24]—elements listed by Behrends as including raw materials, management, and markets.[25]

The experience of these Americans with the corrupt politics and governmental prodigality of the "Great Barbecue" made them chary of the political side of socialism. Socialization of land, resources, capital, and means of production seemed an unwarranted centralization of power. The notion of state ownership stood directly athwart the current of late nineteenth-century ideology. The eminent Unitarian Minot J. Savage pointed out that governmental management of business in this country had not been "especially encouraging,"[26] while Joseph Cook asked an applauding Boston Monday Lecture audience if there would be any jobbery in politics if "all the lands of the nation" were to be disposed of.[27] The bureaucracy necessitated by socialism would break down of its own weight; its directing com-

21. Newton, *op. cit.,* pp. 512–514.
22. Austin Bierbower, *Socialism of Christ* (Chicago, 1890), chaps. iv, v.
23. Parsons, *op. cit.,* p. 610.   24. Gladden, *op. cit.,* p. 92.
25. Behrends, *op. cit.,* p. 84.   26. Savage, *op. cit.,* p. 111.
27. Cook, *Socialism* (Boston, 1880), p. 26.

mittee would need superhuman wisdom; the inefficiency of the state is notorious and it is absurd to believe that state operation of industry would be more efficient than private management or "free capitalistic coöperation." Whatever the government attempts proves more costly and more wasteful than private enterprise, asserted Behrends.

It was further contended that certain socialistic arguments were fallacious: poverty was not on the increase, although labor had admittedly not shared proportionately in the increase of wealth. The ultimate dominance of the proletariat was attacked as "indefensible and tyrannical." Gladden believed that capital would tend to disappear under socialism because of the lessened force of the motives that led to its accumulation. In addition to these practical contentions, the utopian character of socialism was pointed out. Granted that the dream may be pleasant and even desirable, how could it be effected short of civil war? asked Gladden, while Joseph Cook was convinced it would lead to dictatorship. David Jayne Hill branded socialism as "a dream of impossible remedies for imaginary wrongs," and Behrends declared its basic assumptions "as groundless as a castle in the air." It is discredited, he summarized,

by its assumption that man is a creature of circumstances, that civil institutions rest on force, that the capitalistic form of industrial organization, based upon freedom of contract, has made the rich richer, and the poor poorer, that it is the business of the state to find work for its citizens, and that political power is the prerogative of labor.[28]

Minot J. Savage objected to the unhistorical temper of socialism, declaring that "the idea of radical reconstruction of society at once is sheer nonsense and the baldest absurdity." To be effective, change must be evolutionary, not revolutionary; socialists overlook the fact that society "is not manufactured, but is a growth."[29] One of the shallowest of all delusions, said Savage, is the belief that a group of theorists can reorganize society on paper and introduce the kingdom of heaven by ballot.

The equalitarianism proposed by socialism proved a serious stumbling block to these children of an individualistic age.

28. Behrends, *op. cit.*, p. 83.   29. Savage, *op. cit.*, p. 106.

They held that inequality of endowment and irregularity in social condition are "always present in society" and that any leveling process would hamper the individual's development.[30] The socialist state would simply absorb the individual, while the abolition of private property would remove certain of the strongest incentives to virtue and the development of character. Joseph Cook, a firm believer in "self help," declared that socialism would be detrimental to the lower classes because in fostering dependence on "state help" it would undermine individual initiative. Some believed that genius would be muzzled under the unimaginative rule of a socialist régime, Savage suggesting that a socialist government would never have been wise enough to commission Shakespeare to write *Hamlet* and *Macbeth!* If there is any one trend to be seen in history, he continued, it is the rise of the individual. But the socialists "now ask us to turn right about, and go diametrically in the face of the total course of human progress up to the present hour."[31]

Socialism as a theory of social change was further rejected because these Protestants thought it impossible to effect a genuine social reformation otherwise than through the regeneration of character. Reorganize society as much as you please, said Savage, but men will remain selfish. Rearranging does not change character. The evils of society are the result of the evil in individuals. Lyman Abbott, editor of the *Christian Union* and successor to Henry Ward Beecher in the pulpit of Plymouth Church, Brooklyn, championed many reforms but proposed "to work for the rebuilding of men rather than for the reforming of social organizations; for the change of character rather than of environment."[32] The Reverend Josiah Strong, author of the best seller, *Our Country*, declared in that famous work that socialism "attempts to solve the problem of suffering without eliminating the factor of sin." A San Francisco minister objected to socialism's desire to redeem man through society rather than society through man, while a writer in the *Church Review* held that a truly democratic salvation could only be based upon "the educating fear and trembling of the conscious-

30. Brace, *Gesta Christi* (New York, 1882), p. 418.
31. Savage, *op. cit.,* p. 107.
32. Lyman Abbott, "Christianity versus Socialism," *North American Review,* 148 (1889), 453.

ness of personal freedom" as contrasted with a socialistic salvation worked out by the state for the people.

Only one or two ministers paused in their criticism of the economics and politics of socialism to examine its philosophical
foundation. Edward S. Parsons mentioned "the materialistic,
evolutionary philosophy which is the religion of socialism," but
it remained for Behrends to show that this set of beliefs comprised a consistent system that began with a behavioristic psychology and included materialistic evolution and the economic
interpretation of history.[33] Behrends believed such a union of
materialism and social idealism to be inherently contradictory
and ultimately inimical to the interests of the lower classes. Deliverance of the poor and oppressed will never come from an
evolutionary political economy ignorant of mercy and trusting
only in the survival of the fittest, he asserted. Rather, "the cry
of the poor is just only on the theory that every man is a child
of God and the heir of eternity."[34] Behrends went on to point
out the antireligious and antifamilial temper of socialism, using
as proof-texts quotations from Marx and others, and concluding that "hostility to religion is not incidental to the system,
but deeply rooted and characteristic." This Brooklyn minister
did not merely accuse socialism of atheism. He realized that it
had attacked religion because of the decadence of the religious
life of the modern world; its criticism of the family he similarly
interpreted as founded on "the prevalence of low views of
wedded life and the facility of divorce." Other critics of socialism would doubtless have agreed.

When these diagnosticians proposed remedies for the ills of
which they regarded socialism a symptom, they naturally turned
to Christianity as the great panacea, and their social interpretation of the faith marks this discussion as a significant step
along the path toward a social gospel.

But there were other remedies proposed as well. Coöperation
—which we saw had its appeal in a previous decade—was widely
advocated by ministers who little realized that in so doing they
were tacitly accepting one of the fundamentals of socialism.
Espousal of coöperation was, however, an open protest against
unrestricted competition. Gladden thought that profit sharing

---

33. Behrends, *op. cit.,* pp. 61 ff.   34. *Ibid.,* p. 66.

would "put a new face upon industrial society." The Reverend J. H. Rylance devoted an entire lecture in a series on social questions to coöperation, while another clergyman pointed out the Christian aspects of the Rochdale system.[35]

In concluding his scholarly essay on "Recent American Socialism," from which we have drawn in this chapter, Professor Ely advocated "a higher and more advanced political economy" that would challenge *laissez faire*, and "a wider diffusion of sound ethics." Extreme individualism is immoral, he asserted, and a clearer perception of the duties of property is an ethical necessity. But, said Ely, "it is with satisfaction that one turns from the study of social problems to the teachings of Christ, which seem, from a purely scientific standpoint, to contain just what is needed."[36]

So it appeared to many others who proposed the "Christianization of the present order" by means of a "Christian socialism" or an "applied Christianity." J. H. Rylance asserted that "Christianity itself is a species of Socialism" and therefore naturally sympathetic to all endeavors toward social amelioration. It is the cure for the evils of which socialism complains, said Edwin B. Webb, while Ely declared that the church could do "far more than political economists toward a reconciliation of social classes." Behrends concluded his notable book, *Socialism and Christianity*, with the statement that social regeneration must be sought along such lines of historical progress as are clearly laid down in the Scriptures and in Christian history. Several writers of this period agreed with the German Christian Socialist pastor Rudolph Todt that

Whoever would understand the social question and contribute to its solution, must have on his right hand the works of Political Economy, and on his left the literature of Scientific Socialism, and must keep the New Testament open before him.[37]

Perhaps the attitude of religious leaders of the times was well summarized by the Reverend Forrest F. Emerson of Newport, Rhode Island, who told his Thanksgiving congregation in 1886 that Christianity in its social teachings stands midway between

---

35. Richard Wheatley, "Christian Socialism," *Christian Thought*, 3 (1885), 203.

36. Ely, *op. cit.*, p. 304.   37. Behrends, *op. cit.*, p. xii.

socialism and economics, for it "understands the causes of each and the follies of each, and . . . it is a mediator between them and a remedy for the evils of both."[38]

But the controversy over socialism was but part of the greater problem of industry. We have said that the social gospel began largely as the response of religious leaders to the challenges of socialism and labor. Having examined the first of these we now turn to Protestantism's concern in the labor problem.

38. Forrest F. Emerson, *Socialism and Christianity. A sermon* . . . (Newport, 1886), p. 8.

CHAPTER V

APPLYING CHRISTIANITY TO THE LABOR QUESTION

The gospel is a religion fitted for to-day, and it will answer the social problems of to-day, whether propounded by workman, employer, or consumer.

HARRY W. CADMAN

THE latter half of the nineteenth century witnessed radical changes in the character and status of American labor. With phenomenal speed the industrial revolution converted a peaceful agricultural country almost overnight into an urban nation of bustling factories whose operatives were no longer skilled artisans but machine tenders. Gigantic absentee-owned corporations removed the personal factor from employment while managements nourished on *laissez faire* economics opposed collective bargaining and hired mercenaries to do battle with strikers.

At the close of the Civil War strikes and lockouts had been virtually unknown, but between 1881 and 1894 more than fourteen thousand contests took place involving over four million workers. Technological unemployment, immigration, and other factors combined by 1900 to create a standing army of a million unemployed whereas in 1870 the labor supply had been inadequate. The demands of industry brought millions from the farms and from the old world to the new and crowded cities, expanding the working classes fivefold. Between 1860 and 1890 the national wealth increased from sixteen to seventy-eight and one half billions of dollars, more than half of which was held by some forty thousand families or one third of one per cent of the population. But in the decade 1870–80 real wages, which had never been above the bare subsistence level, had declined from an average of $400 to $300, forcing children into premature labor and driving women to the factories beside the men. The American industrial revolution, in the process of creating wealth such as the world had never seen or dreamed of, produced also a sullen proletariat resentful of the poverty it had obtained as its share of the bounty, and the republic of Jefferson and Jackson now became the scene of the most embittered class wars and the most glaring social contrasts modern times had seen.

The decade of the 'eighties witnessed not only the rise and decline of labor's more radical attempt at organization, but also the inauspicious beginnings of a conservative but more successful federation for collective bargaining. The Noble Order of the Knights of Labor, based on the inclusive principle of organization and definitely hospitable to socialism, grew from a secret society organized in 1869 to a militant membership of over one-half million by 1886. Pursuing an aggressive campaign that did not stop at sabotage, the Knights won many notable encounters and climaxed their success in a decisive victory over the Gould interests, thus demonstrating to a surprised nation the effective power of organization. Intoxicated by such gains their leaders pushed beyond the bounds of reasonable achievement and in the face of a falling market frequent defeats in the late 'eighties brought the decline of the Order.

The American Federation of Labor, whose effective beginnings date from 1886, marked a retreat from radicalism in the philosophy of the labor movement. Organized as a federation, on the craft-union principle, it accepted capitalism and adopted a political policy of reward to its friends and punishment of its enemies. By means of collective bargaining, the eight-hour day, labor bureaus, strikes, boycotts, and agitation against child labor, the Federation sought a partnership for labor in the great American business of acquiring wealth.

Such was in brief the background of the labor problem that became the central concern of social gospelers throughout the last twenty years of the century.[1] The seething pot of industrial troubles that had been so violently uncovered by the great strike of 1877 was kept bubbling by adverse conditions and it not infrequently boiled over. As we have seen, this situation appeared the more serious because of the lurid propaganda of socialism. Thus forced upon the attention of the nation, it elicited the careful concern of clergymen along with many other observers.

1. This chapter carries the discussion of the labor problem to 1900.

When Washington Gladden, who has previously been referred to as an outstanding and representative pioneer of social Christianity, assumed the pastorate of the First Congregational Church of Columbus, Ohio, in 1882, the solution of the social problem seemed to him of vastly greater moment than the current theological controversy at Andover or the impending battle over evolution. Within the next two years there occurred two hard-fought struggles which served the more to impress upon his mind "the critical character of the relations between the men who are doing the work of the world and the men who are organizing and directing it." The conflict consequent upon competition, he said, has produced a state of war "and the engagement is general" throughout industry; the worker compares his own precarious situation, the introduction of labor-saving machinery, and the increasing cost of living with the steadily rising incomes of other classes and is naturally dissatisfied. After careful study Gladden calculated that the real annual wages of labor were little, if any, higher in 1886 than they had been in 1860, whereas during that same period the national wealth increased from sixteen to forty-three billion dollars and the value of manufactured goods trebled. So, he concluded, when the workers are thus denied their just share of the products of their labors, naturally they "complain and rebel" and can see no alternative to organization "for mutual protection and defense."[2] Newman Smyth, minister of Center Church, New Haven, Connecticut, analyzed labor's complaints into five propositions: the laborer's share in the products of his work has been reduced; the use of machinery is creating a working class separated from other social groups; division of labor tends toward its further degradation; capital has unfair advantages; class legislation and other factors will make labor's status progressively worse.[3] While Smyth did not admit the truth of all these, such statements indicate that leading clergymen were aware of the plight of "the other half."

Some religious leaders placed the blame for this state of affairs squarely upon the propertied classes. One Sunday evening

2. Washington Gladden, *Applied Christianity* (Boston and New York, 1886), pp. 103, 120, 123.
3. Newman Smyth, *Social Problems: Sermons to Workingmen* (reprinted from the *Andover Review,* Boston, 1885), pp. 10–13.

shortly after the Haymarket riot, Charles Carroll Bonney, a prominent Chicago layman, told a congregation at the Union Park New Jerusalem Church that one of the basic causes of such outbreaks could be found "in the greed, the selfishness, the neglect and folly of wealth and power."[4] The complaints of labor against capital are not groundless, wrote a contributor to the *Methodist Review* in 1886:

The accumulation of gigantic fortunes by craft and cunning, by fraud and theft. . . . The ruthless seizure and control of the highways of continental traffic, the rape of the world's mineral wealth, the fruits of invention and discovery made instruments of oppression and ministers of greed, these are indeed terrible illustrations of the power, the tyranny, and the cruelty of avarice, as well as of its antagonisms to Christianity. . . .[5]

Another speaker asserted that nearly all the ills of the poor are caused by the rich in monopolizing land and resources and then using the power thus gained to avoid useful labor.[6]

In approaching this social issue, clergymen made short shift of the notion that they ought to restrict themselves to discussion of "spiritual" matters. Newman Smyth told his fashionable New Haven congregation that any subject of vital concern to a number of human beings deserved "just claim to candid and thoughtful consideration in any Christian church." When William Jewett Tucker of Andover Theological Seminary introduced the publication of Smyth's "Sermons to Workingmen" in the *Andover Review* he asserted that "the labor question is more than a question of economics. It comes legitimately within the sphere of Christianity."[7] The Reverend Joseph H. Rylance of St. Mark's Episcopal Church, New York, declared that the avoidance of such subjects had resulted in a loss of prestige by the Christian pulpit and that social questions were neither for-

4. Charles Carroll Bonney, *The Present Conflict of Labor and Capital* (Chicago, 1886), p. 24.
5. *Methodist Review*, 68 (1886), 566. Quoted by K. E. Barnhart, *The Evolution of the Social Consciousness in Methodism* (University of Chicago Ph.D. dissertation, 1924), p. 120.
6. Charles Richardson, *Large Fortunes; or, Christianity and the Labor Problem* (Philadelphia, 1888), p. 80.
7. William Jewett Tucker, "Social Problems in the Pulpit," *Andover Review*, 3 (1885), 299.

eign nor inimical to Christianity. The Reverend A. J. F. Behrends told the students of Hartford Theological Seminary that religious leaders should be conversant with the social problems of the day in order "to be prepared to apply the principles of the New Testament to their solution."[8] Clergymen were chided for neglect of social concerns by Episcopal Bishop Frederic Dan Huntington of Central New York when he wrote in the *Church Review* that the matter of the mutual duties of the classes to one another "is a subject more fully treated in the Gospels than it is by the modern pulpit."[9]

This awakening interest on the part of certain clergymen was more than matched by the frank hostility evidenced by some spokesmen of the masses. Terence V. Powderly, Grand Master Workman of the Knights of Labor, wrote that if the Sermon on the Mount were to be preached without reference to its divine author, in many churches "the fashionable pews would be emptied, the minister of God would be censured and warned never again to repeat the ravings of an utopiast." Powderly went on to accuse religious people of insincerity in praying for the coming of the kingdom of God while they opposed the program of the Knights, who had never presumed to ask that this earth should become a better place than the heaven Christians were accustomed to pray for.[10] C. Osborne Ward, author of *The Ancient Lowly*, a detailed study of labor in antiquity, arraigned the "gilded pulpit" for pagan neglect "of the millions whose toil still supplies its luxuries."[11] Fred Woodrow, a sort of roustabout messiah of the proletariat, called the pulpit "more of a relic than a power," asked whether the poor were as welcome as the wealthy in the churches, and declared "the pure and simple truth of Christianity" to be the "one cure and one corrective" for the gigantic forces of social evil.[12] A New England worker, concerned about technological unemployment, proposed in the columns of the New Haven *Work-*

8. A. J. F. Behrends, *Socialism and Christianity* (New York, 1886), p. v.

9. Frederic Dan Huntington, "Some Points in the Labor Question," *Church Review,* 48 (1886), 1.

10. Terence V. Powderly, *Thirty Ye   ; of Labor* (Columbus, 1889), pp. 669–671.

11. C. Osborne Ward, *The Ancient Lowly* (Chicago, 1888), I, 530.

12. Fred Woodrow, "The Pulpit and the Poor," in *The Labor Problem* (New York, 1886), pp. 322–323, William E. Barnes, ed.

men's Advocate that preachers give thought to this problem. The clergy, he believed, should promote much more than they do the earthly happiness of mankind. "They ought to blush with shame and mortification when they reflect that there is still so much poverty and misery in the world." They ought to investigate the teachings of socialism for themselves and assist the poor in the contest with "soulless corporations, powerful monopolies and unscrupulous rich men whose only God is a dirty dollar."[13] We believe in Jesus and his teachings, wrote a Michigan worker to the *Christian Union*, but not in the teachings of his pretended followers:

A civilization that permits man to be the greatest enemy of man, and allows the hardest and most repugnant toil to draw the lowest pay, is a cheat and a sham; the political economy that permits it is a falsehood and a fraud; and a religion that allows it without constant, earnest, and persistent protest is a humbug.[14]

This type of criticism was rather well summarized in several questionnaires. In 1885 the Reverend Amory H. Bradford of Montclair, New Jersey, reported in the same journal the returns from an inquiry among labor groups. While the results may not have been scientific, they were indicative. To the first question, "How large a proportion of the artisan classes in your region are regular attendants at any church?" Bradford obtained responses varying, for Protestants, from ½ per cent to 10 per cent. Answers to the second query indicated that such attendance was decreasing in all cases but one. The third question asked whether nonattendance was caused chiefly by "unbelief in Christianity as taught by Christ"; the response was a unanimous "No." But "unbelief in Christianity as practised by the churches" was given as a significant cause, along with the statement that "ministers of the gospel do not practice what they preach," and Christians do not "possess what they profess, or at least manifest it in their lives and conduct."[15]

13. W. H. Benson, "A Hint to Preachers," in *Workmen's Advocate,* New Haven (February 26, 1887), unpaged.
14. J. Willett, "Letter from a Workingman," *Christian Union,* 32 (October 19, 1885), No. 18, 7–8.
15. A. H. Bradford, "Why the Artisan Classes Neglect the Church," *Christian Union,* 32 (July 2, 1885), No. 1, 7–8, and (July 9), No. 2, 7–8.

In his *Applied Christianity*, published in 1886, Washington Gladden gave the results gained from a circular letter sent to a large number of workers. There were two principal reasons given for laborers' failure to attend church: inability to dress well enough to appear "in a place as stylish and fashionable as the average church," and their feeling against the injustice they received at the hands of their employers. Gladden found that these two reasons were frequently related, inability to dress well being held due to inadequate wages. Most of his replies assumed that "the churches are chiefly attended and controlled by the capitalist and the employing classes." We quote from one of Gladden's correspondents:

Of course the manufacturers can and should dress better than the laborer; but when we see them so full of religion on Sunday, and then grinding the faces of the poor on the other six days, we are apt to think they are insincere. . . . When the capitalist prays for us one day in the week, and preys on us the other six, it can't be expected that we will have much respect for his Christianity.[16]

In 1898 the Reverend H. Francis Perry, minister of the Englewood Baptist Church of Chicago, asked representative leaders of American labor what reasons workers would give for their absence from the church and what might be done about it. From Samuel Gompers he received this reply:

My associates have come to look upon the church and the ministry as the apologists and defenders of the wrong committed against the interests of the people, simply because the perpetrators are possessors of wealth . . . whose real God is the almighty dollar, and who contribute a few of their idols to suborn the intellect and eloquence of the divines, and make even their otherwise generous hearts callous to the suffering of the poor and struggling workers, so that they may use their exalted positions to discourage and discountenance all practical efforts of the toilers to lift themselves out of the slough of despondency and despair.[17]

John B. Lennon, general secretary of the Journeyman Tailors' Union of America, said that workmen stayed away from church

16. Gladden, *op. cit.*, p. 157. By permission.
17. H. Francis Perry, "The Workingman's Alienation from the Church," *American Journal of Sociology*, 4 (1898–99), 622.

because their employers attended and controlled it, whereas in daily life the workman received "but little of Christian treatment from the employers." The Reverend Herbert N. Casson of the Labor Church of Lynn, Massachusetts—an organization which we shall describe shortly—declared that workingmen recognize in the front pews "the men who grind them in business" and that they "do not see any similarity between Christ and the church." The church errs in justifying present industrial circumstances; it does not treat living issues; it frowns upon labor unions; and its services are stale and uninteresting. A worker wrote to Perry that his fellows were more interested in getting food and clothing and paying the rent than they were in a future life, and that they wanted a heaven on earth instead of after death. Another called the church "a sort of fashionable club" for the entertainment of the rich; its ministers "are muzzled by their masters and dare not preach the gospel of the carpenter of Nazareth"; it has no sympathy with the masses. Perry summarized his correspondents' criticisms under five heads: the church is subsidized by the rich; the ministry does not discuss living issues; the ministry is not well enough informed on economic and social questions; the workingman is not welcome in the churches; the church is not aggressive enough in assisting the workers to secure their rights.[18]

There was at least one temporarily successful attempt made to organize a workers' church prior to 1900. The Labor Church of Lynn, Massachusetts, was founded in 1894 by the Reverend Herbert N. Casson, a Methodist minister who withdrew from that communion because of dissatisfaction with the effectiveness of the organized church in reaching the working classes. Casson, who was characterized by Ernest H. Crosby as "a modern edition of a Hebrew prophet," believed that there could be no real reconciliation of the masses to the church until the latter repented and became converted to a socialized gospel. An ardent socialist, this reformer held that the true church was composed of "all those who are working in the reform movements of the time"; he endeavored to realize in his ministry a sympathy with "the great struggling mass of workingmen."[19]

The Labor Church, of which Casson appears to have been the moving spirit, was founded on four principles:

18. *Op. cit.,* pp. 627–628.   19. *Op. cit.,* p. 624.

To remove religious superstition, and to develop the moral nature of the Labor Movement.

To promote social intercourse, and practical co-operation.

To prepare for the social crisis by educating ourselves and others.

To proclaim the Co-operative Commonwealth as the ideal of society.

The organization described itself as composed of wage earners who believed the social question to be the ethical problem of the day; it maintained socialism "to be the present ideal of industry, and perfect freedom of thought to be the ideal of religion"; it aimed to provide a free meeting place for all reformers working toward collectivism and brotherhood; it paid no regular salaries, exacted no pledges of its members, and claimed that "the more unfortunate a man is, the warmer will be his welcome."[20] The membership card of the church stated that the group sought "to educate, to harmonize, to coöperate, and to experiment as the pioneers of that glad day when there shall be no business but friendship, and no religion but love." Casson was forced to leave Lynn in 1900 on account of his health, but in the few years of its activity his unique society attracted much attention in this country and in England. Labor leaders such as Keir Hardie spoke from its platform. Casson is reported to have addressed a Labor Day mass meeting attended by seven thousand on the Lynn Common in 1894; the next year thirty-five trades organizations were represented on the same occasion.[21] The church declined after Casson left Lynn. The only permanent labor church known to the writer to have been founded prior to the World War is the Labor Temple in New York, begun in 1910 by Charles Stelzle. It will be described in Chapter XVII.

Before these early social gospelers could well prescribe for industrial ills it was necessary to formulate a Christian social ethic. The nebulous character of the resulting statements indicates that the social gospel was still in its youth. Such utter-

20. From pamphlet material in the possession of Mr. C. Francis Willey of Lynn, to whom the writer is indebted for this and other information.

21. Lynn *Daily Evening Item,* September 3, 1910. Eltweed Pomeroy, "The National Social and Political Conference," *The Social Forum* (Chicago), 1 (August 1, 1899), 86. Ernest H. Crosby, "A New Labor Church Booklet," *The Kingdom* (Minneapolis), 10 (May 12, 1898), 585–586.

ances as will be reviewed were, further, not the carefully seasoned propositions of scholars or theologians. They were groping attempts to meet the exigencies of a new situation on the
part of a ministry untrained in social science. For the most part
they were unrealistic and somewhat repetitious general affirma-
tions.

Professor Richard T. Ely, perhaps the most aggressive advocate of the social gospel during the 'eighties, asserted in his
book, *The Labor Movement in America*, that Christian ethics
"contain the principles which should animate the entire labor
movement"; the perfect embodiment of Christian ethics is their
founder, who gave the absolute ideal to the world in the doctrine of human brotherhood.[22] The Reverend Harry W. Cadman of San Francisco, whose book, *The Christian Unity of
Capital and Labor*, received a prize of $1,000 from the Ameri-
can Sunday School Union in 1888, phrased the ideal in terms
of love. The duty of Christianity in the present crisis, he wrote,
"is to infuse industrialism with the spirit of love" derived from
Jesus. This offers "a more efficient remedy than revolution,"
placing in our hands "the key to all industrial problems, the
solvent for all class distinctions, the law for all righteous elevation, the remedy for all remediable social evils and the method
of adjustment for all conflicting interests."[23] George E. Mc-
Neill, who is sometimes referred to as "the father of the American Federation of Labor," wrote in 1886, concluding his book,
The Labor Movement, that

When the Golden Rule of Christ shall measure the relations of
men in all their duties towards their fellows, in factory and workshop, in the mine, in the field, in commerce . . . the promise of the
prophet and the poet shall be fulfilled . . . and peace on earth
shall prevail . . . by the free acceptance of the Gospel that all
men are of one blood. . . .[24]

22. Richard T. Ely, *The Labor Movement in America* (New York, 1886),
pp. 313, 321.
23. Harry W. Cadman, *The Christian Unity of Capital and Labor* (Philadelphia, 1888), pp. 246–247, 255.
24. George E. McNeill, ed., *The Labor Movement: The Problem of Today*
(Boston and New York, 1887), chap. xvii. This book was the first history of
American labor movements.

More realistic was Washington Gladden's interpretation of what he termed "the Christian law." In the injunction, "Thou shalt love thy neighbor as thyself," Gladden analyzed the fundamental obligation as rational self-love, operating as the measure of love to neighbor. The implication was that since one regards himself as a being of essential worth he will likewise view his neighbor as a child of God, and, identifying the interests of the two, "share together the good which the divine bounty distributes to all." In *Applied Christianity* Gladden attempted to relate this principle to society. He held that the social order rests upon a combination of egoism and altruism. Both self-love and self-sacrifice are essential to it: no society can exist on the sole basis of either one. Now, the mutual relations of labor and capital form a type of social order. But the attempt to rest this society—the industrial system—exclusively upon competition is "a social solecism," for society cannot be held together by antisocial bonds. Rather, a stable social order must rest upon the assumption "that it is every man's business to give as much as he can, prudently and safely, and with due regard to his own integrity, to all with whom he deals." In so doing he should neither cripple nor impoverish himself, nor give in such a way as to destroy his power to give.[25] Such was "Christ's law of life" as the practical mind of Gladden translated it into a social principle.

The gospel was to affect society through the converted individual whose changed character would produce a social transformation. This pietistic view was succinctly stated by President David Jayne Hill, now of Bucknell University, in his Newton Lectures of 1887 when he said that "if all men were Christians, the labor problem would melt away and be forgotten in the sense of universal brotherhood."[26] Strikes are symptoms of social disease, wrote Bishop Huntington, and although it may be possible to deal here and there with particular outbreaks, nothing but personal character can avail for social health in the long run.[27] Jesus did not plan to regenerate the

25. Washington Gladden, *Recollections* (Boston and New York, 1909), pp. 298 f., 311.
26. David Jayne Hill, *The Social Influence of Christianity* (Boston, 1888), p. 121.
27. Huntington, *op. cit.*, p. 20.

race in a lump, wrote the Reverend Adam Stump of North Platte, Nebraska, in the *Lutheran Quarterly,* but rather he began with the individual: "as the saviour of the soul . . . Christ becomes the reformer of society." He will thus bring about the millennium.[28]

Naturally, then, many ministers proposed stewardship as a methodology. The wealth of the earth is designed for the public welfare, and its owners must consider themselves agents bound to use it for the benefit of all, maintained President Joseph Cummings of Wesleyan University at the 1886 meeting of the American Association for the Advancement of Science. "The great remedy for social wrongs will be found in the Christian use of money," he added.[29] Professor Norman Fox of New York told the Baptist Congress of 1885 that it was the duty of every man pretending to be a servant of Christ to use his talents for the good of the community. Others spoke of "a right spirit in the rich," "an understanding heart in the laborer," "a just and noble business character,"[30] the consecration of capital to God,[31] and the stewardship of "rank, wealth, learning or cleverness."[32]

Along with this presentation of a new function of Christianity there developed a demand that the church change her attitude toward her task as well as toward the social scene. It was held that the church and her ministers ought to go out to the laborer where he could be found, hear his complaint, and shape their policy to his needs. Newman Smyth stated that it was not the business of the clergy to teach economics, but that they ought to "apply economic science in their teachings and lives to the needs of men in this present life." Just prior to the Haymarket riot the Reverend C. O. Brown of Dubuque, Iowa, proposed that the churches demonstrate their friendliness

28. Adam Stump, "Christ and the Labor Movement," *Lutheran Quarterly,* 20 (1890), 443.

29. Joseph Cummings, "Capitalists and Laborers," *Proceedings* of the 35th meeting of the American Association for the Advancement of Science . . . (Salem, 1887), pp. 352–353.

30. Charles Roads, *Christ Enthroned in the Industrial World, A discussion of Christianity in property and labor* (New York, 1892), p. 49, and chaps. iv, v.

31. Charles Carroll Bonney, "Consecrated Capital," *Christian Union,* 32 (1885), No. 26, 9.

32. Henry Codman Potter, "The Laborer not a Commodity," *Christian Thought,* 4th ser. (1886), 289.

toward the laboring classes by specific means. An immediate declaration along this line "would go a long way toward solving the existing difficulties," he asserted.[33] In 1883 the Reverend R. Heber Newton told a Congressional committee investigating labor conditions that it would be essential for the church "to reform herself" if she hoped to gain the confidence of the working classes.[34] In summarizing the report of his questionnaire described above, the Reverend Amory H. Bradford recommended that the churches "court all classes as well as the rich," going out to those who would not come in to them.

Another insistence was that divinity schools teach economics and sociology. Professor Ely pointed out that theologs were being well trained in theology, or, as he put it, in how to obey the first commandment of love to God, whereas they were left ignorant of how to fulfill the second commandment of love to man, the latter being "the function of social science." In 1886 the eminent economist Edward Atkinson told the alumni of Andover Theological Seminary that the clergy had not kept sufficiently abreast of economic thought and suggested it as a discipline every minister should master.[35] Atkinson went on to warn his hearers against a social gospel founded solely on sentiment, as did a writer in the *New Princeton Review* who remarked that "what we need is not sympathy, but knowledge."[36] Professor Francis Greenwood Peabody of Harvard, probably the first teacher of social ethics in the United States,[37] wrote in the *Independent* in 1886 that "the modern minister needs to have been trained in the study of social reform" because he is coming to be more and more in demand as the natural leader of the charities and temperance work, as a mediator between social classes, and as an adviser of community philanthropies. The modern world has called the church to an ethical revival, Peabody continued, and if the theological schools do not undertake

---

33. C. O. Brown, *Talks on Labor Troubles* (Chicago, 1886), p. 20.
34. R. H. Newton, *Social Studies* (New York and London, 1887), p. 374.
35. Edward Atkinson, *Addresses upon the Labor Question* (Boston, 1886), p. 21.
36. Henry W. Farnam, "The Clergy and the Labor Question," *New Princeton Review*, 2 (1886), 61.
37. James Dombrowski, *The Early Days of Christian Socialism in America* (New York, 1936), p. 63.

the social studies the ministry will be unprepared for its great opportunity.[38] How the schools responded to this challenge will be described in a later chapter.

To the specific problems posed by labor's condition and claims, Protestant leaders responded (1) with the demand that workers receive justice; (2) they refuted classical economic dogmas; (3) trades unions, strikes, and mutual aid were discussed; (4) labor was criticized and admonished; and (5) arbitration and such forms of coöperation as profit sharing were advocated.

Many ministers realized that the fundamental issue in the labor question was the division of the profits of industry, and they insisted that the workers obtain justice, not charity. Gladden, for example, agreed with labor's contention at this point and held it essential to the welfare of the nation "that wage-earners receive their full share of the growing wealth."[39] The Reverend Adam Stump, after emphasizing this same point, asserted that America was in a period of her history in which workers might be "at the same time civic freemen and economic slaves." The Reverend Taral T. Frickstad of Oakland, California, wrote that the problem of the day was not the division of all existing wealth, but "how to distribute to each producer the full value of the product of his labor,"[40] and many others agreed. This insistence unquestionably rested upon the social implications of the Christian doctrine of man. We can do no better than let President David Jayne Hill express the sentiment of the day:

If the laborer has any rights which he can defend by other means than dynamite, if he has any standing before the tribunal of reason, it is because he is a person, because he is that which Christ taught that he is, the image of God, clothed with the majesty of freedom. Christianity solves this problem of the laborer's rights in the light of its conception of man, the conception that has enfranchised the slave, emancipated woman, and snatched the abandoned

38. Francis Greenwood Peabody, "Social Reforms as Subjects of University Study," *Independent,* 38 (1886), 5.

39. Washington Gladden, *Tools and the Man. Property and Industry under the Christian Law* (Boston and New York, 1893), p. 139.

40. Taral T. Frickstad, *From Behind the Scenes: The Churches and the Masses* (Oakland, 1894), p. 21.

child from the eagles and the wolves, to place it in the safety of the cradle and the sunlight of the school.[41]

Classical economics, which rationalized low wages, poverty, and unemployment in terms of supply and demand, was assailed on similar grounds. In accepting the anti-Christian dogmas of the older economists the church has turned traitor to the ethics of Jesus Christ, declared R. H. Newton. Gladden asserted that social and economic laws are not inexorable and that moral forces could affect economic trends. He believed "the maxims of Smith and Ricardo" to be untrue and appealed to the reason and conscience of the Christian community to apply "the Christian law" in their stead.

In the assertion that "the laborer is not a commodity" this attitude was focused upon the industrial problem at the point of greatest humanitarian import. Here again the emphasis was placed upon the doctrine of the worth of man. Bishop Henry Codman Potter of New York, who first gave significant utterance to this proposition in 1886, declared that the division of society into warring classes could never be mitigated until

Capitalists and employers of labor have forever dismissed the fallacy, which may be true enough in the domain of political economy, but is essentially false in the domain of religion, *that labor and the laborer are alike a commodity*, to be bought and sold, employed or dismissed, paid or underpaid as the market shall decree. . . .[42]

The employment of labor is not merely a matter of the production of things, asserted Gladden, it is the life of the nation: "Is that a commodity to be bought in the cheapest market and sold in the dearest?" If the employer can arrange matters so that the moral and intellectual status of his workers is improved by their labor he is a benefactor. But if they are degraded and demoralized, the employer is "a malefactor, a public enemy."[43] A. J. F. Behrends also endorsed this viewpoint, declaring that the laborer "is a man, whose toil may not be purchased or controlled in such a way as to involve the sacrifice of his manhood."

41. Hill, *op. cit.*, p. 85. By courtesy of Silver, Burdett Co., publishers.
42. Potter, *op. cit.*, pp. 290–291.
43. Gladden, *Applied Christianity*, p. 52.

Professor Ely, champion of the new "historical" school of economics as well as protagonist of a socialized Christianity, gave scientific sanction to the criticism of classical economics. The new economics, he declared, does not permit that science to be used "as a tool in the hands of the greedy and avaricious for keeping down and oppressing the laboring classes." It refuses to acknowledge "laissez-faire as an excuse for doing nothing while people starve," or "the all-sufficiency of competition as a plea for grinding the poor." Rather, it holds that there is a place in economic life for love, generosity, and self-sacrifice. "The first duty of man in trade, as in other departments of human employment," maintained Ely, "is to follow the Golden Rule."[44]

Social gospelers of this period were generally agreed that labor had every moral and legal right to organize, although they were somewhat skeptical about strikes and they condemned violence without hesitation. Gladden believed that unions were not only lawful but necessary if labor were to protect itself against the combinations of capital taking place on every hand. The church, he asserted, ought not to censure the labor movement but should encourage it. Lyman Abbott believed strongly in the right of workers to organize and supported their cause in the columns of the *Christian Union*. He not infrequently remarked that if he were a laborer he would belong to his trade union. That labor leaders sometimes betrayed their trust, and unions abused the confidence of the public, did not shake his faith in the rank and file and the justice of their cause.[45] Ely went so far as to say that the trades union was, next to the church, the strongest force in the world making for human brotherhood.[46]

A few ministers ventured to assert in the 'eighties that strikes were not always to be condemned.[47] R. H. Newton believed that strikes and lockouts were not necessarily the inevitable concomitants of the wages system, but he could see no way of avoiding them. Another minister advised strengthening the

44. Richard T. Ely, "The Past and Present of Political Economy," *Johns Hopkins University Studies in Historical and Political Science* (Baltimore, 1884), 2d ser., p. 202.

45. Lyman Abbott, *Reminiscences* (Boston and New York, 1915), p. 415.

46. Ely, *The Labor Movement*, p. 138.

47. J. H. Rylance, *Lectures on Social Questions* (New York, 1880), p. 35.

unions in order to enable them to force capital to arbitrate. Gladden declared that if industrial warfare were the order of the day "we must grant to labor belligerent rights." But the memory of 1877, the Knights' use of sabotage, and the wave of horror following the Haymarket riot precluded much sympathy for strikes. Not until the Federal Council of Churches investigated the Bethlehem steel strike in 1910 did American Protestantism face this problem realistically.

The enthusiasm for coöperation that was evident in the previous decade continued through this period. Mutual aid of various types, notably for relief and insurance, and the Rochdale coöperatives, were heartily approved, doubtless because of their democratic character and their element of what Joseph Cook called "self-help." Many ministers were impressed by the Rochdale Pioneers, among them Walter Rauschenbusch, who long planned writing a book on the subject. The Reverend Charles Roads expressed the thought of many regarding the Christian aspects of coöperatives when he wrote in his book, *Christ Enthroned in the Industrial World*, that when Christ should become the ruler of the world "by the adoption of his law in business" a money economy would gradually be replaced by a coöperative one.[48]

Certain clergymen hastened to reassure labor that Christian principles and the sympathy of the church were on the side of justice, while at the same time they cautioned against excesses. Ely assured the workers that "Christ and all Christly people" were with them for the right. Harry W. Cadman pointed out that Christ was a laborer. T. T. Frickstad declared that the workingman's best friend is the Bible, and the Reverend W. W. Everts cautioned against overlooking the natural inequalities of men. Gladden, who was considerable of a realist, pointed out the dangers of antagonizing the employing class unduly, and stressed especially the need for workers to discipline themselves in the wise use of their newly gained and growing power.[49]

Arbitration was looked upon with favor. When William E. Barns conducted a symposium on the labor problem in 1886 he found a number of well-informed clergymen who believed that

48. Roads, *op. cit.*, p. 287.
49. Gladden, *Applied Christianity*, pp. 139–145.

arbitration and profit sharing offered workable solutions of the conflict between labor and capital.[50] The Reverend W. W. Everts believed that arbitration should be provided for in all disputes; Gladden held that in the case of quasipublic utilities it should be compulsory.[51] Under the present industrial system, he explained, the best way of avoiding strife and securing justice is through arbitration, which will come about at the demand of compact labor unions. The churches ought to throw their influence energetically and constantly behind it.[52]

Profit sharing appealed to many writers of this period as a definitely Christian specific for the maladjusted relationships of industry. Gladden, Josiah Strong, J. H. Rylance, and many others endorsed it, but the most thoroughgoing study was that published in 1889 by Nicholas Paine Gilman, who was later professor of Social Ethics in the Meadville Theological School. In concluding his exhaustive research Gilman expressed the belief that profit sharing would bring industrial peace, add to profits, and give to employers "the consciousness of having helped mankind a little nearer to the kingdom of God"; it would greatly diminish the class selfishness engendered by the wages system. The fraternity thus fostered would be "thoroughly moral, thoroughly Christian." In line with the progress of democracy, profit sharing is a "hearty recognition of human brotherhood and the duties of prosperity." In summary Gilman added: the labor difficulties of the nineteenth century will find no more effectual solvent than a rebirth of the Christian gospel that will bring ethics to the aid of economics and temper the commercial spirit with the Christian sentiment of brotherhood.[53]

Thus it was that the labor question and its related enigma, socialism, elicited a growing concern on the part of an increasing number of Protestant clergymen during the period of the nationalizing of American business. These two problems were the major interests of a youthful social gospel. The many careful analyses of the labor issue, together with the situations of the clergymen we have studied, indicate that most ministers

50. Barns, *op. cit.*, pp. 147 ff.
51. Gladden, *Tools and the Man,* chaps. viii, x.
52. Gladden, *Applied Christianity,* pp. 132, 177.
53. Nicholas Paine Gilman, *Profit Sharing between Employer and Employee* (Boston and New York, 1889), pp. 444–445.

who dealt with it were facing a local issue with which they were reasonably familiar. The early social gospel was thus no academic matter. This note of realism is further borne out by the practical character of the remedies suggested: justice to the workers, challenge of *laissez faire*, approval of the organization of labor, criticism of the lawlessness of some unions and likewise of the plutocracy, endorsement of the coöperative movement and of arbitration and profit sharing. If the proposal of the stewardship of wealth seems sentimental, it should be recalled that this was the era in which John D. Rockefeller asserted that God gave him his fortune and another spokesman for big business defended dictatorial and monopolistic policies on the ground that the wealth of the nation had been given into the keeping of its Christian businessmen.

Although the labor question was central to the new socialized Christianity, it was not its sole concern. Other issues growing out of the industrial revolution also aroused its interest and brought forth an even larger formulation of principles, panaceas, and programs. To these related problems we now turn.

CHAPTER VI

THE KINGDOM OF GOD AND "OUR COUNTRY"

Christianity is primarily concerned with this world, and it is the mission of Christianity to bring to pass here a kingdom of righteousness and to rescue from the evil one and redeem all our social relations.

RICHARD T. ELY

ALTHOUGH the social gospel of the 1880's found itself largely occupied with the problems of socialism and of labor, there were other products of the industrial revolution to which it gave equally serious attention. During this period, when the nationalizing of business was proceeding apace, other changes of equal importance with those affecting labor were being wrought in the American scene. These further concomitants of industrialism were the accumulation of vast new wealth, the consolidation of business, and the emergence of the corporation with its legitimate offspring, monopoly. At the same time the industrial centers grew almost overnight, and without plan or hindrance, into vast sprawling cities whose social, sanitary, and religious problems were as staggering as was their mushroom development.

The last forty years of the nineteenth century saw the wealth of the United States increase from 16 to 126 billions of dollars.[1] One of the chief instruments that helped produce such riches was the corporation. So powerful and efficient did the joint-stock company prove that individually owned firms were gradually but inevitably supplanted, and consolidation for the purpose of eliminating competition became the order of the day. The decade of the 'eighties was marked by the evolution of the interlocking corporate structure through the "pooling" and "trust" stages. Consolidation was taking place during these years in all the major lines of economic endeavor: transportation, communication, and industry; likewise in agriculture, and

1. Ida M. Tarbell, *The Nationalizing of Business, 1878–1898* (New York, 1936), pp. 2, 262.

as we have seen, in labor. The dozen years prior to 1890 brought into being at least fifteen great new combinations organized on a national scale.[2] In the 'eighties, also, the regulation of such monopolies was recognized by Congress as a national problem with the result that the Interstate Commerce Commission was set up in 1887 and the Sherman Antitrust Act passed three years later.

During this period the great industrial and commercial centers grew by leaps and bounds. With their laboring populations recruited from the American farm and from Europe, the extraordinary growth of large cities became one of the marvels of the decade. In the ten years following 1880 Chicago increased in size over 100 per cent to establish itself as the second city of the nation, while the Twin Cities trebled in population, and other mid-Western places expanded from 60 to 80 per cent.[3] By 1890 the Atlantic seaboard had developed a generally urban cast, with New York reaching a million and a half, Philadelphia a million, and Boston, Baltimore, and Washington about a half million each.[4] Crowded with unassimilable aliens and faced by tremendous social problems, these cities were struggling with lawlessness and crime, tenements, crooked politics, delinquency, sanitation, traffic, inadequate religious resources, and a host of other complexities.[5]

In the present chapter we are concerned to show the interest of Protestant clergymen in the ethics of wealth, the dangers of monopoly, the religious problems of the cities, the tenement evil, and other issues created by the gigantic forces unleashed by the industrial revolution. This discussion rested upon what by this time had become a fairly well-articulated set of propositions. The church was criticized for her social impotence and the clergy challenged to a new appraisal of its task. The ethical aspects of Christianity were stressed, with certain emphases upon the moral teachings of Jesus and of the Old Testament. Salvation was phrased in ethical-social terms, and the inclusive ideal described as the kingdom of God on earth. Likewise in this decade this ideology first appeared significantly before the na-

2. *Op. cit.,* p. 89.
3. Arthur M. Schlesinger, *The Rise of the City, 1878–1898* (New York, 1933), p. 64.
4. *Op. cit.,* p. 68.   5. *Op. cit.,* chap. iv.

tion, being discussed at a number of church gatherings but most notably at three great conferences assembled by the Evangelical Alliance of the United States for the purpose of considering "the great perils and needs of the times."

Both socialism and a dissatisfied labor movement had called attention to the vast increase in the nation's wealth during the post-Civil War years. Preachers who were aware of this fact pointed out that the desire to gain sudden riches was leading to more and more unscrupulous methods that tended to force legitimate business into illegitimate practices. Josiah Strong, whose thirty years of leadership in the social gospel movement began in 1885 with the publication of his remarkable survey of American conditions entitled *Our Country*, declared in that book that the spirit of mammonism was corrupting the ballot box, damaging public morals, and fostering a gross materialism. Strong, whose analysis was typical, warned against the dangers inherent in a system that allowed such an enormous concentration of power in the hands of an individual as was held, for example, by Cornelius Vanderbilt, who owned one two-hundred-eighteenth of the wealth of the nation.[6] The extremes of wealth and poverty were regarded by certain writers as not only a disgrace to American civilization but also as a threat to its stability. A contributor to the *Methodist Review* in 1886 expressed serious doubt as to the right of an employer to pay "so small wages and to reserve to himself so large a share of the products of labor, as to accumulate his millions of dollars." The Reverend F. S. Root of Auburn, Maine, pointed out that the control of wealth continued to fall into fewer and fewer hands and charged that the sins of the plutocracy against the people were "so many and so varied that the merest catalog would be a formidable tract."[7]

Analyses of the rise of the corporation were decidedly realistic. We may take the Reverend A. J. F. Behrends' discussion as representative. He admitted the validity of certain of labor's criticisms of vested wealth and pointed out that corporations could "prescribe their own terms to the public" through their

6. Josiah Strong, *Our Country: its possible future and its present crisis* (New York, 1885), p. 123.

7. F. S. Root, *Familiar Vestry Talks on Christ's Christianity as Applied to Economic Questions* (Auburn, Me., 1887), pp. 15–17.

ability to defy competition, break down opposition, and buy up their enemies. The powers of a corporation lay in its impersonality: a creature of law, it should be amenable to law and strictly accountable to governmental inspection, he contended. Quasi-monopolies and holders of public franchises should not be left to purely private management. These public trusts, made possible by public consent, were declared to have responsibilities reaching beyond the welfare of stockholders.[8]

Monopoly, however, loomed as a far more serious threat to democracy than did the mere possession of wealth. Washington Gladden demanded that the government crush "certain outrageous monopolies" such as the coal trust. That half-a-dozen men could control the entire fuel supply of New York and New England Gladden declared "so contrary to public justice and public policy that some way must be found of making an end of it." Likewise, the great arteries of transportation between East and West are controlled by three or four men, and "the oil in the poor man's lamp is heavily taxed by a greedy monopoly"— examples of "iniquitous encroachments upon the rights of the people." Gladden believed it the duty of every Christian, "as the servant of a God of justice and righteousness," to register his objections to such a state of affairs.[9] Behrends pointed out the monopolistic character of patent control, suggested a revision of legislation, and observed that the public had a right to insist that profits from this source should not be extravagant.[10]

But it was the misuse of wealth and power in obviously illegitimate ways that aroused the fiercest ire of these prophets of a socialized Christianity. Stock manipulation and watering, corners in foodstuffs, speculation, bribery, betrayals of obligation, railway exploitation, fraudulent manufacturing, and adulteration of food were roundly condemned. The church was counseled to exert her influence against this "swelling tide of immoral methods of business."[11] Short weight, poor material, corners,

8. A. J. F. Behrends, *Socialism and Christianity* (New York, 1886), pp. 162–163.
9. Washington Gladden, *Applied Christianity* (Boston and New York, 1886), p. 19.
10. Behrends, *op. cit.*, p. 166.
11. J. W. Mendenhall, in *Methodist Review*, 70 (May, 1888), 753–756. Quoted by Kenneth E. Barnhart, *The Evolution of the Social Consciousness in Methodism* (University of Chicago Ph.D. dissertation, Chicago, 1924), p. 119.

and artificial panics were regarded as forms of robbery. Stock and wheat gambling, shoddy manufacture, and adulteration of food represented the unchristian desire to get something for nothing.[12] Gladden looked upon gambling in stocks as a "gigantic public evil that the state must exterminate." He called speculation on margins a form of piracy, comparing it to gambling at a faro bank. Every cent made by this means is dishonestly stolen from the industrial classes, he asserted.[13] Professor Richard T. Ely considered such gambling the essence of theft.[14]

Although Gladden and others recognized the need for governmental regulation of many abuses of wealth, there were advocates of stewardship as a method of control. The church, which is responsible for public opinion on moral questions, must accept both in theory and practice the Bible doctrine of possessions, wrote Josiah Strong, for only this will save us from "the great and imminent perils of wealth."[15] Stewardship was preached by Bishop Henry Codman Potter as an adequate gospel for the rich,[16] while F. S. Root declared that the best remedy was "a close and faithful application of the gospel of Jesus Christ." Another writer noted that Christianity had so far failed to assert its mastery of wealth and declared that a Christian solution of the financial problem must include the wide distribution of property.[17]

In 1870 only a little over one fifth of the nation's population lived in cities. By 1890 the proportion had risen to one third.[18] Protestant leaders were in the vanguard of those who diagnosed the unique situations arising from this rapid development. The cities were rightfully regarded as the focal points of civilization, and Strong voiced a widespread apprehension when he warned that unless Christianized they would in time destroy our free institutions.

The unprecedented religious problems raised by the growing cities elicited the most serious concern. The outstanding and

12. *Methodist Review,* 68 (1886), 566, 771. Quoted by Barnhart, *loc. cit.*
13. Gladden, *op. cit.,* p. 203.
14. Richard T. Ely, *Social Aspects of Christianity,* New York, 1889, p. 21.
15. Strong, *op. cit.,* p. 211.
16. Henry Codman Potter, "The Gospel for Wealth," in *The Scholar and the State* (New York, 1888), pp. 233–248.
17. *Methodist Review,* 68 (1886), 597 ff., 768 ff.; quoted by Barnhart, *loc. cit.*
18. Schlesinger, *op. cit.,* pp. 76, 79.

appalling fact was simply that the masses of the people, particularly the laboring classes, were callously indifferent to the ministrations of the Protestant churches. Probably the most acute analysis of the urban religious dilemma was a series of lectures given at Andover Theological Seminary in 1886 by the Reverend Samuel Lane Loomis of Brooklyn, whose book was later published as *Modern Cities and their Religious Problems*. Loomis showed how an undiscriminating immigration policy had resulted in a heterogeneous population difficult of assimilation; he then demonstrated the concomitant failure of Protestantism to win the working classes who regarded the churches as tools of capital.[19] His thesis was that our Christian civilization depends upon the vitality of faith in the people at large, in the decay of which there lurks a serious moral and social threat. To this collapse he attributed corruption in municipal government, drunkenness, increase of poverty and pauperism, and the desecration of the Sabbath. Further, many churches had removed from downtown districts as their neighborhoods had filled with workingmen and hosts of Catholic immigrants. At the time of Loomis' writing this situation was regarded as a crisis, and although it later brought forth the heroic efforts known as the "institutional church," the situation was to prove beyond the power of Protestantism to meet.

The churches were tardy in their recognition of the tenement question, there being few utterances on this subject in the 'eighties, possibly because of the belief that poverty was largely due to intemperance. Although several articles dealing with it appeared in the *Christian Union* in 1885 and 1886, the Reverend A. J. F. Behrends was one of few ministers to treat the matter with some concern. He pointed out that about 10 per cent of tenement buildings were adjudged to be in good condition, with 5 per cent deserving to be razed, and the remainder ranging between these extremes. He held the primary need to be adequate sanitary legislation that would require and enforce regular and frequent inspection. Such a policy would necessitate continued public pressure, due to the power of the investors and the indifference of tenement dwellers.

The related problem of pauperism found several clergymen placing considerable blame upon society for this evil, holding it

19. Samuel Lane Loomis, *Modern Cities* (New York, 1887), p. 99.

responsible for providing every man an opportunity for "honest endeavor, and of protecting him against the selfish greed of those who make gain of his misery." Behrends took into account both personal factors such as idleness and improvidence and the social factors of illiteracy, intemperance, overcrowding and the absence of a true domestic life. He proposed the scientific organization of charity.[20] Gladden pointed out the duty of charity and suggested that the wealthy invest in model tenements. Loomis saw in the statistics on poverty and pauperism another proof of his thesis that the decay of religion was making itself felt in the "serious decline from the high plane of Christian civilization."[21] Bishop Samuel Smith Harris of Michigan regarded the problem as an inevitable and permanent one and recommended the application of Christian rather than governmental charity in order to throw both rich and poor back on the law of mutual helpfulness and love.[22]

Urban politics also attracted some attention. Loomis felt it unnecessary to enlarge upon the fact that the governments of most important American cities had been for a long time "more or less rotten, and in some cases little more than gigantic systems of fraud." Strong pointed out the prevalence of "boss" rule and observed that in general the larger cities were the worse governed.[23] Such were conditions that Ely remarked that "a man who would talk as Christ did on the streets of Chicago or New York would be in danger of being clubbed by the police, if nothing worse."[24]

Beyond these broader concerns, there was a moderate interest shown by the writers under consideration in the questions of criminology, the family, the social consequences of the saloon, and immigration. These discussions, suggestive at this early date of widening interests on the part of social Christians, may be briefly noted. The treatment of crime and the criminal was regarded as a "soiled and disreputable page in our social history"; Christianity should insist upon reforms in prison procedure, sympathy toward discharged criminals, prison education,

20. Behrends, *op. cit.,* pp. 239–241.   21. Loomis, *op. cit.,* pp. 102–104.
22. Samuel Smith Harris, *The Relation of Christianity to Civil Society* (New York, 1883), p. 182.
23. Strong, *op. cit.,* pp. 135–136.   24. Ely, *op. cit.,* p. 157.

and religious ministrations to convicts.[25] In *Applied Christianity* Gladden pointed out the fundamental physical and
moral importance of the family to society and named certain
causes of its deterioration: an exaggerated individualism,
crowded living conditions, indiscriminate congregation of men
and women in factories and amusement places, meager wages,
and uncertainty of employment.[26] The saloon was not a primary
concern of what is generally meant by the social gospel, but its
recognition as a social force is noteworthy. Gladden held it and
the liquor traffic to represent "a highly unsocial proceeding,"
while Loomis read both the causes and effects of urban degradation in the saloon evil.[27] The hordes of immigrants arriving
on our shores during these years were not unnoticed. Strong
devoted a significant chapter of *Our Country* to this problem,
wherein he indicated the generally low moral and religious
character of immigrants and showed from statistics that many
who belonged to the pauper and criminal classes were further
demoralized by the process of migration itself. Immigration
was further charged with bringing "continental ideas of the
Sabbath" and a liking for liquor. Strong also saw it as nourish-
ing socialism, contributing to the "liquor vote," and furnishing
the rabble upon which the boss-ridden corruption of the cities
flourished.[28]

In the course of this widespread discussion, which was vastly
greater than our abbreviated review has indicated, there
emerged the first articulate rationalizations of social Christianity. We have seen the religious origins of this ethical current
in the "new theology" and the humanitarian impulses of the
more liberal groups. Prerequisite to the new viewpoint was (1)
certain criticism of orthodoxy's traditional otherworldly and
individualistic outlook. Social Christianity (2) founded its
claims upon a fresh emphasis on the social and humanitarian
aspects of the second commandment and stressed the need for
the development of an adequate sociological technique with

25. Potter, *op. cit.,* p. 177. See also William M. F. Round, *Our Criminals and
Christianity* (New York), reprinted from the *Homiletic Review,* n.d. D. J. Hill,
The Social Influence of Christianity (Boston, 1888), chap. viii.

26. Gladden, *op. cit.,* pp. 194–197.

27. *Op. cit.,* p. 187; Loomis, *op. cit.,* p. 101; Behrends, *op. cit.,* p. 200.

28. Strong, *op. cit.,* chap. iv.

which to apply the law of love to the complexities of modern society. Christian ethics (3) based on the teachings of Jesus and the Old Testament were discussed as the norm for social standards. Salvation was conceived (4) in ethical-social terms, and (5) the inclusive religious social ideal was described as the kingdom of God on earth. The church and her ministers (6) were summoned in the name of God and humanity to the leadership of the new social crusade.

The first influential effort on the part of a prominent American to state "the social side of the Church's mission" was Professor Ely's book, *The Social Aspects of Christianity,* published in 1889. Ely's criticism of the social outlook of orthodoxy was representative. He believed the commonly held otherworldly conception of Christianity to be an "unfortunate error" that would explain many historical aberrations such as persecution and formalism, while accounting at the same time for the church's failure to appeal to the working classes.[29] The so-called "simple gospel of Christ" Ely branded "a one-sided half-gospel," the corrective of which would be the whole truth that included "a social as well as an individual gospel" that proclaimed both regeneration and salvation for society as well as for the individual. The church will find her opportunity when she abandons the "narrow, negative, individualistic attitude" that has restricted the Christian message to "saving souls," and when she preaches the entire gospel of Christ. As proof of his contention Ely held up the strongly "social and national" emphases of the Psalms against the individualism and frequent selfishness of the hymns of his day.[30] The Reverend Edward Everett Hale of Boston contrasted a "Christian" church that directed men to bring in the kingdom of God with a "medieval" church that stressed the salvation of individuals.[31]

Ely further charged the church with having neglected the study of social science. As a result of her preoccupation with theology the church has lost the leadership of sociology, he asserted. Socialism has consequently become materialistic and communism infidel. Without careful examination the church

29. Ely, *op. cit.,* pp. 63 ff.   30. *Op. cit.,* pp. 26–27, 148–150.
31. Edward Everett Hale, "Can our Churches Be Made More Useful?" *North American Review,* 148 (1889), 379.

has hastily condemned both of these to please the rich. While the clergy manifest some interest in problems of the day, their ignorance of social science frequently renders them blind leaders of the blind. Another Episcopalian, the Reverend Julius H. Ward, warned the church that the masses of the people would continue to ignore it until its leaders should give to Christianity a fresh insight into "the present ordering of life" and display some mastery of its conditions. The church, he added, "has made the mistake of separating in its thought and management the industrial and social from the moral and spiritual life."[32]

The social reformers of Christianity insisted that new stress must be laid upon the much neglected application of the second commandment. Spiritual progress in our time, wrote John Bascom, president of the University of Wisconsin, "lies for each and all in the passage from the first to the second commandment, from the love of God to the love of our neighbor."[33] The gospel of the Son of Man, said Ely, "is the Gospel of Humanity." Christ gave a *new* commandment—"that ye love one another"—the implications of which the church has lost sight of but which now need to be carried into all the relations of life. Christianity in essence is love toward God and toward man: the two are inseparable. The law of love is epitomized in the golden rule, which is "the highest formula of social justice."

Although the golden rule may be repeated often enough by preachers, its application in the real world of affairs is not easy. Love to God is piety and the science dealing with this aspect of Christianity is theology, wrote Ely. Love to man is philanthropy, and the science that deals with this part of the gospel is sociology. Therefore, if we would know how to apply the golden rule we must "devote ourselves long and carefully to the study of the science of human happiness, social science." This much neglected second branch of the gospel of Christ ought to be pursued with diligence equaling that devoted to theology. Gladden and R. H. Newton were among the first to recognize the close relationship between social Christianity and sociology,

32. Julius H. Ward, *The Church in Modern Society* (Boston and New York, 1889), p. 57.
33. John Bascom, *Sociology* (New York and London, 1887), p. 242.

having discussed the need for the study of social science in
Working People and their Employers and *The Morals of
Trade,* both of which series of lectures were given in 1876.

Gladden believed that ministers could use the findings of sociology in solving problems that came before them and that they
could thus gain valuable points in methodology. Ely proposed
that half of theological students' time be devoted to social science and that divinity schools be the chief intellectual centers
for sociology. The church should call to her service in this field
the greatest intellects of the age to guide the study of a philanthropy that in its positive and preventive aspects would embrace "the individual, the family, the community, the state, the
nation, and finally humanity." By a preventive philanthropy
Ely meant social reform, holding it far better to diminish the
need of reformatories and hospitals, for example, than to build
such institutions. The abolition of child labor as a method of
preventing disease, crime, and poverty was suggested by Ely as
philanthropy "of the kind especially recommended by Christ."[34]
Thus the emphasis upon the law of love carried at once beyond
a sentimental mouthing of the golden rule to the demand for
scientific discipline and definite social reform.

The social character of Christianity may be found in the
teachings of Christ, who proclaimed a social as well as an individual salvation, and who condemned the social sins of his generation, claimed Ely, who went on to suggest that the fundamentally ethical attitude of Jesus and his disciples led them at
once to the heart of the social questions of their time. In Christ's
emphasis on love and service Ely found "the most convincing
evidence" of his divinity.[35]

This apologist for social Christianity was likewise deeply impressed by the social ethics of the Old Testament, recommend-
ing the spirit of the economic and industrial laws of Moses to
the consideration of his own generation. Ely pointed out the
subordination of the individualistic element to the social in the
Psalms, and frequently quoted Scripture at length to show both
the sweeping generalizations that "include the whole duty of
man within the compass of a few words," and their detailed application in such matters as interest, weights and measures, justice, and charity. Beyond a doubt, he concluded, there runs all

34. Ely, *op. cit.,* p. 89.   35. *Op. cit.,* p. 59.

through the Bible the distinct aim of the abolition of poverty and the establishment of general social welfare.[36]

Although most prophets of the social gospel would probably have acquiesced in Ely's attempt to ground the new faith in the ethics of Christ and of the Old Testament, it was for a later generation to provide the most complete intellectual foundation for the movement in the social teachings of Jesus, which discovery came at the end of the century. During the 'eighties the ideal of the kingdom provided a frame of reference frequently appealed to, as we shall see. Although this likewise was to reach its apogee later (in the writings of Walter Rauschenbusch), these two patterns were to provide social Christianity with its most useful settings.

Salvation was expressed in social-ethical terms by these leaders of Protestant social thought. Ely declared that salvation meant "positive righteousness in all the earth," while preaching the gospel involved "a never-ceasing attack on every wrong institution, until the earth becomes a new earth, and all its cities, cities of God."[37] Gladden claimed Christianity as something broader than all its divisions: it is the kingdom of God in the world—a comprehensive salvation of both soul and body.[38] "There is a most important sense in which religion is for politics and social life and for them primarily," asserted John Bascom in his *Sociology*, published in 1887.

But social salvation was really included within the broad universalism of the kingdom of heaven on earth, a conception now beginning to emerge definitely as the ideal of a perfected human society. Realizable in the historical process and embodying the weal of humanity, yet essentially a spiritual entity that nevertheless shaped material things and events, the kingdom became the complete social goal for both the individual and the social organism. It was a spiritual kingdom, yet built on the earth—the true synthesis of the physical and spiritual universe of God, according to John Bascom.[39] The sphere of religion in the modern world, declared Minot J. Savage, is here—in New York, in London—not in ancient Jerusalem, and the business of religion is to lay the foundation and build the superstructure of the city of God, which in the nineteenth century has be-

36. *Op. cit.*, p. 155.   37. *Op. cit.*, p. 73.
38. Gladden, *op. cit.*, p. 212.   39. Bascom, *op. cit.*, pp. 263–264.

come the city of man. The perfect condition of man is a perfect reconciliation with all the laws of God.[40] For Ely, salvation was achieved through service to the kingdom. For the Reverend Leighton Williams of New York City, a founder of the Brotherhood of the Kingdom, the kingdom ideal was the fruition of the millennial hope—"the golden age to come, when society shall be what the Christian church teaches it ought to be."[41] In his Lyman Beecher Lectures at Yale in 1890 A. J. F. Behrends declared the historic triumph of Christianity to be the great object of Christian preaching and the "present prosaic earth" the territory wherein "the reconstruction of humanity" will take place.[42] In the next decade the kingdom idea was to be exhaustively explored by Walter Rauschenbusch and his colleagues of the Brotherhood of the Kingdom.

The general nature of the social ideal was further revealed in the summons to the church to take up the new crusade. Running through this challenge was the note of crisis, a characteristic of the social gospel throughout its development. It was maintained that the church should assert the moral leadership of society, for whose ethics it is responsible. As lineal successors of the Hebrew prophets, ministers of Christ should denounce wrong, explain right, and so lead the people to a realization of duty, declared David Jayne Hill.[43] The church is most needed today as the guide and inspiration of human society; it must push out beyond the needs of its own members to a "broader identification with all the interests of life," declared the Reverend Julius H. Ward in his book, *The Church in Modern Society*.[44] Christianity must assert its right to rule "this kingdom of industry as well as all the other kingdoms of this world," for the Christian law is the only standard upon which society can rest in security and peace, said Gladden.[45] Religion is for the body as well as for the soul, for time as well as eternity; it concerns the affairs of the present life, both with respect to individuals and to the masses. The church will be unable to re-

40. Minot J. Savage, *Social Problems* (Boston, 1886), p. 23.
41. Leighton Williams, *The Established Tendencies toward Social Reform* (New York, 1888), pp. 16–17.
42. A. J. F. Behrends, *The Philosophy of Preaching* (New York, 1890), pp. 45–47.
43. Hill, *op. cit.*, p. 191. 44. Ward, *op. cit.*, p. 68.
45. Gladden, *op. cit.*, p. 173.

solve itself of blame if the widely heralded social cataclysm overtakes us, warned the Reverend Frederick H. Wines.[46]

All these viewpoints, and others indicative of the future development of the social gospel, were stated in 1880 by a writer whose brilliant and pioneering outline for a *Christian Sociology* deserves special mention. The Reverend J. H. W. Stuckenberg, a distinguished Lutheran liberal,[47] laid out in this treatise the first, and one of few, significant American formulations of social theology, in comparison with which the writings of Ely, for example, seem almost childish. Unfortunately, Stuckenberg's book received but scant notice. The groping young social gospel was thus deprived of the rare guidance of a mind well trained in both theology and sociology, with the result that twenty years or more passed before the movement fully realized principles advocated by this pathfinder of whom it had the misfortune to be unaware.

Disturbed by the popular tendency to ignore "the social elements of the gospel," Stuckenberg essayed an appraisal of "the social laws and duties" growing out of the relations of Christians to one another and to the world, holding that such principles must be formulated before the church could be expected to exert a social influence. The science of Christian sociology, a special branch of theology, would systematize the social teachings of the New Testament, with particular emphasis upon the equal importance of the second commandment with the first; it would protest the contemporary divorce of morality from religion; and it would propose Christian solutions for social problems. Why, asked Stuckenberg, leave the most important civil and social questions of the day to a godless economics? Rather, "why not make the ethics of the New Testament the test of all social theories?" While there are of course many situations upon which the New Testament has no direct bearing, nevertheless the general principles are there and should be applied. The church must now assume a role similar to that of the

46. F. H. Wines, *The Restoration of the Criminal. A sermon* . . . (Springfield, Ill., 1888), p. 16.

47. Stuckenberg taught theology at Wittenberg College, was at one time minister of the American Church in Berlin, and wrote distinguished but never popular books on philosophy, history, and sociology. See John O. Evjen, *The Life of J. H. W. Stuckenberg—Theologian—Philosopher—Sociologist* (Minneapolis, 1938).

prophets; but at the foundation of such activity there must be a properly developed social science.[48] Stuckenberg's most unique and prophetic note was his insistence that the teachings of Christ are adaptable to all the needs of men, in which viewpoint he antedated by two decades the adoption of the social teachings of Jesus as the religious basis for a maturing social gospel.[49]

The decade of the 'eighties was distinguished in social-gospel history by a plethora of discussion of aims and principles and a notable lack of technique and organization. These characteristics have been sufficiently apparent in the foregoing analyses to need no further emphasis, but a concluding survey of two further phenomena of the period will serve to reinforce this generalization. There is no better evidence of the serious interest of Protestantism in this newest expression of the historic faith than the fact that the theme of "Christianity Practically Applied," which had originated as the concern of a few scattered individuals, began in this decade to appear on the agenda of important church meetings and to attract on its own occount conferences of national significance.

The Episcopal Church Congress, founded, as previously noted, in 1874, maintained its interest in social problems throughout the 'eighties. It continued to devote a generous share of every meeting to certain social issues—including civil service, charity organization, the tariff, free churches, the race question—hearing these discussed by such leaders as William Graham Sumner, W. S. Rainsford, Seth Low, and Robert Treat Paine. An annual gathering similar in spirit and method was the "Baptist Congress for the Discussion of Current Questions," an unofficial denominational forum that held its first meeting in 1882. Regarded by its leaders as a good-natured battlefield "for the holy warfare of ideas," the Congress, which never omitted social issues from its program, early provided a sounding board for the social gospel of several young ministers destined to become leaders of social Christianity—notably Walter Rauschenbusch of New York, who first occupied its platform in 1888. Others were Leighton Williams, Samuel Zane Batten, Shailer Mathews, Charles R. Henderson, E. B. Andrews, Nor-

48. J. H. W. Stuckenberg, *Christian Sociology* (New York, 1880), pp. 16, 21.
49. See chap. xii, below.

man Fox, P. S. Moxom, Francis Wayland, and W. H. P. Faunce.

When American Methodists gathered at Baltimore to celebrate their centennial in 1884 the social note was repeatedly struck by speakers anxious to bridge the gulf between the masses and the church. Social matters not infrequently interested the small but select and influential American Institute of Christian Philosophy, before whose regular meetings and summer schools were given many notable addresses later widely circulated, such as Bishop Potter's pastoral letter entitled "The Laborer not a Commodity."[50] When the American Congress of Churches (a premature effort at federation) met for its second session at Cleveland in 1886, the speakers included Washington Gladden, Henry George, a representative of labor, and such leaders of modernized church work as the Reverends W. S. Rainsford and Samuel W. Dike.

One of the most dynamic advocates of social Christianity was the Reverend Josiah Strong, who began his career as a home missionary in Ohio but sprang into national prominence in 1885 upon the publication of his book, *Our Country*—which tract was written for the American Home Missionary Society. In December of that year, Strong, then pastor of the Central Congregational Church of Cincinnati, called an "Inter-Denominational Congress" in his church for the purpose of discussing current problems. To this meeting came such advocates of social Christianity as Lyman Abbott, Richard T. Ely, Washington Gladden, and Amory H. Bradford, to present the issues of the hour: the urban situation, socialism, the indifference of the working classes toward the churches, a religious program for the immigrant population, and a religious census. At the close of the five-day session another meeting was planned and the suggestion offered that religious surveys be made in as many cities as possible.[51]

Strong, whose ability as a promoter was now recognized, became the general secretary of the hitherto semimoribund Evangelical Alliance of the United States the next year. Under his leadership the three most significant conferences ever held in

50. *Christian Thought,* 4th ser. (1886), 289–291.
51. *Christian Union,* 32, No. 26 (December 24, 1886), 6–8.

the United States in the interest of social Christianity were assembled in 1887, 1889, and 1893. The first of these, which met in Washington, was announced in an address to the Christian public signed by William E. Dodge as President of the Alliance and seventy leading ministers, teachers, and laymen, including James McCosh, Phillips Brooks, Mark Hopkins, James B. Angell, John H. Vincent, and Lyman Abbott. This "call," sounding the note of crisis much as had *Our Country*, mentioned the major problems of the time and asserted that the church had not yet fully recognized its "relations to the entire life of the community and the nation." The conference would study three questions: the "perils and opportunities of the Christian church and of the country," denominational coöperation to meet these, and means of securing such coöperation and of awakening "the whole church to its responsibility."

Some twelve to fifteen hundred delegates responded and for three intensive days were bombarded in long sessions with facts, challenges, and methods by a scintillating group of Protestant leaders. The *National Perils and Opportunities* surveyed, as the printed report of the conference was titled, were the problems with which we have dealt in this decade—perils of the city, dangers to the family, the issue between labor and capital, immigration, and the misuse of wealth; the opportunities were chiefly the possibilities available through the coöperation of religious bodies utilizing the underlying Christian resources of the country. The most practical result of the meeting was a concerted effort to study local situations by means of organized visitation, and the development of a scheme for the affiliation of local coöperating groups with the national Evangelical Alliance. Although the comment of one delegate that the conference "was perhaps the most important gathering of Christians since the Council of Nice" is to be discounted, it certainly "made a deep impression on the country," as Strong wrote.

The following year local conferences dealing with *The Religious Condition of New York City* and *Vital Questions* affecting the welfare of Montreal were held in those two cities by the Alliance. The next great national gathering took place in Boston in 1889, where in addition to the local attendance there came five hundred delegates representative of sixteen denominations and twenty-three states. The gathering was concerned largely with progress in coöperation since the Washington meeting, but it also discussed crime, and church and state, and heard various papers on the methods being developed in expanded church work. Its report, *National Needs and Remedies*, was much more optimistic than had been the summary of the Washington meeting.

The climax of Strong's efforts in this direction was reached in the conference held at Chicago in connection with the World's Columbian Exposition in 1893. Here perils and needs were taken for granted; the great object was "to point out the social mission of the church" and to discuss methods of accomplishing it. Of the four divisions of the program, that devoted to the church and social problems received by far the most attention. Twelve major addresses dealt with the function of the church in a changing social order, while sectional conferences discussed various phases of religious social work such as the institutional church, athletics, tenement reform, politics, boys' clubs, and social settlements. In addition to many familiar names there appeared new leaders and new gospels at this week-long conference: the Reverend Charles H. Parkhurst, anti-Tammany crusader; Professor George D. Herron and President George A. Gates of Iowa College; the Reverend W. S. Rainsford of St. George's, the pioneer institutional church of New York; Charles R. Henderson of the University of Chicago; John R. Commons, then of Indiana University; Jane Addams, Robert A. Woods, and Dean George Hodges—all of whom we shall meet in our study of the next decade. In commenting upon the conference, Josiah Strong stressed its practical emphases and the importance of scientific techniques and trained workers. He felt that the churches were beginning to see their duty "to the entire man and to the entire life" and to recognize their social function. In this he read a "coming Christian renaissance" that sprang from "a clearer and truer vision of the Christ and his mission," and that would "apply his salvation to body as well as soul, and to society as well as to the individual."[52]

The stage set by the Chicago exposition provided for the meeting of another important group of social gospelers. Several days of the very popular sessions of the famous World's

52. In John Henry Barrows, *The World's Parliament of Religions* (Chicago, 1893, 2 vols.), II, 1449.

Parliament of Religions were devoted to the relations of the churches to social questions. Addressed by Professors Francis Greenwood Peabody, Charles R. Henderson, Richard T. Ely, and Albion W. Small, and the Reverends Anna Garlin Spencer, Edward Everett Hale, and Washington Gladden, this forum heard presentations of social-gospel theory, the problems of criminology, labor, the ethics of wealth, and denominational co-operation.[53]

It remains to describe an event that provides a useful summary of the various trends discussed in this chapter. The interest of many ministers in sociology and the demand that Protestantism develop a scientific technique for carrying into effect the second commandment led to the participation of certain social gospelers in the founding of the American Economic Association in 1885. Professor Ely, who was perhaps the leading spirit in the group, found generous support for his new historical school of economics among the clergy who as we know had joined the "revolt against the laissez-faire theory"—in which attitude the Association found its chief *raison d'être*. One of the four brief principles presented by Ely at the first meeting of the Association was a recognition of the church, the state, and science as agencies whose combined efforts should be enlisted in the solution of the "vast numbers of social problems" brought into prominence by the conflict of labor and capital. Ely and his colleagues hoped "to accomplish certain practical results in the social and financial world," and believing that their task lay "in the direction of practical Christianity," they appealed to the church, "the chief of the social forces in this country," for aid.[54] Later Ely wrote in the Boston *Congregationalist* that the Association's purpose was to investigate the problems of social science, to give no opinions but to strive to discover "the underlying principles of industrial society," and to diffuse information among all classes of people. In brief this meant the serious study of "the second of the two great commandments . . . and thus to bring science to the aid of Christianity."[55] This viewpoint appealed strongly to leaders of the social-gospel movement, with the result that many of those

53. Barrows, *op. cit.*

54. Richard T. Ely, "Report of the Organization of the American Economic Association," *Publications* of the Association, 1 (1886), No. 1, 9, 18.

55. Reprinted in *Social Aspects,* pp. 24–25.

whose names appear in these pages were charter members of the Association: Lyman Abbott, Washington Gladden, Leighton Williams, Amory H. Bradford, Newman Smyth, R. Heber Newton, J. H. Rylance, and Professors E. Benjamin Andrews, Edward W. Bemis, William DeWitt Hyde, Jesse Macy, and Jeremiah W. Jenks.[56]

In Part II we have seen the development of the occasional questionings of the 'seventies into an enthusiastic and widespread trend that by 1890 was verging upon organization. The motivation for this distinctly religious movement was supplied chiefly by the ethical impulses flowing from a progressive theology. In turn the social demands of a newly industrialized age forced Protestantism not only to defend itself but to rethink its ideology and reform its methods. Of the many perplexing issues growing out of industrialism those that concerned the relations of labor and capital and their interpretation by socialism so largely dominated the interests of socially minded clergymen in this decade that the social gospel may without question be described historically as the response of Protestantism to those specific situations. The centrality of the labor problem in all realistic discussions of urban religious conditions adds further weight to this definition. The problems of an industrial civilization remained the central interest of social Christianity.

We have interpreted the decade as the phase in the development of the religious social movement in which activity was largely limited to discussion. The new school had entered the national forum, but not as yet the national arena. Although spurred by religious idealism, reformers of this period were consciously hampered by the excessive individualism of the age and by their ignorance of sociology and their lack of scientific techniques. We have reviewed a few pioneer efforts to supply these needs. Characteristic emphases of the movement as it continued to grow were to be assertions of the social viewpoint with attempts to synthesize it with individualism, and demands for the teaching of sociology and the fabrication of scientific methodologies. The foundations for all such future developments had now been laid.

56. It is hardly necessary to add that this evangelistic fervor did not remain a permanent characteristic of the Association.

PART III: 1890–1900
THE SOCIAL GOSPEL COMES OF AGE

The object of Christianity is human welfare; its method is character-building; its process is evolution; and the secret of its power is God.

LYMAN ABBOTT

How shall come the kingdom holy,
In which all the earth is blest,
That shall lift on high the lowly,
And to weary souls give rest?
Not with trumpet call of legions
Bursting through the upper sky,
Waking earth thro' all its regions
With their heav'n-descending cry.

Not with dash or sudden sally,
Swooping down with rushing wing;
But, as, creeping up a valley,
Come the grasses in the spring;
First one blade and then another,
Still advancing are they seen,
Rank on rank, each by its brother,
Till each inch of ground is green.

Thro' the weary days of sowing,
Burning sun and drenching show'r,
Day by day, so slowly growing,
Comes the waited harvest hour.
So the kingdom cometh ever,
Though it seems so far away;
Each high thought and true endeavor
Hastens on the blessed day.

MINOT JUDSON SAVAGE

INTRODUCTION

THROUGHOUT the brisk years of the 'eighties a youthful social Christianity had been becoming increasingly aware of the maladjustments with which the industrial revolution and the birth of a new social order had supplanted the once-peaceful serenity of a rural America and her provincial moral guardian, conventional Protestantism. Embattled industry and socialistic agitators had very nearly absorbed the interests of progressive ministers who were inclined to diagnose conditions around them, although the dire threat of vast unchurched populations in the newly big cities also elicited the profoundest concern. These problems, seriously analyzed and debated throughout the decade, were finally taken into the forum of national discussion in conferences that sought to assay the perils facing the nation. The chief prescription was an application of practical Christianity. These many enthusiasms of an adolescent movement were nonetheless those of a relatively small group and the actual usefulness of their proposals hardly passed beyond the stage of blueprints.

The last decade of the century brought the sobering realization that good intentions were not sufficiently powerful to reform an unchristian civilization. Many and various organizations sprang into being, some to broadcast the seed of ideas and disappear, others to act as hotbeds for the germination of subsequently pervasive influences, and some to agitate for practical reform in the name of religious humanitarianism. Others banded together to lay a sociological foundation for religious reform activity. A group of enthusiasts made the radical Christian ethic of love the basis for what proved to be one of the most unique experiments in practical communism in American history. On the left of the movement socialism again presented its claims and in this decade made many converts. Even those who did not go as far as the Christian Socialists challenged the sufficiency of the traditional doctrine of stewardship to control the reckless power of triumphant capitalism.

The ruling theological ideology of the day accepted an evolutionary kingdom of God to be built upon earth by men of good will, such a kingdom being the end result of an almost inevitable progress. At the same time the social gospel often marched hand in hand with the muckrakers of the period. A popular literature of fictional exhortation that attempted to bring Christ's healing touch into the sore spots of American civilization sold into the millions of copies. In the Middle West the most advanced school of religious radicalism found itself closely related to the revolt of the farmers against the entrenched plutocracy.

In brief, the 'nineties may be regarded as the great flowering period in the history of American social Christianity, when it was coming of age but had not yet reached maturity.

CHAPTER VII

EVOLUTION AND THE KINGDOM

The immanence of Christ, the vital unity of the race, the presence of the kingdom—these truths give to life a new sacredness and to duty new cogency.

WASHINGTON GLADDEN

THE last decade of the nineteenth century witnessed the whole-hearted acceptance of the Darwinian theory of evolution by progressive American theologians. The consequent accommodation of liberal religion to the leading scientific concept of the century produced three clearly related ideas that together constituted a logical and unified frame of reference for social Christianity. These were the immanence of God, the organic or solidaristic view of society, and the presence of the kingdom of heaven on earth. This religious rationalization of contemporary ideologies emphasized the ethical aspects of the faith, particularly in its views of Jesus and of salvation, and it linked moral and religious improvement to the current optimistic belief in progress. All of these conceptions had been long growing, and although no one of them was in itself strikingly new or unique, their formulation by Protestant leaders bespoke the acclimatization of Christianity to the modern world with its scientific and humanitarian sanctions. In such a religious climate the social gospel, itself the child of the new era, was to come of age.

The doctrine of the immanence of God assumed the divine presence in nature and in human society, broke down traditional distinctions between sacred and secular, and regarded Christianity as a natural religion. "God is in his world," said Washington Gladden and Lyman Abbott, though it might have been Emerson speaking. To look reverently at the face of nature is to look in the face of Christ. Nature is the constant revelation of the presence and power of God—"the outward utterance of himself."[1]

1. Washington Gladden, *Ruling Ideas of the Present Age* (Boston and New York, 1896), pp. 280, 290. Lyman Abbott, *The Evolution of Christianity* (Boston and New York, 1892), p. 245. Granville R. Pike, *The Divine Drama. The*

Immanence also characterized the spiritual and social realms. God lives through all the ranks of his creation, whether in angels or amœbas, in men or in the Christ, said the Reverend James Morris Whiton of New York.[2] God is truly, yet not completely revealed in the universe, in history, in man, and in Christ. Although above and beyond history, he indwells the processes of human society, giving man his ideals and sending the race to its highest achievements,[3] asserted the Reverend George A. Gordon of Boston, leading pastor-theologian and successor to Theodore T. Munger as spokesman of progressivism.[4] Such conceptions were a marked change from the time when, as President Eliot of Harvard noted, God had been thought of as "an angry deity whose chief functions were punishment and vengeance." The God of this incipient modernism was "one of supreme power and love, filling the universe, working through all human institutions, and through all men" and promoting joy and happiness.[5]

The presence of the divine in society naturally tended to level the old barriers between sacred and secular. The value of this universalizing conception to a social gospel that had long been advocating the broadening of the field of religion is apparent. The vision of God unfolding himself in human institutions lent religion a new immediacy, expanded its sphere of activity, and reinforced the organic bonds integrating the individual with society.[6] Gladden declared that the doctrine of immanence rendered the old distinction of sacred and profane "meaningless and almost blasphemous" in view of the sanctity of all life.[7] There is no sacredness about the church that ought not to be attached to the chamber of commerce, declared Philip S.

manifestation of God in the universe. An institute of social theology (New York, 1898), Preface.

2. James Morris Whiton, Gloria Patri, or our talks about the Trinity (New York, 1892), p. 91. Whiton's Yale Ph.D. of 1861 was the first such degree conferred in the United States.

3. George A. Gordon, "The Theological Problem for Today," in The New Puritanism (New York, 1898), pp. 156–157. Also Gordon, The New Epoch for Faith (Boston and New York, 1901), p. 12.

4. See John Wright Buckham, Progressive Religious Thought in America (Boston and New York, 1919).

5. Charles William Eliot, American Contributions to Civilization and other essays (New York, 1897), pp. 64–65.

6. Pike, op. cit., p. 175.   7. Gladden, op. cit., p. 295.

Moxom, the progressive minister of the First Baptist Church of Boston.[8]

The doctrine of the immanence of God carried the further corollary that Christianity is a natural religion. In *Ruling Ideas of the Present Age* Gladden claimed that the basic laws of the faith can be verified inductively and that religion itself is the product of evolution: in this universe we find humanity the crown of the creation; Christ, as the head of humanity "completes and explains the revelation that began with the beginning of the creation." The union of the heavenly and the earthly is thus as natural as that of soul and body. We therefore stand on solid, scientific ground in proclaiming the gospel.[9] In *The Evolution of Christianity* Lyman Abbott similarly traced the growth of revelation through the Old Testament to Christ and asserted that the development thus described was the outcome of the actual working of the same evolutionary principle as is operative in the physical realm.[10]

It was a logical step from the doctrine of the immanence of God to an organic theory of society. "The vital unity of the race," as Gladden referred to the solidaristic view, was established by the indwelling of the divine Father in all men. In contrast to the excessive individualism of Calvinism this liberal attitude embraced a "broad, healthy, social philosophy of human nature" that bound the race in an organic brotherhood. While such a view may have derived in part from contemporary sociological theory such as Herbert Spencer's notion of society as an organism, it was fundamentally a religious conviction, though sometimes supported by arguments from physical science.

Gladden devoted a chapter of *Ruling Ideas* to the complementary nature of the relationships between the individual and the social order. The organic idea has been present in Christianity since the writing of St. Paul's epistles, he said, but it has been narrowly construed to mean only the church. In reality the relations of men in society are not contractual, but "vital and organic." We are members one of another. No man lives or dies or attains happiness apart from his fellow men.[11] The organic view held not only for the relations of individuals, but

8. Philip Stafford Moxom, *The Religion of Hope* (Boston, 1896), p. 66.
9. Gladden, *op. cit.*, pp. 294–295.   10. Abbott, *op. cit.*, pp. 255–256.
11. Gladden, *op. cit.*, p. 285.

also for social institutions and events. Lyman Abbott pointed out that there is a science of history and of sociology just as truly as there is of astronomy or biology, and that therefore humanity possesses a unity and a continuity similar to that of nature. Cause leads to effect in the spiritual as in the material realms; there is a God in history quite as in the physical universe.[12] The Christian God who created the heavens and the earth likewise "made all men of one blood," asserted Gordon.

Here, then, was a sociological rationalization of the doctrines of the fatherhood of God and the brotherhood of man—a formulation of fundamental importance to the social gospel. Some thinkers interpreted these views in terms of the incarnation. James M. Whiton saw this central Christian dogma as expressing an eternal act of God taking place in all humanity as well as in the Christ and therefore reinforcing human kinship and sympathy.[13] Gordon showed how the plain humanity of the Master revealed a new relationship for the race in demonstrating "the great commonplace of brotherhood supreme over all inequalities and diversities." On this basis Christianity converts social and economic situations into moral and humanitarian concerns, because it refuses to regard men simply as "creatures of the seen and temporal" but persists in viewing them "as brothers in a grand community of duties and privileges" under the providence and moral discipline of a common Father.[14]

This school tended to replace the older exaggerated individualism with definitely social views of man and of salvation. Gordon claimed that the traditional theological map was completely changed at a single stroke by this new demand that redemption cover the entire race. Moxom believed that the work of Jesus included the creation of a new social order as well as of a new man. The kingdom of God is the regenerated society, just as the child of God is the regenerated individual, he said, as had Jesse Henry Jones two decades before him.[15] Josiah Strong wrote in *The New Era* that the two great commandments rep-

12. Abbott, *op. cit.*, p. 247. See also William Jewett Tucker, *The New Movement in Humanity from Liberty to Unity* (Boston and New York, 1892), and Buckham, *op. cit.*, pp. 158–161.

13. Whiton, *op. cit.*, p. 78.

14. George A. Gordon, *The Christ of To-day* (Boston and New York, 1895), pp. 217, 219.

15. Moxom, *op. cit.*, p. 85. Jones's views were described in chap. ii, above.

resent man's relations to God and to his fellow men: obedience to the first saves the individual, while observance of the second would save society.[16] Redemption, said Abbott, is not the restoration of man to a state of innocence; it is the process of spiritual evolution by which God is creating a new humanity in Christ.[17]

The implications of these reforms for the social gospel were pointed out by the Reverend Granville Ross Pike in his "institute of social theology," *The Divine Drama*. In the "broad, underlying, organic oneness of humanity," he wrote, the church will find strength and vitality for every duty, whether it devote itself to relieving social distress, subjecting wealth to the service of poverty, creating homes for the homeless multitudes, redeeming art and science and trade, or bringing the saving influences of Christianity into vital touch with the masses by new methods.[18] The Christian ideal gives the ultimate order for human existence, said Gordon, for behind all institutions, all types of business, and beneath the entire life of mankind there is "the moral order that includes all men in one brotherhood subject to the Divine Fatherhood."[19]

The inclusive religious social goal toward which these conceptions all pointed was the kingdom of heaven on earth. We have observed the gradual humanizing of the kingdom in previous decades, but as Walter Rauschenbusch was to point out later, the form of this doctrine with which we are now concerned was a religious version of evolution. Freed of its traditional catastrophic setting and its background of demonism, and coupled to the dogma of progress, the kingdom was now at home in the naturalistic atmosphere of the modern world. "Evolution," said Rauschenbusch, for whom the kingdom and the social gospel were practically synonymous, "has prepared us for understanding the idea of a Reign of God toward which all creation is moving."[20] In addition to its evolutionary aspect the "solid reality" and the ethical nature of the kingdom are to be noted.

16. Josiah Strong, *The New Era, or the Coming Kingdom* (New York, 1893), pp. x–xi.

17. Abbott, *op. cit.*, p. 257.   18. Pike, *op. cit.*, p. 183.

19. Gordon, *op. cit.*, p. 219.

20. Walter Rauschenbusch, *Christianizing the Social Order* (New York, 1912), p. 90.

In the thought of Jesus the kingdom of God was here and now on earth, wrote Newman Smyth in his *Christian Ethics:*

The Christian conception of life and its supreme good rests on this fundamental fact which Jesus announced, that the kingdom of God is not something wholly future, or remote from our present participation in it, but it is a real power and an actual reign of God already begun on earth—a kingdom of heaven into which we may now enter, and which offers through citizenship in it some immediate possession of the highest good and present part in the eternal life.[21]

Philip S. Moxom interpreted the coming of the kingdom as "the advancement and completion of a process now going on," the salvation of the organic life of society here in a world "fair enough and great enough for the consummate flowering and fulfillment of a redeemed and heavenly life."[22] The kingdom is not in some remote sphere to be anticipated by asceticism, utopian visions, or otherworldliness, maintained President William DeWitt Hyde of Bowdoin College in his *Outlines of Social Theology;* it is made of the stuff of human life—"the appetites, impulses, passions, pursuits, interests, affections and aspirations of man," whether these be happy homes, cheerful schoolrooms, faithful work, honest business, wholesome food, beautiful parks, official integrity, public libraries, refined social intercourse, or abundant recreation. Such positive elements are essential to the realization of the kingdom for it and the well-being of man are two sides of the same thing.[23] Thus in place of the mansions on high, these prophets of a social faith dreamed of a heaven on earth as the goal of the human race.

The ethical character of the kingdom hardly needs to be pointed out. One minister, the Reverend Laurence H. Schwab of New York, who gave the Bohlen Lectures in Philadelphia in 1897, described the kingdom as the realization of the leadership of Christ in the two aspects of the Christian life—the religious and the ethical. Acknowledging his indebtedness to the German

21. Newman Smyth, *Christian Ethics* (New York, Scribner's, 1892), p. 98. By permission.
22. Moxom, *op. cit.,* pp. 49, 64, 66.
23. William DeWitt Hyde, *Outlines of Social Theology* (New York, 1895), pp. 252–254. By permission of The Macmillan Company, publishers.

theologian Albrecht Ritschl, Schwab, displaying a distinctly ethical interest throughout his eight addresses on *The Kingdom of God*, attempted to illumine Christianity by the light of what Christ did rather than by what theologians or historians had said he was.[24]

In addition to embracing these three specific ideas, liberal Protestantism of the late nineteenth century stressed the ethical aspects of religion and interpreted the meaning of Jesus and of salvation in ethical terms. It did not, however, lose its firm hold upon theism, although it regarded Christianity as a process of evolution and so identified it with progress.

"There is no religion which is not ethical," declared Lyman Abbott, echoing Gordon's demand for "an ethical faith." President Eliot pointed out the growing tendency on the part of the churches to view their task in moral terms. While the progressive churches were the leaders in this trend, even the conservative plainly exhibited the tendency to work for "the improvement of character and conduct in the individual, in society, and in the state during the present life," wrote this distinguished observer.[25]

The social and ethical nature of salvation was shown by P. S. Moxom in a sermon on the kingdom of God in which he pointed out that the salvation of society is the salvation of the individual extended throughout his relationships. This would include "the regeneration of the social personality, the quickening and enlargement of the social intelligence, the purification and refinement of the social character, the development of all the social activities, and the realization in social forms of the spiritual graces of love, truth, and righteousness."[26] According to Gordon's theology salvation was "righteous character, and nothing else." G. R. Pike defined it as "the present process of realizing our ideal of life."

Though such views had their obviously humanistic implications, the school remained definitely theistic, interpreting God in Christocentric terms and clothing the whole in an evolution-

24. Laurence H. Schwab, *The Kingdom of God. An essay in theology* (New York, 1897). Beside Rauschenbusch, this Episcopal clergyman was the only figure discovered in the present research who acknowledged or in any way appeared to be directly influenced by Ritschl.

25. Eliot, *op. cit.*, p. 66.

26. Moxom, *op. cit.*, p. 66. By permission of Little, Brown & Co., publishers.

ary philosophy. The spirit of Christ is the essence of Christianity and reveals the real character of God, asserted one writer, while Gordon, the outstanding theologian of the decade, conceived of God in personal, human terms: "The humanity of God is given in the humanity of man; it is given supremely in the humanity of Jesus. We ascend to God through man and his sovereign leader; through man and his sovereign leader we receive God."[27] Newman Smyth defined Christian ethics as "the unfolding and application to human life in all its spheres and relations of the divinely human Ideal which has been historically given in Christ."[28] Christ comes, said Lyman Abbott, not merely to reveal divinity to us but to evolve the latent divinity implanted in us. He is a door through which the divine enters humanity and man enters into the divine. He is "the secret of spiritual evolution," the pattern of the ideal to be wrought in humanity when spiritual evolution is complete. The incarnation is not an isolated episode, but rather the beginning of a perpetual work.[29]

The religious rationalization of evolution carried with it the uncritical assumption of the corollary belief in progress. Many Protestant thinkers saw the process of development at work in the religious and moral realms as well as in nature. Progress was held to be real and evolution to provide cosmic sanction for trust in the ultimate triumph of good. In *The Evolution of Christianity*, Abbott spoke of a "growing spiritual life in man, beginning in the early dawn of human history, when man first came to moral consciousness, and to be consummated no one can tell when or how."[30] Gladden saw this force gradually freeing the world of superstition and prejudice, purifying its social attitudes, changing customs for the better, and slowly modifying laws with higher ideals of justice. In spite of setbacks and disasters, progress is sure, for God is in his world. This great movement down the centuries was for Gladden the kingdom of heaven.[31] Said Lyman Abbott: "The object of Christianity is human welfare; its method is character-building; its process is evolution; and the secret of its power is God."[32]

27. Sermon, "The Humanity of God," in *Through Man to God*, p. 41, quoted by Buckham, *op. cit.*, p. 109.

28. Smyth, *op. cit.*, p. 57. By permission.   29. Abbott, *op. cit.*, pp. 250–251.

30. *Op. cit.*, pp. 255–256.   31. Gladden, *op. cit.*, pp. 290, 298.

32. Lyman Abbott, "What is Christianity?" *Arena*, 3 (1891), 46.

Those who held these ideas found both theoretical unity and practical dynamic in the hope of the kingdom of God on earth. So great was the appeal of this ideal that, after the manner of Christians in all ages, certain converts to it formed in 1892 a "Brotherhood of the Kingdom." Their purpose was "to reëstablish this idea in the thought of the church, and to assist in its practical realization in the world." The almost Franciscan quality of the Brotherhood's quest evidenced the fundamentally religious nature of the growing social gospel; and the group provided the forum in which was formulated much of the epochal social Christianity of Walter Rauschenbusch. The Brotherhood of the Kingdom was perhaps the most important social-gospel society in a period remarkable for organizations.

The Brotherhood originated in a friendship among three young Baptist ministers of New York in the late 1880's: Walter Rauschenbusch, Nathaniel Schmidt, and Leighton Williams.[33] Influenced by a proposal made by Williams' father and by the infectious enthusiasms of another young Baptist preacher, Samuel Zane Batten, who "had been led to dwell much upon the teaching of Jesus regarding the kingdom," the group, by then expanded to nearly a dozen, gathered at the Williams summer home near Marlborough, New York, in August, 1893, to read and discuss papers written in contemplation of a book of essays on the kingdom. This meeting proved "so helpful and inspiring" that it was made an annual affair, and so until 1915 the problems of the world were brought each summer to "this consecrated hill" to be considered prayerfully in the light of the kingdom ideal.[34] In subsequent years the widening of the invitation reduced the group's Baptist majority and brought to its occasional fellowship many, if not most, of the leaders of the religious social movement. While it never became large, its influence was pervasive, carried out primarily through the personal evangelism and writings of members.[35]

"The Spirit and Aims of the Brotherhood," as formulated at

33. From 1889 to 1891 Williams and Rauschenbusch, with J. E. Raymond and Elizabeth Post, edited *For the Right,* a pioneer social-gospel journal "published in the interests of the working people of New York City."
34. None of the first group of papers survived, but many later addresses were printed as pamphlets and in the *Reports* of the conferences.
35. Average attendance was about thirty-five. The Brotherhood regarded its task as the propagandism of an idea, not of an organization.

the first conference, declared the purpose of the society to be the propagandism of the kingdom idea both in word and deed. Every member pledged himself to exemplify obedience to the ethics of Jesus in his personal life, to propagate "the thoughts of Jesus to the limits of his or her ability," to "lay stress on the social aims of Christianity"—especially Christ's teaching on wealth—to "take pains to keep in touch with the common people and to infuse the religious spirit into the efforts for social amelioration." The bond of fellowship was to be strengthened by correspondence, by frequent meetings for prayer and discussion, and by exchange of written articles. In conclusion, the brothers promised to support one another "in the public defense of the truth" and to guard jealously the principle of freedom of discussion.[36] These principles, with few slight modifications, were the Brotherhood's only constitution.

Though in the course of its twenty conferences the group was to wrestle with most of the social issues of the times, its primary interest was the kingdom. This, "the most splendid idea that has ever enriched human thought and inspired human effort," a "new revelation" of Scripture and of the thought of Jesus himself, was at once a theological and a social ideal, a theme for study, and a focus for worship. In one of the Brotherhood's first pamphlets Rauschenbusch pointed out the defects of current views of the kingdom—which were heaven, the inner life of the spirit, the church, the millennium, the missionary enterprise. Each and all such definitions were inadequate. Like a chemical compound that is more powerful than the sum of its parts, the kingdom is more than a synthesis of these elements. It stands for the totality of divine and righteous forces on earth, embracing "all pure aspirations Godward, and all true hopes for the perfection of life."[37] The Brotherhood's view of the kingdom as well as its own purpose was comprehensively stated by Rauschenbusch in another early pamphlet:

We desire to see the Kingdom of God once more the great object of Christian preaching; the inspiration of Christian hymnology; the foundation of systematic theology; the enduring motive of

36. This statement frequently appeared in Brotherhood literature.
37. Walter Rauschenbusch, *The Kingdom of God, Brotherhood Leaflet No. 4*; quoted by Leighton Williams, *The Brotherhood of the Kingdom and its Work, Brotherhood Leaflet No. 10*, p. 10.

evangelistic and missionary work; the religious inspiration of social work and the social outcome of religious inspiration; the object to which a Christian man surrenders his life, and in that surrender saves it to eternal life; the common object in which all religious bodies find their unity; the great synthesis in which the regeneration of the spirit, the enlightenment of the intellect, the development of the body, the reform of political life, the sanctification of industrial life, and all that concerns the redemption of humanity shall be embraced.[38]

The conferences did not restrict themselves to the consideration of theoretical problems. They discussed socialism, the ethics of business, monopolies, the labor question, social work, and the single tax—to name a few—all with reference to the kingdom. The conference of 1897 sent a resolution of sympathy to striking coal miners; that of 1908 drew up a remarkable address to the churches of America in which the necessity for a religious foundation for the social movement was emphasized. Cultivation of the spiritual life was a central concern. For its meditations the Brotherhood turned to the saints and prophets —Wycliffe, St. Francis, Mazzini, the figures of the Old Testament, the seventh earl of Shaftesbury, Jeremy Taylor. Williams, whose mysticism later led him into the Episcopal church, was ever reminding the fellowship of the primacy of the religious as distinguished from the moral element of Christianity. Our emphasis on righteousness, he warned, should not blind us to the reality of the inner life and the importance of its nourishment. We seek the coming of the kingdom, but that kingdom is more than equitable social adjustments; it is the high spiritual realm of the saints, the reign of the new humanity transfigured by the spirit of Christ.[39] And yet Samuel Zane Batten reflected the spirit of the Brotherhood with equal faithfulness when he asserted that it ought to go without saying that "every believer in the kingdom is interested in everything that makes for the temporal and eternal well being of man."[40]

In 1907 the publication of Rauschenbusch's *Christianity and*

38. Williams, *op. cit.,* p. 14.
39. Leighton Williams, *Our Duty to Cultivate the Spiritual Life* . . . (Marlborough, 1913).
40. Samuel Zane Batten, *The Brotherhood of the Kingdom* . . . p. 6, pamphlet.

the Social Crisis, which established its author as the leader of the social-gospel movement, brought the Brotherhood's major ideas to the attention of English-speaking Protestantism. Regarding the popularity of the book as a vindication of its efforts "to establish the social nature of Christianity," the group seriously considered disbanding, but Williams pointed out further tasks that held it together for another eight years. The kingdom idea was central to Rauschenbusch's further challenge, *Christianizing the Social Order,* as it was to his interpretation of the teaching of Jesus in his most widely circulated work, a study manual on *The Social Principles of Jesus.* The Rochester branch of the Brotherhood was a stimulus in the writing of his *Prayers of the Social Awakening.*[41] The kingdom was again set at the heart of what was perhaps his greatest effort, *A Theology for the Social Gospel,* the Nathaniel William Taylor Lectures at Yale in 1917. The Brotherhood's ideology exerted a significant influence upon the early social-service activities of the Northern Baptist Convention, largely through the leadership of Samuel Zane Batten, whose books *The New Citizenship, The Christian State,* and *The Social Task of Christianity* were widely read and studied. E. Tallmadge Root, Nathaniel Schmidt, Leighton Williams, William Newton Clark, and other members likewise evangelized for the kingdom.

The Franciscan quest of these Brothers of the Kingdom visioned their goal as "the great central idea and hope of the Christian revelation"—the reign of God in and over men, illustrated in the life of Christ, and progressing according to "the law of growth and development" by powers now resident in humanity.[42] Thus did the kingdom of social Christianity evolve at the end of the nineteenth century.[43]

41. The first edition of this book was entitled *For God and the People.*
42. *Report of the fifth annual conference* . . . (New York, 1897), p. 36.
43. For a detailed account of the Brotherhood, see the writer's article in *Church History,* 7 (1938), 138–156.

CHAPTER VIII

THE CHURCH FACES A NEW AGE

The world in this sociological age needs a new social ideal to direct the progress of civilization. Let the church fully accept her mission and she will furnish this needed ideal, viz., her Master's conception of the kingdom of God come upon earth.

JOSIAH STRONG

ONE of the evidences of maturity that accompanied social Christianity's coming of age in the last decade of the nineteenth century was an attitude of serious questioning on the part of the church with respect both to the task imposed on her by an age of transition and to the ability of her traditional techniques to meet the new needs. As a result of this gradual awakening there appeared a vast literature of analysis, prescription, and challenge, of which the most unique form was the immensely popular social-gospel novel. Although most social Christians of the period were critical of the church's failures, many examined her message and methods with great care. Usually optimistic, but driven by a sense of crisis, they described the forces in modern civilization hostile to religion, pointed out the errors committed by the church herself, outlined what they believed to be her true function, and exhorted her to pursue it in order to restore her lessened prestige and retain her historic hold upon society.

Spokesmen of an expanded Christianity who stressed the urgency of the crisis held that the opportunity was unprecedented "for the church of Christ to make felt its power for righteousness and peace."[1] The Reverend E. D. Weigle voiced a typical viewpoint when he argued that the age demanded "new applications of the truth and the adoption of methods unknown to former times," and asserted that in such a crisis the pulpit could not dare to be indifferent to the forces threatening the

---

1. Merrill E. Gates, "Social Problems and the Church," *Chautauqua Monthly,* ns9 (1893), 136–142.

very foundations of society.[2] Likewise the Reverend S. D. Mc-Connell declared that the church was entering upon a new epoch in which her place and function in society were rapidly undergoing radical change. But, he warned, "we are disputing among ourselves like a lot of Roman pedants while the barbarians are at the gates."[3]

A very able treatment of the problem came from the pen of the Reverend J. H. W. Stuckenberg. This eminent Lutheran showed how a secular culture had been evolved out of various modern currents: the rise of the masses to consciousness and power through the educating influence of the schools and a popular press, the trend toward cosmopolitanism resulting from similar factors and the growth of great cities, the leveling effects of political and religious liberty, the impact of science and its techniques, and the "practical materialism" seen in the widespread pursuit of pleasure and in the low level of political life.[4] Josiah Strong's less philosophical mind led him to enumerate the physical factors producing the industrial revolution and to point out the fluid character of modern society. He also noted the rise of democracy, the spread of working-class discontent with its consequent concern for industrial and social conditions, the growth of socialism, labor organizations, and corporations, and the trends toward centralization of population, political power, production, and capital. Strong saw beyond the marvels of his age to the wider effects of industrialism that would completely alter the nation's future.[5]

But it was said that the church had failed to keep abreast of these dynamic changes largely because of its traditional adherence to an unnatural dichotomy between sacred and secular, a division that had divorced doctrine and conduct, alienated the masses, and developed a selfish individualism and an unchristian organization of society.[6] Good works have been subordinated to sanctification, said Professor Charles A. Briggs of

2. E. D. Weigle, "The Ministry and Current Social Problems," *Lutheran Quarterly*, XXIV (1894), 467, 472.

3. S. D. McConnell, "The Church in Modern Society," *Outlook*, 58 (1898), 177–180.

4. J. H. W. Stuckenberg, *The Age and the Church* (Hartford, 1893), pp. 21–88.

5. Strong, *The New Era, or the Coming Kingdom* (New York, 1893), chap. i.

6. *Op. cit.*, chap. vi.

Union Theological Seminary: in a practical age that judges the church by its fruit it has not been distinguished for its Christlikeness, it has limited its notion of salvation to a future life, and it has failed to comprehend the catholicity of Jesus' conception of redemption. Such preoccupations have rendered it unresponsive to the needs of modern life, with the result that most humanitarian enterprises have been carried on outside the church and sometimes against the opposition of its leaders.[7] Religion, said Strong, has been made a mere adjunct of life and not its inclusive purpose. The church has not applied the law of Christ to society as well as to the individual. It has failed in its duty to teach and apply the doctrine of brotherhood. Briggs held up the curse of denominationalism—which he called the outstanding sin of the modern church—as the most conspicuous example of this shortcoming. He added that individual churches do not attempt to reconcile the masses to the church universal because they function merely as "select religious societies" from which the people as such are excluded.[8]

Left-wing ministers and reformers who believed in religion but not in the church were definitely antagonistic. One preacher saw the church as fully occupied with defense of the *status quo*, merely mollifying the power of evil, and never rising at all to an aggressive ethical faith. Benjamin O. Flower charged the churches of Boston with responsibility for the condition of the poor in that city, while Henry Demarest Lloyd described institutional religion as restricted to "intermittent moods of emotional fervor embellished with occasional charities and surrounded by the accessories of song and stained-glass windows." Singing, praying, and listening to sermons seemed to Lloyd atheism rather than piety when all about there rose the cries of "those being murdered, plundered, betrayed, by an unethical social order."[9]

Constructive statements of the function of the church in society may be analyzed into three propositions, taking as an outline an address given in 1899 by Professor Graham Taylor of

7. Charles A. Briggs, "The Alienation of Church and People," *Forum,* 16 (1893), 375.
8. *Op. cit.,* p. 375.
9. As quoted by James Dombrowski, *The Early Days of Christian Socialism in America* (New York, 1936), pp. 126–127.

the Chicago Theological Seminary before the International Congregational Council in Boston. As his primary principle Taylor held that the task of the church is formative rather than reformatory—the creative, prophetic stating of the divine ideal of human life, which is "individual and social for itself and all men" and must be so recognized in the churches. Life consists in large part of its relations; religion is relationship; the church is in society to make it Christian and must therefore embody the social ideal. This involves a science of Christian society—"sociology with God left in it."[10] The best service the church can render the labor situation, for example, is "the setting forth, not of regulations, but of eternal principles," declared Dean George Hodges of the Episcopal Theological School in Cambridge.[11] Professor Shailer Mathews of the University of Chicago described the basic function of the church as religious and dynamic rather than regulative.[12]

Secondly, the churches should "initiate social movements and agencies for the realization of their ideals, but not . . . be their executive." They must preach the ideal of righteousness and equality, but without identifying their organizations with particular reforms or agencies. As a religious institution, said Mathews, the church is especially fitted to educate and direct the social impulse.

The third social function of the church is to supply the sacrificial service necessary for the regeneration of society. The heart of the social question, maintained Taylor, is the issue between the competitive system of our industrial society and the simple ethics of the golden rule. This dualism must be challenged by Christendom and it must be faced in local crises by churches and individuals who accept the full implications of "the moral monism of the kingdom of God."[13] This gospel of social salvation through sacrifice was preached with fervor throughout the land in this decade by the most unique and the

10. Graham Taylor, "The Church in Social Reforms," *Proceedings* of the Second International Congregational Council . . . Boston, 1899 (Boston, 1900), pp. 143–145.

11. George Hodges, *The Heresy of Cain* (New York, 1894), p. 65.

12. Shailer Mathews, "The Significance of the Church to the Social Movement," *American Journal of Sociology,* 4 (1898–99), 608. See also John Bascom, *Social Theory* (New York and Boston, 1895), p. 525.

13. Taylor, *op. cit.,* p. 149.

most radical figure to step upon the social-gospel platform in all its history, George D. Herron, to whom we shall devote a later chapter.

The church was challenged from all sides to assume these several functions. "The thorough application of Christian ethics to social life is an imperative necessity of the times," editorialized the *Methodist Review*, while E. D. Weigle declared the paramount question of the day to be not philosophy or theology but "Christianity as applied to the various relations of life."[14] In his book *The New Era*, Josiah Strong faced the church with her social responsibility. He wrote:

Our existing social system . . . is destined to undergo great changes before the sociological problems of the age are solved. And as their solution must come through the application of Christ's teachings, this surely is the opportunity of the centuries for the church to mould the civilization of the future by taking to heart the teachings of her Lord in all their fulness. "The conversion of the church to Christian theory must precede the conversion of the world to Christian practice."[15]

Beyond such generalities of exhortation these prophets of a social faith demanded an attitude of "Christian realism"—an objective facing of the actualities of modern life in place of "empty speculations on divine subjects." Stuckenberg pointed out that realism meant the adoption of scientific methods, the development of actual social influence by the church, a definite program of education, and the personalizing of religious-social idealisms.[16] Others echoed these contentions. The realistic note was sounded by the insistence that "whatever is essentially unjust or selfish is anti-Christian," as Strong asserted.[17] The demand for a scientific attitude raised again the persistent call for the study of sociology and the development of modern methods of church work, as we shall see. A great deal of emphasis was placed upon the educational function of the church: "It must teach that the question of right and wrong must have

14. Weigle, *op. cit.*, p. 468.
15. Strong, *op. cit.*, p. 134. By permission of the Misses Strong, owners of copyright.
16. Stuckenberg, *op. cit.*, chap. vi.
17. Strong, *op. cit.*, pp. 241–242. See also Gates, *op. cit.*, p. 139.

its answer from the counting-room as well as from the pulpit";
it must train its members to follow the Christian standard of
ethics; for if there can be no regenerate society without regenerate men, "neither can there be regenerate men without a regenerate society," wrote Mathews.[18] The Christian church should
be found at the forefront of all the great movements that tend
to the elevation of the individual, the home, and society, and to
the improvement of the social and physical as well as the spiritual welfare of man—directing, encouraging, inspiring, and
sharing the never-ending struggle, asserted President A. Gaylord Slocum of Kalamazoo College before the Michigan Political Science Association.[19]

The most unique form of this challenge was the social-gospel
novel. Great causes have almost invariably produced a popular
propagandist literature, and to this rule American social Christianity was no exception. Just as Charles Kingsley's *Yeast* and
Alton Locke had stimulated the British Christian Socialist
movement of a previous generation, there now appeared in the
United States an avalanche of fiction dramatizing the claims of
the social gospel. The most successful of these novels was a
"sermon story" by the Reverend Charles Monroe Sheldon of
Topeka, Kansas, entitled *In His Steps: What Would Jesus
Do?* which ranks with *Uncle Tom's Cabin* and *Ten Nights in a
Bar Room* among the greatest American tracts. These sentimental stories, whose Algeresque characteristics were not foreign to the literary standards of the denominational periodicals
in which many of them first appeared as serials, based their appeal on religious idealism, sympathy, the novelty of the panaceas proposed, and above all, stewardship.

The first notable bit of pamphleteering of this sort was a
"prophetic dream-story" written by Washington Gladden for
the *Century Magazine* and published in book form in 1883 as
The Christian League of Connecticut. Superior to most of the
literature that was to follow it, this crisp conversational narrative recounted the organization of an imaginary interdenomi-

18. Mathews, *op. cit.,* p. 620.
19. A. Gaylord Slocum, "The Relation of the Church to Political and Social
Science," *Publications* of the Michigan Political Science Association, 1 (1894),
87.

national league and its social effects upon an ordinary factory town. The story, which aimed at "the Christianizing of our churches," was Gladden's most successful journalistic effort up to that time, and exerted considerable influence toward church coöperation and consolidation.[20] Two years later a "sequel" to *The Christian League of Connecticut* entitled *The Union League Club* was published by R. E. Porter, who proposed that churches unite on what they held in common but preserve their separate ministers and beliefs as far as necessary. Another significant tract by a famous minister was Edward Everett Hale's *How They Lived in Hampton*, an essay presenting in narrative form the advantages of industrial coöperation, a principle its author regarded as "essential to all Christian civilization." Subtitle "Christianity applied to manufacture," this book by the writer of *A Man Without a Country* made a strong plea for industrial democracy and for the building of a coöperative commonwealth.[21] In 1889 there came from the pen of Katherine Pearson Woods a novel of social protest with a strong religious color, entitled *Metzerott, Shoemaker*. Frequently quoted, this story was dedicated to the clergy and the workingmen of America in the hope that they might "work and pray together for the coming of the kingdom of Christ." The next year saw the publication of *Murvale Eastman, Christian Socialist*, by Albion W. Tourgee, carpetbagger, lawyer, and author of *A Fool's Errand* and other novels of the Civil War era. The titular hero of this "powerful discussion of real Christianity and its relations to the turbulent questionings of our times" was the popular pastor of a fashionable church, who had disguised himself as a horsecar driver in order to study a strike at first hand, and who later successfully organized a "League of Christian Socialists" in his church. The principles of the league were hardly socialistic, but the publication of this book almost simultaneously with W. D. P. Bliss's organization of his Society of Christian Socialists in Boston was an indicative coincidence.[22]

The social-gospel novel achieved its greatest success in the hands of a journalistically inclined mid-Western minister who in

20. Washington Gladden, *Recollections* (Boston and New York, 1909), p. 275.
21. Edward Everett Hale, *How They Lived in Hampton: A Study of Practical Christianity* (Boston, 1888), p. 281.
22. See chap. x below.

1891 tried the experiment of reading serial sermon stories to his Sunday-evening congregation of young people. Charles M. Sheldon, son of a South Dakota farmer-minister, was educated at Phillips Academy, Brown University, and Andover Theological Seminary. While at Brown he contributed to the *Youth's Companion;* upon graduation from divinity school he refused an offer from Lyman Abbott to join the staff of the *Outlook,* preferring to enter the ministry. In 1889 he accepted a call to what proved a lifetime pastorate of the newly formed Central Congregational Church of Topeka. Upon arrival in the city Sheldon set out to learn as much as possible about its social conditions. Living a week each with various social groups, he investigated unemployment, made himself familiar with the status of such classes as railroad men, college students, professional people, Negroes, and newspaper workers. This firsthand knowledge of all types and classes provided a realistic background for the novels that were to bring him world-wide recognition.

The first sermon story, entitled *Richard Bruce, or the life that now is,* was followed by *Robert Hardy's Seven Days, The Angel and the Demon, The Crucifixion of Phillip Strong,* and various shorter stories, all of which were published serially in a Chicago Congregational paper, the *Advance.* "Phillip Strong" was a young minister who chose a call to a church in an industrial city rather than one to a college town, and who not only carried on an aggressively social type of ministry but dramatized his sympathy for the lower classes by living in humble quarters in a tenement district. The story closed with the hero's collapse and death in his pulpit at the climax of a sermon on the meaning of the cross—his last message to a church that had requested his resignation. This story, along with more than thirty others to flow from Sheldon's pen, was published in book form and enjoyed a moderate popularity. It was accorded the distinction of several reprints and a dramatic adaptation.[23]

The most successful of Sheldon's works was written and read to his congregation in 1896, and sold to the *Advance* for $75. Demand for *In His Steps* was such that it was printed in book form. By June, 1897, the sale had reached 100,000 copies, when enterprising competitors discovered the copyright to be defective. Within two months sixteen American publishers were at-

23. By Anna Newell Atkins, Boston (Baker), 1935.

tempting to meet a sale that showed no signs of abating. Thirty British firms issued the book. In 1933 Sheldon estimated that a total of 23,000,000 copies had been sold throughout the English-speaking world, while translations had been made into twenty-one foreign languages.[24] In 1913 he wrote a sequel entitled *"Jesus Is Here!"* and in 1921 recast his social philosophy as *In His Steps To-day*. A motion picture was based on *In His Steps* in 1936.

The story opened with a dramatic incident the like of which has doubtless occurred to many an absent-minded listener to a dull sermon. At the close of a smooth sermon on following Jesus the contented congregation of the First Church of "Raymond" was startled by the sudden appearance of a "dusty, worn, shabby-looking young man" who arose from the front row and quietly told his hearers a tale of unemployment and want. "Of course," he said, in effect, "you can't all go out hunting up jobs for people like me, but what I am puzzled about when I see so many Christians living in luxury and singing 'Jesus I my cross have taken, all to leave and follow thee,' is what is meant by following Jesus? I remember how my wife died gasping for air in a New York tenement owned by a member of a church. I suppose I don't understand, but what would Jesus do?"—and the questioner collapsed in the center aisle of the church.[25]

Cared for in the pastor's home, the young man died the next Sunday morning. Shortly after, the deeply stirred minister challenged an unusually large congregation with the implications of the previous Sunday's question. Interpreting the stranger's query as "a challenge to Christianity as it is seen and felt in our churches," the pastor asked his hearers to join him in a pledge "not to do anything without first asking 'What would Jesus do?'" and then "to follow Jesus as exactly as [they] knew how, no matter what the results. . . ." Among the fifty volunteers were an heiress, a gifted soprano, the president of the local college, a railroad superintendent, a newspaper editor, and a leading merchant. The efforts of these characters to live out the pledge comprised the narrative of *In His Steps*—with the embellishment of several romances.

24. Charles M. Sheldon, *His Life Story* (New York, 1925), p. 97, and "The Ethics of Some Publishers," *Christian Century*, 50 (1933), 1206–1208.
25. Sheldon, *In His Steps* (Chicago, 1898), p. 14.

The singer refused an alluring offer to go on tour, giving her voice to rescue mission work. The editor dedicated his newspaper to the kingdom of God instead of to profit and drew up a code of ethics for a "Christian daily" that would lack sensational features and questionable advertising, while providing "news of the Christian world" and "the news that people ought to know."[26] This policy so reduced the paper's income that an endowment became necessary. It was conveniently provided by the heiress and her converted brother, who further invested their now-consecrated wealth in rebuilding the tenement district of the town. The railroad superintendent resigned his position after finding the company engaged in illicit practices, for which it was indicted on his evidence. He found reëmployment in his old occupation as a telegraph operator. The college president forsook his aloofness to run for mayor on a prohibition platform; his failure revealed to the reformers the power and unscrupulousness of the liquor interests. The merchant reorganized his business according to a paternalistic policy of "intelligent unselfishness" that provided profit sharing for his employees. These and other effects of the pledge upon the life of the First Church and of "Raymond" gradually crept into the newspapers and spread to other churches with the result that a national revival of social religion seemed imminent.

Sheldon continued to write his sermon stories. In 1898 he published *The Redemption of Freetown*, a novel describing the influence of a church settlement upon a slum neighborhood. The story, said its author, was an account "of actual conditions in hundreds of cities in Christian America," written in hopes that "the young men and women who have been willing to do as Jesus would do would actually go and live (under the direction of wise leadership) in the social settlements the churches could create."[27] Numbers of other novels appeared, among them *Born to Serve*, *The Reformer*, and *The Heart of the World: A Story of Christian Socialism*, but none rivaled *In His Steps*.

Although their efforts never attained the popularity of Sheldon's stories, other writers continued to propagandize for social Christianity through the medium of fiction. In 1893 Wash-

---

26. As a result of this proposal Sheldon edited the Topeka *Daily Capital* for a week in 1899, at the owner's invitation. See *His Life Story,* chap. v.

27. *Christian Endeavor World* (July 7, 1898), p. 827.

ington Gladden again entered the field, this time with an account of municipal house cleaning carried out by a group who organized *The Cosmopolis City Club* for the improvement of urban government and social life. The next year there appeared anonymously an odd but symptomatic book entitled *Christ the Socialist*, whose author presented in a sort of parabolic form the claim that Christ was "the greatest, truest, purest socialist the world has ever seen" and that socialism was simply Christianity reduced to practice.[28] In 1900 Florence Converse published *The Burden of Christopher*, a somewhat realistic story concerning a radical young clergyman who succeeded in inducing a wealthy shop owner to adopt a fair wage scale. Such novels ran even in the obscure magazines, an example being "A Modern Minister" by George S. Eddy, a serial in *The Coming Age* at the turn of the century. In 1903 Professor Vida Dutton Scudder of Wellesley College used the conversational device to express her thought on such questions as labor, slums, socialism, and religion in a book called *A Listener in Babel*. The same year saw the printing of *Ronald Carnaquay, a commercial clergyman*, by Bradley Gilman, a story contrasting the fashionable and commercial aspects of Protestant church life with the ideal of social service.

In 1907 three books of this type appeared. Incredibly naïve was *Maud Muller's Ministry, or the claims of Christian Socialism*, by the Reverend James L. Smiley of Annapolis. W. J. Dawson's novel, *A Prophet in Babylon, a story of social service*, recounted the organization of. a "League of Social Service" at Madison Square Garden by a socially minded minister whose zeal for religious and humanitarian reform captured the imagination of the metropolis, with sweeping results in social betterment.[29] The most interesting of these last three works was the fictionized autobiography of Jesse Henry Jones, founder of the pioneer Christian Labor Union of Boston described above in Chapter II. Under the title *Joshua Davidson, Christian*, Jones set forth once more "the sphere of the Gospel of the Kingdom of God, as Jesus proclaimed it." Violently critical of many as-

28. Archibald McCowan, *Christ the Socialist* (Boston, 1894), p. 335.

29. Evangelists for this fictitious movement preached on street corners and wherever they could obtain a hearing, as did the actual Social Crusaders to be described in chap. xi.

pects of capitalism, Jones here restated his earlier beliefs and dramatized the rejection of his own message by concluding the biography with the lynching of "Joshua Davidson" by a mob angered at his condemnation of legalized vice.[30]

One item in this flood of popular literature differed considerably from the rest in that it was founded on fact and that it proposed at least some realistic remedies. In 1893 the crusading British journalist William T. Stead, founder of the *Pall Mall Gazette* and the *Review of Reviews* visited the exposition at Chicago. Fascinated by the metropolis, he plunged into an investigation of its social conditions. The moment seemed to him ripe for some kind of action to bring the city to the crest of the rising civic revival then apparent throughout the nation, and Stead was asked by a citizens' committee to lead the crusade. The first step was a gigantic mass meeting, to which all classes and races were invited. Stead surprised the audience by opening his address with a simple prayer for understanding of "something of the love that is in the heart of our brother Jesus." He then asked: "If Christ came to Chicago today, what would he think of it?" To Graham Taylor, sitting on the platform, the speaker "seemed to rise to the stature of one of the Hebrew prophets" as for an hour he answered his own question, describing various evils and abuses he had found. In conclusion Stead told his hearers that if they wanted to make Chicago a moral place they must unite "all the forces which make for righteousness, which make for love." The Chicago Civic Federation was the outcome of this challenge.[31]

When his stenographers failed him, Stead wrote a 460-page tract reporting the meeting and its results, but chiefly presenting a detailed exposé of conditions in the Windy City. Titled *If Christ Came to Chicago! A plea for the union of all who love in the service of all who suffer*, the book was an instantaneous sensation. Viciously denounced by the press, it mysteriously disappeared from Chicago stores,[32] but nevertheless sold several hundred thousand copies in this country and in England. Maintaining that our belief in Christ is shown not by what we say

30. Jesse H. Jones, *Joshua Davidson, Christian* (New York, 1907).

31. See Graham Taylor, *Pioneering on Social Frontiers* (Chicago, 1930), chaps. iv–vii, and Albion W. Small, "The Civic Federation of Chicago," *American Journal of Sociology*, 1 (1895–96), 79–103.

32. Taylor, *Pioneering*, p. 35.

about him, nor by the temples built in his honor, "but by the extent to which we succeed in restoring in man the lost image of God," Stead proposed to indicate "how a living faith in the Citizen Christ would lead directly to the civic and social regeneration of Chicago."[33] All phases of social conditions were dealt with in a devastatingly realistic manner: jails, prostitution, liquor and politics, graft, the plutocracy, lawless contempt for human life by the railroads, tax dodging, the churches, labor, black lists, and so through the catalogue of municipal evils. The assistance of the government is indispensable to improvement, asserted Stead: all roads out of the social quagmire lead to the city hall. At the end of his book he asked:

If Christ came to Chicago what would He wish me to do? . . .

He would have you follow in His footsteps and be a Christ to those among whom you live, in the workshop, in the city and in the State. . . .

Are you willing to help? If Christ came to your city would He find you ready?[34]

The similarity of this to the proposal of *In His Steps* was pointed out by Stead. In the Preface to the London, 1899, edition of *If Christ Came to Chicago!* its author declared the two books to be alike in diagnosis and remedy except for Sheldon's interest in the saloon problem and Sunday journalism, and asserted that *In His Steps* might well have been written to popularize the teaching of his own book. This same edition also appropriated Sheldon's subtitle, "What would Jesus do?" and was labeled "The precursor of *In His Steps.*" Another amusing incident followed Stead's tract. The aging Edward Everett Hale read it with some alarm, and fearing that it might cause ill-informed people to decide "that Christ's plans have failed badly," wrote a humorless pamphlet entitled *If Jesus Came to Boston.* In this story Jesus visited Boston in the guise of a Syrian traveler seeking a long-lost relative, whom he located after a tour of the city's welfare agencies. So well impressed was he that he left shortly, sending this telegram to his host: "I have gone to Chicago. I find I have other sheep there. What

33. William T. Stead, *If Christ Came to Chicago!* (London, 1894), p. xiv.
34. *Op. cit.,* pp. 432–434.

you in Boston have been doing to the least of these my brethren and sisters, you have done it unto me."[35]

For the most part this literature reflected the ideology we have described as characteristic of the period. Sentimental and usually mediocre, the social-gospel novel was basically critical of the church's failure to recognize the new needs of the urban areas. The leading figure of *In His Steps* dreamed of "the regeneration of Christendom" when there would be a church "without spot or wrinkle." "Phillip Strong" believed that the church would respond to a vision of "the Christ as he would act today"; Sheldon's criticism lay in the fact that his young preacher's social message was rejected by a church that thus crucified its pastor.

The central feature of this fiction was its emphasis upon stewardship. The dedication of person and resources to the task of social betterment, while relying upon a traditional methodology, nevertheless marked a step toward a social religion in that its ultimate aim was a changed status of society as well as saved individuals. A "new exhibition of discipleship" called not only for consecration of wealth but for personal self-sacrifice. Probably this modernized version of pietistic self-denial was in part responsible for the wide appeal of novels such as Sheldon's.

But the utopian nature of these stories was doubtless the real secret of their success. They revealed how the simple adaptation of a familiar method would quickly accomplish the reforms for which the times so passionately yearned. A panacea such as that proposed by *In His Steps*, while realistic in its description of conditions, was at the same time utopian in its grasp of the forces producing those conditions, and in its prescriptions. Asking for charity while unaware of the need for justice, this literature was a plea for a socialized Christianity, not for a Christian socialism—a distinction worthy of note.[36] Fully awake to the social emergency, its evangelistic fervor yet failed to project social goals and techniques commensurate with the demands of the crisis. Nevertheless, the social-gospel novel brought social religion to the attention of millions of laymen who might never have heard of it otherwise.

35. Edward Everett Hale, *If Jesus Came to Boston* (Boston, 1894).
36. See Henri Georges Chevrin, *Socialisme Chrétien ou Christianisme social, étude comparative entre Herron et Sheldon* (a University of Paris thesis, Paris, 1901).

CHAPTER IX

SOCIAL PROBLEMS IN THE LIGHT
OF CHRISTIAN ETHICS

. . . Our present problems . . . are Christian because they have
to do with character. . . . Sanitation, and the administration of
the city, and politics, and rent, and wages, and the conditions generally under which men work and live between Sundays, are of direct concern to the Christian religion.

GEORGE HODGES

IF the critical note sounded by the social-gospel novel was an
evidence of approaching maturity in the life of the movement
we are following, further proof of the fact may be seen in the
increasing number of ministers giving attention to social issues
as the nineteenth century drew to a close. In 1895 *The Dawn*
magazine published the names of seven hundred clergymen
"who had shown their interest in the labor movement by some
public utterance, or joining some society for the study of social
problems."[1] Two years later the Episcopal Christian Social
Union counted one thousand members, and the American Institute of Christian Sociology claimed to be reaching as many
more in all churches.[2] Coming of age was also indicated by increasingly realistic attitudes that recognized the effects of environment and developed the new techniques of "institutional"
church and religious social settlement. Organizations of various
types sprang up, all devoting their energies to some phase of
the social situation, notably labor. The perennial demand for
the study of sociology began to bear fruit not only in the entrance of social science into the curricula of a significant number of theological schools, but by its inclusion in the programs
of conferences, its popularity with societies organized for social
education, and also in renewed attempts to formulate a "Christian sociology."

1. William D. P. Bliss, ed., *The Encyclopedia of Social Reform* (New York,
1897), p. 258.
2. *Op. cit.*, p. 275.

As had been the case during the two previous decades, the labor issue continued in the 'nineties to be regarded by social prophets as "the most urgent question before the country."[3] We have previously analyzed much of their thought concerning it (in Chapter V) but certain advances in the attitude toward this key problem are to be noted. The demand for justice became more insistent. Lyman Abbott, for example, asserted that even a living wage might not be the consummation of justice if industrial democracy did not prevail.[4] The existence of an ethical dualism in popular attitudes toward labor disputes was again pointed out by Richard T. Ely, while Walter Rauschenbusch asked his fellow ministers at the Baptist Congress of 1898 to work for the elimination of social inequalities, to back legitimate strikes, and to "strengthen public opinion in its demand for justice and humanity." The worker, wrote Josiah Strong in *The New Era*, is not receiving his share of the benefit of recent material progress, nor is the division of property between capital and labor just.[5] Unions were likewise regarded with increasing favor, such leaders as Gladden and Abbott reiterating their belief in the trades-union principle. E. Winchester Donald, rector of Trinity Church, Boston, went so far as to say that federated labor virtually amounted to a new expression of extra-ecclesiastical religion.[6] Such remedies for industrial unrest as coöperation, profit sharing, and arbitration continued to be favored by religious writers, who also maintained their hostility to classical economics.

Several group efforts to deal with the labor problem indicated the temper of the times. In many respects the most remarkable organization in the half century of social Christianity's growth, with the exception of the Federal Council of Churches, was the Church Association for the Advancement of the Interests of Labor.[7] This Episcopal society not only typi-

3. The socialism of this decade will be examined in the next chapter.

4. Lyman Abbott, "Industrial Democracy," *Forum,* 9 (1890), 658–669.

5. Josiah Strong, *The New Era* (New York, 1893), chap. vii.

6. E. W. Donald, *The Expansion of Religion* (Boston and New York, 1896), chap. iv.

7. This account is an abstract of chap. iv of Spencer Miller and Joseph F. Fletcher, *The Church and Industry* (New York, 1930). By permission of Longmans, Green & Co., publishers. See also Maurice B. Reckitt, *Faith and Society* (New York, 1932), pp. 190 ff.

fied the advanced social thought of that communion but was a specific example of the transfer of British experience to America through the medium of Anglican influence.[8] "C.A.I.L."* came into being in New York City in 1887 as an attempt to translate into action a deep-seated belief that as a part of her universal ministry to mankind the church had a genuine concern in the welfare of those involved in industry. The Association's constitution set forth certain fundamental principles: the essence of Christ's teaching is the fatherhood of God and the brotherhood of man; God is the sole possessor of the bounty of the earth and man is his steward; labor, defined as "the exercise of body, mind, and spirit in the broadening and elevating of human life," is the duty of every man and should be the standard of social worth; when all men are enabled so to labor, one great cause of present distress will disappear. C.A.I.L.'s methods were to be prayer, sermons on the relevance of the gospel to social problems, printed propaganda, lectures and addresses, and encouragement to conscientious use of the ballot. As special duties each member was to read at least one labor periodical and to study the social questions of the day in the light of the incarnation. Under the leadership of such men as Bishops Frederic Dan Huntington and Henry Codman Potter, the Association soon spread across the country and was often accepted by labor as a friendly ally, as examples of its activities indicate. In 1890 three sizable mass meetings were held at which labor's problems and their solutions were discussed. That year the group endorsed the efforts of the Working Women's Society of New York toward the improvement of the status of women and children workers in retail stores, and it recommended successfully to the diocese of New York that its printing be given only to firms paying standard wages. C.A.I.L. instituted in Episcopal churches the first observance of Labor Sunday in America, also in 1890. In 1893 a plan for mediation in labor difficulties

* Pronounced "cail."

8. No systematic study of the influence of English social-gospel thought upon American social Christianity has been made in connection with the present research. Such channels as the Christian Social Union and other Anglican–Episcopal contacts are obviously the best examples of it. In all cases, however, such foreign stimuli simply crystallized indigenous strivings. For a list of British books read widely in this country, see the writer's forthcoming classified bibliography.

was proposed to Bishop Potter. The resulting impartial committee served for many years and Potter's name became a symbol for fair judgments.[9] The next year sweatshop and tenement committees were formed to agitate against those evils by various means such as posters and other forms of propaganda. In 1895 was begun the publication of *Hammer and Pen,* a rather remarkable quarterly that dealt frankly with strikes, legislation, and general reform news. A sort of subsidiary of C.A.I.L. was the Actors' Church Alliance, organized in 1899 to support the efforts of the Actors' Society for one day of rest in seven. Actually pursuing a broader program, by 1905 the Alliance had enlisted Episcopal ministers in more than four hundred towns and cities as "chaplains" to traveling actors.

Local chapters of C.A.I.L. frequently stimulated their parishes to useful social services. That in St. Michael's Church of New York, for example, held meetings for the discussion of such matters as the single tax, woman suffrage, prison reform, tenements, sweatshops, and other phases of the labor problem. This chapter had three standing committees: that on tenements inspected all buildings in the parish and reported violations of the law; the labor-organization group—chaired by a member of the bricklayers' union—acted for justice in controversies; and a sweatshop committee published a "white list" of clothing firms that paid living wages and treated employees fairly.[10]

C.A.I.L. was active for forty years. With its sister organization the Church Social Union it was instrumental in securing the adoption of social-service measures by the General Convention of the Episcopal Church, as will be pointed out in Chapter XVII. It voluntarily disbanded in 1926 when a secretary for industrial relations was made a regular member of the staff of the denomination's Department of Christian Social Service.

One of the earliest open forums under religious auspices in the United States was the "Christian Workingmen's Institute," an adjunct of Leighton Williams' Amity Baptist Church in West Fifty-fourth Street, New York.[11] Membership in the In-

9. For a typical case illustrating Potter's prestige, see Harold U. Faulkner, *The Quest for Social Justice, 1898–1914* (New York, 1931), p. 56.

10. "What One Parish Is Doing for Social Reform," *Open Church Magazine,* 1 (1897), 45–47.

11. From materials supplied the writer by Mrs. Leighton Williams. The date was prior to 1894.

stitute was open to "any workingman above eighteen years of age who endeavors to conform his life to the moral teaching of Jesus"—which teaching it held affords "a perfect solution" of the social problems of the times, inasmuch as it declares "the intrinsic principles of personal and social righteousness which form the firm basis of the Common Weal." The Institute described its "free discussions every Sunday afternoon" as aimed at impressing this belief upon both laboring people and the churches in order to end the estrangement between them. Said a leaflet:

We aim to enthrone Christliness as the dominant principle in industrial, commercial, social and political as well as in individual action.

The Kingdom of God on Earth is the right Social Order wherein every one gets the full reward of his labor and the fullest enjoyment of all his possessions.

Attempting "the moral, social, and intellectual improvement of its members" through discussion of questions of current interest, the Institute brought to its platform over a period of years many outstanding labor leaders and spokesmen for social Christianity, among them Josiah Strong, W. D. P. Bliss, Charles Cuthbert Hall, and Hugh Lusk of New Zealand.

When Protestant leaders faced the urban situation in this decade, their understanding of its complexity was deepened by an increased awareness of the effects of environment. Whatever the inheritance, wrote Amory H. Bradford in *Heredity and Christian Problems*, it may be changed by good environment; Christianity must therefore provide helpful surroundings as well as correct doctrines for those it would aid. Gladden held that the success of Christian work depended upon a balance between the improvement of the social order and the conversion of individuals. After conversion men should be provided with a Christian society to live in if the conversion process is to be meaningful.[12] Such a viewpoint led the Reverend Frank Mason North,[13] founder and editor of *The Christian City*, to de-

12. Washington Gladden, *Tools and the Man, Property and Industry under the Christian Law* (Boston and New York, 1893), pp. 2, 4. See also George Hodges, *Faith and Social Service* (New York, 1896), pp. 142–143.
13. Author of the hymn, "Where Cross the Crowded Ways of Life."

clare that urban conditions made their own plea for a distinctly evangelistic and humanitarian approach rather than an ecclesiastical and edificatory program: the object of Christian solicitude must be human need of every kind.[14] North was but one of many Protestant leaders calling upon the church to face the urban crisis. Josiah Strong, who in a previous decade had outlined "national perils and opportunities," now analyzed the problems of *The Twentieth Century City*. These two men, with Charles L. Thompson, Charles A. Dickinson, John B. Devins, Leighton Williams, Gaylord S. White, and Elias B. Sanford, organized in 1894 the "Open and Institutional Church League"[15] to agitate for enlarged church work in the cities. With Sanford as its indefatigable secretary, this organization, a significant forerunner of the Federal Council of Churches, published *The Open Church* and held important conferences on the new methodology. These workers hoped to bring about social salvation by means of an aggressive evangelistic, educational, and "institutional" program; during the 1890's such proposals were actualized in the institutional church[16] and the religious social settlement.

The institutional church was primarily an effort to recoup the ground lost by Protestantism when its churches moved out of the crowded working-class areas of the great cities and at the same time betrayed the confidence of those classes. Although William A. Muhlenberg and Thomas K. Beecher had pioneered along this line, institutional features were significantly inaugurated in this country at St. George's (Episcopal) Church, New York, by the Reverend William S. Rainsford, who in 1882 began the abolition of pew rents, continuous weekday use of his plant, and the development of a program to meet the needs of the immediate neighborhood. Rainsford stated the aims and method of the expanded church work when, after objecting to the uptown location of the Cathedral of St. John the Divine, he proposed

14. Frank Mason North, "City Missions and Social Problems," *Methodist Review*, 75 (1893), 238.

15. See chap. xix, below.

16. The term "institutional" originated in a chance remark of William Jewett Tucker. See Josiah Strong, *Religious Movements for Social Betterment* (New York, 1900), p. 42.

. . . two or three large free churches, built on cleared spaces, on east and west down-town sites, always open to the public, provided with real preachers, and having each a large kindergarten, a swimming bath, and a gymnasium . . .[17]

Undoubtedly influenced to some extent by the Young Men's Christian Association and the Salvation Army, the institutional churches from simple beginnings developed elaborate social-service programs. By 1897 St. George's had a $60,000 annual budget, four pastor's assistants, four deaconesses as well as specialists in charge of athletic and industrial departments, and a large number of volunteer workers. There were 6,690 persons on its parish lists of whom only half were communicants.[18] Institutional churches in the 'nineties supported kindergartens, gymnasium classes, boys' and girls' clubs, libraries, dispensaries, the free-pew system, open forums, employment service, clinics,[19] study classes, popular lectures, sewing and cooking schools, loan funds, "penny provident" banks, game rooms, soup kitchens, deaconess homes, hospitals, and colleges.[20] Berkeley Temple, the first institutional church in Boston, trained its workers from the church's membership; as unique services it provided a legal bureau and a boarding-house register. Several churches maintained mutual-benefit societies within their memberships. Churches providing many of these features were to be found in most large cities. Gradually certain of their functions were absorbed by other agencies (Rainsford predicted that sooner or later the state would take them over) leaving perhaps the greatest single influence exerted by this movement as the "socializing" of churches all over America by the simple process of adapting institutional methods to the average neighborhood.

17. W. S. Rainsford, "What Can We Do for the Poor?" *Forum,* 11 (1891), 125. For Muhlenberg, see page 6, above. For Beecher, see Lyman Beecher Stowe, *Saints, Sinners, and Beechers* (New York, 1934), pp. 370–374.

18. F. M. North, "The New Era of Church Work in the City of New York," *Open Church Magazine,* 1 (1897), 7–8. For a detailed description of St. George's, see George Hodges and John Reichert, *The Administration of an Institutional Church* (New York, 1906).

19. More than 6,500 cases were treated in one year at the clinic of St. Bartholomew's, New York; North, *op. cit.*

20. Temple University was an outgrowth of Russell H. Conwell's Grace Baptist Church, Philadelphia.

The institutional church had been the result of a final realization that mission halls were inadequate to the religious needs of the slum areas, particularly in view of the social gospel's demand for a social and ethical ministry to the needs of the whole man. But even these greatly expanded programs soon proved ineffective without the residence of workers among the people with whom they labored. Recognition of this fact led in the 1890's to the establishment of numerous social settlements with religious objectives. Paralleling the college-settlement movement, to which it owed a great debt, this newest Protestant effort to reach the masses, like its secular counterpart, derived great stimulus from similar British experiments, notably Toynbee Hall. But the rapid growth of such settlements, many in connection with institutional churches, indicates that this movement was indigenous—the response to a deep-seated and deeply felt need. Its details lie beyond the scope of the present general survey, but the influence of the religious dynamic upon the history of social service in America is amply demonstrated in the fact that by 1905 more than seventy settlements were being supported by Christian groups.[21]

Every organization that has developed in these latter days for bettering the condition of the people has its roots in the doctrines of the churches [wrote Lillian W. Betts in 1902]. Workers and money come from the people who receive their impulse from the teachings of Christ. These organizations are as truly as the churches the expression of brotherly love; the positive declaration of the consciousness that no man liveth to himself.[22]

The second permanent men's social settlement in the United States was opened in Boston in January, 1892, as Andover House, later South End House, and dedicated "to the special ends of Social Christianity." Planned by Professor William Jewett Tucker of Andover Theological Seminary, the venture was sponsored by a group of Andover alumni. Its head resident was Robert A. Woods, an Andover graduate who had just spent

21. Caroline W. Montgomery, *Bibliography of College, Social, University and Church Settlements* . . . (Chicago, 1905, 5th ed.).

22. Lillian W. Betts, *The Leaven in a Great City* (New York, 1901), pp. 142–143. By permission of Dodd, Mead & Co., publishers.

a year in London at Toynbee Hall.[23] Woods also aided in the founding of Kingsley House in Pittsburgh, where he had grown up. The Reverend George Hodges, then rector of Calvary Church, had visited Toynbee Hall and was acquainted with Woods, whose book, *English Social Movements*, seemed to him to describe "just the sort of thing for us in Pittsburgh." Named for the British Christian Socialist Charles Kingsley, because of his pioneer recognition that "the gospel of Jesus Christ has a message to the whole of life," this settlement's history has been notable testimony to the force of the motto over its doorway: "Together we labor for God and for humanity."[24]

In 1894 the Chicago Commons settlement was founded by the Reverend Graham Taylor, who recently had left a remarkable social ministry in Hartford and a professorship in the Hartford Theological Seminary to accept (and create) the first chair of "Christian Sociology" in the country at Chicago Theological Seminary. Religious motives and techniques were important in the work of the Commons; it became a laboratory for Taylor's classes; and not long after its founding Taylor accepted the pastorate of a struggling neighborhood church which was later housed in the settlement building.[25] Another such institution is the Union Settlement Association, organized by alumni of Union Theological Seminary in 1895 "for the maintenance of Settlements in New York City for the assertion and application, in the spirit of Jesus Christ, of the principles of brotherhood along the lines of educational, social, civic, and religious well-being." For many years under the headship of the Reverend Gaylord S. White, the Union Settlement is one of New York's most significant social-service establishments.[26]

23. Andover House Association, *Circulars* No. 1 to 8. William J. Tucker, "The Work of the Andover House in Boston," *Scribner's*, March, 1893. Eleanor H. Woods, *Robert A. Woods* (Boston and New York, 1929).

24. Kingsley Association, Pittsburgh, *The Meaning of the Social Settlement Movement* (Pittsburgh, 1909), pp. 33–34; same, *Kingsley House and the Settlement Movement* (Pittsburgh, 1933), pp. 15–16. Also Julia S. Hodges, *George Hodges, A Biography* (New York, 1926).

25. From early issues of *Chicago Commons*, or *The Commons*, published by the settlement from its inception. Also Taylor, *Pioneering on Social Frontiers* (Chicago, 1930); and *Chicago Commons Through Forty Years* (Chicago, 1936).

26. Union Settlement Association, *Seventh Report* (1902), pp. 9 ff., and *Twentieth Report* (1915), pp. 19, 36–38. Also Gaylord S. White, "The Social Settlement after Twenty-five Years," *Harvard Theological Review*, 4 (1911), 20–21.

Similar descriptions might be continued at some length. There were, for example, eleven church settlements in Chicago in 1905, four in Boston, five in Buffalo, and twenty-four in New York. Maintained by churches, Epworth Leagues,[27] home-missionary societies, in some cases partly by charity organizations, and by individuals, local church federations, women's religious societies, men's clubs, and associations such as those supporting South End House and the Union Settlement, these residences, of which many were destined not to be permanent, indicated a widespread concern over the urban situation—a concern felt by laity as well as by clergy, and attributable largely to the maturing social gospel.[28]

The attitude of Protestant leaders toward poverty and the slums was characterized in this decade by a realism not evidenced in earlier periods, notably in the realization that poverty is not an isolated social phenomenon. This was the judgment of Professor John R. Commons and of George Hodges, who pointed out that poverty results from combinations of causes—industrial, ethical, and physical. To study it is but to open the door to further investigation of labor, moral reform, and the city, wrote Hodges.[29] Gladden believed the abolition of the slum to be as feasible and as imperative as the drainage of a swamp. The most sensational exposure of tenements and home sweatshop conditions in the 'nineties was an investigation by the Reverend Louis Albert Banks of South Boston, published in 1892 as *White Slaves, or the oppression of the worthy poor.* Banks demanded improved inspection of tenements, regulation of concerns letting out piecework, "a revival of conscientious landlordism," playgrounds, and boys' and girls' clubs.

The widespread and shameless corruption of municipal government elicited a great deal of interest on the part of the clergy in this decade. Gladden was content to deal with the problem in one of a series of lectures published as *Social Facts and Forces,* wherein he lay the blame upon the public for fail-

27. There was an Epworth League House both in Boston and in Chicago.
28. Partly popularized, no doubt, by the social-gospel novel.
29. George Hodges, *Faith and Social Service* (New York, 1896), pp. 142–143. See also John R. Commons, "The Church and the Problem of Poverty in Cities," *Charities Review,* 2 (1893), 347–348.

ing to take a deep interest in the government;[30] Strong sought the solution in men of character and intelligence;[31] but others chose a course of direct action. We have mentioned the development of the Chicago Civic Federation out of the investigations of the underworld and its environs by William T. Stead. What was probably the most famous case of religious muckraking in American history was inaugurated in 1892 when the Reverend Charles H. Parkhurst of the Madison Square Presbyterian Church in New York undertook to expose Tammany Hall and its "lying, perjured, rum-soaked, and libidinous" city administration.

As president of the New York Society for the Prevention of Crime, Parkhurst had found the police department the chief obstacle to the enforcement of laws against vice and gambling. Convinced that the police protected and even fostered crime and profited from it, Parkhurst charged the city government not only with obstructing the course of justice but with frustrating every effort "to improve character in this city, every effort to make men respectable, honest, temperate, and sexually clean." If, he asserted, it is the church's task to try to convert Third Avenue alcoholics, then it is the church's duty to strike at an administration that fosters alcoholism. "If it is proper for us to go around cleaning up after the devil, it is proper for us to fight the devil."[32] Challenged to support his generalizations, Parkhurst spent a month personally "traversing the avenues of our municipal hell," and obtained affidavits proving 284 cases of law violation. This response to Tammany produced first a grand-jury presentment against the police department. Later came the Lexow Committee's investigation, the election of a reform administration, and ultimately a whole era of reform.[33]

Lyman Abbott bespoke the concern of ministers over the social evil when in *Christianity and Social Problems* he maintained that the Christian approach to this issue was not permis-

---

30. Washington Gladden, *Social Facts and Forces* (New York and London, 1897), pp. 189–190. These lectures were given in Chicago and at Iowa College.
31. Strong, *The New Era*, p. 330.
32. Charles H. Parkhurst, *My Forty Years in New York* (New York, 1923), pp. 109–116. Also *Our Fight with Tammany* (New York, 1895).
33. Lincoln Steffens, *The Autobiography of Lincoln Steffens* (New York, 1931), I, 215.

sion and regulation, segregation and protection, prohibition and penalty, "but the method of compassion and cure."[34] An epochal step toward an understanding of the problem was made in Chicago shortly after the turn of the century, largely on the initiative of Dean Walter T. Sumner of the Episcopal Cathedral, whose parish chanced to include one of the three areas in which police segregated and regulated vice resorts and their inmates. On the basis of his own observations, Sumner asked the Chicago federation of churches to endorse his proposal that the mayor appoint a commission to investigate the social evil. Thirty citizens were named, among them Graham Taylor, Charles R. Henderson, and four ministers, with Sumner as chairman. The results of a year of fearless and exacting labor were incorporated in a report that created a sensation across the country and awoke other cities to a similar situation.[35]

A less spectacular approach to the metropolitan situation was the "Municipal Programme Conferences" begun at Amity Church, New York, in January, 1894. To the catholic mind of Leighton Williams, their chief sponsor, the "reformatory and progressive elements of all classes, parties and organizations" needed to be united toward the realization of a concrete program.[36] The weekly meetings looking toward this end had as their immediate objective the promotion of intelligent interest in municipal government and the constructive discussion of current topics. To the Amity platform came such leaders as Professor Franklin H. Giddings, Miss Grace H. Dodge, Theodore Roosevelt, Lyman Abbott, Charles H. Parkhurst, W. S. Rainsford, Albert Shaw, John B. Lennon, Walter Rauschenbusch, Professor E. R. A. Seligman, Jacob A. Riis, and many others, to present issues as various as public bathhouses, the single tax, and paved streets. The Amity conferences were a constructive influence for a number of years.[37]

Limitation of space prevents the presentation of other indi-

34. Lyman Abbott, *Christianity and Social Problems* (Boston and New York, 1896), pp. 346–347.

35. Taylor, *Pioneering,* chap. vii. Also, Vice Commission of Chicago, *The Social Evil in Chicago* (Chicago, 1911).

36. Leighton Williams, "Municipal Reform: The Need of a Positive Program," *Arena,* April, 1894; reprinted as *Municipal Programme Leaflet No. 1,* p. 1.

37. This material is based upon data obtained from Mrs. Leighton Williams.

viduals and movements dedicated to municipal betterment in these years, notably the "Christian citizenship" agitation by the Evangelical Alliance, various local church federations, Christian Endeavors, and organizations such as the National Reform Association. The issues of Sabbath observance, regulation of the liquor traffic, opposition to gambling, law enforcement, purification of politics, and education and participation in municipal affairs tended to focus in the cities, with the natural result that it was there that the churches began to learn in this decade that those who "differed theologically could sociologically unite" to fight the devil. Coöperation in reform was thus another step along the pathway toward church federation that had started at the Evangelical Alliance conference of 1887 and was to lead to the organization of the Federal Council of Churches in 1908.

The ethics of wealth were interpreted in this period in terms of a modified doctrine of stewardship. The older belief that riches should be administered charitably and with a certain paternalism was amended by the view that "all wealth is to be held and administered as common wealth."[38] The notion that private property in land is something peculiarly sacred and interference with it piracy has no basis in history or reason, said Gladden with reference to Henry George's single tax: "The land is held by the state for the whole people, and the right of private proprietors cannot be allowed to override or obstruct the rights of the whole people."[39] This challenge to an extreme individualism went on to assert that "no man's right of private property in land can be so sacred as every man's right to standing room. . . ." Land is the bounty of the creator, for the benefit of all. This, however, does not mean communism, but rather the sharp restriction of monopoly and speculation. Foreseeing an era of increasing socialization, Gladden applied his version of stewardship to the corporation: if it can administer its wealth in accordance with ethical standards it will be tolerated; otherwise the nation will be forced to establish "a firm supervision" over it.[40] An example was the railroads, a natural monopoly which had been allowed to operate on a competitive basis. In the case of this type of business, the federal govern-

38. Abbott, *op. cit.,* p. 99.   39. Gladden, *Tools,* pp. 71–72.
40. Gladden, *Social Facts,* p. 114.

ment must take the lead in enforcing certain reforms and regulations.[41] The Reverend George C. Lorimer of Boston, alarmed at the prospect of corporate control of American life, recommended industrial coöperation.[42] President E. Benjamin Andrews of Brown University saw the prospect of great harm to society in the development of monopolies "save on the condition of men's moral improvement."[43]

In addition to these major social-gospel interests, preachers of the 1890's displayed an uneven concern in the problems of crime, war and imperialism, divorce, international arbitration, civil-service reform, socialism and populism. We shall deal with the last two of these in the following two chapters; certain others lie beyond the scope of the present study. The problem of the treatment of the criminal is a perennial but minor social-gospel interest. In the 'nineties Lyman Abbott reiterated the religious approach to it: the vindictive or retributive system of punishment is entirely wrong, he asserted, and in its place a redemptive method must be developed. Since the criminal is the enemy of society he must be treated as Jesus declared our enemies should be: in the spirit of love. Abbott then indicated reform measures that he believed would translate this ideal into practice.[44]

John R. Commons once declared that "people need not only the heart of love, but also the knowledge to guide their love," and that such understanding could be "derived only from the science of sociology." As the century neared its close, a growing awareness of the complexity of its task led the social Christian movement increasingly to the study of social science, in classes and schools for that specific purpose, in additions to theological school curricula, and in efforts to formulate an adequate Christian sociology. The sociological character of the age and the increasing use of social-study materials were nowhere more apparent than in the literature that has been examined in this

41. *Op. cit.,* chap. iv.
42. George C. Lorimer, *Christianity and the Social State* (Philadelphia, 1898), pp. 246–248.
43. E. Benjamin Andrews, *Wealth and Moral Law* (Hartford, 1894), p. 49.
44. Abbott, *op. cit.,* pp. 310–311. See also Henry L. Myrick, *The Importance of the Scientific and Practical Study of Crime to the Clergy* (New York, 1893). For references to problems not treated here, see the writer's forthcoming classified Bibliography.

chapter. While in 1885 a lecturer such as A. J. F. Behrends had been content to name in the Preface to his *Socialism and Christianity* a few books that had influenced him, ten years later works of this type almost invariably included pages of references to the best materials available. In 1895 Wilbur F. Crafts's *Practical Christian Sociology* appeared, the first American attempt to systematize reform information, bibliographies, outlines for study, and propaganda between the covers of one volume; the first edition in 1897 of the monumental *Encyclopedia of Social Reform*, edited by the Reverend W. D. P. Bliss, was the first convenient compilation of sociological data published in this country.[45]

The popularity of social science was attested by its inclusion in Chautauqua programs. By 1890 the summer conferences held at Lake Chautauqua in western New York had become a national institution of immense prestige.[46] Retaining throughout this period its original religious complexion, Chautauqua contributed greatly to the spread of social Christianity. Although social topics had been discussed incidentally at Chautauqua as early as 1877, the social gospel entered this forum in earnest with the season of 1889, when Richard T. Ely gave three courses and Washington Gladden, Lyman Abbott, H. H. Boyesen, and F. W. Gunsaulus all lectured on social themes. In the next dozen years labor reform, social problems, money, social ethics, introductory sociology, social psychology, socialism, public opinion, and similar subjects were taught or lectured on by Ely, E. W. Bemis, Jacob Riis, Graham Taylor, Theodore Roosevelt, Carroll D. Wright,[47] John R. Commons, George E. Vincent, Charles R. Henderson, E. R. L. Gould, Josiah Strong, George Dana Boardman, Jeremiah W. Jenks, Francis G. Peabody, Washington Gladden, Jane Addams, Charles Zueblin, and others—a representative roster of America's leading social thinkers.[48]

45. Both Crafts's book and Bliss's *Encyclopedia* were published by Funk and Wagnalls, the former being reprinted four times in a dozen years, the latter once in 1908.

46. For a general account of Chautauqua see Jesse L. Hurlbut, *The Story of Chautauqua* (New York, 1921).

47. Wright's *Industrial Evolution of the United States* was written as a Chautauqua textbook.

48. This compilation is based upon catalogues, periodicals, etc.

Local Chautauquas reflected widespread interest in social questions during the years of populist discontent. Graham Taylor, who lectured at numerous regional Chautauquas in the summer of 1896 (at the height of the Bryan–McKinley campaign[49]) reported the attendance and attention given to classes in the social teachings of the Bible, to lectures on the labor movement and other similar problems, as "simply astonishing." Everywhere he was impressed by the "growth of social consciousness." At Ottawa, Kansas, he spoke thirty times, whereas eighteen lectures had been scheduled; fifty pastors were present "eagerly discussing the social aspects of their own and the Church's ministry"; a late evening question hour drew almost as large a group as did regular lectures. At Des Moines Taylor was unable to meet the demands for appointments; at every conference he was amazed by "the tremendous moral earnestness" with which the social aspects of the coinage question were discussed.[50]

This interest was manifested in other institutes and summer schools,[51] notably those held at Iowa College under the leadership of Professor George D. Herron. As might be expected, in addition to summer assemblies there were numerous efforts to organize groups for study and propaganda. One that attracted considerable attention and yet was short-lived was the "American Institute of Christian Sociology," founded at Chautauqua in July, 1893, by Professor Ely, who was followed as its president in turn by Josiah Strong and George D. Herron. Claiming an ultimate social authority for the Christian law, the Institute proposed "to study in common how to apply the principles of Christianity to the social and economic difficulties of the present time" and to present the kingdom of Christ as "the complete ideal of human society to be realized on earth."[52] This goal, the statement of which was borrowed from that of the Christian Social Union, was to be achieved "by publications, by lectures, and addresses, by the establishment of libraries, pro-

49. For the issues in the free-silver campaign, see Ida M. Tarbell, *The Nationalizing of Business, 1878–1898* (New York, 1936), chap. xiv.

50. Graham Taylor, "The Social Propaganda," *Chicago Commons* (July, 1896), p. 2.

51. See for example *The Commons* (May, 1897), p. 19.

52. "American Institute of Christian Sociology," *Encyclopedia of Social Reform.*

fessorships, etc., and especially by the formation of local institutes following prescribed courses of study." Several summer assemblies were held at Chautauqua and one at Grinnell, Iowa. Local gatherings were fostered in various places, the most important being a series of lectures in Chicago by Professor Herron.[53] For a time the Institute maintained a regular column in *The Kingdom*, the most widely circulated social-gospel paper published prior to the World War. Local institutes in a dozen states and a membership of over one thousand were once claimed by this group.

Organizations of this type were not limited to the area where agrarian discontent rendered social radicalism popular. Another well-planned but perhaps overly ambitious effort, destined to fail from lack of funds when its guarantors realized the inherently critical character of its instruction, was the "Hartford School of Sociology," a venture in adult education carried on by members of the faculty of Hartford Theological Seminary between 1894 and 1896. Designed as a three-year graduate course including research and field work, the curriculum listed such subjects as the family, social history, population, and the evolution of custom. The visiting faculty included John Bascom, Lester Ward, Alice Freeman Palmer, Edward W. Bemis, Charles M. Andrews, Dana C. Munro, J. Franklin Jameson, and William Z. Ripley. Popular at first, the School was forced to close after its second year.[54]

The most notable educational organization in social Christianity's growing years was the Episcopal Christian Social Union, founded in 1891 as the direct outcome of British stimulus to a felt American need for the "scientific study and analysis of social problems."[55] Adopting its principles from its Anglican parent, the Union proposed:

1. To claim for the Christian law the ultimate authority to rule social practice.

53. John R. Commons, *Myself* (New York, 1934), p. 51.
54. Data obtained by the writer from Professor Emeritus Curtis M. Geer, who was a member of the School's staff.
55. This account is derived in part from Miller and Fletcher, *op. cit.*, chap. v. By permission of Longmans, Green & Co., publishers. The Rev. R. A. Holland was the real founder of the Union; Ely, Potter, and F. D. Huntington were influential in its organization.

2. To study in common how to apply the moral truths and principles of Christianity to the social and economic difficulties of
the present time.

3. To present Christ in practical life as the Living Master and
King, the enemy of wrong and selfishness, the power of righteousness and love.

Conceiving its task as purely educational, the Union left practical activities to the older Episcopal society, "C.A.I.L." and
devoted itself to the publication of literature and the dissemination of information through conferences and lectures. Its
monthly *Publications*, always of a high order, were widely distributed. Often quoted, they were not infrequently reprints of
articles or addresses of particular moment by recognized authorities. An early pamphlet, for example, was a reissue of
John R. Commons' *Popular Bibliography of Sociology* that
had been compiled in 1892 by this young Oberlin professor "to
furnish the general reader, especially the Christian minister
and worker, a list of the best available books on important sociological problems."[56] The Union printed statements of social-
gospel theory by Anglican leaders such as B. F. Westcott and
Charles Gore, whose emphases were usually upon the social
meaning of the incarnation and of the church universal. The
Publications, of which there were more than one hundred, dealt
with such diverse subjects as "Arbitration and Conciliation in
Industrial Disputes," by W. D. P. Bliss, "Rights and Duties.
Passages from the Writings of Joseph Mazzini," and "The
Church's Opportunity in the City To-day," by W. S. Rainsford.[57] Beginning about 1894 the group held annual conferences at which it discussed the researches of committees and
planned its year's work in advance. Courses of lectures in Episcopal schools were carried out with fair success. The most important publicity effort engaged in was the call in 1897 of
W. D. P. Bliss as traveling secretary, a venture to be described

56. John R. Commons, "A Popular Bibliography of Sociology," Oberlin College Library *Bulletin,* I, No. 1 (January, 1892), 3. Commons believed that
ministers should devote half their time to sociology. See his *The Christian Minister and Sociology. Publications* of the C. S. U., n.p., 1891. This was reprinted
in his *Social Reform and the Church* (New York and Boston, 1894).

57. An extended account is impossible here. See the writer's forthcoming
Bibliography of Social Christianity.

in our next chapter. Continual pressure was exerted upon the General Convention of the denomination for the recognition of the claims of social Christianity, and when this was granted in 1910 by the appointment of a permanent Commission on Social Service and validated the next year with a full-time secretary, the Union voluntarily disbanded.

More important than any of these attempts to indoctrinate Protestants with social science, or social facts, was the gradual acceptance by certain theological schools of their responsibility for the sociological education of the clergy. In *The Early Days of Christian Socialism in America,* Dr. James Dombrowski has shown that the teaching of social Christianity in American divinity schools began to arouse interest in the 1870's, was pioneered effectively at Harvard and at Andover during the next decade, and became fairly widespread in the early 'nineties. The first definite instruction in social ethics in an American theological school was begun at Harvard by Professor Francis Greenwood Peabody in 1880.[58] During the following decade Professor William Jewett Tucker developed at Andover Theological Seminary what was unquestionably one of the most thoroughgoing courses of its kind ever given in this country.[59] Other significant beginnings were made by Graham Taylor at Hartford Theological Seminary in 1888;[60] in 1892 when Charles R. Henderson was called to the University of Chicago as chaplain and assistant professor of sociology; and at the Chicago Theological Seminary the same year when Taylor filled the first chair of Christian Sociology in the United States.[61] William F. Blackman was called to Yale as professor of Christian Ethics in 1894; he was greatly interested in social issues.[62] In 1895 Robert A. Woods was appointed lecturer in sociology at the Episcopal Theological School in Cambridge, a position he held for twenty years. Also in 1895 Nicholas Paine Gilman

58. See James Dombrowski, *The Early Days of Christian Socialism in America* (New York, 1936), p. 69, and *The One Hundredth Anniversary of the Harvard Divinity School* (Cambridge, 1916), pp. 47 f.

59. For a complete outline of Tucker's course, see *Andover Review,* beginning in XI (1889), 85–89, and continuing to XII, 437–438.

60. See Graham Taylor, "The Practical Training Needed for the Ministry of To-day," Hartford Seminary *Publications,* No. 2 (new ser.), Hartford, 1888.

61. Taylor, *Pioneering,* pp. 6, 383.

62. See W. F. Blackman, "The Study of Social Science in Theological Seminaries," *Christian Thought,* 9 (1891–92), 362–377.

began his distinguished career at the Meadville Theological School. Within a few years after the turn of the century such instruction was being given at well over a dozen leading theological schools.

These pioneer teachers of a complex subject found themselves plowing virgin soil. As Dombrowski points out, Peabody used the case-study method as an inductive approach to ethics, his purpose having been the illustration of ethical principles rather than exhaustive sociological research or understanding.[63] Tucker followed an entirely different procedure. Concerned with methods of bringing "the untrained, the disheartened, the dangerous classes [criminals] into moral relations to society,"[64] he studied specific problems intensively. His course covered the social evolution of labor, crime, and the criminal classes, and the treatment of pauperism and disease.[65] Each of these was developed under twelve subheads such as "the factory system," "prison labor," "the present sources of poverty," or "the problem of the tenement house." The subdivisions were discussed exhaustively, with constant reference to the best historical, sociological, and economics sources. In addition to classroom procedure Tucker arranged six-week periods of field work for advanced students, some of whom ranged as far as New Haven and Pittsburgh, and reported original research concerning "labor organization in America," "the wage system," "the ethics of socialism," or "Christianity and the social economy."[66]

The pioneer character of this teaching was well illustrated in Graham Taylor's efforts to develop a Biblical Sociology. Hampered both at Hartford and later at Chicago by the absence of materials, he nevertheless developed his course into a well-rounded survey of Christian sociology.[67] Printed in 1900, his *Syllabus of Biblical Sociology* outlined its data in five divisions. Subject and method were defined as ". . . the attempt to collate and classify the social phenomena and relationships referred to in, or inferable from, Scriptural data and teachings, and to apply the inductions from the same to the development of life, individual and social, in accordance with the Di-

---

63. Dombrowski, *op. cit.,* pp. 69–70.   64. *Op. cit.,* p. 66.
65. See note 59, above.   66. Dombrowski, *op. cit.,* pp. 67–68.
67. Taylor, *op. cit.,* pp. 390–391, 398 f., 422.

vine ideal . . ."[68] Such a methodology would be based upon the life and words of Christ, particularly in his conception of the kingdom of God. The second part of the course traced the origins of the kingdom idea in the Old Testament, and the third outlined a Christian social order as disclosed by Christ, taking up his social ideals. Next the social life and teachings of the early church were studied, and lastly the fundamental social concepts of the Bible synthesized. Taylor pointed out to his students that the important spheres of social life there delineated were the family, the neighborhood, and the areas of economic, political, and religious activity. Of these "the source and norm of society" and "the primary unit of state and church" were the family.[69] Field work was carried on at Chicago Commons, which Taylor had founded partially to provide a clinic for his students.[70]

A popular method of acquainting theological students with social conditions was pioneered by Nicholas Paine Gilman at the Meadville Theological School at about the turn of the century, when he began taking groups of seniors to New York City on tours of the social-service agencies and institutions. Scheduled at Christmas vacation, these trips usually included some two weeks in New York, during which the students visited Ellis and Blackwells Islands, the state parole office, the municipal lodging house, public baths, Ossining, the East Side, and the headquarters for organized charity. Groups were domiciled at such places as the University Settlement, and on at least one occasion visited the reformatory at Elmira en route to Meadville. One student writes that this experience was "one of the most instructive and inspiring two weeks" of his life and of inestimable value to him in a later ministry.[71]

These further evidences of the increasingly serious temper of the Christian social movement were in themselves its most careful attempts to formulate a Christian sociology. They embraced the study of the Bible and of social science, and endeavored to apply the resulting synthesis to the social problems of the day. All the efforts to deal with current issues as surveyed in this

68. Graham Taylor, *Syllabus in Biblical Sociology* (Chicago, 1900), p. 2.
69. Taylor, *Pioneering,* pp. 390–391.   70. *Op. cit.,* pp. 277 ff.
71. Letter from Professor Charles Lyttle of Meadville Theological School to the writer, November 11, 1936.

chapter might be classified in the right wing of the movement. But its most dramatic and perhaps widely heralded expressions belonged definitely to the left wing or socialistic side. We now turn to the radical versions of the social gospel of the late nineteenth century.

CHAPTER X

CHRISTIAN SOCIALISM

The Dawn stands for Christian Socialism. By this we mean the spirit of the Socialism of the New Testament and of the New Testament church. In man's relations to God, Jesus Christ preached an *individual* gospel; accordingly, in their relations to God, Christ's disciples must be individualists. In man's relations to man, Jesus Christ preached a *social* gospel; accordingly, in these relations, his disciples must be socialists.

The Dawn

ONE of the outstanding facts distinguishing the 1890's from the previous decade of social-gospel development was a marked change in attitude toward socialism. Unanimously rejected in the 'eighties, socialism nevertheless served as a powerful stimulus to the socializing of Christianity. In the last years of the century, however, its aims and program were examined with distinctly less hostility, much good was found in them, and an appreciable number of clergymen embraced a Christianized version of socialism as the ideal formulation of the religious social goal. This phenomenon was an integral part of the strivings of an age believing in evolution, in an organic society and in social salvation, and that was coming to appreciate the significance of environment and the power of organization.

Although Jesse Henry Jones had declared in 1875 that Christ's kingdom possessed two "wings"—individual regeneration and social reorganization—nearly two decades passed before this view reappeared in a refined form that reflected a better understanding of social forces. Individual regeneration alone is not enough, wrote the Reverend C. M. Morse in the *Methodist Review* in 1891: to be socially effective conversion must be to an ethical, socialized religion. The participation of Christians in war, slavery, and sharp business practices is evidence enough that faith in Jesus alone will not change society. If every individual in the United States were "regenerated" in an hour, asserted Morse, not a single reform in the industrial or social world would result, because our social system, which is contrary both in spirit and practice to the teachings of the Bible, is grounded in custom and is naturally looked upon as right and just. The church must exert her function as a moral teacher and present "the sociological doctrines of Jesus" if genuine social change is to result.[1] Morse did not propose socialism as a method of modifying the social order, but his fundamental assumption was that upon which the "Christian Socialism" of the period built: certain aspects of capitalism are contrary to Christian ethics; the duty of the church is to oppose and supplant them.

A further step was taken by those who found much of value in socialism but did not therefore call themselves Christian Socialists. This viewpoint was well expressed by the Reverend Frank Mason North, who contributed four articles on "Socialism and the Christian Church" to *Zion's Herald* in 1891. Pointing out the similarity of Christianity and socialism, North declared that "the common brotherhood of man is at once the Gospel of Christianity and the gospel of socialism." Citing certain aims of the Knights of Labor as definitely Christian, he held that Christianity and socialism agreed in their general attitude toward the distribution of wealth. For the most part socialism "is not the foe, but the brother of Christianity."[2] Through socialism the spirit of the age demands that the church prove the truth of its faith and apply its morals to life: "the whole force of Christian thought and action should be turned upon the world's wrongs and miseries."[3] Christian Socialism cannot be ignored, declared the Reverend J. E. Scott before the Presbytery of San Francisco in 1895: its essential ideas are cooperation and a just apportionment of the fruit of toil and the common bounties of nature. Competition is contrary to Christianity; how long can the church uphold an economic and social system based on the philosophy of every man for himself? Christian Socialism must be given a sympathetic hearing, for

1. C. M. Morse, "Regeneration as a Force in Reform Movements," *Methodist Review*, 73 (1891), 923–931, 74 (1892), 876–883. See also Alexander Kent, *The Needed Regeneration* (Washington, 1895).

2. Frank M. North, "The Christianity of Socialism," *Zion's Herald*, 69 (January 28, 1891), 25.

3. North, "Socialism of Christianity," *Zion's Herald*, 69 (February 4, 1891), 34.

Christianity, hitherto applied to individuals, is adapted to a kingdom, and a kingdom means organic society.[4] This view was not far from the Christian Socialism of the Reverend W. D. P. Bliss and his Boston followers, whose story forms the central theme of this chapter.

William Dwight Porter Bliss, son of an American missionary, was born in 1856 at Constantinople, where his education began at Robert College. After further study at Phillips Academy, Amherst College, and Hartford Theological Seminary, Bliss began his ministerial career as a Congregational pastor in Denver, where he remained only a short time on account of his health. Settled at South Natick, Massachusetts, he became interested in socialism in 1885 as a result of observing the village life of the working classes and reading Henry George and the series of articles on social problems that were featured in the *Christian Union* that year. Attracted by the catholicity of the Episcopal Church as better suited to his expanding social philosophy,[5] Bliss in 1886 entered that communion, where he felt that he could enjoy greater freedom of thought and action.[6] For two years he ministered to St. George's Church of Lee, Massachusetts, during which time he joined the Knights of Labor and became Master Workman of the local Assembly. In 1887 he was sent as a delegate to the Union Labor Convention in Cincinnati and the same year aided in the founding of the Church Association for the Advancement of the Interests of Labor (C.A.I.L.). Settled over Grace Church in South Boston in 1888, Bliss was nominated by the Labor party for lieutenant-governor of the state, but declined to run. The next year he was one of the founders of the first "Nationalist" club, and later organized the Society of Christian Socialists.

The Nationalist movement was the popular following attracted by Edward Bellamy's utopian novel, *Looking Backward, 2000–1887*, a powerful tract presenting the concept of the socialized totalitarian state to American readers for the first time and with a religious halo. The story concerned the adven-

---

4. J. E. Scott, *Socialism, What Is It?* . . . (San Francisco, 1895), p. 20.

5. See Bliss's article, "Anglican Position on Social Reform," *Encyclopedia of Social Reform* (New York, 1897).

6. James Dombrowski, *The Early Days of Christian Socialism in America* (New York, 1936), pp. 96–97.

tures of a young Bostonian who awoke from a hypnotic sleep in the year 2000 to find himself in a "national-coöperative" civilization where all men were economic equals. In this fictitious commonwealth work was neither for wages nor by contract, but "all alike were in the service of the nation working for the common fund, which all equally shared" even to medical care. Such wonders had been accomplished by the simple expedient of "replacing private capitalism by public capitalism" and organizing production and distribution on a coöperative or national rather than a profit basis.

As had been the case with Henry George, Bellamy found himself the center of a widespread reform movement as Nationalist clubs sprang into being throughout the country, the first of which was in Boston where Bliss, Edward Everett Hale, the Reverend Philo W. Sprague, and several other ministers were charter members. Nationalism, which appealed strongly to clergymen, not infrequently described itself as an applied Christian ethics. We have found a new basis for the reconstruction of the very nature of society and business, which is "Christian socialism, or nationalism," exulted a convert.[7] The Reverend F. S. Root of Auburn, Maine, regarded Bellamy's indictment of existing society as "powerful and unanswerable" but he distrusted the utopian character of the remedies proposed. However, said Root, the best of all remedies "is a close and faithful application of the gospel of Jesus Christ"—which is a "simple, clear, and efficient" cure.[8]

A similar conviction on the part of a group of Boston clergymen dissatisfied with the secular character of Nationalism brought forth the Society of Christian Socialists, largely under Bliss's guidance, in the spring of 1889. Asserting in their "Declaration of Principles" that "all rights and powers are gifts of God . . . for the benefit of all," these reformers believed that "all social, political and industrial relations should be based on the Fatherhood of God and the Brotherhood of Man," because God is the source and guide of all human prog-

7. Charles F. Goss, "Christian Socialism," *The Statesman* (Chicago), 6 (October, 1889), No. 1, 19. See also Jacob Edson, *Christian Socialism* (Boston, 1890?).

8. F. S. Root, *The Vision of Edward Bellamy* . . . (Auburn, Me.), n.d. (1888?), pp. 17–18.

ress. Their indictments of the extant social order were: concentration of ownership of resources and inventions, planless production resulting in business crises, concentration of control of industry in the hands of a dangerous plutocracy guiding the destinies of the masses, and the consequent prevalence of moral evils such as mammonism, overcrowding, prostitution, crime. The Society then declared that "united Christianity must protest against a system so based and productive of such results," and demanded a reconstructed coöperative social order wherein distribution and production would benefit everyone. The possible dynamics of such a society could be seen in contemporary trends toward business combination. The practical objects of the Society were:

To show that the aim of Socialism is embraced in the aim of Christianity.

To awaken members of Christian churches to the fact that the teachings of Jesus Christ lead directly to some specific form or forms of Socialism; that therefore the Church has a definite duty upon this matter and must, in simple obedience to Christ, apply itself to the realization of the social principles of Christianity.[9]

Among the officers of the Society were the prominent Baptist minister O. P. Gifford, the Reverend Philo W. Sprague, and Mrs. Mary A. Livermore. The movement spread to a number of small groups in scattered cities, but the only organization outside of Boston concerning which adequate information is available was that in New York, formed in February, 1890, of which the Reverends R. H. Newton, James M. Whiton, and Leighton Williams were charter officers.[10]

The Boston Society was hardly established when Bliss commenced the publication of *The Dawn*, a monthly journal for the propagation of the socialistic faith. Excepting *Equity* and *Labor-Balance* this was the first paper devoted exclusively to

9. *The Dawn*, I, No. 1 (May 15, 1889). The Declaration was often printed in the Society's literature. It may be found in the 1897 edition of the *Encyclopedia of Social Reform*, p. 258; in Ely, *Socialism* (New York and Boston, 1894); Appendix vii; and in Dombrowski, *op. cit.*, pp. 99–100.

10. H. H. Brown, *For the Right* (New York), I, No. 6, 8, and No. 7, 7–8. For the further spread of organizations, see *The Dawn* for November, 1889, May, 1890, and December 4, 1890. For another such church see "A Christian Socialist Church," unsigned article in *The Outlook*, 58 (1898), 90.

the cause of social Christianity in the United States, and was to serve for seven years as the chief publicity agent of Christian Socialism. Its first issue voiced a creed similar to the "Declaration of Principles" but perhaps more critical: "Business itself today is wrong. . . . It is based on competitive strife for profits. But this is the exact opposite of Christianity. . . . We must change the system. . . ." Christian Socialism was to be the cure for plutocracy, mammon worship, pauperism, poverty, and unbelief. *The Dawn* proposed "no magic panacea" but rather an evolutionary, experimental progress toward a co-operative society that would be characterized by fraternity and democracy; that would provide for the development of "true individuality"; that would hold land and all resources "under some system as the gift of God equally to all his children"; and that would control capital and industry for the benefit of the entire community. *The Dawn's* editor refused space to questions of theology or church government; he advocated "the gradual and careful change of the present industrial and financial system from its competitive basis to one of democratic and fraternal association"; and he planned to propagandize for his ideal principally through the church, in which he heartily believed. Associate editors of the paper were at first O. P. Gifford, P. W. Sprague, Hamlin Garland, Edward Bellamy, R. H. Newton; later the names of Reverend J. O. S. Huntington and Miss Frances E. Willard were added. Throughout its life *The Dawn* manifested a lively interest in the broad field of social reform, the catholic nature of Bliss's interests including all progressive concerns. Contributors, in addition to the above, included such leading social thinkers of the day as Daniel De Leon, George D. Herron, Washington Gladden, Edward W. Bemis, and Albion W. Small.

The Society considered its function to be primarily educational. *The Dawn* was its strong arm at this point, printing articles, courses of study, and bibliographies. A department headed "Our Library" presented classified references on various phases of socialism, the land question, etc., keeping up to date as new literature appeared. Study courses were worked out with great care by a special committee; in 1890 two series had been outlined, the first of which began with a review of *Looking Backward*, which book was, incidentally, offered as a premium for subscriptions to the paper. Labor, the competitive system, coöperation, the land question comprised the subject matter of these studies. Articles were reprinted, as for example an essay on the labor problem by Lawrence Gronlund, foremost literary interpreter of Marx in America. These leaflets were called "The Dawn Library" and Bliss, Edward W. Bemis, Vida D. Scudder, and Florence Kelley contributed to it. The prestige of the Society was aided by the publication in 1890 of Rogers' history of English labor, edited by Bliss. In reviewing this work, Richard T. Ely congratulated the Christian Socialists on their "zeal in the dissemination of useful information" that would "lay a solid basis for social reconstruction." The most complete statement of the Society's beliefs came from the pen of the Reverend P. W. Sprague in 1891, as *Christian Socialism, What and Why?* In 1895 Bliss published an admirable *Handbook of Socialism*, which, incidentally, did not deal with Christian Socialism. The members of the Society also spread their views by lecturing, and at times joined with Nationalist clubs in conferences and discussion groups.[11]

But these proponents of Christian Socialism were not content with a purely educational program. The first issue of *The Dawn* suggested as legislative measures the nationalization of land, railroads, telegraph, telephone, and all resources; public ownership of local transit, light, and heat systems; woman suffrage, compulsory education, the eight-hour day; and prohibition. On another occasion the editor of *The Dawn* elaborated a plan of action for clergymen and the churches. The church's needs, he said, are a simplified theology, a return to Christ, recognition of social duty, and a sacrificial practice of Christian love. To this end every preacher should remember that he is the minister of Christ, not the hired man of a parish; he should read, study, and preach social Christianity; every church should be a Christian brotherhood and an army of Christian workers with a chapter of Christian Socialists organized to evangelize the world for social Christianity.[12]

The adoption of these principles in his own ministry led Bliss in 1890 to resign his parish in order to form the Mission of the Carpenter as "an effort to carry out, in church life, the principles of Christian Socialism." No better proof is needed of the

---

11. Dombrowski, *op. cit.,* p. 101. 12. *The Dawn*, III, No. 1, 9.

spiritual character of this type of reform than the fact that the Society of Christian Socialists gradually became the Church of the Carpenter, a regularly constituted Episcopal mission. Avowedly a Christian Socialist church, this communion nevertheless did not formulate an economic creed, although its pastor professed to believe in "straight Socialism, in the spirit of Jesus Christ."[13] The notice announcing the formation of the Mission declared that "the Church of Christ, in her true spirit, is a Christian Socialist Church," her one Foundation being the Divine Carpenter "who taught of 'The Father who is in heaven,' and that all we are brethren." Pointing out the "true socialism in the service and sacraments of the Church," Bliss invited especially those who did not believe in the church, whether rich or poor, to his meetings. He affirmed his loyalty to the Episcopal communion by whose rules he was content to abide and whose Even-song would constitute his Sunday service. Rather than a new denomination or sect, the Mission would be "a humble effort of a Church that is, to bring it back to what seem largely forgotten or ignored truths."[14] Sunday-afternoon services were followed by informal "agapae" featured by ham and pickles, "socialist songs and free talk," and often distinguished guests such as W. S. Rainsford, Percy S. Grant, and William Dean Howells. The tiny congregation included George E. McNeill, one of Bliss's converts to Christian Socialism, the confirmed "Socialist churchwoman" Professor Vida D. Scudder of Wellesley College, and Robert A. Woods of Andover House. Bliss long afterward reminisced that "other lesser leaders came to the Church of the Carpenter—more leaders than led—and women, a few, among them some earnest young women from the settlements who sympathized and wondered and some of whom have since given their brilliant minds and devoted lives to the gospel."[15] In the course of "flitting from hall to hall in search of less rent," Bliss and his family at one time attempted a sort of social settlement in connection with the church, but only at the cost of impaired health and serious illness. "Reform and tragedy walk together," he remarked afterward. The end of the

13. Bliss, "The Church of the Carpenter and Thirty Years After," *Social Preparation for the Kingdom of God,* IX, No. 1 (January, 1922), 12–15.
14. *Ibid.*
15. *Ibid.* Also Vida D. Scudder, *On Journey* (New York, 1937), p. 165.

little society came in 1896 when Bliss was called to the larger opportunity of "seed-sowing" throughout the land as traveling secretary of the Christian Social Union.

The varied activities of the pastor of the Church of the Carpenter during his seven years in Boston were all directed toward religious social reform. He maintained his membership in the Knights of Labor, yet joined the Masons to avoid being identified solely with labor. He was a member of a section of the Socialist party when it met "upon a sofa and three chairs." He spoke in Episcopal churches and clubs, at the Cambridge Theological School, and sat on the platform of Tremont Temple when Father McGlynn appeared there in behalf of the single tax. In 1895 Bliss founded *The American Fabian,* in the editorship of which he was aided by Edward Bellamy, Henry Demarest Lloyd, and Frank Parsons.[16] All this time he was writing and assembling the materials for the epochal *Encyclopedia of Social Reform,* which came from the press in 1897.

The appointment as secretary of the Christian Social Union opened a ten-year period of lecturing across the continent, in Canada, and in England. Bliss spoke before churches, clubs, colleges—in fact wherever he was offered a hearing. In San Francisco in 1898 he filled the city's largest auditorium every night for two weeks, occupied the pulpit of one of the wealthiest Episcopal churches, was denounced by the papers as "an anarchist tramp preacher from Boston," and organized the "Union Reform League" that was merged the next year in the "Social Reform Union" set up at Buffalo by himself and others who hoped to unify the reform elements of the nation.[17] Bliss received his warmest welcome in Los Angeles where he preached, it seemed to him afterward, "in every Protestant church of the city." Later he was twice sent to Europe by the government to study unemployment, and held various pastorates near New York. After the turn of the century he was associated with Josiah Strong in the American Institute of Social Service and edited, at least in part, the widely studied Bible lessons in social Christianity published as *The Gospel of the Kingdom.*[18] Dur-

16. Dombrowski, *op. cit.,* p. 105.
17. The Union Reform League published *The Social Economist* for a time. For an account of it see articles by Bliss in *The Arena,* 22 (1899), 78–89, 111–114, 272–275.
18. See chap. xvi, below.

ing the World War Bliss worked among French and Belgian soldiers in Switzerland. At his death in 1926, this untiring missionary from the Church of the Carpenter had devoted forty years to the propagandist ministry of Christian Socialism.[19]

The Christianized fabianism of Bliss and his followers was a compound of religion, evolution, and socialism. Accepting uncritically the "ruling ideas" of the day—an immanent God, the organic view of society, and the present reality of the kingdom of heaven—these crusaders developed an evolutionary reform philosophy that included the spiritual values of socialism and many of its critical and constructive elements, but that rejected its materialistic and atheistic aspects. The Boston Christian Socialists were first of all Christians, and socialists secondly and only insofar as socialistic goals could be "embraced in the aim of Christianity."

Socialism, as Sprague interpreted it, meant in a strict sense the collective ownership and control of land and capital. He looked for the realization of this goal by evolutionary means when society—a conscious, self-determining organism—would decide to "perfect its own life and accomplish its own destiny" by organizing "against the common enemies of all its citizens— hunger, thirst, cold, and want."[20] Bliss was equally idealistic. Referring his readers to the encyclopedias for detailed definitions of socialism, he declared it to be "fraternalism, co-operation, organic collectivism, not paternalism or governmentalism at all." It is not a scheme, a system or status, but "a theory, a philosophy," he asserted in a Dawn Library tract, *What is Socialism?*

Perhaps the most realistic note of Christian Socialism was the acceptance of the familiar socialistic critique of capitalism.

19. The church, he said, "found its largest audience when it ceased to meet."

20. Philo W. Sprague, *Christian Socialism, What and Why?* (New York, 1891), chap. ii.

Another more realistic treatment of the relations of socialism and Christianity was *Socialism from Genesis to Revelation,* by the Rev. Franklin M. Sprague of Springfield, Mass., whose book was published in 1893, apparently without knowledge of the existence of the Boston group. This writer regarded socialism as a new economic theory, the object of which was "to realize the ethics of the religion of Jesus Christ in the possession of economic goods." Capitalism, said Sprague, has become "the arch enemy of this ethical principle."

Our industrial system, built upon private control of land and capital and actuated by individual self-interest, results in the spoliation of the masses, wrote Sprague in a study-course leaflet, *The To-morrow of Labor*. Religious objections were added to the economic strictures of orthodox socialism. Competition or "systematic robbery," Sprague declared in his *Christian Socialism, What and Why?* "is plainly not loving our neighbor." The present organization of the industrial world makes it impossible for a Christian to follow the ethics of Jesus in business; the consequent dualism between theory and practice is resulting in the loss of moral leadership on the part of Christianity. Sprague also challenged the capitalistic assumption that man exerts himself only for selfish ends, on the ground that it assumed "an utterly incomplete and imperfect conception of human nature"—a conception that overlooked the brotherhood of man resting upon the fatherhood of God.

Collectivism would provide the economic basis for a fuller individual and social life and would make possible obedience to Christ in the business world. It would remove from our society the evils of poverty, intemperance, and injustice that are contingent upon the capitalistic system. Socialism would foster such conditions of moderate wealth as to best develop character and under which "incentives of labor, of art, of thought, of service" would have new effectiveness because freed from the pressure of economic competition, declared Miss Scudder before the Society in 1891:

Then, as now, will be scope for moral struggle; for the choice between love and self. Only in this struggle the men of the future may, if they will, be strengthened with a new power; for the socialistic state will render possible what is hardly possible now,—literal obedience to the commands of Christ.[21]

The socialism proposed was to be "stripped of all those accidental and undesirable features which have too often marred the name of Socialist"—namely, of its irreligious aspects. While founded on the general principles of coöperation and of joint ownership of means of production, it would of necessity be "socialism in the name and according to the spirit of Jesus Christ."

21. Vida D. Scudder, "Socialism and Spiritual Progress," *Andover Review*, 16:49–67. Quote from page 19 of reprint. See *On Journey*, p. 168.

In its general economic aim Christian Socialism would not differ markedly from orthodox socialism, but it believed that the coöperative goal could be attained only "by starting from Christ." Socialism, wrote Bliss in *What is Socialism?* is an idle dream "unless realized through union with Christ, living from Him, and applying His law of brotherhood to society, politics, industry—productive and distributive." In the Preface to his *Handbook of Socialism*, Bliss asserted his agreement with the socialistic analysis, its economic program and ideal, but he differed with it "radically," "at the root," in insisting that it be "grounded in Christ."

This view, nowhere clearly explained, appears to have been Bliss's way of saying essentially what the Brotherhood of the Kingdom was similarly attempting to point out: because men are God's children and therefore brethren the kingdom of Christ is the most complete social goal. Said Bliss in *What is Christian Socialism?*: Christ preached a kingdom on earth—a kingdom having a law, subjects, and a realm. Christ came, therefore, to save individual subjects but also to harmonize their social relations—in other words to save society. Man is to carry out the program of the kingdom—to actualize true brotherhood in the social order. Socialism enters here as the technique whereby this can be actualized. The Christian Socialist program would aid all changes pointing toward this goal: "It is many reforms on one principle." Thus it would support the eight-hour movement, direct legislation, woman suffrage, government ownership and operation of railroads, telegraph, and express, and land reform. Appealing especially to the church, Christian Socialists held that "the solvent of social problems is the love of God."[22]

Thus weaving a socialized version of the Christian doctrine of man into contemporary reform ideologies, the Christian Socialists compounded an inclusive social philosophy of gradualism so broad that Nicholas Paine Gilman characterized them as "something like a society for the propagation of virtue in general."[23] Finding their rationale first in religion and second in

22. Bliss, *What Christian Socialism Is*, The Dawn Library, No. 1 (Boston, 1894). P. W. Sprague's position was similar; see chap. vii of *Christian Socialism, What and Why?*

23. Nicholas Paine Gilman, "Christian Socialism in America," *Unitarian Review*, 32 (1889), 351.

ethics, and but incidentally in scientific socialism, they seemed to Richard T. Ely to be motivated by "a certain spirit rather than a fixed creed." The fundamental purpose of Bliss and his colleagues was to awaken the church to her social duty, not to win converts to Marxism.[24] In contrast to socialism itself, Christian Socialism specified no particular organization of society, being committed rather to a method of change: "the attempted realization of some of the doctrines of Christ in an environment more or less unconformable with them," as Professor Paul Monroe of the University of Chicago analyzed it.[25] Christian Socialism may mean many things, said Ely, but it always insists that a spirit of brotherly love is an essential part of Christianity.[26] We may point out in conclusion that this emphasis was based upon belief in "the brotherhood of the race, the pre-eminence of personality over all material conditions, and the effectiveness of other than economic motives."[27]

Thus what might have been the weakness of Christian Socialism was perhaps in the long run its strength: socialism became a spiritual means to a social end. Concerned more with method than with goal, it sought "the application to society of the way of Christ."[28]

24. See P. W. Sprague, *op. cit.*, pp. 183–184.
25. Paul Monroe, "English and American Christian Socialism, An Estimate," *American Journal of Sociology*, 1 (1895–96), 56.
26. Ely, *op. cit.*, p. 89.   27. Monroe, *op. cit.*, p. 67.
28. Many orthodox socialists held a similar view. Lawrence Gronlund wrote in the *Homiletic Review* that socialism would "realize the kingdom of heaven on earth. . . . Socialism leads straight up to God. . . . You should be socialists because you are Christians, and thus make your religion, joined to socialism, the strongest social motive force." 22 (1891), 375.

CHAPTER XI

GEORGE DAVIS HERRON: SOCIAL REDEMPTION THROUGH SACRIFICE

The kingdom of heaven is at hand in America . . . I believe God has sent me with this message of a new redemption.

HERRON

THE most dramatic chronicle in American social-gospel history was the passage of George D. Herron across the stage provided in the last decade of the nineteenth century by the widespread social unrest that reached its peak in populism and the symbolic free-silver campaign of 1896. The revolt of the West was marked by a religious fervor that provided the fertile soil in which the gospel of this modern Jeremiah readily took root. The child of his age, Herron preached a God at work in the world redeeming an organic society destined to become progressively the kingdom of heaven on earth, while his radicalism pushed beyond that of all other prophets of the social faith and made him a national figure to be denounced or idolized. In the enigmatic and mystical personality of this "speaker of God" there were somehow embodied most of the characteristics of social prophets: crusading zeal, religious insight, a martyr complex, fervid advocacy of the reign of God, and sensitiveness to social wrong.

Born in Indiana in 1862 of devout Scotch parents whose ancestry rooted deep in the religious heritage of the Reformation, Herron was a mystic from infancy. "I may have been converted before I was born. . . . I have never been without the inner consciousness of God's compelling and restraining presence," he testified. A delicate child, Herron was largely taught by his father, "a humble man who believed in the Bible and hated unrighteousness." At the age of ten the boy had read Bancroft's history of the world, but behind that panorama he was even then conscious of the Divine Reality. Of his early years Herron later said:

. . . I was a slave . . . to the idea of God. I knew little of childhood or play. But the Kingdom of God and its righteousness were tremendous realities. I could not dissociate a picket on a fence from the moral kingdom. God was my confidant. I never thought of myself as other than His child. I talked with him over my books and on my walks. He answered my prayers. The words and deeds of His servants were my recreation. Joseph and Elijah and Daniel, Cromwell and John Wesley and Charles Sumner, were my imaginary playmates. Thus I grew up in the company of God, with a daily deepening sense of a divine call which sooner or later I must obey.[1]

Herron first united with the church at the age of thirteen, already away from home at work in a print shop. Here there was formed a strange but dynamic friendship between the boy and one McCleod, a temporarily reformed relative of the James brothers of wild West fame. McCleod, who had appeared at the shop a penniless tramp, became foreman and befriended Herron. An educated man, he taught the youth to read Shakespeare, introduced him to the gnostic philosophies, and inspired in him a great love for the Greek classics. Suddenly McCleod disappeared; Herron later learned of his death at the hands of a United States marshal and fifteen deputies he had held at bay in a wild encounter.[2] Knowledge of the printing trade enabled Herron to attend the preparatory department of Ripon College for three years, but the end of his school days did not interrupt his education. An omnivorous reader, he studied widely in economics and philosophy, especially Hegel and Lotze, and contemporary German theology, and was also influenced by Maurice, Edwards, Calvin, Newman, and Mazzini.[3] In 1883 he was married and entered the Congregational ministry.

Herron appeared on the social-gospel horizon in 1890 following an address given in Minneapolis before the Minnesota Congregational Club. Entitled "The Message of Jesus to Men of Wealth," this sermon contained the germs of Herron's later

1. Charles Beardsley, "Professor Herron," *Arena*, 15 (1896), 786.
2. William T. Stead, *Chicago To-day, or the Labour War in America* (London, 1894), pp. 156–158.
3. Beardsley, *op. cit.*, p. 794. Also W. H. Denison, "Professor George D. Herron, D.D.—A Sketch of His Life and Character," *The Social Gospel*, I, No. 6 (July, 1898), 18.

gospel, but doubtless obtained an enthusiastic reception on account of its unique and impassioned presentation of the doctrine of stewardship. Our social questions, began Herron, are as old as the problem of human association and may be reduced to the issue raised by Cain's query, "Am I my brother's keeper?" But history and prophecy have always pointed toward a time of industrial peace and social brotherhood. However, that day seems distant, and the blood of Abel cries out through the toiling millions. Our civilization cannot answer this complaint, for it is motivated by greed. Based on self-interest and maintaining itself through competition it is inherently unable to render justice; its ends are material, not moral. God's answer to Cain's question and to our social questions is the cross, said Herron. The law of self-sacrifice asserted in Christ is the law of life: it is the message of Jesus to every man, but especially to the wealthy because theirs are the larger opportunities and possessions to sacrifice. The men of wealth in our churches can begin the solution of our pressing social problems any time they choose, "by simply being disciples of the Lord Christ" and living sacrificially in the service of men. Quoting Franklin, Herron told his audience that "whoever introduces into public affairs the principles of primitive Christianity will change the face of the world." This is the opportunity opening before the Christian businessmen of America, who can "bear the weak in their arms . . . give work to the wageless, teach the thriftless and ignorant," seat the poor in the best pews of their churches, and so be "the makers of the new earth."[4]

From the many calls received as the result of the wide circulation of this sermon, Herron chose that of the First Congregational Church of Burlington, Iowa, where he was installed as pastor December 30, 1891. On that occasion, in reviewing his religious experience, Herron professed a general accord with evangelical theology but asserted that his views had been formed "as the product of moral conflict." As to his preaching the gospel, he avowed: "I could not help it. I dared not do else." The seventeen months of Herron's Burlington pastorate witnessed his rapid rise to national recognition. His sermons were widely

4. George D. Herron, "The Message of Jesus to Men of Wealth," *Christian Union,* 42 (1890), 804–805. Also in *The Dawn,* January 1, 1891; reprinted in *The Christian Society* (New York, 1894).

read, being published as *The Larger Christ, A Plea for the Gospel,* and *The Call of the Cross.* He carried on a socialized church program, lectured, and in 1892 held a minister's retreat at Iowa College, at Grinnell. The next winter he gave a series of addresses in his church on such themes as labor, capital, wealth, and poverty. Well attended by the working classes the lectures were officially approved by union labor and strongly criticized by business interests.

The most important incident of Herron's Burlington pastorate was his contact with a Mrs. E. D. Rand and her daughter, Carrie Rand, wealthy members of his church. Through the instrumentality of President George A. Gates,[5] Mrs. Rand endowed a "chair of applied Christianity" in Iowa College at Grinnell (later Grinnell College), to which Herron was called. He entered upon his duties in the autumn of 1893. In resigning his pastorate, Herron vouchsafed to the Burlington church his intuition regarding the crisis being forced upon American Christianity by contemporary events, in which he saw the coming of the kingdom of heaven. The Rand chair opened the way for him "to speak to the church at large." In no sense was he merely resigning one position to take another: "I go to witness to the righteousness of Christ as the righteousness of society and the nation. I have no choice in the matter . . . I go to suffer for the truth and the name of Christ."[6] Herron's benefactors also moved to Grinnell, and Carrie Rand was subsequently appointed dean of women of the college.

The call to speak "to the church at large" materialized at once. Herron's classes became so large that they had to be held in the college chapel. His first series of addresses away from Grinnell, at Ann Arbor, attracted three thousand people. During the first winter of his professorship Herron spoke at Union Theological Seminary in New York, in Indianapolis, in Brooklyn, and at Lawrence, DePauw, Indiana State, and Princeton universities. These addresses were published as *The New Redemption* and *The Christian Society.*[7] The first summer school was held at Grinnell in 1894.[8] *The Kingdom,* a weekly journal sponsored by friends as a mouthpiece for his ideas, was also es-

5. Later president of Pomona College, and of Fisk University.
6. Beardsley, *op. cit.,* p. 793.   7. See note 4, above.
8. Attended by some four hundred persons, this institute lasted a week, dis-

tablished that year. Wherever this "man of power" went he was the center of tremendous and usually controversial interest. When he lectured in Montreal a reporter compared the sensation to the explosion of a bomb in a public square of the city. After a commencement address at the University of Nebraska Herron was publicly challenged by the governor of the state. A similarly dramatic episode occurred when he visited San Francisco in 1895, the opposition being violently denunciatory and his support equally vocal.[9] Some of that year's lectures were published as *The Christian State*. In Boston Herron attracted audiences of five hundred to a course of afternoon lectures and filled fourteen other speaking engagements in a week. The Boston addresses had previously been given at Chicago Commons and were later published as *Social Meanings of Religious Experiences*. The last such production of the Grinnell period was *Between Caesar and Jesus*, a series given in Chicago in the fall of 1898 under the auspices of the National Christian Citizenship League. In addition to this output, Herron wrote regularly for *The Kingdom*, met his classes, and lectured far and near at every opportunity.

The gospel of the prophet of Grinnell began as "a call to the church to reconstruct society" according to the ethics of Christ, and eventuated in a complete avowal of socialism. A highly spiritualized appeal for religious social reform sounded against a background of widespread unrest, Herron's message held no practical concern for specific remedies, such as trades unions or regulation of monopoly, of the sort that appealed to Washington Gladden. Nor would Christ save the world "by a scientific study of the economic conditions of society." Dissimilar also to W. D. P. Bliss's Christian Socialism, Herron's evangel was of "the political appearing of Christ"—a religious theory of the nature and purpose of the social state. Although cer-

cussed the social gospel in general, and featured as speakers T. C. Hall, Jesse Henry Jones, John R. Commons, B. Fay Mills, Charles James Wood, John P. Coyle, William H. Tolman, Josiah Strong, and Jesse Macy. A smaller group came to Grinnell again the next summer. Such conferences were held in several cities, as well. See *The Kingdom* (Minneapolis), 7:209, 212, 220–222, 506; 8:198–199, 203; 9:306–307.

9. *The Kingdom,* May 10, May 17, June 7, November 1, 1895. See also the symposium published in the *Arena,* 14 (1895), 110–128.

tain isolated segments of Herron's thought might be labeled anarchism, mysticism, or communism, and some critics have placed him on the lunatic fringe, to the present writer this version of the social gospel appears to have been a deeply religious interpretation of the contemporary social revolt, phrased by a prophetic genius of tremendous spiritual dynamic.

Built upon those theological assumptions of the day that we have previously examined, Herron's "system" was, in brief, a challenge to the church not to reform but to reconstruct society in accordance with the standards of Jesus. This essentially socialistic proposal involved criticism of the existing order and of the church, and demanded social justice. The goal was outlined as a "Christian state" to be based upon the principle of social sacrifice. Herron's strictures against capitalism were neither gentle nor tactful. Rooted in traditional Protestant and democratic ideology, his critique traced the widespread poverty and discontent of the times to the centralization of wealth and control of business by an irresponsible industrial despotism created by a false science of society.[10] The unwarranted and unethical assumption that natural law must be allowed to run its course has produced "the unspeakably corrupt world of 'business,' now the chief danger to the nation and the greatest enemy of human life."[11] Competition is not law, but anarchy; this magnification of selfishness into a universal principle is resulting in social disintegration. It is social imbecility, economic waste, the atheism of civilization, and hell on earth. Monopoly is its natural fruit and the whole social issue is rapidly resolving itself into a question of whether or not capital can be controlled by law.[12] Our industrial order is wicked and doomed; the social traits we once lauded have become vices and tyrannies.[13]

To approve of such a civilization is to reject Christ and all that he stood for, said Herron. Any man who believes that a Christian life can be lived in the present order is either profound in ethical ignorance or he deliberately lies. "The worst charge that can be made against a Christian is that he attempts to justify the existing social order."[14] The church, whose duty

10. *The Christian Society*, pp. 16–17.
11. "The Social Failure of Political Economy," *The Kingdom*, 8 (1895), 587.
12. *The New Redemption* (New York, 1893), pp. 16–18.
13. *The Christian State* (New York and Boston, 1895), p. 110.
14. *The New Redemption*, p. 143.

it is to proclaim righteousness, is subservient to wealth; its efforts to reconcile the business morality of modern industrialism with the ethics of Christ is treason to the kingdom of God.[15] The prevailing forms of conservative Christianity are a gigantic moral heresy; as an institution the church is not Christian. A caste religion, Protestantism misrepresents Jesus Christ, does not know what he taught, and believes his teachings impractical.

Loyalty to Christ means rejection of the prevailing economic morality by individual, church, and society. If we believe that Jesus' doctrines are true we must take fundamental issue with those who assume that man's first duty is to gain a living. To be a Christian is to make righteousness the chief pursuit of life: the application of Christianity is the church's opportunity. No infidelity is so terrible as that of the so-called Christian who fails to exert himself toward the regeneration of social conditions, and no atheism is so frightful as the belief that society must remain as it is. The church is a means to an end—the kingdom of God, a just social order. Its work is the salvation of society. It was sent to be a sacrificial and redemptive life in the world. Not the cross, but the church that bears and offers no cross is turning men from Christ.[16]

The central theme of Herron's evangel was the principle of sacrifice, which we saw was related but subordinate to the doctrine of stewardship in "The Message of Jesus to Men of Wealth." The notion of social self-denial gradually assumed more importance in his thought and led him finally to socialism. What is needed, said Herron, is not successful men, but a generation great enough to fail according to worldly standards. The imperative of the hour is the assertion of the cross as the eternal principle of all divine and human action. The driving forces of the universe are sacrificial and redemptive. "Christianity is the realization of the universal sacrifice, of the philanthropy of God, of the redemptive righteousness of Christ, in society. . . . The fulfillment of Christianity will be the mutual sacrifice of God and his world in the society of a common need. . . ."[17] This is not merely the old Hebrew principle of loving

15. "The Opportunity of the Church," *Arena*, 15 (1895–96), 47.
16. *The New Redemption*, p. 150.
17. *The Christian Society*, pp. 25–26. By permission of Fleming H. Revell and Co., publishers.

one's neighbor as much as oneself: the true Christian is he who makes his life an offering to human need. Likewise a society that partakes of this sacrificial and redemptive quality will thus become Christian.[18]

Such a society would be a socialistic one. The connecting link between socialism and the principle of sacrifice was provided in Herron's belief that "every religious and political question is fundamentally economic." Economic relations concern the social prophet because they are the root of spiritual life, which can flourish only in soil enriched by the equal opportunity provided by social justice. The growth of monopoly and governmental corruption is turning the economic question into a moral one, because conscience demands the right to organize material things as the foundation of spiritual freedom. Unemployment, scarcity, and poverty, due to monopoly and organized selfishness, will be wiped out only by a changed economic system. Herron stated this view in a commencement oration in 1898:

Some of us believe that the public ownership of the resources and means of production is the sole answer to the social question. In order that each may have according to his needs, and be secure in the private property wherewith to express his individuality, the resources upon which the people in common depend must by the people in common be owned and administered. The common ownership of the earth, with industrial democracy in production, is the only ground upon which personal property and liberty can be built, the only soil in which individuality may take root.[19]

Such an arrangement would be the political appearing of Christ, "manifest in the increasing social functions of the state, and the socialization of law"; paralleling this development Herron observed around him an increasing appreciation of Christ's law of sacrifice as "the fundamental law of society."[20]

Although privately a supporter of the Socialistic Labor party throughout this period, Herron did not advocate political socialism as a religious creed, for he distrusted it as he did other panaceas such as the single tax because at best they could

18. *Op. cit.*, pp. 27–28.
19. "The Social System and the Christian Conscience," *The Kingdom*, 10 (1898), 827.
20. *The Christian State*, p. 31.

incarnate the teachings of Jesus only in part. Herron was, however, ready to follow any man or program that would take even the blindest first steps toward the organization of "the peace of goodwill among men."[21] Thus he could assert that "a pure socialism becomes the only form through which religion can express itself in life and progress," once the fundamental character of sacrifice is acknowledged. Human justice and peace, order and harmony are but a dream save through apprehension of sacrifice as the law of social and universal coherence. Religion becomes superstition and tyranny unless translated into social values and manifested in social justice.[22] The demand for social justice and industrial democracy was often repeated by Herron. The revival we need today is "the restitution of stolen goods, of wealth gained through oppression, extortion, and economic atheism."[23] There is no justice as long as capital is allowed to do as it pleases without regard for the welfare of society as a whole. Democracy, good for the state, is also good for industry. George III's taxation of Americans without representation was no more unjust than the practice of claiming advantages from society on the part of corporations that refuse society a voice in their affairs. "An industrial democracy would be the actualization of Christianity. It is the logic of the Sermon on the Mount, which consists of the natural laws by which industrial justice and social peace can be obtained and established."[24]

Herron's "Christian state," based upon "a clear line of Christian teaching" begun by Jesus Christ, was his answer to the problem of how to effect an economic organization that would express in material form the highest spiritual forces. It was to represent society organized for the good of all its members, and serving no selfish ends of its own. If the state is thus to fulfill the present longings of the masses, it must become Christian, wrote Herron:

21. "A Confession of Social Faith," *The Kingdom*, 11 (1898), 203–204. Herron was greatly indebted to Henry George, and believed the single tax the best form of taxation, but he distrusted it as he did any panacea short of Christian brotherhood, chiefly because he felt it would merely provide a new basis for individual freedom rather than association. See *The Kingdom*, 10 (1897), 243.

22. *Social Meanings of Religious Experiences* (New York, 1896), p. 44.

23. *Op. cit.*, p. 79. See also *The New Redemption*, p. 21.

24. *The New Redemption*, p. 34.

Except the state be born again, except it be delivered from pagan doctrines of law and government, from commercial and police conceptions of its functions, from merely individual theories of freedom, it cannot see the divine social kingdom. . . . If the state would be saved from the wrath of the rising social passion, it must believe in Christ as its Lord, and translate his sacrifice into its laws. Our institutions must become the organized expression of Christ's law of love, if the state is to obey the coming social conscience that is to command great moral revolutions in political thought and action. For society is the organized sacrifice of the people.[25]

To Herron this was not merely mystical or utopian. The state would not need to legislate in religious terminology in order to become "the social organ of the Christian life of the people." It would simply embody "the common faith and will of men to fuse their differences, justify their inequalities, universalize their interests, communize their aims and efforts" by translating Christ's principles into "political association and collective action." It would provide "a new social machinery in order that love and conscience (might) organize the world for the common good of all." In such a society Christianity would supply "the forces that can procure social justice," which forces can be actualized only through the agency of the state.

In the social stirrings of his day Herron saw "the beginnings of a great political movement, inspired for the purpose of translating the righteousness of Christ into the legislation of the nation, and the making of his mind the national political sense." Spurred by his feeling of crisis Herron's preaching bore the prophetic note of urgency: the assertion of the cross as "the eternal principle of all divine and human action" was the imperative of the hour.[26] Herron felt that near at hand there was a religious movement unlike anything in the past—the beginnings of a new spiritual development, churchless, the bringer of liberty, springing from "the seed of Christ" in the soil of common humanity. The social revolt likewise portended the retribution of the Lord: "The kingdom of the Christ is coming among men as a divine judgment, deep and swift, sudden and unob-

25. *The Christian State*, p. 62.
26. *A Plea for the Gospel* (New York and Boston, 1892), Preface.

served, straightening out the crooked things of the earth. It hurls upon us vast problems, travailing with the destinies of nations and civilizations. . ."[27] "Weighed down, almost overwhelmed by the sense of coming woe," this prophet of the social revolution seemed to W. T. Stead, who visited him in 1893, to combine in a unique way "the passion of the Socialist with the faith of the Christian." Never in our day have we had the moral foundation and spiritual law of a Christian society preached with such prophetic fervor and power, said another British commentator.

Among Herron's many supporters none was more staunch than President George A. Gates of Iowa College, who secured the endowment for the chair of Applied Christianity and who successfully stemmed the tide of abuse poured upon the college by Herron's opponents. Not the least of Gates's services was the sponsoring of a paper to serve as the mouthpiece of the "new religious movement" of which Herron was the obvious spokesman. The first issue of *The Kingdom, a weekly exponent of applied Christianity,*[28] April 20, 1894, announced an editorial board composed of Gates, Herron,[29] T. C. Hall,[30] Josiah Strong, B. Fay Mills, John R. Commons, H. W. Gleason, and four others.[31] In a sort of salutation, Gates, convinced that "here is a voice which cannot be stilled, and a message which will be read," outlined some of the features of "the movement for the kingdom" and acknowledged Herron's leadership. The paper was published for exactly five years,[32] and at one time ob-

27. *The Larger Christ* (Chicago and New York, 1891), p. 41. By permission of Fleming H. Revell & Co., publishers.

28. *The Kingdom* was formerly the *Northwest Congregationalist;* it continued to be published in Minneapolis. The new paper was the result of reader sentiment expressed following a symposium in the *Northwest Congregationalist* in January, 1894.

29. Herron had no organic connection with the paper.

30. Then a Presbyterian pastor in Chicago, Hall was later professor of Christian Ethics in Union Theological Seminary, New York.

31. The names of John Bascom, Robert A. Woods, Washington Gladden, and Charles Zueblin were added at various times. This list meant simply that these men contributed to the magazine with some regularity. Gleason was the managing editor. None of the editors received any compensation.

32. Gates was the cause of the demise of *The Kingdom.* In 1897 he wrote a booklet, *A Foe to American Schools,* exposing the mid-Western "book trust," the American Book Company. Because the tract had been printed by The Kingdom Publishing Co., the magazine was involved in litigation brought by the

tained a circulation of twenty thousand.[33] It was the most outstanding social-gospel journal in the half century covered by the present study.

Although strongly influenced by Herron, whose ideas were simply repeated by Gates, *The Kingdom* was in general tone considerably less radical than the prophet of Grinnell himself, as the diversity of its editorial group would suggest. It took a progressive attitude toward the problems of the day, frequently presenting both sides of a question. On the occasion of the Pullman strike of 1894, the Reverend George D. Black editorialized that a national system of compulsory arbitration should result from the controversy. John R. Commons compared Pullman, Carnegie, and corporations in general to Charles I or Louis XIV, and asserted that both employees and the public have rights that capital must recognize.[34] The free-silver campaign of 1896 was fought in a war of articles and correspondence, precipitated by John Bascom's disapproval of "16 to 1" on the moral ground of the sacredness of contract.[35] Others saw the ethical issue as between the plutocracy and democracy, with gold and silver merely symbols. One contributor declared that McKinley's victory had not advanced the kingdom of God.[36] Occupying for the most part a position on the leftward side of contemporary social-gospel trends, *The Kingdom* reflected a tremendous interest in social Christianity on the part of a following spread across the nation.

The Kingdom was the means of bringing together a diverse group whose subsequent venture in establishing the "Christian Commonwealth Colony" in Georgia was one of the most unique communistic experiments in American history.[37] Beginning in November, 1895, a series of articles and letters finally eventuated in the colonizing of one thousand acres in Georgia by some

book company. The suits were really won by the defense, but technicalities forced *The Kingdom* to suspend. Clarence Darrow was one of the lawyers for the defense, and Henry Demarest Lloyd its treasurer.

33. Bliss, *Encyclopedia of Social Reform* (New York, 1897), p. 258. This figure may be inaccurate. Gleason once referred to the magazine's 10,000 readers.

34. "Democracy vs. Paternalism," *The Kingdom*, 7 (1894), 233–234.

35. John Bascom, "The Morality of 16 to 1," *The Kingdom*, 9 (1896), 257.

36. *The Kingdom*, 9 (1896), 275–276, 498.

37. The following account is condensed, with the author's approval, from James Dombrowski, *The Early Days of Christian Socialism in America* (New York, 1936); chap. xii, which is a definitive account.

three to four hundred people between November, 1896, and the spring of 1900. Motivated by "a curious mixture of ideas drawn from Karl Marx, St. Francis and Jesus"—by way of Herron and Tolstoi[38]—these comeouters proposed to "organize an educational and religious society whose purpose is to obey the teachings of Jesus Christ in all matters of life, and labor, and in the use of property." The last point was the significant one: everything was owned in common, and everyone who came was equally welcome, whether tramp, college professor, minister, or one-legged man with nine children. Communism plus Christian brotherhood would equal the kingdom of God and demonstrate the practicality of the ethic of Jesus on an island of coöperation surrounded by the corrupt sea of capitalistic competition. Impressed by Herron's doctrine of social salvation through sacrifice, the colonists proposed to demonstrate the power of love as a working principle. All went well for a time. The colony was the recipient of numerous beneficences and the object of much interest. But nonresistance proved powerless against a few malcontents who slandered the group for selfish ends. Decimated by typhoid and discouraged by a heavy winter, the colonists disbanded in the spring of 1900, still financially solvent.

This bizarre incident has a peculiar significance for the history of social Christianity in that the Georgia Commonwealth coined and spread abroad the name "social gospel." When the experiment was well established, Ralph Albertson, one of the leaders, conceived the notion of printing a paper of some sort. The outcome was *The Social Gospel, a magazine of obedience to the law of love,* published for more than three years and read by liberals across America and to some extent abroad. A monthly of some thirty-six pages, *The Social Gospel* not only became one of the colony's chief means of support but was in itself an excellent paper, well printed and frequently illustrated. It carried articles by such writers as Graham Taylor, Henry Demarest Lloyd, Keir Hardie, Tolstoi, J. Stitt Wilson, and B. O. Flower. Among its two thousand readers *The Social Gospel* popularized its title, which gradually became the accepted name for social Christianity. Although the phrase had occurred

38. Tolstoi's doctrine of nonresistance was arousing great interest in this country at the time.

incidentally before this time,[39] it now spread and was later approved in high places when Shailer Mathews used it in 1910 as the title of his study manual on the social teachings of Jesus and their modern application.[40]

When *The Kingdom* ceased publication in 1899, a Chicago paper entitled *The Social Forum*, published by the National Christian Citizenship League, aspired to be its successor. This journal proposed to "stand for all *The Kingdom* stood for," but went considerably further when it declared that "the only true economic and political outcome of Christianity is socialism." Its sponsors believed in socialism "as an essential part of true religion," called themselves Christian Socialists, and professed their delight in preaching "the social gospel of Jesus Christ."[41] These magazines indicate the widespread interest of the times in religious social reform. *The Social Forum* once claimed a circulation of five thousand and during its brief career of seventeen months absorbed the *Truth Teller* of Lincoln, Nebraska, published "in the interests of applied Christianity," and *Conscience*, "another fine organ of applied Christianity," of Berthoud, Colorado.[42]

In 1899 *The Social Forum* became the mouthpiece of the "Social Reform Union," founded that year at Buffalo by W. D. P. Bliss and others who hoped to unite the reform parties of the nation in an organized effort to defeat the Republicans in 1900.[43] Needless to say this excursion into politics was unsuccessful. The educational program of the group was noteworthy,

39. See for example, C. O. Brown, *Talks on Labor Troubles* (Chicago, 1886), p. 9. *The Dawn,* supplement for June, 1890.

40. Shailer Mathews, *The Social Gospel* (Philadelphia, 1910).

41. In commenting upon Charles M. Sheldon's issues of the Topeka *Capitol,* the editor of *The Social Forum* criticized Sheldon for calling himself a Christian Socialist when "his plea was for charity rather than justice, whereas the Christian Socialist looks for the remedy of the poverty and distress caused by social conditions not in the palliating and aggravating application of pauperizing charity, but in the removal of the conditions. . . ." For Sheldon, see chap. viii, above.

42. Limitation of space prevents an examination of the social gospel of the Bible belt as expressed in the writings of the Rev. James M. Converse of Morristown, Tenn.: *The Bible and Land, Uncle Sam's Bible, or Bible teachings about politics,* and a paper, *The Christian Patriot,* which proposed to discuss "the teachings of the Bible in regard to social science, political economy, law, taxation, etc."

43. See chap. x, above.

however. It planned several types of correspondence courses in economics, to be handled by recognized teachers. This scheme blossomed as a "College of Social Science" whose faculty comprised several liberal professors recently ousted from Kansas State Agricultural College, among them Edward W. Bemis and Frank Parsons.[44] The most significant part of the Union's educational program was the preparation, by Bliss, of "Bible Lessons in Social Reform," designed for adult and for primary classes, and to supplement the International Sunday School Lessons for 1900. Typical subjects were "Christ's method in reform," "Christ and the people," "The Pharisee's home"; Bible readings, questions, references, and suggestions were included. This was the first attempt of its kind, and while only about nine months' lessons were published,[45] it provided a background of experience for Bliss's later studies for the American Institute of Social Service, beginning in 1908.[46] In all these movements and activities the influence of the prophet of Grinnell was apparent.

The trend of Herron's liberalism toward an avowedly socialistic position made his tenure at Grinnell more and more difficult. President Gates might have been able to fend off the increasingly severe attacks upon the college, had it not been that Herron's distrust of all "coercive institutions" gradually expanded to include marriage. He lived with the Rands as much as in his own home; gradually he became alienated from his wife. A trip abroad in the winter of 1897–98 afforded his enemies their opportunity and not long after his return he resigned, ended his teaching in the winter of 1899–1900, and went again to Europe.[47]

Learning that American socialism was "in the melting-pot" he returned to the United States in the spring of 1900 to give his support to the party in that year's campaign. Although he regarded political socialism as far from perfect, Herron told a mass meeting of the Social Democratic party in Chicago that he

44. *The Social Forum* (Chicago), October, 1899, April, 1900. Also Dombrowski, *op. cit.*, pp. 162–163.
45. *The Social Forum* ceased publication in October, 1900.
46. See chap. xvi, below.
47. *The Commons*, 4 (1899), 67–68. Also, Herron, *Why I Am a Socialist* (Chicago, 1900), p. 5.

stood before it to commit himself publicly to the political socialist movement as "the only collective expression" of the things
he had preached from the same platform in the name of Christ,
and he expressed his belief that the "new religion" whose
prophet he had been for a decade was itself converging into the
socialist movement.[48] He made one of the speeches nominating
Eugene V. Debs for the presidency that year.

One of the most unique of many groups motivated directly
or indirectly by the new socialistic religion of Herron was the
"Social Crusade" organized by J. Stitt Wilson. This fraternity
first enters printed history in its journal, *The Social Crusader*,
"a messenger of brotherhood and social justice" begun in 1898
by Wilson and Thad S. Fritz. Wilson, later to become mayor
of Berkeley, California, had resigned his pastorate in order to
enter the social arena more vigorously. The little paper was
fervid with a primitive religious zeal. The Crusaders preached
on street corners and wherever they could obtain a hearing.
Martyrdom had come through being jailed. As many as fifty
meetings had been held in one month. Enthusiastic conferences
gathered in many mid-Western cities, some "succeeding beyond
our hopes."[49] Wilson listed the "five fundamental truths" of his
movement as the kingdom of heaven on earth the eternal social
ideal, the principle of sacrifice its fundamental law, the teachings of Jesus "the eternal laws of social health," coöperative
industry the immediate social hope, and the inspiration of the
divine spirit the dynamic of the faith.[50]

Herron, anxious to infuse socialism with the religious spirit,
joined Wilson's Crusade in January, 1901. Miss Carrie Rand
became its treasurer. The preachers of the new gospel now sym-
bolized the religious nature of their mission by reorganizing as
the "Social Apostolate." *The Social Crusader* referred to Herron as "the Isaiah of our times" to whom the group looked "as
the natural leader of the spiritual forces making for economic
righteousness." Early in 1901 Herron gave a series of twelve
sermons in Chicago under the title, "The Economics of the

48. *Why I Am a Socialist,* pp. 9–10.
49. Worth M. Tippy, "The Terre Haute Campaign," *Social Crusader* (July
1, 1899), p. 14. Tippy supported the Crusade by remaining in his pastorate and
contributing financially. Other members of the group were W. H. Wise, J. H.
Hollingsworth, Benjamin F. Wilson, Franklin H. Wentworth.
50. *The Social Crusader,* I, No. 1, 9.

Kingdom of Heaven," in which he presented "a religious synthesis of the forces and elements that are making for the new world." In this rationalization of his avowal of socialism Herron pointed out lines of convergence between socialism and the teachings of Jesus, holding the socialistic goal of economic unity to be "the only foundation" upon which the principles of Jesus could be realized in "a truly free and spiritual society." But Herron would not stop with socialism. Beyond it he visioned a completely free social order based upon love and needing no coercive institutions.[51] Other lectures were given at Rochester, Cincinnati, St. Louis, and various Michigan cities. The band increased in size, a notable recruit being the Reverend William Thurston Brown, pastor of the socialistic Plymouth Church of Rochester, New York.[52]

Suddenly all this activity ceased. In 1901 Mrs. Herron secured a divorce. The prophet of applied Christianity was promptly deposed from the ministry by the Congregational group at Grinnell. His leadership of the social Christian movement collapsed. The last number of *The Social Crusader* was issued in June of that year. In September Herron and Miss Rand were married by Brown in a liberal ceremony in which they "took each other for man and wife," thus dramatizing their opposition to coercive institutions. Shortly afterward this "self-sacrificing advocate of social revolution," now branded an advocate of free love, sailed away to Italy, there to live with his new wife and Mrs. Rand in a villa near Fiesole.[53] Such was the tragic end of the most brilliant episode in social-gospel history.

51. *The Commons* (January, 1901), pp. 3–4.
52. Brown had previously held a pastorate at Madison, Connecticut. He was the author of several religious-socialistic tracts: *The True Meaning of Christianity, The Real Religion of To-day, After Capitalism What?, How Capitalism Has Hypnotized Society,* and *The Relation of Religion to Social Ethics.*
53. Hospitality to prominent guests gained for Herron such a knowledge of men and international affairs that he was assigned an important diplomatic mission by Woodrow Wilson at the Peace Conference of Versailles, and it is chiefly for this service that he is remembered. For his part in the European peace settlement see Mitchell P. Briggs, "George D. Herron and the European Settlement," Stanford University *Publications,* III, No. 2, 225–402.

PART IV: 1900–1915

MATURITY AND RECOGNITION

The social gospel . . . is no longer a prophetic and occasional note. It is a novelty only in backward social or religious communities. The social gospel has become orthodox.

WALTER RAUSCHENBUSCH

Where cross the crowded ways of life,
Where sound the cries of race and clan,
Above the noise of selfish strife,
We hear thy voice, O Son of Man.

In haunts of wretchedness and need,
On shadowed thresholds dark with fears,
From paths where hide the lures of greed,
We catch the vision of thy tears.

From tender childhood's helplessness,
From woman's grief, man's burdened toil,
From famished souls, from sorrow's stress,
Thy heart has never known recoil.

The cup of water given for thee
Still holds the freshness of thy grace;
Yet long these multitudes to see
The sweet compassion of thy face.

O Master, from the mountain side,
Make haste to heal these hearts of pain;
Among these restless throngs abide,
O tread the city's streets again.

Till sons of men shall learn thy love,
And follow where thy feet have trod;
Till glorious from thy heaven above,
Shall come the City of our God.

FRANK MASON NORTH, 1903

INTRODUCTION

WITH the turn of the century the social gospel entered upon the final stage of the career that has now been followed through three decades. As had been the case during the 1890's when the evangel of George D. Herron was borne upon the wave of populist discontent, the first dozen years of the twentieth century witnessed the rise of another surge of reform—progressivism—in the sweep of which the social gospel was carried to the climax of its development. The spirit of progress expressed itself in the vigorous "trust-busting" of Theodore Roosevelt and the idealistic crusades of Woodrow Wilson. The direct primary, woman suffrage, the initiative, referendum, and recall were being widely discussed and voted upon, while the older populist agitation against the plutocracy ripened into accomplished reform in the establishment of the Federal Reserve System, the income-tax amendment to the Constitution, the tightening of the Interstate Commerce Commission's control of the railroads, and the assumption of the policy of public ownership of unexploited forests. On the crest of this liberal flood social Christianity rode to its high-water mark.

But the apogee of the movement we have so far followed was aided by internal factors as well as the progressive climate of the day. The quest of the historical Jesus led to the discovery of his social teachings and their enthusiastic avowal as the ethical and authoritarian foundation that social Christianity had previously lacked. Likewise the growing force of socialism and its increasingly effective appeal to the clergy acted as a leavening agent of no mean power. The developing techniques of sociology and the religious interests of certain popular sociologists added both methodological effectiveness and scientific sanction to a movement now rapidly becoming acceptable, while a factor of no mean significance was the inspired formulation of social-gospel philosophy by its greatest prophet, Walter Rauschenbusch.

The confluence of these streams resulted in the formal recognition of social Christianity by Protestant denominations and by their representative association the Federal Council of the

Churches of Christ in America, which latter was brought into being largely as the result of social-gospel influences. These bodies developed social-service programs that were carried out by official agencies manned by paid workers, and they issued statements of the new social faith that assumed classic import as the "Social Creed of the Churches." As the social gospel thus came to maturity and widespread approval its official pronouncements were at first largely concerned with the problems of industry, an interest that had characterized it from its beginnings in the 1870's, but with the aid of sociology and the sobering influence of experience the social creed and viewpoint gradually assumed a more comprehensive and seasoned outlook.

CHAPTER XII

THE DISCOVERY OF THE SOCIAL
TEACHINGS OF JESUS

The new civilization, with its social problems, has led us to search for the social teachings of Jesus, which had been long neglected; and we find that those teachings fit modern conditions as a key fits its lock.

JOSIAH STRONG

THE confluence of several currents that resulted in the discovery of the social teachings of Jesus around the turn of the century provided the maturing social gospel with a permanently valid scriptural and authoritarian basis. Although a few pioneer social Christians—notably Professor Stuckenberg[1]—had pointed out the necessity of basing a "Christian sociology" upon Christ's teachings, the ideal of the kingdom nevertheless continued to be the accepted religious foundation of the social goal until about 1900. During the early years of the new century American theology's debt to Darwin remained an open account and the "ruling ideas" of the 1890's—the immanence of God, the solidarity of society, and the earthly presence of the kingdom—were assumed as corollaries to the doctrine of progress. However, in the latter years of the 'nineties continental New Testament scholarship, mediated through British scholars and a few Americans who had studied in Germany, began to make itself felt in the United States. This discovery of the Jesus of history furnished the growing social-gospel movement with ethical and religious formulae according to which it eagerly constructed for itself a rationalistic and autonomous foundation that not only rested the kingdom hope upon the ethics of Jesus but afforded a frame of reference within which either a theistic or a humanistic social creed might be phrased. With

1. J. H. W. Stuckenberg, *Christian Sociology* (New York, 1880), chap. iii. See also John Bascom, *The Words of Christ as Principles of Personal and Social Growth* (New York and London, 1884), p. 153 and chaps. viii, ix. Austin Bierbower, *Socialism of Christ* (Chicago, 1890). Minot J. Savage, *Jesus and Modern Life* (Boston, 1893), chapter on the kingdom of God.

the outstanding exception of Walter Rauschenbusch and others of the Brotherhood of the Kingdom, exponents of social Christianity now rationalized the new faith in terms of the social teachings of Jesus rather than the kingdom ideal.

Most of the literature to be examined in this chapter was written by those seeking a religious key to the problems of civilization, not by the eminent scholars of the day. In 1896 Lyman Abbott published in the *Outlook* a series of his sermons discussing "Christ's Teaching on Social Topics," which were later more appropriately titled *Christianity and Social Problems* when printed in book form. At the same time, Shailer Mathews' essays on "Christian Sociology" in the *American Journal of Sociology* were better described by their subsequent book title *The Social Teachings of Jesus*. This volume, printed in 1897, was the first American work devoted exclusively to its subject and was reprinted seven times in a dozen years.[2] In 1899 the first specialized study of its kind appeared, *"The Profit of the Many." The Biblical Doctrine and Ethics of Wealth*, by the Reverend E. Tallmadge Root.[3] Professor Francis Greenwood Peabody's *Jesus Christ and the Social Question*, released in 1900, was perhaps the best of these essays; a generation later Mathews spoke of it as even then "one of the most comprehensive and sanest treatments of its field." In *Christ's Social Remedies*, also published in 1900, Harry E. Montgomery declared that "without a clear and accurate knowledge of the teachings of Christ upon the great social and industrial questions of to-day, we will be unable to fulfil our highest duties as American citizens." Two years later the eminent Biblical scholar Orello Cone brought out a careful study of *Rich and Poor in the New Testament*. In 1906 the first edition of *The Political and Social Significance of the Life and Teachings of Jesus*, a popular study course by Professor Jeremiah W. Jenks of Cornell University, met with a ready response. A notable contribution followed in 1907 in Joseph A. Leighton's *Jesus Christ and the Civilization of To-day*, a study of the ethics of Jesus in relation

---

2. See, for example, Shailer Mathews, *New Faith for Old. An Autobiography* (New York, 1936), pp. 123–124.

3. It was described by the *Outlook* as one of the "six best books on sociology." See, in comparison, Edward Tallmadge Root, *Bible Economy of Plenty* (New York, 1939).

to modern culture. In 1910 Lyman Abbott gave the George Dana Boardman Lectures at the University of Pennsylvania under the title, *The Ethical Teachings of Jesus*. The last of the more significant works of this kind during the period came from the pen of Walter Rauschenbusch in 1916 as a study manual on *The Social Principles of Jesus*.[4]

The discoverers of the social teachings of Jesus were agreed that such social implications as flowed from the Master's thought depended upon and were incidental to his religious presuppositions. This evidence of the basically religious character of the social-gospel movement was well phrased by Professor Peabody when he declared that the doctrine of fatherhood was the cardinal point of Jesus' teaching and that the idea of the brotherhood of man depended upon it.[5] Jesus was primarily concerned with the relation of the human soul to God.[6] He taught that the goal of humanity is "the realization of brotherhood interpreted in the light of the common fatherhood," wrote Amory H. Bradford.[7] Jesus' basic conviction was that love is at the heart of the world, said President Henry C. King of Oberlin,[8] while the Reverend S. D. McConnell of New York declared that Christ held God to be the eternal principle of love.[9]

All writers, from the socialistic interpreter who regarded Christ's ideal as a reign characterized by economic justice,[10] to

4. This highly selected list makes no attempt at inclusiveness, nor does it mention such general works as those by Marvin R. Vincent, Henry S. Nash, Benjamin W. Bacon, George B. Stevens, T. C. Hall, Henry M. Herrick, William DeWitt Hyde, Charles A. Briggs. For further references, see the writer's *Bibliography of Social Christianity* (forthcoming).

5. Francis Greenwood Peabody, "The Message of Christ to Human Society," in *The Message of Christ to Manhood* (Boston and New York, 1899).

6. Peabody, *Jesus Christ and the Social Question* (New York, 1900), p. 77. This book, which was reprinted five times by 1903, was a good example of the effect of German scholarship upon the American social gospel, as it abounded in references to German critics, notably Beyschlag, Holtzmann, Harnack, and Wendt. The same was to a less extent true of Mathews' *Social Teaching of Jesus*. Professor Cone and Nathaniel Schmidt (*The Prophet of Nazareth*, 1905) were perhaps the best American scholars of the time in this field; they were conversant with all foreign literature. Other foreign influences came into American thought through such British writers as F. D. Maurice, B. F. Westcott, W. H. Fremantle, A. B. Bruce, W. Sanday, S. R. Driver, A. M. Fairbairn.

7. Amory H. Bradford, *The Age of Faith* (Boston and New York, 1900), p. 135.

8. Henry Churchill King, *The Ethics of Jesus* (New York, 1910), p. 273.

9. S. D. McConnell, *Christ* (New York, 1904), p. 212.

10. Austin Bierbower, *Socialism of Christ* (Chicago, 1890), p. 7.

Josiah Strong who saw the kingdom as an ideal for the present world,[11] agreed that in the mind of Jesus the love of God was to evidence itself in human affairs in the coming of the kingdom. The kingdom, said Lyman Abbott, will be wrought by men, on earth;[12] it will be "an ideal social order in which the relation of men to God is that of sons, and to each other that of brothers"; for Jesus it was neither materialistic nor supramundane, neither a political state nor an individual way of life.[13] The apocalyptic character of the kingdom was rejected as a justifiable interpretation of Jesus' use of the phrase. Peabody claimed that Jesus did not share the eschatological ideas of his age; he must be understood "above the heads of his reporters."[14] The kingdom of Jesus would come "as the seed grows and the leaven exerts its power silently but persistently by the help and guidance of God," wrote Harry E. Montgomery.[15] The coming of the kingdom is a gradual process, said Mathews: Jesus meant evolution (although he could scarcely have been expected to use that word), and his use of biological analogies indicates that he presupposed an organic society.[16] Such was the force of the "ruling ideas" of the day.

From Jesus' religious position, and from his ideal of the kingdom, certain basic principles were to be inferred. According to Josiah Strong the three laws of the kingdom were those of service, sacrifice, and love.[17] The Reverend David Beaton of Chicago found the rules of the kingdom in several words implying social obligation: righteousness, love, faith.[18] For Rauschenbusch "the axiomatic social convictions of Jesus" were the value of life, the solidarity of the human family, and the necessity for the strong to "stand up for the weak"—the last a

11. Josiah Strong, *My Religion in Everyday Life* (New York, 1910), pp. 37–50.

12. Lyman Abbott, *The Ethical Teachings of Jesus* (Philadelphia, 1910), p. 70.

13. Shailer Mathews, *The Social Teaching of Jesus* (New York, 1897), p. 54.

14. Peabody, *Jesus Christ and the Social Question,* p. 96.

15. Harry Earl Montgomery, *Christ's Social Remedies* (New York, and London, 1900), pp. 119–120, 135.

16. Mathews, *op. cit.,* chap. ix.

17. Josiah Strong, *The Next Great Awakening* (New York, 1902), pp. 7–8.

18. David Beaton, "The Program of Christ," *American Weekly,* 3 (1902), 894–895.

variation of Herron's doctrine of social sacrifice.[19] Joseph A. Leighton summarized Jesus' social principles as a life of service, rendered according to need and from the motive of personal love, of which last the evidence is forgiveness or an infinite good will. The true ethical and spiritual life for the individual is genuinely social. In the ordering of the universe there is an ethical law of compensation.[20]

These interpreters of Jesus found the heart of his social teaching in the idea of the worth of or reverence for personality. The historic dogma of individual freedom now became the principle of the value of the individual and hence an authoritative basis for social reform. The fundamental principle of Jesus is "the absolute worth of every human individual"; this is the ultimate norm by which all social institutions and the social activity of the individual are to be measured, wrote Leighton.[21] Professor Cone declared that in the gospel of Jesus "the worth and welfare of the human soul are of such inestimable importance that the individual should not be made the slave of the institutions that men establish."[22] These several central concepts were admirably stated by Rauschenbusch:

The God of Jesus was the great Father who lets his light shine on the just and the unjust, and offers forgiveness and love to all. Jesus lived in the spiritual atmosphere of that faith. Consequently he saw men from that point of view. They were to him children of that God. Even the lowliest was high. The light that shone on him from the face of God shed a splendor on the ranks of men. In this way religion enriches and illuminates social feeling.[23]

Social regeneration is to come about through the dissemination of the spirit of reverence for personality throughout society. Beginning with individuals it will proceed to groups and institutions, pervading them with the Christ spirit of brotherli-

19. Walter Rauschenbusch, *The Social Principles of Jesus* (New York and London, 1916), Part I.

20. Joseph A. Leighton, *Jesus Christ and the Civilization of Today* (New York, 1907), pp. 106–115.

21. *Op. cit.*, p. 117.

22. Orello Cone, *Rich and Poor in the New Testament* (New York, 1902), p. 223.

23. Rauschenbusch, *op. cit.*, p. 9.

ness. It is an evolutionary process. According to Jesus, said Peabody, social salvation is to be accomplished neither through organization alone nor through inspiration alone, "but by the application to organization of the personal power inspired by Jesus Christ."[24] The regenerative force in human society is that "innumerable company of unknown men and women who have been transformed into the image and likeness of Christ" and who quicken the world simply by living this new life, wrote S. D. McConnell. However, David Beaton pointed out that the personal and social obligation accepted by one who tries to follow Christ involves something more than the performance of duties in a manner unrelated to society. A perfect society cannot be created from an imperfect people, said Mathews. The process of transformation is of necessity gradual; it starts with the individual, but not in an atomistic sense. Jesus began by winning separate souls, not by righting political wrongs. The expanding Christian society will consist of little groups of men and women possessed of the spirit and method of life of their Master—groups he likened to leaven. Jesus foresaw that the long slow progress of the Christian society in the world would depend upon the effectiveness of these nuclei of Christians.[25]

These writers pointed out carefully that Jesus was neither a socialist nor a reformer and that he did not and could not legislate for modern civilization. He simply antedated the complexity of modern life. He did not plan to realize his kingdom by the improvement of the external conditions of life. He had no plan of attack upon the institutional vices of his own age— polygamy, slavery, and tyranny.[26] The New Testament supplies ideals and inspiration rather than systems of belief or outlines of social policies, declared Professor Cone, who went on to show that the apocalyptic hopes of the age led Jesus to minimize social evils, an opposite view to that taken by most writers of the period. Taking Herron and others to task for trying to find the program of socialism in the New Testament, Cone asserted that an unbiased exegesis revealed "neither a social philosophy, nor the foundations, nor the outlines of a social system." The New Testament teachers were idealists with definite conceptions of the ethical ends of the individual life. They were

24. Peabody, "Message, etc.," p. 79.   25. Mathews, *op. cit.*, chap. ix.
26. Beaton, *op. cit.*, p. 894.

not social reformers.[27] Peabody agreed with this view, holding that Jesus was not a reformer but a revealer, an idealist with a vision, not an agitator with a plan. But, said David Beaton, it would be a shallow interpretation to infer from this absence of specific social concerns that Jesus was indifferent to "the material and political interests of men, and that his religion does not furnish the principles and inspiration of all reforms."[28]

Limitation of space prevents an exhaustive analysis of the specific social teachings of Jesus as these interpreters understood them. The significance of their writings for the history of the social gospel lies in wider implications rather than in detailed findings. It is noteworthy that the utterances of Jesus concerning property and riches elicited perhaps the most interest evidenced in any phase of his thought. At a time when the ethics of wealth were being discussed on every hand, Rauschenbusch wrote that Jesus' teaching on questions of property would exceed in mere bulk his concern for any other ethical matter.[29]

The search for and use of wealth is a moral matter, said Mathews. Jesus had nothing to say about financial trusts, but his denunciation was unsparing of those who grow rich at the expense of souls, or who use wealth to make themselves independent of social obligation.[30] E. Tallmadge Root interpreted the Master's attitude toward wealth as follows: "Jesus showed that it is the life-purpose that determines the character and destiny of society and individual; that the purpose to seek riches for self is false and pernicious; and that the true purpose to 'seek first the Kingdom' should control all use of wealth."[31] Professor Cone pointed out that on the whole Jesus and other New Testament teachers were unfriendly toward wealth because their spiritual insight indicated to them its perils for the life of the spirit. Their message appeared to have been "somewhat harsh and one-sided" on this subject; what they would say today would be suggested by the permanently valid aspects of their thought. This would probably be that those who show

27. Cone, *op. cit.*, p. 221.   28. Beaton, *loc. cit.*
29. Walter Rauschenbusch, "Social Ideals in the New Testament," *Treasury*, June, 1899.
30. Mathews, *op. cit.*, p. 157.
31. E. T. Root, *"The Profit of the Many"* (New York, 1899), p. 267. By permission of Fleming H. Revell & Co., publishers.

themselves spiritual sons of God must demonstrate that profession in terms of kindness and sympathy and in the abolition of all class distinctions attendant upon possessions or other external factors.[32] Peabody pointed out that Jesus' awareness of the insidious peril to the Christian life lurking in the love of money led him to declare that no man could have two masters: the service of the kingdom demanded the whole of one's loyalties—possessions as well as mind and heart. "The teaching of Jesus permits in no case the sense of absolute ownership." A man does not own his wealth; he owes it. As a follower of the Master he is a trustee of all he possesses. And if he becomes aware that selfishness is getting the better of his trusteeship, renunciation is the only course.

But Peabody went on to show that in the view of Jesus mere economic justice was not enough. Wealth should be a means of redemption. The modern attack on riches would be satisfied if a more equitable distribution of profit could be achieved. But Jesus does not ask merely for a fair proportion of our earnings. "He asks the whole of one's gains—and the life which lies behind the gains—for the service of the kingdom." Thus the matter of economic distribution expands in his teachings into the greater problem of spiritual regeneration and preparedness. In short, Jesus does not present a scheme of economic rearrangement: he issues a summons to the kingdom.[33] The similarity of this interpretation to the traditional conception of stewardship hardly needs to be indicated. And yet it provided the basis for a more radical form of this belief. We need a Christian ethic of property perhaps more than anything else, declared Rauschenbusch. "The wrongs connected with wealth are the most vulnerable point of our civilization. Unless we can make that crooked place straight, all our charities and religion are involved in hypocrisy."[34]

To follow these interpreters of Jesus as they analyzed his attitude toward other social problems would require a volume in itself. They discussed his teaching on the family, the state, the industrial order, society, nonresistance, crime and the criminal,

---

32. Cone, *op. cit.,* pp. 206–208.
33. Peabody, *Jesus Christ,* etc., pp. 214–215. See also Rauschenbusch, *Social Principles,* etc., p. 125.
34. Rauschenbusch, *op. cit.,* p. 127.

pleasures, poverty, and democracy.[35] The enthusiasm created by the discovery that the Christ had spoken on matters related to everyday American life brought about a demand for courses of study explaining his social utterances. Probably the most famous early outline of this type was by Professor Jeremiah W. Jenks of the economics faculty of Cornell University, entitled *The Political and Social Significance of the Life and Teachings of Jesus.*[36] Originating as a series of Sunday-morning talks before the university Christian Association, Jenks's course dealt with many of the topics listed above. In 1904 Shailer Mathews had prepared a series of studies on *The Social and Ethical Teaching of Jesus* for the American Institute of Sacred Literature. At this time the International Young Men's Christian Association was using similar courses by Professor Edward I. Bosworth of Oberlin College, although these were less concerned with social questions than with personal religion. In 1912 Professor Edward S. Parsons of Colorado College wrote a twelve-lesson outline of *The Social Message of Jesus* for the national Young Women's Christian Association, in which he dealt with the family, the state, social classes, the rich, and the poor. Perhaps the best known of these manuals today is *The Social Principles of Jesus*, written in 1916 by Walter Rauschenbusch. The most widely circulated of his books, this classic was used extensively by the Student Christian Movement. In it Rauschenbusch placed the doctrine of the kingdom at the heart of Jesus' message and related this ideal to contemporary problems.

In conclusion, we may summarize certain major emphases that were distinct features of this literature. Most writers would have agreed with President Henry Churchill King of Oberlin College when he declared that the Sermon on the Mount is a summary of Jesus' teaching. The entire body of his ethical and religious doctrines stands upon his faith in God as a father; therefore love is the highest life and the greatest possible good is the reign of God (the dominion of love) both in the individual and in society. Every man is a child of God and of infinite worth.[37] Joseph A. Leighton stressed the principle of reverence for personality as the heart of Jesus' social ethic. From "this notion of the transcendent aspect of the individual life"

35. For detailed references see the writer's forthcoming *Bibliography*.
36. Published in New York, 1906.   37. King, *op. cit.*, p. 271.

spring the social principles of Christianity.[38] But the application of such fundamentals would best be left to students of social science, in the judgment of Professor Cone, who stated his own findings thus:

Jesus confined his social teachings to expressing sympathy with the poor, to enjoining the duties of the brotherhood of man, to enforcing the practice of kindness, helpfulness, and charity, and to setting before men the supreme example of the divine benevolence. He also indicated in unmistakable terms his hostility to the selfish greed that accumulates riches to the injury of the weak . . . and to wealth itself as one of the evil powers of a wicked age.[39]

However, we shall see that social gospelers were not willing to delegate the task of religious social reform only to those suggested by this scholar!

After three decades of groping for a valid intellectual foundation, social Christianity now rested securely, it believed, upon the rationalistic and autonomous doctrines here examined, and so found itself at home in a pragmatic world. Oddly enough, the higher criticism that had once damaged the older supernaturalistic sanctions of religion now provided this newest branch of the Christian tradition with an essentially Protestant rationale that substituted ethical and humanitarian motives for traditional logical and theological interests.[40] However, the greatest prophet of the social gospel deliberately chose to base his proclamation not upon the teachings of Jesus, but preferred to state it in terms of the spiritual goal of the kingdom of God. We turn now to Walter Rauschenbusch's epochal statement of the new social faith.

38. Leighton, *op. cit.*, p. 119. See also Henry C. King, *The Moral and Religious Challenge of Our Times. The guiding principle in human development: reverence for personality* (New York, 1911).

39. Cone, *op. cit.*, p. 219. By permission of The Macmillan Company, publishers.

40. For a contemporary discussion of the ethicizing process, see Henry C. King, *Theology and the Social Consciousness* (New York, 1902), chap. vii. Also John Wright Buckham, *Christ and the Eternal Order* (Boston, 1906).

CHAPTER XIII

WALTER RAUSCHENBUSCH FORMULATES THE SOCIAL GOSPEL

My sole desire has been to summon the Christian passion for justice and the Christian powers of love and mercy to do their share in redeeming our social order from its inherent wrongs.

RAUSCHENBUSCH

THE prewar years of the twentieth century saw the rise of an immense body of literature stating the philosophy of social Christianity. Prominent metropolitan ministers and obscure country preachers, college and theological school professors, religious journalists and certain social scientists shared in this widespread concern. Most of the leaders with whose names we are familiar added to the swelling chorus and many new converts professed faith in the social gospel and wrote books and articles proclaiming it.[1]

Above this clamor of many voices the classic statement of

1. Chronologically, the most important books might be listed as follows: For a complete list see the writer's forthcoming *Bibliography of Social Christianity.*
Josiah Strong, *The Next Great Awakening* (New York, 1902).
Washington Gladden, *Social Salvation* (Boston and New York, 1902).
W. N. Sloan, *Social Regeneration* (Philadelphia, 1902).
Charles R. Brown, *The Social Message of the Modern Pulpit* (New York, 1906).
Samuel Plantz, *The Church and the Social Problem* (Cincinnati and New York, 1906).
Shailer Mathews, *The Church and the Changing Order* (New York, 1907).
Washington Gladden, *The Church and Modern Life* (Boston and New York, 1908).
Charles D. Williams, *A Valid Christianity for Today* (New York, 1909).
Shailer Mathews, *The Social Gospel* (Philadelphia, 1910).
William J. Tucker, *The Function of the Church in Modern Society* (Boston and New York, 1911).
Henry C. King, *The Moral and Religious Challenge of Our Times* (New York, 1911).
Charles R. Zahniser, *Social Christianity, the Gospel for an Age of Social Strain* (Nashville, 1911).
John Haynes Holmes, *The Revolutionary Function of the Modern Church* (New York, 1912).
Scott Nearing, *Social Religion* (New York, 1913).

American social Christianity is that of Walter Rauschenbusch, whose works were undoubtedly the most significant religious publications in the United States if not in the English language in the first two decades of the new century. Rauschenbusch, "perhaps the most creative spirit in the American theological world," unquestionably influenced the religious life of his time more deeply than did any other individual.[2] His books, which were translated into eight foreign languages, provided Protestantism with a vital, stimulating, and unsurpassed formulation of the Christian Sociology it had so long sought.

Walter Rauschenbusch was born in Rochester, New York, in 1861, in which city he spent his life, save for the decade of his ministry in New York City. Educated in Rochester and in Germany,[3] Rauschenbusch prepared himself for the foreign missionary service, but was rejected because of a suspected flaw in his Old Testament theology. The seventh of a line of ministers in a family whose religious heritage rooted deeply in pietism, young Rauschenbusch accepted at the age of twenty-five the pastorate of the Second Baptist Church in West Forty-fifth Street, New York, at an annual salary of $600. The eleven years spent in ministering to this poverty-stricken congregation proved to be the great dynamic experience of Rauschenbusch's life. Here the conventional pietism of his fathers failed to meet the complete needs of the endless procession of men "out of work, out of clothes, out of shoes, and out of hope," that wore down the threshold and wore away the hearts of the sensitive young pastor and his wife.[4] In the turmoil and toil of the great American metropolis the new gospel came to Rauschenbusch, writes his intimate friend, Professor F. W. C. Meyer of Rochester:

Henry George and Bellamy and Mazzini and Karl Marx and Tolstoi influenced him some, but above all the crying need of the com-

2. The statements concerning Rauschenbusch's influence were made by Mr. Edward C. Marsh, secretary of the Macmillan Company, Rauschenbusch's publisher. See F. W. C. Meyer, "Walter Rauschenbusch, Eine Wertung seines Lebenswerkes," in *Das Theologische Seminar der Deutschen Baptisten, Fünfundsiebzigstes Jubilätum* (Rochester, 1927), p. 27.

3. Rauschenbusch attended the Rochester Free Academy, the gymnasium at Gütersloh, the University of Rochester, and the Rochester Theological Seminary.

4. Ray Stannard Baker, *The Social Unrest* (New York, 1910), p. 268.

fortless multitude and the senseless inadequacy of competitive strife, the apparent possibility of cooperative service and the jubilant remedy of the message of the Kingdom took hold of his susceptible soul.[5]

Rauschenbusch himself confirmed the fact that Henry George in 1886 first awakened him to the world of social problems.[6] From 1889 to 1891 he joined with Leighton Williams, Elizabeth Post, and J. E. Raymond in the publication of *For the Right*, a monthly paper devoted to "the interests of the working people of New York City," whose problems it discussed "from the standpoint of Christian-socialism."[7] In 1891 Rauschenbusch traveled and studied abroad, devoting considerable time to sociology and to the teachings of Jesus while in Germany; he was so impressed by the British coöperative movement that he contemplated writing a book on it. Unquestionably one of the greatest influences in his development was the intimate fellowship of the Brotherhood of the Kingdom—"a powerful support and stimulus in those early days of isolation"—in whose discussions were clarified many of the ideas and arguments that afterward appeared in his books.[8] In 1897 Rauschenbusch returned to Rochester to teach in the German Department of the Rochester Theological Seminary. Five years later he became professor of Church History in the English division of the school, which position he held until his death in 1918. Such was his civic activity during these years that at his passing it was said that "Rochester has lost its first citizen."

Rauschenbusch's preëminence as a prophet of the social gospel rested as much upon his unique personality as upon the force of his ideas. Deeply and sincerely religious, he shared the mysticism but none of the fanaticism we have seen in George D. Herron. He lacked the urbanity of Lyman Abbott and the practicality of Washington Gladden, but he surpassed both in

---

5. F. W. C. Meyer, "Walter Rauschenbusch, Professor and Prophet," *The Standard* (February 3, 1912), p. 662 (with slight alteration).
6. Rauschenbusch, *Christianizing the Social Order* (New York, 1912), p. 394.
7. The only known available file of *For the Right* is that recently acquired by the Library of the Yale Divinity School.
8. See chap. vii, above. For a detailed account of the influence of the Brotherhood of the Kingdom on Rauschenbusch see the writer's article in *Church History,* VII (1938), 138–156.

popular appeal and in sense of humor. He possessed the earnest-ness of W. D. P. Bliss but more vividly and with deeper insight. Poet, mystic, seer, and teacher, Rauschenbusch kept close to humanity while reaching the heights of idealism in his message. "He was a modern saint as glorious as any of the distant past," said Harry Laidler.

With all his interest in socialism and in social reform Rausch-enbusch was ever and fundamentally a spiritual prophet. In "An Affirmation of Faith," perhaps as much of a creed as he ever avowed, Rauschenbusch said simply:

I affirm my faith in the reality of the spiritual world . . . I re-joice to believe in God . . .

I affirm my faith in the Kingdom of God and my hope in its final triumph . . .

I make an act of love toward all fellow men. . . . If any have wronged or grieved me, I . . . here and now forgive. I desire to minister God's love to men and to offer no hindrance to the free flow of his love through me.

I affirm my faith in life. I call life good and not evil. I accept the limitations of my own life. . . . Through the power of Christ which descends on me, I know that I can be more than conqueror.[9]

Such was the personal belief of "one of the great social prophets of America, and one of its true noblemen."

Although Rauschenbusch had been a prolific writer of maga-zine articles for twenty years and had frequently appeared on the platform of the Baptist Congress, he attracted little atten-tion beyond the Baptist fold prior to the publication in 1907 of *Christianity and the Social Crisis*, which established him at once as the recognized leader of the social-gospel movement. No one was more surprised at the electric effect of the book than Rauschenbusch himself. He now assumed the role of an evan-gelist and traveled the country over in response to requests for lectures before churches, student groups, the Y.M.C.A., theo-logical schools, summer conferences, and forums of every kind.

---

9. From a reprint. The whole may be found in *Prayers of the Social Awaken-ing* (Boston, 1925), pp. 148–149. Copyright, The Pilgrim Press. Used by per-mission.

Written in two vacation periods of six weeks each, *Christianity and the Social Crisis* showed "the learning of the scholar, the vision of the poet, and the passion of the prophet." Crisp and sometimes whimsical in style, yet borne upon a deep undercurrent of religious fervor, the book was an admirable statement of theoretical and practical Christian Sociology. Beginning with an analysis of the social and ethical aspects of the religion of the Old Testament, Rauschenbusch pointed out neglected areas in Biblical interpretation and asserted the interest of the Hebrew prophets in morals, in the social and political life of their nation, and in the condition of the poor and oppressed. Jesus he saw as the divine founder of a new society, whose plan for salvation included "all human needs and powers and relations." Rauschenbusch then contrasted the contemporary social impotence of Christianity with the social power of the early church, analyzed the place of the church in modern society, and concluded with a chapter on "What to do." *Christianity and the Social Crisis* was most recently reprinted in 1937.

His second book was well described by its title. *For God and the People: Prayers of the Social Awakening,* first published in 1910, was the outcome of a conviction that the social movement needed to be grounded in religion and that the new type of religious experience ought to find conscious and social expression. Marked by their author's poetic feeling, the prayers were for days and seasons, for social groups and classes, for the kingdom of God, for "prophets and pioneers"; "prayers of wrath" were against war, alcoholism, mammon, and impurity; those for "the progress of humanity" included the city and the coöperative commonwealth.

The next of Rauschenbusch's works came from the press in 1912. "Wholly without a note of hatred," *Christianizing the Social Order* was nevertheless "a day of judgment" in the eyes of many. The central feature of this book was a careful examination of "our semi-Christian social order"—a frankly socialistic critique of capitalism, and the statement of a religious foundation for social reform. Although he recognized the value of the Christian doctrines of stewardship and charity, Rauschenbusch insisted upon social justice and economic democracy as minimum requirements upon which a Christian social order could be built. In 1916 he wrote a little manual on *The Social*

Principles of Jesus, which proved the most popular of all his books, as we have seen in Chapter XII.[10]

The last and probably the greatest of Rauschenbusch's books was *A Theology for the Social Gospel,* his Nathaniel W. Taylor Lectures at the Yale Divinity School in 1917. Sensing the danger to both theology and the social gospel if the social movement should lose its religious character, Rauschenbusch proceeded upon the assumption that "we need a systematic theology large enough to match the social gospel and vital enough to back it." Although he devoted much attention to the social implications of sin and salvation, Rauschenbusch also discussed in this light the doctrines of revelation, inspiration, prophecy, baptism, the Lord's Supper, eschatology, the atonement, and the conceptions of God and of the Holy Spirit. Again, as in all his books, he placed the kingdom at the center of his argument, here presenting it in more exact form than previously.

Rauschenbusch's style was easy and at times brilliant. Whatever subject matter he used seemed to fit itself to his purpose. As Professor Meyer said, "history became his story." But journalistic methods did not rob his works of solidity. His economic thought followed the leading authorities of the day: R. T. Ely, John Graham Brooks, Nicholas Paine Gilman, John R. Commons, John A. Fitch, F. H. Giddings, Robert Hunter, J. W. Jenks, Tom L. Johnson, Graham Taylor, and Émile de Laveleye. In theology Rauschenbusch acknowledged his debt to Schleiermacher and Ritschl; Royce's philosophy of loyalty influenced him considerably; we have previously noted his debt to Henry George; he not infrequently referred to E. A. Ross, Werner Sombart, John Spargo, Jacob Riis, and Adolph Harnack; he was profoundly affected by the socialism of the English nonconformist minister Richard Heath, as expressed in *The Captive City of God.*

A child of his age, Rauschenbusch shared those "ruling ideas" that we have seen provided the background of the theological climate at the turn of the century. He described the social order in solidaristic terms, declaring St. Paul's comparison of the church to the human body to be "the highest possible

10. The International Y.M.C.A. distributed 20,000 copies of this book the first year of its publication. Royalties on it far exceeded the total for all his other books.

philosophy of human society": the ideal social order is an organism.[11] So integrated is society that when one man sins, others suffer; when one social class sins, others are involved; such sufferings are solidaristic.[12] God was for Rauschenbusch "the common basis of all our life"—the ground of the spiritual oneness of the race and of the hope for its future unity. The consciousness of solidarity is therefore of the essence of an ethical and social religion. "We love and serve God when we love and serve our fellows, whom he loves and in whom he lives. We rebel against God and repudiate his will when we set our profit and ambition above the welfare of our fellows and above the Kingdom of God which binds them together."[13]

Rauschenbusch's central concept was the kingdom of God, which he believed to have been the heart of Jesus' teaching. Aware of the influence of Darwinism upon theology, he declared that the kingdom idea was the result of translating the theory of evolution into religious terms.[14] He saw the kingdom as a collective conception involving the whole social life of man. The doctrine "is itself the social gospel." Without it the notion of social redemption will become but an annex to the orthodox scheme of salvation. Rauschenbusch based both his criticism of modern society and his program for its reformation on his belief in an immanent, active God upon whose indwelling could be predicated the solidarity of that human society whose progressive perfection would realize the divine kingdom of righteousness and justice.

Rauschenbusch's case against capitalism rooted in religion and ethics. Well read in socialism, he stripped that critical weapon of its crasser features and used it to demonstrate the unchristian character of a social order that "tempts, defeats, drains, and degrades, and leaves men stunted, cowed, and shamed in their manhood."[15] However, there are in our society certain institutions that have been partly Christianized: the family, the church, the agencies of education, and politics insofar as it has been democratized. These aid the trend toward a

---

11. Rauschenbusch, *Christianizing,* etc., p. 366.
12. *A Theology for the Social Gospel* (New York, 1917), p. 182.
13. *Op. cit.,* p. 48. By permission of The Macmillan Company, publishers.
14. *Christianizing,* etc., p. 90.
15. This critique of capitalism is an outline of Parts III and IV of *Christianizing the Social Order.*

Christian society in that they provide surroundings that exert upon individuals dynamic influences for good. Largely the product of Christianity, their accomplishments afford optimistic ground for further effort in similar directions. Present social ills are bred in the unchristianized areas of modern life, notably in the business world. In commerce and industry "we encounter the great collective inhumanities that shame our Christian feeling, such as child labor and the bloody total of industrial accidents." Prostitution, poverty, and political corruption are also chronic ailments of the social order produced by the industrial revolution. The process of Christianizing society, as Rauschenbusch saw it, was therefore the strengthening of its fraternal and coöperative elements, and their extension into the competitive and hence primitive realms.

First of the basic tenets of capitalism to come under Rauschenbusch's scrutiny was competition—"the law of tooth and nail." One nation after another has been forced to restrict the murderous effects of this shortsighted and suicidal policy. It is a denial of fraternity and when allowed full freedom brings back the savage era, dechristianizing the social order. It has brought into play the lower instincts of selfishness, covetousness, and craft, rather than mutual interest, good will, comradeship, and solidarity—the marks of a Christian social order.

Secondly, Rauschenbusch saw "the last entrenchment of autocracy" in the dictatorial and monopolistic character of great corporations. The primary ethical problem of the age was the universal and perennial unrest of labor, due to "some constitutional maladjustment in the moral relations" between the managing and employing classes and the workers. He saw the crux of the problem as the lack of industrial democracy—the antithesis of modern trends toward freedom and equal rights for all. "Every business concern is a little monarchy." Workers comprise a subject class, owning no tools, having no voice in industrial management, and holding no control over their own production. This "contradiction of American ideals" Rauschenbusch regarded as a menace to American institutions and a barrier to Christianizing our social order. Power must be shifted from the ruling class to the people, in industry as well as in politics.

Rauschenbusch's third count against capitalism cited the evil effects of modern economic organization as evidenced in adulteration of foods, short weights, spurious advertising, overproduction, and similar practices perilous not only to the consumer but also to business and national morality. The manifold forms of dishonesty met with in business are the natural result of a relation based almost wholly on individual selfishness, and hardly at all on fraternity or solidarity. In this system where the middleman is the controlling factor the dominant motive is not to supply human needs but to make a profit.

The subserviency of capitalism to the profit motive stamped it, as Rauschenbusch's fourth point, "a mammonistic organization with which Christianity can never be content." Insofar as profit is the just reward for able work it is entirely legitimate. But when it becomes large and dissociated from hard work "it is traceable to some kind of monopoly privilege and power." To the extent that it is derived from low wages, high rates, or unsocial practices "it is tribute collected by power from the helpless, a form of legalized graft, and a contradiction of Christian relations."

Capitalistic business is thus to be distinguished from the home, the school, the church, and the democratized state "as an unregenerate part of the social order, not based on freedom, love, and mutual service, as they are, but on autocracy, antagonism of interests, and exploitation." This is not to condemn the moral character of men in business; they have made it endurable by their high qualities. Likewise the state has pulled a few teeth and shortened the tether of greed. At the same time capitalism has invaded several of the regenerate spheres. The life of the masses has been kept low by poverty. Beauty has been sacrificed to profit. The home, sanctuary of God's gift of love, has been broken into and crippled; prostitution multiplies. Capitalism sets private good before public weal—corrupting our legislatures, executives, and courts, influencing the press, and vindictively opposing those who stand up for the common good. It has generated "a spirit of its own which is antagonistic to the spirit of Christianity; a spirit of hardness and cruelty that neutralizes the Christian spirit of love; a spirit that sets material goods above spiritual possessions."

Religion declares the supreme value of life, said Rauschenbusch, while business worships profit. By splitting society into warring classes capitalism reduces the Christian ideal of unity and solidarity to a harmless sentiment. Based on the principle of autocracy, it suppresses the Christian sense of the worth of personality, the love of freedom, and independence of action. Christianity proclaims all men equal; capitalism perpetuates inequality by its distribution of property. Jesus bade us strive for the reign of God and its justice; capitalism urges us to work for personal enrichment and to cultivate the love of money for its own sake; it rewards most generously "those who use monopoly for extortion." If we can trust the Bible, God is against capitalism, its methods, spirit, and results.[16]

To balance this Christian version of the socialist critique of capitalism, Rauschenbusch laid down five fundamental requisites of a Christian economic order: social justice, collective property rights, industrial democracy, approximate equality, and coöperation. The most striking of these was the demand for justice, which underlay all the others and which he regarded as "the fundamental step toward Christianizing the social order." Particularly in three areas ought injustice to be corrected: private property in land and resources, private control of transportation and communication, and private monopoly of inventions and industrial processes—all of which situations had been intensified by the rise of corporate combinations able to fix prices and dictate wages.[17] The first of these could be eliminated by adequate taxation of land values. Public ownership or the restriction of corporations to fair incomes would control the second, while a public grant or royalty system would remedy the third.

Rauschenbusch believed in "property and a job as a means of grace" for the common man. Property is needed for the support of the well-rounded life. Therefore, he declared,

A condition in which millions of people have no share at all in the productive capital of the nation, and hardly enough even of furniture, clothing, and food to cover their nakedness and nourish their bodies, debases humanity, undermines the republic, and desiccates religion.[18]

The workingman needs property, but today ownership must acquire new forms, consisting in "a small share of and a right

16. *A Theology*, etc., p. 184.   17. *Christianizing*, etc., p. 337.
18. *Op. cit.*, p. 341. By permission of The Macmillan Company, publishers.

in a collective accumulation which belongs to a larger group jointly." Extension of this principle would provide sickness and old-age protection. The worker's minimum-property right in industry must be recognized in his tenure of a job as long as he does honest and efficient work.

Further, there must be industrial democracy. "Political democracy without economic democracy is an uncashed promissory note, a pot without the roast, a form without substance." Rauschenbusch frankly favored labor in its struggle with capital. Employers resisting the workers' demand for the democratic conduct of industry he likened to Louis XIV, and declared that labor organizations had never inflicted as much wrong as they had suffered. Not only should unionization be tolerated, but the law ought to recognize, facilitate, and regulate it. The transition to industrial democracy will test both the Americanism and the Christianity of employers. In his demand for democracy and approximate equality, Rauschenbusch asserted that we ought at least to be able to refrain from perpetuating and increasing the handicap of the weaker groups by the existing enormous inequalities of property. The growth of the great fortunes he saw as "an institutional denial of the fundamental truths of our religion."

An economic basis of coöperation is necessary for the realization of genuine social fraternity, said Rauschenbusch, who regarded contemporary trends toward business combination as evidences of a gradually evolving coöperative system. However, he declared, the unsocial perversity of capitalism holds us back unduly, as is illustrated in many cities where a genuine desire for coöperative management of utilities is frustrated by a group bent on profit. Capitalism likewise opposes labor's efforts to achieve solidarity. Business itself would like to unite even more than it has, but the public has found that dangerous. And so our public life has become "a huge tragi-comedy in which we are all trying not to do what we all know we shall have to do anyway. This is the enchanted maze into which the wily Devil of Profit has conjured us. . . ."

As a specific program, Rauschenbusch advocated measures designed to aid in the conservation of life, the socializing of property, the control and management of monopolies and utilities by the community, the improvement of the condition of the working class, and a revival of social religion. With respect to the first of these, he suggested limitation of the hours of labor, establishment of minimum wages, prevention of industrial diseases, protection from dangerous machinery, industrial accident insurance, care of the aged, and proper housing. But before such a program could be made truly effective it would be necessary to socialize property in order that it be "more directly available for the service of all." Social change has made evils out of institutions once regarded as basic rights: private development of natural resources, formerly legitimate and useful, "is now becoming a dangerous encroachment on the rights of society." The great necessities—coal, iron, watersheds, harbors, etc.—must be owned by society for the common good. This is not to suggest that the area of private property for use be invaded. The idea that there can be absolute ownership in a mine, as in a coat, is preposterous. Were the rocks of Pennsylvania stored for the benefit of a few stockholders or for the use of a great nation? Along with the socialization of property there would go an increase in public functions, accompanied by a rise in public spirit. The natural monopolies must become public property not only for the sake of efficient and coherent management but for the impetus to civic morality and public spirit.

The most important factor presaging a Christian social order was, in Rauschenbusch's mind, the rise of the working class. The labor movement is the salient fact of present history, "and if the banner of the Kingdom of God is to enter through the gates of the future, it will have to be carried by the tramping hosts of labor."[19] Although he discussed various aids to the workers, Rauschenbusch's major emphases were upon security, property rights, and economic democracy. He was greatly impressed by the ethical character of the labor movement: "The working class embodies an immense fund of moral energy which we need to equip the Christian social order." The virtues stressed by labor are distinctly praiseworthy; collectively the leaders of labor stand for a higher morality than does business.

Rauschenbusch's attitude toward socialism has been suggested, but it is worthy of note that although he regarded collectivism with great favor he was not a "party man" in the sense in which Bliss and Herron supported the political Social-

19. *Op. cit.,* p. 449. By permission.

ist movement. His sympathy with the socialistic viewpoint appeared as early as the first issue of *For the Right* in 1889. In 1894 he told the German Young Men's Christian Association of Philadelphia that one would be a better Christian for being a socialist, and a better socialist for being a Christian.[20] In *Christianizing the Social Order* Rauschenbusch declared that regardless of party shortcomings socialism was a tool in the hands of the Almighty. We may assume that his mature judgment on socialism was that expressed in terms of Christian Socialism in his article under that title published posthumously in the Mathews–Smith *Dictionary of Religion and Ethics* in 1921. Differentiating between socialism and Christian Socialism, Rauschenbusch declared the latter to be "a peculiar genus of Socialism":

The Christian sense of the sanctity of life and personality and of the essential equality of men re-enforces the Socialist condemnation of the present social order. The religious belief in the Fatherhood of God, in the fraternal solidity of men, and in the ultimate social redemption of the race through Christ lends a religious quality to the Socialist ideals.[21]

Christian Socialism is in conscious antagonism with orthodox socialism in that it sets positive religious faith against a materialistic philosophy; it believes in the value and social possibilities of the churches; it stresses religious regeneration as a factor in the salvation of society; while accepting economic determinism it asserts the reality and independent power of spiritual forces; it recognizes the influence of social environment while pointing out the moral responsibility of the individual; and it stands for the sanctity of the family and the radical Christian attitude regarding intoxicants.

But Rauschenbusch was concerned with the economic system because he looked upon it as "the strategical key to the spiritual conquest of the modern world." Near the conclusion of *Christianizing the Social Order* he declared that although much

20. Rauschenbusch, *Kann ein Christ auch ein Socialist sein?* . . . (Philadelphia, 1894), pp. 28–29.
21. Rauschenbusch, "Christian Socialism," in Shailer Mathews and G. B. Smith, *A Dictionary of Religion and Ethics* (New York, 1921), pp. 90–91. By permission of The Macmillan Company, publishers.

of his argument had seemed to sag "down to the level of mere economic discussion," such an estimate would be superficial, for this was "a religious book from beginning to end," its sole concern being for the kingdom of God and the salvation of men. Within the inclusive religious and social framework of the kingdom ideal Rauschenbusch formulated his criticism of the church and of theology, and stated his program for the reorientation of the church to her task. His mature thought concerning the kingdom was compressed into a pivotal lecture in *A Theology for the Social Gospel*. Here was the final statement of the vision first seen during the trying but formative struggles of the New York pastorate—a conception shaped by study as a teacher of church history and in the spiritual mold of the Brotherhood of the Kingdom.

The doctrine of the kingdom of God is itself the social gospel. It was the center of Jesus' teaching. He always spoke of it, "and from it looked out on the world and the work he had to do." He certainly never thought of founding the institution that has grown up in his name. But when his disciples united in a society their chief interest naturally began to flow toward the church, and the kingdom ideal gradually faded. This process was completed by Augustine; the Reformation failed to replace the kingdom hope in its proper context; its present revival is due to the historical study of the Bible and to the social gospel. The withdrawal of the kingdom idea caused theology to lose its contact with Jesus and to become to a certain extent incapable of understanding him, so that his teachings had to be rediscovered in our day. Since his ethical principles were largely the outgrowth of his conception of the kingdom, loss of the latter from theology involved the disappearance of the former from Christian practice. When theology placed its emphasis upon the church, which is a fellowship for worship, the religious enthusiasm that might have saved mankind from its greatest sins was diverted to ceremonialism. The kingdom is a fellowship of righteousness, and when it ceased to be the dominating religious reality, the church became the *summum bonum* and its promotion the promotion of Christianity. The result was the removal of moral restrictions from ecclesiastical policies and the growth of such dogmas as the medieval conception of the supremacy of the church over the state. In the absence of the kingdom's ethical dynamic, unjust social conditions were allowed to develop, the practical program of the church remained narrow, and theology was confined to unproductive pursuits.

The hope of the kingdom contains the revolutionary force of Christianity. Had it remained active through the ages, the church could not have "been salaried by autocratic class governments to keep the democratic and economic impulses of the people under check." Without it, movements toward democracy and social justice were left without religious support. Even today many Christians can see no religious significance in social justice and fraternity because these neither increase the number of conversions nor fill the churches. Secular life has been belittled in comparison with ecclesiastical; services rendered the church are rated higher religiously than those performed for the community; thus the normal activities of the common man as well as prophetic contributions to the social weal are denied religious value. Apart from the notion of the kingdom individual salvation is seen only in relation to the church and the future life, and not with respect to social salvation. And finally, theology has been deprived of the inspiration of the great ideas bred by the kingdom hope and by labor for its realization. "The Kingdom of God breeds prophets; the Church breeds priests and theologians." The kingdom is to theology what outdoor color and light are to art.

As the starting point of a positive statement concerning the kingdom Rauschenbusch declared the chief contribution of the social gospel to theology to be the giving of new vitality and importance to the kingdom ideal as (1) "divine in its origin, progress, and consummation." Initiated by Christ, it is "sustained by the Holy Spirit and it will be brought to its fulfillment by the power of God in his own time." So slender are its human resources against the powers of evil that the only explanation of it satisfactory to the religious mind is that which sees its miraculous character as "the continuous revelation of the power, the righteousness, and the love of God." Further (2) it contains "the teleology of the Christian religion," that is, it is a dynamic conception that looks to ends to be accomplished rather than to rites that must be preserved. As long as there is evil in the world, the kingdom will be engaged in conflict. (3) Since God is in it, it is in both present crisis and future possibility: "It is the energy of God realizing itself in human life": we see "the Kingdom of God as always coming, always pressing in on the present, always big with possibility, and always inviting immediate action. . . . The Kingdom is for each of us the supreme task and the supreme gift of God. . . ."[22]

(4) Although before Christ men had caught fleeting glimpses of the kingdom, it receives its distinctive interpretation within our religion from him. He emancipated it from previous limitations, making it world-wide and spiritual. He made the purpose of salvation essential in it, imposed his mind, will, personality, and love on it, and not only preached it but initiated it by his life and work.

(5) The kingdom is humanity organized according to the will of God. It tends toward a social order that will best guarantee the highest development of personality, in accordance with Christ's revelation of the divine worth of human life. It likewise implies the progressive reign of his law of love in human affairs.[23] As the supreme purpose of God, the kingdom (6) must be the end for which the church exists: its institutions, "its activities, its worship, and its theology must in the long run be tested by its effectiveness in creating the kingdom of God." So also (7), must all problems of personal salvation be considered from the point of view of the kingdom. The two are to be synthesized; such an orientation will also give us a new understanding of the redemptive work of Christ.[24] Lastly (8), the kingdom is not confined within the church:

It embraces the whole of human life. It is the Christian transfiguration of the social order. The Church is one social institution alongside of the family, the industrial organization of society, and the State. The Kingdom of God is in all these, and realizes itself through them all. . . . The Church is indispensable to the reli-

22. *A Theology,* etc., p. 141. By permission.

23. The highest expression of love is the free surrender of what is truly our own: "No social group or organization can claim to be clearly within the Kingdom of God which drains others for its own ease, and resists the effort to abate this fundamental evil. This involves the redemption of society from private property in natural resources of the earth, and from any condition in industry which makes monopoly profits possible." *A Theology,* p. 143. By permission. The similarity of this to Herron's doctrine of social sacrifice is obvious.

24. Compare with the Anglican emphasis on the incarnation as expressed in the popular book by Canon W. H. Fremantle, *The World as the Subject of Redemption* (New York, 1895).

gious education of humanity and to the conservation of religion, but the greatest future awaits religion in the public life of humanity.[25]

In the light of this ideal Rauschenbusch contended for a reevaluation of the church's mission and a new interpretation of theology. Specifically this meant the rejection of "the fictions of capitalism" and in general it inferred adoption of the program of social Christianity. The task of the church is to preach the "Word of God," but in no narrow or traditional manner. The gospel of Christ touches all life and is quick and piercing like a sword; wherever wrong is done to the weak or an opportunity offers to advance Christian principles, there "the church has a word of the Lord to men."[26] It should aid in the preservation of American ideals of the family, democracy, individual development, education, leisure, and the home. It should mediate between classes, uphold the spiritual ideal against mammonism and materialism, and champion the principles that will produce a Christian social order.

In *A Theology for the Social Gospel* Rauschenbusch interpreted many traditional Christian doctrines in social terms. His treatment of sin and salvation is illuminating, inasmuch as it rested upon the solidaristic view of society. From the individual standpoint, he began, sin is selfishness. A democratic idea of God will render this conception realistic, however, because humanity is always involved in sin of any kind and God is identified with humanity. We love and serve God as we love and serve our fellows. But sin is more than individual; it is transmitted socially through custom; the institutions of society acquire what may be called "the superpersonal forces of evil."[27] The salvation of these entities is to be accomplished by bringing them under the law of Christ. Saved institutions—the family, education, the church, coöperatives—are democratic, whereas unsaved ones—corporations, monopolies, war, the agencies of competition—are autocratic. One class is under the law of Christ, the other under the rule of mammon.

25. *A Theology*, etc., p. 145. By permission.
26. Rauschenbusch, "The Church and Social Questions," in *Conservation of National Ideals* (Chicago, 1911), p. 120.
27. At this point Rauschenbusch acknowledged his debt to Josiah Royce's *Problem of Christianity.*

The fundamental step of repentance and conversion for professions and organizations is to give up monopoly power and the incomes derived from legalized extortion, and to come under the law of service, content with a fair income for honest work. The corresponding step in the case of governments and political oligarchies, both in monarchies and in capitalistic semi-democracies, is to submit to real democracy. There-with they step out of the Kingdom of Evil into the Kingdom of God.[28]

The doctrine of the atonement might also be interpreted in terms of social solidarity. Some half-dozen public sins combined to kill Jesus, and insofar as the personal sins of men have built up these corporate sins, Jesus came into collision with the totality of evil in mankind. No legal fiction of imputation is necessary to show that "He was wounded for our transgressions"; solidarity explains it.[29]

Such, in brief, was the social gospel of Walter Rauschenbusch. For him it was "the old message of salvation, but enlarged and intensified" so as to "bring men under repentance for their collective sins and to create a more sensitive and more modern conscience."

The social movement is the most important ethical and spiritual movement in the modern world, and the social gospel is the response of the Christian conscience to it. Therefore it had to be. The social gospel registers the fact that for the first time in history the spirit of Christianity has had a chance to form a working partnership with real social and psychological science. It is the religious reaction to the historic advent of democracy. It seeks to put the democratic spirit, which the Church inherited from Jesus and the prophets, once more in control of the institutions and teachings of the Church.[30]

28. *A Theology*, etc., p. 117. By permission.
29. *Op. cit.*, p. 248.
30. *Op. cit.*, pp. 4–5. By permission.
The writer wishes to acknowledge his indebtedness to Mrs. Walter Rauschenbusch, to Dr. D. R. Sharpe (the official biographer of Rauschenbusch), to Professors F. W. C. Meyer and C. H. Moehlman, to the Rauschenbusch Lectureship Committee of the Colgate-Rochester Divinity School, to The Macmillan Company, and The Pilgrim Press, and to Dr. Vernon P. Bodein, whose Yale Ph.D. dissertation of 1936, *The Relation of the Social Gospel of Walter Rauschenbusch to Religious Education*, is the most careful study of its kind to date.

CHAPTER XIV

THE CHRISTIAN SOCIALIST
FELLOWSHIP

In our Christian Socialist Fellowship the Fatherhood of God, the Brotherhood of Man, the Earth for all, and loyalty to the International Socialist Movement as the means of realizing the social ideal of Jesus, seem the essential points.

The Christian Socialist

IT has been repeatedly pointed out that the two foci of social-gospel interest during the fifty years covered by this study were socialism and the labor situation. Prior to 1890 socialism was rejected unanimously by the clergy, although the validity of certain of its claims was admitted. The utopian Christian Socialism of the 'nineties proved in practical terms to be little more than a minority emphasis upon the social aspects of Christianity. However, with the advent of the new century left-wing Christian Socialism became both Marxist and political. The central feature of radical social Christianity during the prewar years of the twentieth century was a group of enterprising clergymen who organized the Christian Socialist Fellowship both to obtain the adherence of the churches to the principles of international socialism and to secure their allegiance to the Socialist party of America as the political means of accomplishing the Christian revolution.

Conservative ministers continued to reject socialism on grounds that are sufficiently familiar to need little repetition. The Reverend Edward R. Hartman declared socialism to be "anti-Christian and one of the greatest deceptions of the age" because it sought to establish brotherhood by force, because it eliminated the need for the sacrifice of Christ and proclaimed man's ability to save himself, and because it substituted "the fallible reasoning of human minds" for the plan of the Creator.[1] Another student of the problem took Herron to task for

1. Edward R. Hartman, *Socialism versus Christianity* (New York, 1909), p. 243.

calling Jesus a social agitator or the Sermon on the Mount a treatise on political economy, and declared the weakness of socialism to be its failure to realize the necessity of moral transformation; making no appeal to character, it never urges purity, love, or self-restraint; it errs in relying on externals to change human personality. All it desires is "a well-filled larder, a good bank account, a home, with books and pictures, and a moderate amount of time for rest and enjoyment." But Jesus said that if one has all that and has not developed his soul, his life is a failure.[2]

As had been true of previous eras, liberal clergymen found certain values in socialism. In *Christianity and Socialism* Washington Gladden declared that neither individualism nor socialism furnished a safe principle of social organization but that the needed peaceful evolution could well be achieved through the coördination of the two. The true spirit of socialism is manifest "in the habit of regarding our work . . . as a social function."[3] Professor Henry C. Vedder of Crozer Theological Seminary pointed out that Jesus' realistic approach to the social problem was from within, while socialism in attempting to solve it from without follows an illusory method. But the two need not be hostile; socialists and Christians are natural allies. The changes proposed by socialism "are a wholly desirable complement to the spiritual change contemplated by Jesus." His kingdom and the ideal society anticipated by socialists are indistinguishable in their material base. The moral power of socialism is due to elements borrowed from the ethics of Jesus; the golden age of equity and equality to which it looks forward "is essentially the millennium of Jewish prophets and Christian sages." While Jesus and socialism follow different methods, "they are neither contradictory nor mutually exclusive, but rather complementary."[4] The Reverend Charles Stelzle of the Presbyterian Department of Church and Labor declared that the church ought to recognize socialism and give it credit for what

2. Gerald D. Heuver, *The Teachings of Jesus Concerning Wealth* (Chicago, 1903), p. 122.

3. Washington Gladden, *Christianity and Socialism* (New York and Cincinnati, 1905), chaps. iii, iv. See also Percy S. Grant, *Socialism and Christianity* (New York, 1910), p. 22.

4. Henry C. Vedder, *Socialism and the Ethics of Jesus* (New York, 1912), p. 386.

good it possessed, at the same time asserting the right of others than socialists to interpret the social principles of Jesus; the working classes should be informed that the church does not endorse the present social system.[5]

A Syracuse, New York, minister held that rejection of political socialism did not release the clergy from the obligation to be social Christians or Christian Socialists, for the half-truths of socialism are to be harmonized in the latter.[6] Professor Vida D. Scudder, frankly a political Socialist, hoped to reconcile the conservative Christian and the revolutionary socialist by showing the similarity between the thought of Jesus and that of the socialist. To claim Jesus as a socialist in the modern sense is a sentimental fallacy, she declared. He took no account of economic forces, but he planted an ideal that "bears a subtly intimate relation to each successive stage of social progress." If his church can now recover the kingdom ideal as a practical social program it may itself survive through the transformation of the rising social democracy into the ideal commonwealth.[7] But though it may provide the material foundation, socialism will never be that beloved community, for the consummation of the kingdom of God is in eternity and not in time. Had the movement we are now to examine preserved the sane enthusiasm of this socialist Christian, it might have proved more than a specious propagandism.

The Christian Socialist Fellowship came into being when a few former members of the Social Crusade,[8] heartened and unified by reading *The Christian Socialist*, organized in 1906 "to permeate churches, denominations and other religious institutions with the social message of Jesus; to show that Socialism is the necessary economic expression of the Christian life; to end the class struggle by establishing industrial democracy and to hasten the reign of justice and brotherhood upon earth." *The Christian Socialist* had been started in 1903 by an obscure minister of Webster City, Iowa, who shortly merged his interests

5. Charles Stelzle, *Christianity's Storm Center* (New York, 1907), pp. 34–38.
6. Herbert G. Coddington, *Christianity and Socialism* (Syracuse, N.Y., 1905), pamphlet.
7. Vida D. Scudder, *Socialism and Character* (Boston and New York, 1912), p. 400. Miss Scudder was greatly indebted to Rauschenbusch for her argument in this book.
8. See chap. xi, above.

with those of the Reverend Edward Ellis Carr of Danville, Illinois,[9] where the paper was subsequently published as a biweekly with George Willis Cooke, George E. Littlefield, and J. Stitt Wilson among its eight associate editors. Many religious radicals were added to this list from time to time. Carr, who assumed the editorship, declared *The Christian Socialist's* message to be "to the Church, urging ministers and people to advocate the Real Gospel of Christ, and to the Socialist Party, urging members and leaders not to ignore or belittle the tremendous importance of religion."[10] His crusade, compared with those of the Middle Ages, would be to rescue "the glorious gospel from the whited sepulchre of modern capitalism, which is the worst infidelity of all time." Avowing its class consciousness as well as its religious character, the paper was admittedly more concerned to reach Christians than socialists.[11]

An eight-page sheet featuring indiscriminate socialist propaganda, reform news and articles, poetry, and comments, *The Christian Socialist* was able to claim two thousand clergymen subscribers by 1909 and a peak circulation of some twenty thousand prior to its collapse in the postwar antisocialist reaction. Although, as in the case of *The Dawn,* many of its articles were reprints, contributors included Graham Taylor, Walter Rauschenbusch, Edwin Markham, Eugene V. Debs, Charles Stelzle, Rufus W. Weeks,[12] and John Bascom. In 1906 the paper began a series of socialistic Sunday School lessons, prepared by the Reverend Frederick G. Strickland, a former editor of *The Social Forum.*[13] The next year the editorial staff was augmented by the addition of J. O. Benthall, previously a Baptist minister, whose conversion to socialism caused him to resign from the Anti-Saloon League in order to administer the "Chicago Christian Socialist Center."[14] A unique publicity program

9. In 1907 it moved to Chicago, remaining there. There are no biographical data of any sort available concerning Carr.
10. "Knights of the Cross," *Christian Socialist,* II, No. 5, 3. Hereafter this paper will be referred to as *CS.*
11. *CS,* II, No. 7, 4.
12. Weeks sometimes wrote under the pseudonym of "William Whately." A vice-president of the New York Life Insurance Company, he appears to have been the intellectual leader of the Fellowship, and probably to have supported it financially to quite an extent.
13. See chap. xi, above.
14. See the *Arena,* 37 (1907), 307, 600–604.

carried out by *The Christian Socialist* was the publication of special denominational issues featuring socialistically inclined leaders of the communion in question which were sent to all the clergy of that church throughout the country. The Baptist supplement, for example, gave chief place to Walter Rauschenbusch and contained articles also by Leighton Williams, J. Peter Brunner, and Harvey Dee Brown. In time all the important religious groups were thus propagandized—even the Catholics and the Swedenborgians; seventy-five thousand copies of a special temperance edition were circulated, in which Frances Willard was claimed as a socialist.

The Christian Socialist Fellowship developed out of an exchange of ideas printed as letters in *The Christian Socialist*, much as the Christian Commonwealth Colony had been recruited through the correspondence column of *The Kingdom* a decade earlier.[15] Agitation for a rebirth of the Social Crusade of J. Stitt Wilson was begun in *The Christian Socialist* in June, 1905, with a proposal by Lucien V. Rule of Goshen, Kentucky, for some kind of organization of religiously minded socialists. Such was the interest displayed by readers of *The Christian Socialist* in the suggestion of this former comrade of Wilson that a regular department was devoted to plans for the new Crusade. On August 15 a tentative statement of principles was printed, looking toward "a Fellowship of brothers and comrades pledged to the support of the International Socialist Movement as the means of hastening that good time of God and Man, which we believe to be very near at hand." The next June a "Christian Socialist Conference" was held in Louisville, to which were invited all men and women "who thoroughly believe in the Christianity of Socialism and the Socialism of Christianity—who are loyal to *the Socialist party* and believe that socialism should also have *a distinctly religious expression.*"[16] Delegates from seven states attended the meeting, which proved to be the first annual conference of the Christian Socialist Fellowship. In addition to the promoters of the gathering—Carr, Rule, W. H. Ramsey, and W. L. Wilson—the indefatigable W. D. P. Bliss was there with an address on "The Gospel for Today."[17] A resolution was adopted declaring the adherence of

15. See chap. xi, above.   16. *CS*, III, No. 9 (May 1, 1906), 1.
17. See chap. x, above.

the Fellowship to "the principles of International Socialism" and endorsing "the platform and present organization of the Socialist Party of America." We have quoted the statement of purpose above.

The active propagandism of the Fellowship spread widely during the next year, *The Christian Socialist* reporting the interest of hundreds of ministers. In June, 1907, a second conference was held in Chicago, with Jane Addams among the speakers. Resolutions were addressed to the churches and to the socialists of America. The following year was marked by considerable activity on the part of district secretaries scattered from Boston to Montana, while an intellectual achievement of some note was the translation by Rufus W. Weeks of the German social democratic tract of Herman Kutter, *They Must (Sie Müssen)*.[18] The Fellowship's high-water mark seems to have been reached with its third conference which met in New York in May, 1908, the chief feature of which was a mass meeting attended by an audience of more than three thousand who sat for over four hours under the spell of Eugene V. Debs, Rose Pastor Stokes, and Edwin Markham. The names of Bliss, Charles P. Fagnani, Rabbi Wise, John Spargo, Morris Hillquit, and Rufus W. Weeks appeared on the conference program, while congratulatory messages were read from Episcopal Bishop Franklin S. Spalding of Utah[19] and the veteran liberal R. Heber Newton. Enthusiasm ran high and the gathering was cited by the *Outlook* as plain proof of the growth of socialistic sentiments in the churches.[20] Here it developed that the strongest locals of the Fellowship were in and near New York.[21] Under the aggressive leadership of the Reverend John D. Long, who

18. *CS,* V, No. 2 (January 15, 1908) was devoted to an abstract of the translation.

19. Spalding was an uncompromising and outspoken socialist, whose influence seems to have been much less than his ability deserved. See *CS,* V, No. 1 (February 1, 1908), and John Howard Melish, *Franklin S. Spalding, Man and Bishop* (New York, 1917).

20. "Christian Socialism," the *Outlook,* 89 (June 13, 1908), 319.

21. At this time there were branches in Chicago, San Diego, Boston, Denver, Pittsburgh, Newark, Milwaukee, Philadelphia, Buffalo, and several other cities. Delegates to this meeting took their socialism seriously; Carr was once addressed as "Brother Reverend Comrade." The *Outlook* noted that "the Christian spirit was manifest enough, though Christian wisdom and knowledge were not so fully apparent."

in the summer of 1908 held conferences at Old Orchard, Maine, and Asbury Park, New Jersey,[22] the New York faction tried to gain control of the Fellowship the next year at the fourth conference, held in Toledo. The organization never recovered from this typically socialistic internal disruption. Although its Pittsburgh convention of 1910 drew 380 delegates, the subsequent history of the Christian Socialist Fellowship was a gradual decline.

Various affiliations of the Fellowship suggest the extent to which the ideology represented by this group was spread throughout the country. A loosely constituted "group of persons of diverse views" constituted "The Collectivist Society" of New York, among whose members were Rufus W. Weeks, W. J. Ghent, Owen R. Lovejoy, and Leighton Williams. Although their statement of principles did not indicate a religious interest, the members wrote and published such tracts as *The Socialism of Jesus*, by "Discipulus," and *An Exposition of Socialism and Collectivism*, by "A Churchman."[23] The "Co-operative Fellowship" of Westwood, Massachusetts, was a plan for "cooperative production and exchange on cost basis" and for the spread of socialism. It hoped "to unite all who are interested in the economic, social, moral, and spiritual betterment of man —the socialization of humanity."[24] At the Fellowship's Louisville conference in 1906 J. Eads How of St. Louis was seated as a fraternal delegate from the "Brotherhood of the Daily Life." In 1910 *The Christian Socialist* took over *The Christian Bugle*, which had been published by the Reverend E. H. H. Gates of Walnut, Kansas; in 1915 it absorbed *Good News to the Poor*. Christian Socialist in tone also were *Cestos News* of Cestos, Oklahoma; *Vorwärtz* of Hillsboro, Kansas; and *The Pitchfork*, edited by M. A. Smith at Dallas, Texas.[25] The Christian Socialist Fellowship felt some kinship with similar move-

---

22. Long claimed to have attracted audiences of 1,000 per night to tent meetings at Coney Island.

23. See "Collectivist Society," *Encyclopedia of Social Reform* (New York, 1908); also "Christian Socialism" and "Collectivist Society," *Social Progress Yearbook* (1905), Josiah Strong, ed., New York, 1905, pp. 186, 304.

24. *CS*, II, No. 12 (June 15, 1905), 7.

25. See Paul F. Laubenstein, *A History of Christian Socialism in America* (New York, 1925), p. 78. This is an unpublished S.T.M. thesis in the library of Union Theological Seminary, New York.

ments abroad; in 1907 Carr was sent to a conference at Stuttgart. He reported founding a branch of the Fellowship in Paris, and for some time afterward the activities of this and other European groups were mentioned in *The Christian Socialist*.[26]

The Fellowship once attempted to carry out its plan of "permeating churches, denominations and other religious institutions" by sending fraternal delegates to national religious gatherings. While some church bodies treated the socialist emissaries with good-natured tolerance, the attitude of Protestantism at large was probably reflected in the action of the General Synod of the Reformed Church in the United States when it refused to seat a delegate and later declared the spread of socialism not to be its "duty or province," inasmuch as such propagandism would be subordinating "to a secondary place the great spiritual truths and saving faith of the Gospel of Christ." Also to be deeply deplored was "the reckless criticism of the Church and her ministry, in which so many Socialist agitators indulge." Such matters should be left to the individual citizen.[27]

The leading notions of this brand of Christian Socialism were quite simple. They were the enthusiasms of religious idealists who had been converted to the socialistic gospel by reason of its spiritual and humanitarian appeal and whose conclusions were those of reformers rather than careful students. They would have agreed with the socialist spokesman John Spargo that socialism was "a great, vital and vitalizing religious principle" in which they might find inspiration, solace, and hope. They believed the religious life to be impossible under capitalism, where brotherhood is negated by strife and life is bound down to "ledger accounts of profit and loss."[28] A Christian Socialist manifesto signed by 160 ministers expressed the belief that the existing social system, based "upon the sin of covetousness," made "the ethical life as inculcated by religion impracticable," whereas socialism would create an environment favorable to the practice of religion.[29] The Reverend J. O. Benthall wrote in the

26. Eliot White, "The Christian Socialist Fellowship," *Arena*, 41 (1909), 53. See also *CS*, December 1, 1907, and the *Christian Century*, 32 (June 10, 1915), 414, the latter descriptive of a socialist church in Pittsburgh.

27. *General Synod of the Reformed Church in the United States, 1911*, p. 421.

28. John Spargo, *The Spiritual Significance of Modern Socialism* (New York, 1908), p. 17. See also John M. Scott, *The Soul of Socialism* (Chicago, 1911), p. 18.

29. *Arena*, 40 (1908), 510. This was published in *CS*, April 15, 1908.

Arena in 1907 that socialism, "the material side of that of which Christianity is the religious," would make it possible for one to earn a living without violating the Christian law of love, because in a coöperative society the normal course of life would naturally be ordered according to the golden rule.[30]

Thus, the Fellowship's goal was "to show that socialism is the economic expression of the religious life." Unconcerned about the practicability of socialism, these preachers endorsed Marx and joined the Socialist party in order "to end the class struggle by establishing industrial democracy, and to hasten the reign of justice and brotherhood upon earth." Requisite to the realization of this goal was the removal of the antireligious stigma from socialism, a task requiring the demonstration to Christians that socialism embodied "the most scientific and wise plan so far devised for conforming modern industry and business to the teachings of the Master."[31] The ethi- of Jesus are incompatible with competition and the profit motive. A Christian who engages in "worldly affairs" must compromise with his conscience. To the extent that the church supports the capitalistic system it is trying to serve both God and Mammon.

But although *The Christian Socialist* printed a lengthy abstract of Marx's *Capital*, and the Fellowship asserted its loyalty to the Socialist party of America, the tenets of socialism were rarely if ever examined, the revolutionary classics were never listed among the books recommended, and the Fellowship's own literature carried such titles as *A Christian View of Socialism, What the Christian Socialists stand for*, and *The Socialism of Jesus*.[32] In the first named, George H. Stroebel declared that in socialism God had revealed a plan for the redemption of our earthly life:

It is so wonderful that it creates all the old impassioned fervor of the early Christians. It is sent as of old to the poor and lowly, and

---

30. J. O. Benthall, "Why I Am a Christian Socialist," *Arena*, 37 (1907), 600–604.

31. White, *op. cit.*, p. 47.

32. A list of "the best things to read" also suggested *Love, Hate, and the Class-Conscious Struggle*, by Prof. T. C. Hall of Union Theological Seminary; *Frances E. Willard's Endorsement of Socialism* (a collection); *The Religion of Labor*, by Harvey Dee Brown; *The Captive City of God*, by Richard Heath; *Maud Muller's Ministry*, by James L. Smiley; *Christianity and the Social Crisis*, by Rauschenbusch, "the latest and best American book on Christian Socialism."

the witness of the Holy Spirit is not wanting in this new dispensa-
tion. Those touched by this holy zeal are like the first mar-
tyrs. . . .

For the first time in the history of the world there is an intelligent
and systematized movement toward the conscious organization of
a just society. It is the Socialist movement now on its way to a
speedy triumph. . . .[33]

Socialism will redeem the church and make her the power for
good she was intended to be, declared Benthall.

The mission of the Fellowship was to the Socialist party as
well as to the churches. On one occasion a pronouncement was
sent to the party, in which it was declared that Christian Socialists accepted "the economic interpretation of social and political causes" and had no revisionist motives. But they were
fully convinced that the party ought to avoid "every form of
religious and anti-religious theory or dogma."[34] They believed
in using Christianity to further the influence of socialism because for them socialism represented the cause of justice and
right; it was nonetheless an economic and not a religious movement. Moses and Jesus were against exploitation; Biblical ideas
harmonized with Marxian views of social revolution. But how
they harmonized no one troubled to state.

The purpose and philosophy of the Fellowship were well
phrased by Rufus W. Weeks at the New York conference of
1908. Christian Socialism, he declared, does not stand for a
Christian version of socialism, for there is no such thing. Socialism is a political force based on economic fact: there can be
but one kind of it. Christian Socialists are simply Christians
who accept and adhere to the Marxist doctrine "that economic
mass-interest is the impelling motive, the driving force, which
alone can be depended on to work the great world-change demanded." What then differentiates them from other socialists?
Weeks pointed to these distinctions: the Christian Socialist is
animated in part by love of the church, which he labors to en-
lighten in order that she may take her rightful place in the
caravan of progress. The Christian Socialist derives his passion for social justice from his desire to follow Jesus, whom he

33. Quoted by White, *op. cit.*, p. 50.   34. Quoted by White, *op. cit.*, p. 47.

interprets as having stressed the economic aspects of the kingdom of God. Lastly, the Christian Socialist is devoted to the theistic ideal, which he would make "acceptable and adorable" to the exploited masses. To do this it is necessary that the human race be organized into an "economic whole" where "fair and equal" conditions will provide for individual security and reasonable living standards: "This necessarily means the coöperative commonwealth, as the Socialists picture it; and the Christian Socialists believe that this is Jesus' 'Kingdom of God' in the fundamental plane of life, the economic. . . ."[35] In working toward this goal Christian Socialists believe they are doing their bit toward the establishment of "the modern experimental proof of God's goodness."

Here was an endorsement of political socialism for religious reasons. In a previous decade the Reverend W. D. P. Bliss had advocated a Christian Socialism, he himself being a party member, but he had differed from orthodox socialism "at the root." Walter Rauschenbusch proclaimed a Christian Socialism that was "a peculiar genus of socialism." A member neither of the party nor of the Fellowship, he did not commit the shortsighted error of identifying the kingdom of God with a specific human program. But when the Christian Socialist Fellowship equated the Christian hope of the kingdom with the socialistic dream of economic perfection it jeopardized its Christianity and rendered the social gospel liable to the charge of being "mere humanism."

The last chapter of the story of Christian Socialism in this era was written by an Episcopal society, the Church Socialist League.[36] As had been the case with "C.A.I.L." and with the Christian Social Union,[37] this group came into being as the result of contact with a similar Anglican organization. In 1911 the Reverend B. I. Bell of Grace Church, Chicago, gathered a nucleus that was to include Bishop Franklin S. Spalding of Utah and his successor the Right Reverend Paul Jones, the Right Reverend Benjamin Brewster, Bishop of Maine, and

35. Quoted by White, *op. cit.*, pp. 50–52. See also *CS*, June 1, 1908, p. 2.

36. This paragraph is condensed from Spencer Miller and Joseph F. Fletcher, *The Church and Industry* (New York, 1930), pp. 93–96. By permission of Longmans, Green & Co., publishers.

37. See chap. ix, above.

Professor Vida D. Scudder. There was little organization of the League at first, although in 1912 it commenced the publication of a quarterly, *The Social Preparation for the Kingdom of God.* By 1916, with a membership of less than one hundred, the League was conscious of the spiritual danger to America inherent in the World War, and it endeavored to warn the church that the economic causes of war were fundamental ones that would ultimately submerge her program of Christian work if not challenged. With America's entry into the War the League found itself disintegrating over differences of opinion among its members regarding participation. Its last outstanding act was defense of its president, Bishop Jones, against criticism of his pacifistic position. Typical of its varied activities were forums on economic problems at the General Convention. In 1919 it joined with the Society of the Companions of the Holy Cross[38] in urging clemency for imprisoned conscientious objectors. Postwar antisocialist hysteria made the League's career a "practical futility"; *The Social Preparation* ceased to appear, and in 1924 the group voluntarily disbanded.

The unsuccessful efforts of socialism to capture the church can hardly be regarded as a failure. Beyond the catalytic effect of liberal theology itself no single force so stung American Protestantism into social action as did this gadfly of capitalism. From the rude jolt it gave some of the pioneers of the 1870's, to its integral place in the gospel of Walter Rauschenbusch, socialism was a factor of primary importance in the socializing of Christianity. Religion likewise had a marked effect upon socialism, even if only through supplying the movement with leaders such as George D. Herron and Norman Thomas. Although the Christian Socialist fire of each era flickered and went out, the pilot light somehow remains aglow and from time to time rekindles the flame—at present (1938) in the "Fellowship of Socialist Christians."[39] And it is not unfair to suggest that socialism, the midwife and nurse to the social gospel, is today its traveling companion.

38. This is a group of Episcopal women "inwardly dedicated to the Way of the Cross and to intercession for social justice." Until 1920 it was entirely private.
39. This nondenominational group publishes the magazine, *Radical Religion.* See also the *Christian Century,* 52 (1935), 1319, and the *World To-Morrow,* 17 (1934), 297–298.

CHAPTER XV

PROBLEMS OF THE NEW CENTURY

. . . It is imperative that a point of friendly contact be established between organized Christianity and the millions who in the present crisis are severed from the Church chiefly through misunderstanding. This demand can be fully met by the fearless proclamation of the social teachings of Jesus and the scrupulous application of those doctrines to the problems which vex our social system.

GEORGE P. ECKMAN

WHEN socially minded clergymen analyzed the problems of American life in the early years of the twentieth century, their interests followed lines now familiar to the reader of this study but their attitudes and prescriptions were marked by a new realism. Again labor and the industrial situation received the most attention, with the cities following closely. Immigration, charity, the family, democracy and the socialized state, and the ethics of wealth were examined.[1] This discussion was notable for a new use of sociological techniques and data, such as surveys, investigations, and statistics. Attempts to deal with problems were rendered more effective by the creation of denominational agencies and of the Federal Council of the Churches of Christ in America. The remainder of our study will be concerned with these aspects of a maturing movement; in the present chapter the representative literature devoted to specific problems will be examined.

The generalization that the social gospel was historically the reaction of liberal Protestantism to the industrial problem was amply demonstrated in this period. Not only was the literature of this subject larger than that of any other social concern, but the rights of labor and the question of social justice held a predominant position in the thinking of the denominations as they

---

1. The country church, the race problem, and amusements were also noticeable features of this literature. For references see the writer's projected *Bibliography of Social Christianity.*

appointed social-service commissions and in the philosophy of the Federal Council of Churches as it formulated the "Social Creed of the Churches." Naturally enough the religious and ethical aspects of the issue stood out in the minds of clergymen. To Professor Francis Greenwood Peabody labor agitation was "the penalty we are paying for not being Christian." Outwardly the social problem may be economic, legislative, and educational, but in its essence it is "ethical, spiritual, religious, a call to moral redemption, a summons to a better life," he asserted. The great peril overshadowing American life is not corporations, unions, or economic controversies: it is the menace of "a commercialized, and materialized civilization, in which the ideals that support Democracy may fail of vitality and strength."[2] In his last book, *The Labor Question*, Washington Gladden repeated in 1911 his contention first stated in 1876 in *Working People and Their Employers:* "The labor question is in part an economic question, and . . . all economic questions are fundamentally religious questions; there are no purely spiritual interests, since the spiritual forces all incarnate themselves in the facts of every-day life . . ."[3]

By this time the leaders of Protestant social thought were accepting trades unionism almost without question, an attitude we have examined in the writings of Walter Rauschenbusch. "The union is as inevitable as the weather; to refuse to recognize it is like refusing to recognize the wind and the rain," declared Dean George Hodges of the Cambridge Episcopal Theological School in 1904.[4] This attitude was also indicated in the demand for industrial justice, which, according to C. Bertrand Thompson of the Harvard Business School, was "almost the only ethical problem which the churches have not already settled to the practical satisfaction of all."[5] Churchmen must insist upon social justice everywhere, all the time, and at any cost, declared William M. Balch in *Christianity and the Labor Movement*. The church needs to stand for the justice that removes

2. Francis G. Peabody, "The People," in *Organized Labor and Capital* (Philadelphia, 1904), pp. 221–223. See also Lyman Abbott, *The Rights of Man* (Boston and New York, 1901), p. 369.

3. Washington Gladden, *The Labor Question* (Boston, 1911), p. 153. By permission of The Pilgrim Press, publishers.

4. George Hodges, "The Union," in *Organized Labor and Capital*, p. 140.

5. C. Bertrand Thompson, *The Churches and the Wage Earners* (New York, 1909), p. 180.

the causes of our social ills, not for a charity that merely allevi-
ates them. And, he continued, every demand of labor, whether
wise or unwise, should be heard with friendliness and judged
without prejudice. Professor Henry C. Vedder asserted that
the gospel of Jesus could not tolerate one set of ethics for the
workers and another for their employers; it does not permit a
man to live at the expense of his fellows, and ultimately it will
convince us that all forms of profit are profoundly immoral.[6]

In his book, *Religion in Social Action*, Professor Graham
Taylor outlined several specific areas of that field. Realization
of the need for social justice ought to lead to certain types of
coöperation between religion and labor, he asserted, and proposed also a plan for concerted activity between industry and
religion, which he believed had much in common. The latter
might investigate jointly conditions of labor and housing,
gathering facts impartially. But in such coöperative ventures
the churches ought never to ally themselves with one side more
than with another: ministers have no more claim or right to belong to a labor union than to a manufacturers' association. The
church stands for all; its ministry is mediatorial. However, this
intermediary position should "allow of no weak, non-committal,
timidly compromising spirit." It calls for "a stern sense of justice, a squaring to facts, a peacemaking, with emphasis upon
the making. It means insistence upon fair play, and the free
speech and the full hearing of the other side, without which
nothing is fair." Open forums would aid at this point. If such a
program seemed to daunt the individual church, Taylor recommended united action. In surveys, parish policies, and federated
efforts, new bases are being laid for the levers of religion's old
power, he pointed out. The churches should join with the National Child Labor Committee and such organizations to secure
the enactment and enforcement of improvement legislation.
They should "organise within their denominations to educate
their own fellowship"; the Federal Council should represent
their interdenominational attitude and action.[7]

6. Henry C. Vedder, *The Gospel of Jesus and the Problems of Democracy*
(New York, 1914), p. 69.

7. Graham Taylor, *Religion in Social Action* (New York, 1913), pp. 193, 210.
See also his address "Industry and Religion," in *The Social Application of Religion* (Cincinnati and New York, 1908); his autobiography, *Pioneering on Social Frontiers* (Chicago, 1930), and *Chicago Commons Through Forty Years*
(Chicago, 1936).

Charles Stelzle of the pioneer Presbyterian Department of Church and Labor delineated several areas in which the church and labor might coöperate, but stressed particularly the futility of methods by which the church was attempting to reach the worker from above. Let us talk less about service and helping and more about exchange, he proposed. Both labor and the church feel they have a mission in the world; neither "can afford to look upon the other with a spirit of patronage."[8] Thompson believed the church might do well to side with labor occasionally. Although the clergy are equally bound to rich and poor, he wrote, the greater need of the poor and the relative disadvantage of their position should not infrequently enlist the pastor as the champion of labor. The churches must continue an active opposition to the grosser forms of practical materialism. Stelzle endorsed this general view.[9] Thompson declared that when the churches could be observed fostering the spirit of mutuality preached by socialism then the workers' confidence in them might be restored.

Woman and child labor received the careful attention of several writers. After a study of the wages and hours of these groups, Stelzle concluded that the inevitable result of long hours for women would be "lower standards of living and a lower state of morality" that would undermine the home, the state, and the church. He proposed "a fair law" and efficient inspection as a remedy.[10] Vedder took a more radical view, asking whether such a situation as he reported could possibly "accord with the Gospel of Jesus, the gospel of equality, of brotherhood, of deliverance." A complete solution of the problem of women's wages must be something radical, he asserted, something that goes "to the very bottom of our social evils and deals with primary causes." Although a minimum wage and an eight-hour day will provide relief at the points of greatest pressure, only full justice will cure the evil. "The Church will ere long have to make its ultimate choice between exploiters and exploited, between those who do and those who suffer wrong. . . ."[11]

8. Charles Stelzle, *The Church and Labor* (Boston and New York, 1910), pp. 92, 94.

9. Stelzle, *The Gospel of Labor* (New York, 1912), pp. 85–86.

10. Stelzle, *American Social and Religious Conditions* (New York, 1912), p. 189.

11. Vedder, *op. cit.*, p. 330. By permission of The Macmillan Company, publishers.

Problems of this kind are in the domain of social ethics, wrote Thompson, proposing social preaching as a methodology. The need of the day is discussion of social and economic matters from the highest ethical and religious point of view. "The churches must train a new conscience to meet the new temptations of a commercialized age." Preaching marked by "absolute and unflinching justice" must provide the basis for effective co-operation on the part of the churches with other agencies in the molding of public opinion that will effect reforms.[12] Similarly, Lyman Abbott told the students of the Philadelphia Divinity School in 1905 that they ought not to regard a social message as aside from the regular work of the ministry, which might well include "an understanding of political conditions and a condemnation of political methods . . . a study of social and industrial conditions and a comprehension of social and industrial methods . . . an understanding of popular ethical standards and a condemnation of them because they are unchristian. . . ."[13]

William M. Balch proposed certain more specific methods of closing the gap between the church and the working class. He suggested that representatives from labor groups be invited to church brotherhoods, that units be organized for the study of the industrial problem, that the churches endeavor to be "uncompromisingly democratic." Workingmen should be active in churches; Christian men should join unions whenever possible; fraternal delegates should be exchanged—a program remarkably like that being carried out among Presbyterians by Charles Stelzle and his Department of Church and Labor.[14] In his Merrick Lectures at Ohio Wesleyan University in 1908 the Reverend George P. Eckman of New York asserted that ministers should study sociology, acquaint themselves with working people, and attempt to apply the social teachings of Jesus as a preventative of violent class prejudices and favoritism.[15]

Again in this period the second great problem was the complex tangle of social and religious needs presented by the modern city. Josiah Strong, Frank Mason North, and Charles

12. Thompson, *op. cit.*, pp. 180–183.
13. Lyman Abbott, *The Industrial Problem* (Philadelphia, 1905), p. 194.
14. See chap. xvii, below.
15. *The Social Application of Religion*, p. 135.

Stelzle were perhaps the most widely read among the many who dealt with this situation. In *The Twentieth Century City* and *The Challenge of the City*, Strong diagnosed and prescribed much as he had done two decades previously in *Our Country*.[16] North's influence was exerted chiefly through Methodist circles and his paper *The Christian City*. Stelzle, whose analysis may be considered representative, regarded the city as the focal point of the industrial problem. In *Christianity's Storm Center. A study of the modern city*, he called attention to the crucial character of the urban religious situation as demonstrated in Manhattan, where forty Protestant churches had left the district below Twentieth Street while 300,000 immigrants and workers moved into that area. In the face of her greatest opportunity the church has sounded a dismal retreat, said Stelzle.

In the city as the center of modern economic and industrial development he saw a concentration of forces challenging the church. Business dishonesty, competition, and greed stand as threats against which the church must fight, he asserted. Equally dangerous is the failure to recognize the effect of physical and social conditions upon those whom the church is attempting to reach:

The filthy slum, the dark tenement, the unsanitary factory, the long hours of toil, the lack of a living wage, the back-breaking labor, the inability to pay necessary doctor's bills in time of sickness, the poor and insufficient food, the lack of leisure, the swift approach of old age, the dismal future,—these weigh down the hearts and lives of vast multitudes in our cities. Many have almost forgotten how to smile . . . their souls—their ethical souls—are all but lost. No hell in the future can be worse to them than the hell in which they now are. . . .[17]

The church will be tested in meeting the needs of such as these. Further challenges lie in the sharp class distinctions dividing such urban groups as immigrants, white-collar classes, and women workers. Above all other social forces confronting the church the labor movement has become the most effective. Here are developed to a marked degree three great principles for

16. See chap. vi, above.
17. Stelzle, *Christianity's Storm Center* (New York, 1907), p. 22. By permission of Fleming H. Revell & Co., publishers.

which Christianity stands: the value of human life, the care of the human body, and the development of the human soul. Lastly, the greatest political and economic force among the masses is socialism; its protagonists have adopted the vocabulary of the church, and the worthwhile elements of their cause should be recognized.

There are, however, certain hopeful factors in the situation, said Stelzle. Workers are naturally religious; they honor Jesus Christ; their vision of the social problem—frequently wider than that of the churches—acknowledges its religious character. On the church's part there should be sociological study of a humanitarian sort, such as community surveys appraising the forces influencing the lives of the people. The ordinary services of the church will not reach the working classes; an aggressive evangelism must touch them at as many points as possible. The church plant should be open every night and a good part of the day. Its ministry is for the needs of the people, not merely to bring them to it. To aspire to such a work the church must be absolutely sincere, completely democratic, and must deliver a distinctly social message in a prophetic spirit. It will find that the trades union is blazing its way and that through such methods as observance of Labor Sunday, use of the labor press, and exchange of fraternal delegates the problem of the alienation of the urban masses will be transformed into an opportunity.[18]

In describing programs designed to meet urban needs, Stelzle listed certain outstanding institutional churches such as St. Bartholomew's of New York, Emmanuel Baptist in Chicago, and the Forward Movement of the Methodist Episcopal Church in New York. He outlined the work of social settlements, the Y.M.C.A., municipal centers, and child-saving agencies. Stelzle pointed out how the pressing social needs resulting from changing conditions demanded new techniques and attitudes. He described the institutional program of St. Bartholomew's Church for a typical year. The agencies of this organization held over two hundred meetings per week; its communicants numbered 2,952; 1,610 attended its Sunday Schools. There were 249

---

18. Stelzle, *op. cit.*, chap. iii. These proposals were integral parts of his own program as developed in the Presbyterian Department of Church and Labor. See chap. xvii, below.

paid workers and 896 volunteers. Foreign-language services were conducted in four tongues. Fifteen thousand patients had been cared for in the dispensary the previous year, with over fifty thousand consultations. A loan association received over $100,000 and dispensed $91,000 during the year. Club membership totaled 2,796. An employment bureau had filled 2,531 situations. However, a less pretentious institutional program could be begun at an added annual expense of as little as $100. Its value is proven, declared Stelzle, by the fact that Congregational institutional churches have six times as many additions on confession of faith as do the noninstitutional churches of that denomination. He concluded his book with a chapter on an aggressive evangelism, asserting that although individual evangelism might be inadequate to the social and ethical needs of the day, it was nevertheless requisite to the establishment of right relationships.[19]

Problems related to the basic questions of industry and the cities were immigration, charity, and the family. Stelzle, while convinced that "the peril of the immigrant" had been overemphasized, nevertheless maintained that it constituted such a challenge as the church had never before faced. In *American Social and Religious Conditions* he proposed the study of social and moral factors among the foreign populations, their tenements, saloons, lodges, labor unions, and other natural groupings; provision of attractive places for worship; an educational program; cultivation of the spirit of play in native dances and carnivals; special ministries to the foreign women and children; classes and clubs for boys and girls; the use of music and pictures; and religious services in native languages. "This enterprise is big enough to stir the enthusiasm of every Christian man and woman. Religion, patriotism, philanthropy, education, social service—all these are needed, and the very best of them all, to answer the challenge of the immigrant to our Christianity."[20]

Discussions of charity in this period turned chiefly on economic causes and the development of scientific programs of re-

19. For further detailed references on the problem of the city in this period, see the writer's forthcoming *Bibliography*.

20. Stelzle, *American Conditions*, p. 120. By permission of Fleming H. Revell & Co., publishers.

lief. George Hodges stressed the need for training, knowledge, sympathy, consideration, judgment, and other requisites to an "efficient philanthropy."[21] In his book, *The Burden of Poverty. What To Do*, the Reverend Charles F. Dole of Boston located the roots of this evil in the injustice of the industrial system. Professor Henry C. Vedder likewise discovered the causes of poverty in exploitation of the poor and demanded as a cure the modification of the capitalistic system.[22]

The family received careful attention at the hands of Professor Graham Taylor in *Religion in Social Action*. Along with others, Taylor called attention to the strategic importance of the family unit in the social structure and the intimate connection between home life and religion. He saw in the family "the terms and types by which are revealed our relations to God and each other." The family is not more dependent upon religion than religion is upon the family, he wrote. The hope of one is identified with that of the other. Preservation of the family is therefore a primary religious duty.

A problem not discussed in previous decades was the relation of the increasingly socialized state to democracy and Christianity. In an essay entitled *The Christian State*, Samuel Zane Batten, a founder of the Brotherhood of the Kingdom, called attention to the enlarging sphere of the state's activities and asked whether it might become "the medium through which the people shall co-operate in their search after the kingdom of God and its righteousness." Such might be possible if the purpose of the state could be formulated and a Christian program of social and political action agreed upon. As specific efforts toward this end Batten suggested a "steady pressure against all things that are harmful to man and hurtful to society"; "the administration of justice with a saving purpose" and the "continuous and collective determination to maintain justice throughout society"; attempts toward realization of the spirit of brotherhood; "the collective and unchanging will to secure for every person the conditions of a full, human, moral life"; and a "steady effort to give each person a fair inheritance in society." There is no reason either in the will of God or the nature of

21. George Hodges, *Efficient Philanthropy . . . An Address . . .* (New York, 1911).
22. Vedder, *op. cit.*, chap. ix.

things for all the waste of modern society and for the presence of a large disinherited class, declared Batten. The purpose of God for his children must define the policy of the state in its social action: it is to provide education, and its total resources are to be held in trust for all. "The State that is becoming Christian will regard this work as a social mission and not alone as an individual task." Social policy should exalt man and make wealth a means rather than an end. All these aims may be summarized as "the political vision of the Kingdom of God and the collective effort to realize that kingdom on the earth."

Episcopal Bishop Chauncey B. Brewster of Connecticut warned against plutocracy as a menace to democracy and called upon the church to assert ethical standards that would counteract its influence. He asserted that the church must be true to the democratic ideal—in its administration, its ministry, its music, in providing free pews, and in the recognition of "what is common in its own aims and those of the trade-unions." At best democracy is beset by grave problems and there is need of the principles, vision, ideals, and inspirations to be found in Christianity and furnished by the Christian church.[23] Similarly Professor Vida D. Scudder wrote that the only means by which working people at large could be convinced of the genuineness of Christianity would be through "the true socializing of the church" and by the practice on the part of the rich and prosperous of a simple life and "a social fellowship visibly independent of class divisions." The church should exemplify "that spiritual democracy of which our fathers dreamed, and in the faith of which our republic was founded."[24]

Through all this discussion a marked criticism of the current ethics of wealth was apparent. This attitude was dramatized in 1905 by Washington Gladden, then moderator of the National Council of Congregational Churches, when he opposed the acceptance by that denomination's foreign mission board of a gift of $100,000 from John D. Rockefeller. Gladden interpreted the immediate issue as a compromise between a Christian stand-

23. Chauncey B. Brewster, *The Kingdom of God and American Life* (New York, 1912), p. 57.
24. Vida D. Scudder, "Democracy and the Church," *Atlantic,* 90 (1902), 521–527.

ard of honest gain and the "iniquity of conscienceless and predatory wealth." The church could not be a party to profits held "by no better moral title than the booty of the highwayman." Calling attention to the exposure of the methods of the Standard Oil Company by Ida M. Tarbell, Gladden warned Congregationalism that it could not expect to retain the respect of workers or the loyalty of its own critical young people if by accepting tainted money it failed to testify against "oppressors and despoilers of the people."[25] Of the wider issue of the morals of business he said:

If there is any meaning in the ethics of the Christ for whom the Church is supposed to stand, the industrial order which holds the dollar higher than the man is not Christian but pagan; there is no paganism in Asia or Africa in more deadly hostility to the Kingdom of Christ; and the first business of the Church is to storm it and subdue it and revolutionize it, in the name and by the power of the Christ.[26]

Professor Vedder's strictures were more pointed. " 'Business enterprise' is the euphonious name of all manner of rottenness and wickedness, and 'business success' involves violation of every law, human or divine, that stands in the way, by men of steel-wire nerves and asbestos morals," he stormed. Getting rich is possible only by robbery of one's brother, spoliation of the helpless, and exploitation of the weak. According to this Baptist teacher Rockefeller's wealth rested upon his power under the law "to diminish the real wealth of the coming generation" and his ability to control the labor of other men through his ownership of the means of production.[27] His arbitrary sway over the lives of countless thousands raises the question whether this kind of authority is "founded on any equitable principle in the first place, and whether it is a safe power in a democracy. Or . . . whether a democracy is possible where such economic despotism exists." Vedder's point of view was considerably re-

<hr>

25. Washington Gladden, *Recollections* (Boston and New York, 1909), pp. 402–409; *The New Idolatry and Other Discussions* (New York, 1905), pp. 48–49.

26. Gladden, *The Labor Question,* p. 171. By permission.

27. Vedder, *op. cit.,* p. 293.

moved from the exhortations to stewardship that had characterized the utterances of social-gospel pioneers forty years earlier!

Although further evidence for the fact will be adduced in following chapters, it may be suggested once more in summary that for the most part the social gospel was occupied with the same set of questions throughout the half century it has been traced in this study. Owing its origin to the concern of liberal religious leaders over the social maladjustments attendant upon the struggle between capital and labor and to socialism's interpretation of this crux of capitalism, social Christianity kept the problems of the industrial order at the center of its interest. It then turned to conditions in the cities and only subsequently and secondarily to other matters. While its sympathies tended to broaden as it developed, issues other than those related to industrialism remained on the periphery of its concern.

CHAPTER XVI

SOCIOLOGY IN THE SERVICE OF RELIGION

As fast as social laws are "made known and obeyed, the life of society will become normal; and it can be demonstrated that the fundamental laws of society are identical with the fundamental laws laid down in the social teaching of Jesus."

JOSIAH STRONG

THE need for knowledge of social science and for the development of sociological techniques was a persistent and realistic social-gospel emphasis that came to practical fruition in the period now under consideration. After the turn of the century both program and philosophy utilized increasingly the expanding resources of sociology. Individuals and organizations systematically collated information of every conceivable sort that had any possible bearing upon community welfare. Social-gospel lessons for the Sunday School were founded upon the Bible and "references to various economics books as lesson helps." Open forums became less forensic and more dependent upon recognized authorities in the social disciplines. Prominent social scientists lent their influence, wrote books on social Christianity, and evangelized for reform in the name of religion and of science; some outlined the social character of religion and its institutions and attempted to evaluate its place in modern society in terms of valid sociological concepts. And in this period the churches developed the techniques of social service to such a degree that in the eyes of professional organizations they came to occupy a significant place among the nation's agencies of social welfare.

I. SOCIAL FACTS FOR RELIGIOUS EDUCATION

In the 1890's sociology and reform were quite compatible partners and the social gospel was a happy ally of both. Its first attempt to meet a growing demand for easily available information was the amazing and poorly arranged medley of bare facts, propaganda, and bibliographies entitled *Practical Christian Sociology*, compiled by Wilbur F. Crafts in 1895, and of which there were four editions in a dozen years.

The real pioneer among sociological reference books appeared two years later as the *Encyclopedia of Social Reform*, edited and largely written by W. D. P. Bliss, aided by specialists in many fields.[1] It was well described by the New York *Times* as containing "an endless number of topics relating to political economy, political science, sociology, and statistics, covering Anarchism, charities, civil service, currency, land and legislation reform, penology, Socialism, social purity, trades unions, woman suffrage, and numberless other subjects." Embodying much factual material, the *Encyclopedia*, a large quarto volume of some fourteen hundred pages, was nevertheless well described by its title. "Individualists and socialists, gold monometallists, bimetallists, and believers in free silver, protectionists and free traders, prohibitionists and high-license advocates, believers and disbelievers in woman suffrage, appear in this encyclopedia side by side," wrote its editor. Along with articles on agriculture, the boot-and-shoe industry, coöperation, the Negro, railways, or taxation, Bliss wrote on "the Anglican position in political and social reform," "Christ and social reform," "the church and the working man," "the church and social reform," "the Congregational Church and social reform" —and so through the alphabet. For the most part the content of the *Encyclopedia*, largely written by Bliss, was accurate, informative, and well documented, but hardly scholarly.

One reviewer declared that Bliss had performed a monumental task and that his book would stand in the future as "an epitome of the social and economic conditions and the state of human progress in the last decade of the nineteenth century." This it unquestionably does, having provided a mine of materials for the present study. But as a source of information for current reform it was soon out of date. In 1904 Josiah Strong

1. Among the contributors were E. Benjamin Andrews, Edward Atkinson, Edward Bellamy, E. W. Bemis, John R. Commons, William Lloyd Garrison, Franklin H. Giddings, Nicholas Paine Gilman, Arthur T. Hadley, Edward Everett Hale, Benjamin Kidd, Henry D. Lloyd, Frank Parsons, Carroll D. Wright.

—whose "American Institute of Social Service" is to be described shortly—secured Bliss's aid in editing a "year book and encyclopedia of economic, industrial, social and religious statistics" entitled *Social Progress*. Intended to bring the *Encyclopedia* up to date, these annuals "for the needs of the practical reform worker" were 300-page volumes containing "general demographic," vital, commercial, financial, industrial, educational, and religious statistics; surveys of poverty, crime, intemperance; accounts of reform movements all over the world; carefully selected bibliographies; and directories of social welfare and reform organizations and workers in the United States and foreign countries. Well indexed but badly ordered, *Social Progress*, published in 1904, 1905, and 1906, made available between the covers of one book a questionably usable mass of statistics and a rapid-fire summary and directory of social service and reform.

In 1908 Bliss, aided by Dr. Rudolph M. Binder, produced a revised edition of the *Encyclopedia*. A slightly smaller volume than its predecessor, the new source book claimed to contain data on "all social reform movements and activities, and the economic, industrial, and sociological facts and statistics of all countries and all social subjects"—a statement indicative of ten years' shift in emphasis from propaganda toward solid factual study. The book was a "distinct improvement" over its forerunner; the list of contributors contained many illustrious names.[2] Yet partisan and moralistic viewpoints were decidedly in evidence and excessive quotation and incomplete revision prevented the work from being "really expert through and through." Nonetheless, as Graham Taylor has remarked in his autobiography, Bliss's volume aided in blazing the trails of progress that twenty years and more afterward were to merge into the broad highway surveyed by the *Encyclopedia of the Social Sciences*.[3]

The outstanding agency motivated by a definitely religious drive that was dedicated to the collection and dissemination of

2. Among those who had not written for the first edition were Jane Addams, Percy Alden, W. J. Bryan, Cardinal Gibbons, David Starr Jordan, Edwin Markham, John Mitchell, Upton Sinclair, Oscar S. Straus, Josiah Strong, Booker T. Washington, Sidney Webb, Clinton R. Woodruff, and Charles Zueblin.
3. Graham Taylor, *Pioneering on Social Frontiers* (Chicago, 1930), p. 406.

sociological data for reform purposes was the "League for Social Service" later the "American Institute of Social Service," founded in New York in 1898 by Josiah Strong and William Howe Tolman. Strong had been a leader in the social-gospel movement since the publication of *Our Country* in 1885. As general secretary of the Evangelical Alliance of the United States he had organized the great conferences of 1887, 1889, and 1893 that had called the attention of the nation to social Christianity.[4] When he later planned an ambitious program of popular education in social issues the Alliance refused to follow him. Strong resigned and founded the League, of which the purpose was to gather data "regarding everything that tends to the social betterment of humanity, and to disseminate facts by means of its bureau of information, league leaflets, and the lecture bureau."[5] Its prestige established by a distinguished group of sponsors,[6] the League provided six services: consultation and investigation, library and archives, "propagandism and practical demonstration," publication, service and information, and an institute of social service. Specifically it proposed to accumulate and interpret "the studies of specialists" for the benefit of the practical man of affairs; it would also "act as counsellor to employers of labor and others who desire to enter upon social work, but who have not the time to make the investigations or studies which should precede such action."

The League set about the accomplishment of a task that it regarded chiefly as a process of education by means of several types of printed materials. Strong continued *Truths for the Times*, a series of tracts planned for the Evangelical Alliance and intended for popular distribution. These pamphlets were devoted to good citizenship, abstracts of state laws, education, anti-Mormonism, arbitration, municipal reform, and nature study. A similar but short-lived publication, *Social Engineering*, issued monthly, outlined the League's services, described its activities, contained annual reports, and noted general items

4. See chap. vi, above.
5. William Howe Tolman, "The League for Social Service," *Arena,* 21 (1899), 474.
6. Among Strong's supporters were Washington Choate, Robert C. Ogden, Mrs. Margaret E. Sangster, Albert Shaw, Jane Addams, R. Fulton Cutting, Richard Watson Gilder, Washington Gladden, Frederic D. Huntington, Alice Freeman Palmer, Charles H. Parkhurst, Henry C. Potter, and John H. Vincent.

of a semipropagandist nature. The most important early journal was the monthly *Social Service*, which gradually grew into an impressive magazine with a circulation of 37,500 in 1900. It was given to articles describing various types of "industrial betterment" and industrial social service, plans for civic improvements such as public baths and washhouses, the race problem, or the work of the industrial social secretary. The League's lecture bureau boasted fourteen hundred lantern slides in 1899, by means of which "women's clubs, labor unions, charity organization societies, village improvement societies, and the young people's societies in the various churches, can show their respective communities how they may be made better places to live in." Strong and Tolman, and later the Reverend James H. Ecob lectured widely on "present day problems, like public baths, small parks, the Waring system of street cleaning, the George, Jr., Republic, the institutional church, the New York municipal Department of Police, Health, and Docks."

In 1900 the League arranged at the Paris Exposition the American exhibit covering "various movements for improving industrial conditions on the part of employers for the employed, religious movements for social betterment, and the work of cities for the improvement of municipal conditions."[7] In connection with this, Strong wrote *Religious Movements for Social Betterment*, wherein he described the change in religious activity "from the individualistic to the social type"—a transition being reflected in a new church architecture, "the application of religion to everyday life, a strengthened hold of the churches on the masses, the drawing together of all the churches in closer relations, and their general beneficent influence on civilization."[8]

Two years later the League was reorganized as the "American Institute of Social Service," with similar aims but an expanded program and an augmented group of sponsors.[9] It developed the first exhibit of industrial safety appliances in the United States and exerted a strong influence toward legislation

7. United States Senate *Documents*, 28, No. 232, *Paris Exposition of 1900* (56th Congress, 2d session, 1900–01), p. 406.

8. *Op. cit.*, p. 407.

9. New sponsors were Mrs. Andrew Carnegie, Grace H. Dodge, Mrs. Phoebe A. Hearst, Walter H. Page, Mary E. Woolley, Grover Cleveland, Woodrow Wilson, and Francis G. Peabody.

for the protection of workers from dangerous machinery. From 1904 to 1906 the *Social Progress* yearbooks were published, with W. D. P. Bliss acting as secretary of that department.

The Institute's chief service to the development of social Christianity was through another editorial service rendered by Bliss. In October, 1908, there was published by the Institute, under the names of Strong and Dr. Rudolph M. Binder as editors, the first issue of *The Gospel of the Kingdom*, "a course of study on living social problems in the light of the gospel of Jesus Christ." Intended to present "the most common and urgent problems of the new civilization, and to offer as many helps as may be possible in applying to their solution the principles of Christ's teaching," these social-gospel Sunday School lessons attained the widest circulation of any material published in the interest of social Christianity during its first half century, reaching more than 40,000 readers in churches, Y.M.C.A.'s, Y.W.C.A.'s, colleges, universities, and theological schools. Largely or entirely written by Bliss,[10] who had begun a similar series in the ephemeral *Social Forum* in 1900,[11] the studies undertook to "bring out some social teachings" of the Bible passages studied by the International Sunday School lessons.[12]

A more or less obvious development was followed in these studies, wherein Scripture was quoted and Christian teaching elaborated on the problem at point. Topics were recommended for study and discussion and references to useful sociological materials cited. A notable feature of the lessons was the printing of extensive bibliographies from time to time. The topics for the first year were representative: child labor, women in industry, wealth and capital, the organization of labor, housing, civic corruption, public utilities, socialism, immigration, foreign relations, the race question, and labor conditions. In 1910 the magazine was expanded to include a program of "What to Do" to make the lessons effective in actual reform. The addition

10. ". . . I wrote for Dr. Josiah Strong 'Bible Lessons in Social Christianity,' which, as sent to our classes and republished in the *Homiletic Review,* reached over 40,000 readers . . . ," W. D. P. Bliss, "The Church of the Carpenter and Thirty Years After," *Social Preparation for the Kingdom of God* (January, 1922), p. 15.

11. See chap. xi, above.

12. *Gospel of the Kingdom* (January, 1910), p. 2.

of various contributed features swelled the lesson sheet to a 32-page paper by 1912. Its last issue was that for September, 1916, edited by Binder following the death of Strong in April of that year.

However, the *Gospel of the Kingdom* lessons were merely the most popular item in a great body of study materials. The earliest text of this sort was *The Citizen and the Neighbor; or, Men's Rights and Duties as they live together in the State and in Society*, written by the Reverend Charles F. Dole for the Unitarian Sunday School Society in 1885. This was a syllabus dealing with a score of problems, including politics, economics, industry, crime, temperance, internationalism, and war. In 1895, the international Christian Endeavor journal, *The Golden Rule*, carried an extended course of study on good citizenship, written by Graham Taylor. Two years later Samuel Zane Batten published a lengthy series of articles on the same subject in the *Baptist Union*. In 1897 the Chautauqua reading circles pursued a study of *The Social Spirit in America*, a survey of organizations and movements at work in social service, by Charles R. Henderson of the University of Chicago.

Soon after the turn of the century home-missions courses, Y.M.C.A. outlines, and denominational publications[13] began to pour from the press in amazing profusion. Notice of the materials prepared by the churches' social-service commissions will be taken in our next chapter. Outstanding among the first groups of materials was *The Social and Ethical Teaching of Jesus*, written by Shailer Mathews in 1904, the popularity of which called for several reprints. A significant home-missionary course displaying strong social-gospel interest was *The Burden of the City* by Isabelle Horton, published the same year. *The Political and Social Significance of the Life and Teaching of Jesus*, written by Professor Jeremiah W. Jenks of Cornell University and published in 1906 by the International Y.M.C.A., was widely studied in the colleges. In 1909 Professor Henderson completed "a textbook for the study of social problems" entitled *Social Duties from the Christian Point of View*. Really an

13. For a survey of this literature see Clarence D. Blachly, *The Treatment of the Problem of Capital and Labor in Social-study Courses in the Churches* (University of Chicago Ph.D. dissertation, 1920).

introduction to social ethics, this approach dealt with some fifteen problems such as the family, workers, rural conditions, public health, and international relations. The next year Shailer Mathews published *The Social Gospel*, a systematic study of the teachings of Jesus in their relation to modern problems. In this book, which gained a wide reading, Mathews described the family, the state, and economic activity, as well as other fundamental social institutions. In 1911 the Missionary Education Movement of the United States and Canada published *Community Study by Groups*, by Warren H. Wilson, a manual presenting "a practical scheme for the investigation of the problems of the large town or city ward from the point of view of the church and its work." The next year Wilson wrote *Community Study for Cities*. A unique study by Edwin L. Earp, professor of Christian Sociology in Drew Theological Seminary, entitled *The Social Engineer*, was published in 1911. Earp discussed, for the benefit of men's clubs, Bible classes, and similar organizations, the "essentials which any man should know" before choosing religious social service as a career. The book was an able attempt to introduce the religious worker to the facts of social organization as he would encounter them in actual situations. Unquestionably the most widely circulated of all this literature was Walter Rauschenbusch's *Social Principles of Jesus*, written in 1916, of which twenty thousand copies were distributed in the year of its publication, it being immediately popular in the colleges.[14]

Although such materials as these had their vogue, certain groups, often of students, sought a more thorough understanding of social facts as the basis for applying a socialized religion. The most successful church organization to study sociological data was the pioneer "Social Problems Group" begun in the fall of 1906 at Madison, Wisconsin, by the Reverend Richard H. Edwards, Congregational pastor of the University of Wisconsin. Continued by Edwards until 1912, this group developed an effective technique that aided in bridging the gap "between the experts of social science and the general public." The purpose was "to get at the best and freshest statements of the hard facts of our social problems"; to hear and compare

14. See the writer's forthcoming *Bibliography of Social Christianity* for a full list of these materials.

various solutions; and to ask "the question of the reality and extent of the contribution made by Jesus toward the solution of each problem."[15]

Edwards' meetings, held on Sunday following the regular church service, attracted an average of sixty university students. The subject under discussion was usually presented in not more than two fifteen-minute addresses. Although specialists like Jane Addams, E. A. Ross, Raymond Robins, Robert A. Woods, John R. Commons, and Graham Taylor occupied the platform from time to time, the subject matter for discussion was often brought before the group by its own members. To facilitate this procedure extensive bibliographies were developed, covering both the general field and special aspects of the problem, the entire group being provided with the former type of references.[16] Data were analyzed carefully in order to have materials readily available. The method of presentation may be exemplified in the case of poverty. The issue was first stated concisely:

1. The extent and degree of American poverty.

2. Descriptions of actual conditions in congested districts. . . .

3. The main contributing causes, unsteady work, congestion, accidents, liquor, haste of judgment, etc.

4. The effects of poverty upon the individual, the home, the congested area and the community, as to health, morality and industrial efficiency.

Then followed an analysis of possible lines of solution:

1. The old philanthropy, individual gifts, cases uninvestigated.

2. The new philanthropy.

(a) Organized charity.

(b) Thorough investigation of social conditions and the causes of poverty.

(c) Special lines of enlightened action.

(d) Tenement house legislation; public baths, small parks and playgrounds; social settlements, etc.

15. Richard H. Edwards, "The Social Problems Group," *Charities and the Commons,* 21 (1908), 104.

16. The bibliographies were prepared by students of the Wisconsin Library School. They were thorough and scholarly. A general one seen by the writer con-

3. The battle for industrial justice.
4. Private vs. public philanthropy.[17]

The subsequent discussions were often spirited; interest determined the number of meetings (averaging four or five) devoted to each question. The topics considered the first season were the Negro, divorce, excessive wealth and its concentration, poverty, labor, municipal government, increase of crime, and administration of justice. The Social Problems Group attracted wide and favorable notice, and was one of the influences that brought its leader in 1912 to a position of strategic importance in the Student Christian Movement.[18]

In order to make the Group's technique and experience generally available Edwards published seven studies outlining his approach to the liquor problem, the Negro, immigration, labor, poverty, concentrated wealth, and business morals.[19] Compacted into booklets of thirty-two to fifty-six pages, these syllabuses were about equally divided between concise statements of their problem and annotated bibliographies. In brief introductions describing the "Social Problems Group Idea" Edwards asserted the conviction that "enough reliable information about our social conditions has been amassed to stir all thoughtful citizens, were the facts but generally known." Adding that the same was true of proposed solutions he declared it to be an immediate necessity "to get the ear of all right-minded men and to direct their attention to the naked facts of our social conditions till they be stirred to intelligent and persistent action." The Social Problems Group embraced "a definite and tested plan" for a constructive approach to the study of American social questions. Edwards recommended his outlines to debating groups, for personal information, and to "civic organizations, social settlement clubs, betterment leagues, labor unions, Y.M.C.A. classes, granges, men's clubs in churches, business men's associations, and men's clubs in general, where the basis for a constructive study of the problem is desired."[20] Widely circulated

---

tained over 300 titles; specialized lists often named 100 references, all of which were arranged topically.

17. Edwards, *op. cit.*, pp. 105–106.   18. See chap. xvii, below.

19. These were issued, at Madison, between October, 1908, and August, 1910.

20. R. H. Edwards, *The Immigration Problem* (Madison, Wis., 1909), p. 7.

among such groups, these studies were the best examples we have of the use of social science by a mature social Christianity.[21]

A pioneer institution that did much for social Christianity was the "Ford Hall Forum" begun in February, 1908, in Boston, largely through the instrumentality of George W. Coleman, for many years publisher of *The Christian Endeavor World*.[22] Under Coleman's leadership this public forum became a model for other such platforms. It made the best thought of the day available to an immense audience intensely interested in social and economic questions. The method pursued was the simple procedure of following an address or panel presentation with a free discussion. A characteristic season's program was that of 1908–9, during which there were twenty-four meetings, addressed by Thomas Nixon Carver, William M. Salter, Walter Rauschenbusch, Rabbi Stephen S. Wise, Louis D. Brandeis, Lincoln Steffens, Keir Hardie, and others. Among the subjects discussed were socialism, "A Man and His Vote," the ethical character of American standards, "The Tyranny of Majorities," savings-bank insurance, "Other People's Graft," and the reforms accomplished by the British Labor party. The unique aspect of the Ford Hall setup was the question period—"the freest thing in Boston"—which supplied the democratic note that made the institution justly famous. In 1911 a commentator could well assert that there was "no forum in America where social and economic questions are more intelligently, fundamentally, and fearlessly discussed than from this rostrum."[23]

II. SOCIOLOGICAL EVANGELISM

Religious organizations not only studied the social gospel, they invited social scientists to explain it to them. Such teachers as Charles Zueblin and Charles R. Henderson of the University

21. The writer acknowledges his indebtedness to Mr. Edwards for use of materials, advice, and a critical reading of the original (expanded) draft of this section.

22. Ford Hall was the gift of Daniel Sharp Ford to the Boston Baptist Social Union, "for the spiritual and temporal benefit of workingmen and their families" as the Union might see fit to minister to "the welfare of those who are dependent upon the returns from their daily toil for their livelihood and in promoting such welfare through distinctly Christian agencies." George W. Coleman, *Democracy in the Making* (Boston, 1915), p. 16.

23. D. S. Luther, "The Ford Hall Forum," *The Public* (February 10, 1911), p. 127.

of Chicago and John H. Gray of Northwestern University often gave addresses and courses of study to church groups.[24] Many sociologists were deeply interested in social ethics, as we have seen in previous decades in the cases of Richard T. Ely and John R. Commons. The viewpoint of not a few sociologists was definitely colored by their religious or ethical attitudes. This was particularly true of Professor Albion W. Small, founder of the Sociology Department of the University of Chicago, who had originally trained himself for the ministry.[25] J. H. W. Stuckenberg, a less famous but equally reputable social scientist, revealed this attitude when he declared in his *Introduction to the Study of Sociology* that sociology "without ethics is a torso."[26] Henderson had come to the University of Chicago from the Baptist ministry, Professor E. A. Ross of the University of Wisconsin approached social ethics from a definitely religious viewpoint, Professor Scott Nearing of the Wharton School betrayed a crusading interest in reform in his *Social Religion*, and Professor Charles A. Ellwood of the University of Missouri indicated strong ethical concerns in his *Sociology and Modern Problems* and other books.

Certain viewpoints held by such leaders were of considerable importance to the social-gospel movement. True science, wrote Henderson in an essay entitled "Practical Sociology in the Service of Social Ethics," must consist of more than mere description of social facts. "It is only when a law, some common tendency to produce a definite social result, and promote a social end, is sought, that we have a truly scientific discovery." Now, said Henderson, if the discovery of causes and tendencies is a proper object of social science, the formulation of standards for the conduct that "most perfectly corresponds with the known conditions of welfare" ought also to be within its province. Moral laws cannot be clearly discerned and rationally vindicated without social science. For example, Henderson pointed

24. See *The Kingdom* (Minneapolis), 9 (1897), 820, and *The Commons,* May, 1901, p. 11, and April, 1903, p. 1.

25. See, for example, Small's "The Significance of Sociology for Ethics," *Decennial Publications* of the University of Chicago, 1st ser., IV (1903), 111–149, and *Between Eras: From Capitalism to Democracy* (Kansas City, 1913).

26. Stuckenberg dealt specifically with social issues in *The Social Problem* (York, Pa., 1897).

out, the uninstructed conscience of the general public is at a serious disadvantage in competition with well-organized unions or compact financial interests. The task of sociology, as he saw it, was therefore to endeavor to delineate desirable ends of community conduct and coöperation and the methods by which such ends might most successfully be attained. "Moral teaching is often impotent without the aid of a science of social politics," although this did not mean for Henderson that his science should "speak in the imperative mood." It ought simply to show "methods of organization and principles of social conduct which best promote social welfare."

In the first of two small books aimed at a reform philosophy, E. A. Ross pointed out the social nature of evil and the inability of traditional individualistic ethics to cope with it. *Sin and Society*—according to Theodore Roosevelt a "wholesome and sane" book—based its appeal on the muckraking theory that "public opinion, if only sufficiently enlightened and aroused, is equal to the necessary regenerative tasks and can yet dominate the future." Sin, declared Ross, is "conduct that harms another." The old righteousness is no longer adequate to the needs of our social organization. "We need an annual supplement to the Decalogue"—a new code of social ethics adequate to control the impersonal forces of modern society. Good men are not enough; ethical codes must be improved and public judgment focused on social rather than personal sins. In *Latter Day Saints and Sinners* Ross declared that the modern saint "goes about checkmating evil." The true hero of our times gives himself to mending and strengthening good customs, accepted moral standards, the laws, the recognized rights of the individual, the established agencies of coöperation, and all the dykes protecting us "against crime and wrong, against confusion and waste, against disease and strife. . . ."

A more convincing case for *Social Religion* was put by Scott Nearing in his book by that title, the argument of which was based upon three assumptions of a religious nature:

1. That men at bottom are worth while.
2. That the vast majority of people will be normal and virtuous if given an opportunity to lead decent lives.
3. That the provision of that opportunity was the function of

the Social Religion which Jesus preached two thousand years ago, and that it is still the function of a Social Religion to-day.[27]

In the United States, declared Nearing, "there are ignorance, poverty and vice inviting the touch of the Good Samaritan." These are preventable; "if the church wishes to live up to the ideals of its Founder, it must cease dogmatizing and, in pursuance of Jesus' example, it must preach, heal and teach." After devoting his first chapter to the social views of Jesus, Nearing delineated the field of social need in America, with swift, brilliant strokes laying bare whole areas of distress: child labor, poverty, long hours of work, unemployment, women in industry. In conclusion he challenged: "Teach the truth in your churches and your schools—the truth about the appalling maladjustments which threaten the foundations of civilization; about cooperative industry; about the innate goodness and capacity of man; about Social Religion. . . ."[28]

These various aspects of religion and sociology were uniquely blended in the select "Sagamore Sociological Conferences" held at Sagamore Beach, Massachusetts, from 1907 to 1917, at the instigation of George W. Coleman. In a "call," in which Josiah Strong, Samuel B. Capen, Leighton Williams, and Francis E. Clark joined Coleman in inviting some fifty persons to the first gathering, the belief was expressed that "the time is ripe for the establishment of a Conference of Sociology, which shall, in addition to a thorough consideration of the general topic, seek to emphasize and extend, among Christian people, social standards and ideals."[29] A statement explained the purpose of the conference to be the study of "the social organism and man's social obligations in a sympathetic and open-minded way"; attention was to be given to "the study of social conditions, the removal of injustices and the supply of social needs"; the parallel development of a great body of sociological data and of growing unrest called for "careful study on the part of the American people, an honest facing of a serious situation, and an application of the social teachings of Jesus and other great

27. Scott Nearing, *Social Religion* (New York, 1913), p. xv. By permission of The Macmillan Company, publishers.

28. *Op. cit.*, p. 224. By permission.

29. *First Year of the Sagamore Sociological Conference, 1907* (Boston, 1907), p. 5.

teachers of the centuries." It seemed to the conferees that "all men of religious aspiration who really desire the coming of God's kingdom on earth" should consider the questions of the day.

The program of the first year was indicative of the career of this gathering. At this meeting Josiah Strong, Charles Stelzle, Leighton Williams, Robert A. Woods, Bolton Hall, Francis E. Clark, and Edwin D. Mead presented materials for discussion of the individual versus the social interpretation of Christianity, the relation of church and workingman, the kingdom of God, social improvements in the last twenty-five years, the single tax, social conditions in South America, and "present day problems." From this beginning the meetings grew in popularity and prestige. Practically every person named in Part IV of this study was at one season or another Coleman's guest at Sagamore, so that a register of the conferences would provide a directory of progressive American social leadership in this period. Likewise, every important question under public scrutiny in these years was discussed there—adding to the usual social-gospel concerns such widening interests as liquor, democracy, child labor, militarism, syndicalism, the Negro, race psychology, sex, and journalism and advertising. By utilizing the best talent possible, religious reform thus availed itself of the increasing resources of sociology.

III. The Social Function of Religion

Recognition by sociologists of religion as a social force tended to give scientific sanction to the long-standing social-gospel contention that religion needed to be rethought in social terms fitted to the modern world. These sociologists so defined it, or at least pointed out its inherently social implications. Even though the basic religious attitude or experience may be personal, "religious values are built up socially; they are the products, not of one individual mind, but of the collective mental life of a group," wrote Professor Charles A. Ellwood in 1913, in an article later expanded into his book, *The Reconstruction of Religion*.[30] In a "study in Biblical sociology" entitled *Religion in*

30. Charles A. Ellwood, "The Social Function of Religion," *American Journal of Sociology,* 19 (1913–14), 289–307. *The Reconstruction of Religion* was published in 1922.

the Making, Professor Samuel G. Smith of the University of Minnesota asserted that "religion requires the cooperation of the entire social group whether it be small or large," while E. A. Ross described "social" religion (as distinguished from "legal" religion) as "the conviction that there is a bond of ideal relationships between the members of a society and the feelings that arise in consequence of this conviction." These definitions inferred that the social significance of religion lay in its support of custom, moral standards, and moral ideals, as Ellwood phrased it.

Religion was interpreted both as a conservative and as a progressive force. Dr. William Wilson Elwang of the University of Missouri supported this view with anthropological and other data. "Religion is a power of restraint to prevent variations that would destroy the race, but in so doing it also, necessarily, fosters those actions and promotes those variations that tend to perpetuate and to improve it," he wrote. It functions for survival in the guise of a social bond and as a restraint upon antisocial variations.[31] Ellwood, echoing this view, pointed out the effectiveness of religion as an instrument of social control, acknowledging his debt to Lester F. Ward who had defined religion as "the social instinct" for the conservation of existing institutions.

The explanation of religion as a progressive force was the contribution from this discussion having most value for the social gospel. Religion is the only idealistic principle, asserted Elwang; it is the mainspring of all altruism, "the chief mediating principle between the social is and the social yet to be." It and it alone supplies "the universal significance of something absolutely worthful" that renders the impetus to the higher life persistently effective with large masses of men, Elwang reasoned.[32] In this sense religion was regarded as the chief support for ideals. Ellwood wrote:

The supreme role of religion . . . in the higher stages of human culture is to enforce the claim to dominance in the life of man of the ideal social values. That is, it exalts the life in which the indi-

31. William Wilson Elwang, "The Social Function of Religious Belief," University of Missouri *Studies*, 2 (1909), 49–51. See also Ellwood, *op. cit.,* p. 301.
32. Elwang, *op. cit.,* p. 75.

vidual merges his personal interests, desires, and aspirations with his group, or, as in the highest religion, with humanity as a whole. For this reason, so far as we can now see, the death of religion would mean the death of civilization, or, at least of all the higher forms of civilization.[33]

In *Social Control* Ross referred to the social effects of the religious ideal of brotherhood and cited Lecky's *History of European Morals* to prove that the ethical ideals of Christianity had produced "a movement of philanthropy" never equaled in the pagan world.

Religion forms the support for a stable society because it provides the basis for the realization of ideals. Religion has always been connected with social order, where it has lent a powerful sanction to virtue and morality, wrote Professor Frank W. Blackmar of the University of Kansas in his *Elements of Sociology*.[34] Smith declared religion to be one of the great uniting forces of social life, while Ellwood asserted that it had served in this capacity because of its effectiveness in impressing social values upon the individual.[35] Elwang cited the collapse of French society in the Revolution as an example of the decay of religion and the failure of its substitutes to support the social structure. Further, it was held that the survival of modern civilization depends upon the maintenance of religion. A social religion, said Ellwood, is the one thing that can "do most to save human nature from selfishness and brutality, and so solve the social problem." The only true solvent for selfishness is religion, said Elwang: the alarmingly prevalent indifference to the other fellow's welfare will be checked only "through the application to life of the religion which bids us love our neighbor as ourselves."

From this position it was but a step to a practical statement proposing to adapt Christianity to modern needs. A frank attempt to formulate a scientific foundation for religion and to transfer its doctrines "from the traditional basis to the realm of social science" was *The Social Basis of Religion*, by the economist Simon N. Patten. Proposing to restate the historic dogmas,

33. Ellwood, *op. cit.*, pp. 302–303.
34. Frank W. Blackmar, *Elements of Sociology* (New York, 1905), pp. 199–202.
35. Ellwood, *The Social Problem* (New York, 1915), p. 204.

Patten substituted, for example, a conception of social degeneration for the doctrine of the fall of man; regeneration would be accomplished through the reincorporation of outcasts into society; socially it is true that the wages of sin is death, he asserted.[36] Patten speculated on what might have taken place if the life rather than the death of Christ had been interpreted for us by a Plato rather than a St. Paul: "Christ to us would be a social leader, preaching salvation only in terms of love, cooperation and service." If Christ's doctrine is that of salvation through love, said Patten, "the path is open to reconstruct religion in ways that meet modern needs." The lack of a social conception in religion has put the church at a tremendous disadvantage; its social mission "is not to make men religious, but to make them normal." Touching upon one of his economic ideas, Patten declared that the church should do its share in removing men from a pain economy to a pleasure one; the supremacy of Christianity can come only "as civilization and culture are socialized and the economic world so transformed that the minimum of to-morrow's welfare will include more of health and comfort than the maximum of to-day's standards." Thus was a religious motivation linked to Patten's ideal of a pleasure or plenty economy.[37]

This fragmentary review of the sociologists' analysis of religion indicates that the social gospel had succeeded in attracting to its support those social scientists who, in regarding religion as a necessary prop to a stable society, provided the needed rationalization whereby social reform could be based upon this type of social control. In this manner the oft-repeated criticism of the traditionally individualistic ethic of Protestantism obtained scientific sanction, and another evidence of the maturity of the social gospel was written down to its credit.

IV. The Church as a Social Agency

The development of the religious census marked a further step in the ripening of social Christianity into a constructive movement capable of utilizing the techniques of social science. In the period with which we are dealing notable use was made of the community survey, for the purpose of ascertaining the needs

36. Simon N. Patten, *The Social Basis of Religion* (New York, 1911), pp. 4–5.
37. *Op. cit.*, pp. 222–224.

of the neighborhood and planning a church program to meet them. In these years, too, the social-service activities of the churches brought them recognition from the regularly constituted agencies of social welfare as represented by their professional organizations and publications.

The first known religious census taken in the United States was made in New Haven, Connecticut, by the Reverend John C. Collins in 1880, when certain statistics were gathered in order to aid in reaching the unchurched of the city. The information obtained amounted to little more than a numerical count of church members, church goers, nonchurch goers, children in or out of Sunday School, and families having a Bible.[38]

The most significant early socioreligious survey was that of Hartford, taken by the Connecticut Bible Society in 1889 under the direction of Professor Graham Taylor and largely carried out by his students in the Hartford Theological Seminary.[39] This compilation analyzed the population by nationalities and denominations, with a count of families, domestics, and boarders, according to denominational preference and church membership. The relative numbers of Protestants and Catholics, as well as Sunday School statistics, were tabulated in a 40-page report containing many graphic presentations. "Destructive forces" such as saloons were enumerated; some mention was made of prostitution; jail and "town farm" populations were studied; considerable space was devoted to description of preventive, relief, industrial, and social agencies—churches, young people's societies, missions, temperance groups, boys' clubs, the Young Men's and Young Women's Christian Associations, and a number of charitable institutions. An associated charities organization was declared to be Hartford's greatest public need. In concluding the report, Taylor wrote:

This is an age when the study of social science is in its inception. It should be the science of Christian society. Its field is the world, including all classes and conditions of men from all nationalities. Its work is to investigate the conditions of social and personal life, discover the causes of suffering and the sources of inharmonious

---

38. John C. Collins, "Religious Statistics," *Proceedings* of the First Convention of Christian Workers in the United States and Canada, Chicago, 1886.

39. Taylor, *op. cit.*, pp. 418–419.

relations. When Christian sociology has done all this, it will be more possible to adjust differences, and harmonize the varying elements by applying the principles of Christianity.[40]

The most famous religious survey, which did much to stimulate church federation, was that carried on by the "Federation of Churches and Christian Workers in New York City," an organization founded in 1895 largely through the instrumentality of the Reverend J. Winthrop Hegeman, Ph.D. The census of Manhattan was begun about 1897 in the Fifteenth Assembly District, between Forty-third and Fifty-third Streets and Eighth Avenue and the Hudson River. Ten churches and two religious organizations coöperated in this first survey. It was found that in an area containing some 40,000 people, approximately one half were neither church members nor attendants; 10 Protestant churches had a total membership of only 1,798, with but 7 pastors and 2 church visitors.[41]

The Federation soon improved its technique and asserted a position of genuine leadership under the direction of the Reverend Walter Laidlaw, Ph.D., who had been trained in Germany and at New York University. The census next took in a district contiguous to that first surveyed. Concerning its work here the Federation reported in 1899 that two churches had been founded, public baths opened, libraries and a new park established, and "one of the most active and successful industrial settlements in the city" located; the religious life of the neighborhood had been "notably benefited," with pastors and workers meeting monthly to confer on the problems of the district. One minister declared that the survey had "secured a more thorough knowledge of the religious and irreligious condition of the neighborhood" than he had been able to obtain in twenty-five years. Publicity had brought in money and workers; kindergartens, clubs, cooking schools, and libraries had been started.[42]

These were among the first fruits of the Federation's plans

40. Connecticut Bible Society, *A Religious Census of Hartford . . . 1889* (Hartford, 1889), p. 39. The census was reprinted in Hartford Theological Seminary *Publications,* No. 10, February, 1890.

41. Leighton Williams, "Federation of Churches and Christian Workers in New York City," *Open Church Magazine,* 1 (1897), 96.

42. *Open Church Magazine,* unsigned introduction to reprint of the "Third Sociological Canvass" materials, III, No. 2.

for bringing "the organized intelligence and love of our churches to bear upon the material, social, economic, civic, and spiritual interests of the family life of our city, and through interdenominational conference and coöperation to meet its every religious and moral need." The method whereby this was to be accomplished comprised the survey, coöperation of the Federation with existing agencies to meet the needs disclosed, and aid in the creation of new agencies as needed.[43]

In taking the district census workers called upon every family, entering their findings upon carefully prepared cards. In addition to religious facts, information was secured concerning living quarters, length of residence, church affiliation, number and ages of children, occupations of all members of the family, boarders, and domestics, and many other items. The tabulation of this material gave the Federation a tremendously valuable and significant fund of authoritative sociological data concerning many phases of metropolitan life.[44] In time it became a clearing house for information on races, nationalities, housing, and similar matters of great concern to welfare agencies and like organizations. It published studies of various aspects of the areas canvassed, dealing with tenements, saloons, parks, playgrounds, baths, kindergartens, and economic conditions. The Federation furnished churches with information about their parishes, distributed handbooks of the churches and social agencies, interpreted the United States Census, listed and rated various denominational enterprises, provided an exchange for the registry of church-extension schemes, and issued reports of religious and sociological conferences and their findings. Valuable data were published in the quarterly *Federation*, of which a remarkable edition was, for example, that for June, 1902, entitled *Handbook of Population and Religion in New York City*.

The religious purpose of these manifold activities was kept clearly in sight. The philosophy of the organization was once phrased as "devotion to the life which is more than meat . . .

43. From the Federation's constitution; taken from fly-leaf of *Federation,* June, 1900. See also Walter Laidlaw, "Federation," W. D. P. Bliss, *Encyclopedia of Social Reform* (New York, 1908).

44. For example, the report of the third survey required over 100 pages to describe the Twenty-first Assembly District. At one time the Federation claimed to be able to survey one fifth of the city each year.

more than the largest wealth" and "devotion to men, in the midst of commercial processes, rather than to things." Christ's demands upon the church were declared to be "the removal of all traces of the commercial spirit from religion" and "the production of a society which will exhibit and demonstrate to the world the Fatherhood of God." The originating ideal of the Federation had been to utilize all agencies "fitted to bring Christ into the homes of the city."[45] Its attempt to correlate all efforts to improve "the spiritual, physical, educational, economic and social interests" of the families of the nation's greatest metropolis marked this organization as the leader of the forces that were working for church coöperation, and that were utilizing the techniques of social science in the application of the social gospel.

As a result of the development of such techniques as these, and of the ministrations of the institutional church and the religious social settlement, the churches were recognized as significant social-service agencies. In 1907 an entire issue of the *Annals* of the American Academy of Political and Social Science was devoted to *The Social Work of the Church*. Social-gospel theory and descriptions of institutional church work, religious settlements, and social work, and discussions of difficult problems such as the church and the workingman, all written by experts, filled this 128-page volume. In 1911 the National Conference of Charities and Corrections discussed whether the church ought to inspire, interpret, guide, or administer social work. Viewpoints were presented by Washington Gladden and seven other Protestant and Catholic speakers. When the Southern Sociological Conference met for the first time in 1912 it gave a large share of its agenda to the church. Its subsequently published "Social Program" for the betterment of the South stated the desire, among other aims, "for the closest coöperation between the church and all social agencies" for the securing of the various goals to which the Conference was committed. In later meetings this matter was given careful attention, especially in 1913 when the largest section of the program was devoted to the church and social service. Speakers that year included Walter Rauschenbusch, Samuel Zane Batten, Henry A. Atkinson, and Charles S. Macfarland, secretary of the Federal

45. An account of its origins was given in *Federation* for April, 1902, p. 83.

Council of Churches. The Congress itself issued a challenge to the church "to prove her right to social mastery by a universal and unselfish social ministry."[46]

In these varied ways social science, social work, and social reform became the mutual partners of the social gospel. All were the fruits of an age of scientific advance, moral striving, social confusion, and optimism. However romantic certain of its ideologies may have been, the utilization of the techniques of social service was one of social Christianity's chief evidences of realism, while the stimulus it gave to social-welfare activity was one of its noted germinal contributions to the broader social life of the era.

46. Southern Sociological Conference, *The Call of the New South* (Nashville, 1912), and *The South Mobilizing for Social Service* (Nashville, 1913).

CHAPTER XVII

SOCIAL CHRISTIANITY BECOMES OFFICIAL

. . . We summon our great Church to continue and increase its works of social service . . . to patient study of these problems and to the fearless but judicious preaching of the teachings of Jesus in their significance for the moral interests of modern society.

Methodist *Discipline*, 1908

THE social Christianity whose broadening stream has been followed through a generation of American life was in 1900 but an informal current borne upon the convictions of individuals and the interest of voluntary groups. In the first dozen years of the twentieth century most of the larger denominations appointed official social-service—i.e., social action—commissions or agencies. Although this action was the culmination of the movement's long agitation for recognition, it of course did not indicate the full acceptance of social-gospel principles by the rank and file of American Protestants whom the national organizations represented. Nor was it the victory of a majority party. But the accounts of official action here given nevertheless represented the full maturity of the movement and its most significant practical achievements. Such recognition heightened the prestige of social Christianity, opened to it the resources of denominational educational machinery, and provided new access to an immense audience.

The Department of Church and Labor of the Board of Home Missions of the Presbyterian Church in the United States of America was the first official church agency to pursue an aggressive social-gospel campaign through the efforts of a paid secretary. It was not only a remarkable phenomenon in an otherwise conservative denomination, but it acted as a powerful stimulus to the awakening social conscience of other religious bodies. The explanation of its unquestioned success was in the personality of the "superintendent," the Reverend Charles Stelzle. "A son of the Bowery," Stelzle had grown up in New York's East Side and knew the problems of the poor from first-hand experience. After eight years as a machinist he had entered the ministry with the purpose of preaching to working-men. Following study at the Moody Bible Institute in Chicago he held successful pastorates of working-class churches in Minneapolis, New York, and St. Louis prior to being called by the Presbyterian board to "a special mission to workingmen" in 1903.[1]

Stelzle's aim was to improve the relations between the churches and the laboring classes. At the outset frankly evangelistic, he devoted some months to the perfecting of a technique. He spoke to labor groups of every sort, to churches, on street corners, in shops, and in theaters. During his first year he visited a large number of Western cities, remaining in each from a few days to several weeks. His first annual report boasted that the workingman had already "come to a better understanding of the attitude of the Church of Christ toward him, and the Church has been aroused to some deeper interest in seeking the salvation of the sons of toil and their coöperation in building up the Kingdom of the Carpenter." In some cities ministerial associations had appointed fraternal delegates to the central labor body.[2] Within another year such "excellent results" had been obtained that the General Assembly recommended the appointment of local committees to coöperate with Stelzle's Department in the study of the labor problem. Thus there would be created in "every city in America, a board of experts, who may be able to inform the churches with respect to the aims of organized labor, and to inform the workingman concerning the mission of the Church."[3] Thus backed by a sympathetic church, Stelzle organized his work along a number of lines.

Probably the most successful of these was his own speaking.

1. Charles Stelzle, *A Son of the Bowery* (New York, 1926), chaps. i–vi.
2. Presbyterian Church in the United States of America, *Proceedings* of the 116th General Assembly (Philadelphia, 1904), p. 287, also Stelzle, *op. cit.*, chap. vii.
3. Stelzle, *Christianity's Storm Center* (New York, 1907), p. 92.

Membership in the International Association of Machinists gave him access to almost any labor gathering, including the national conventions of the American Federation of Labor, the endorsement of which he obtained at its Pittsburgh meeting in 1905.[4] An equally successful approach was the noon shop meeting at which Stelzle or his local committee members would give brief addresses to workers at lunch; in 1907 he reported 1,000 meetings with a total audience of 200,000.[5] The largest mass meeting arranged by the Department of Church and Labor was held at Kansas City in 1908 during the General Assembly, when an audience of nearly 15,000 people, "at least half of whom were workingmen," heard addresses on religion and labor.

In 1910 Stelzle claimed that the plan of ministerial representation to the central labor body was in operation in 125 cities; in many instances the minister had been elected chaplain and meetings were opened with prayer.[6] Stelzle emphasized Labor Sunday (which had been instituted in Episcopal churches in 1890 by C.A.I.L.),[7] and circulated appropriate sermon materials to 11,000 Presbyterian clergymen; in many localities labor groups marched to church in a body.[8]

A remarkable feature of Stelzle's program was his syndicated press releases, written by himself and published regularly in more than 300 labor papers having a combined circulation of over 3,000,000. In 1907 he claimed to be spreading more literature to the unchurched workingman by this means than was being sent out by all the tract societies in the country. The articles were short but to the point; their chief burden was an ethical religion. Christianity, wrote Stelzle on one occasion, "is not a scheme to increase the population of heaven," but is rather "to bring heaven down to earth"; it is primarily "a character and a life."[9]

Stelzle developed his Department into a clearinghouse for in-

4. Stelzle told the Federation that he stood squarely for organized labor. American Federation of Labor, *Twenty-fifth Annual Convention,* . . . (Washington, 1905), pp. 152, 232.

5. Stelzle, "Presbyterian Department of Church and Labor," *Annals* of the American Academy of Political and Social Science, 30 (1907), 456–460.

6. Stelzle, *The Church and Labor* (Boston and New York, 1910), pp. 29–30.

7. See chap. ix, above.

8. Stelzle, *op. cit.,* p. 33, also *Proceedings* of the 119th General Assembly (Philadelphia, 1907), p. 336.

9. Stelzle, *The Gospel of Labor* (New York, 1912), p. 81.

formation on its problem. Data were gathered from many sources and a series of leaflets issued. One dealt with "the criticisms and misapprehensions of workingmen concerning the Church," while another outlined practical methods of reaching the laboring class with the message of religion. Nearly one-quarter million copies of a pamphlet entitled *Is the Church Opposed to Workingmen?* were circulated.[10] To this literature may be added Stelzle's books, in which he not only reprinted many of the press releases[11] but discussed current problems,[12] and surveyed American social and religious conditions.[13]

In 1909 the Reverend Warren H. Wilson was called as Stelzle's assistant. Specific attention was now devoted to the rural church, and conferences were held concerning it. Wilson later became an acknowledged authority in that field. In 1910 the Department widened its activities to include preaching and conferences on social problems in the colleges and universities. That year Stelzle reported holding a "sociological conference" in New York at which twenty authorities spoke. At this time the *Outlook* declared that the Department of Church and Labor had "virtually revolutionized, within a few years, the attitude of the trades unions toward the Church."

Conservatives forced Stelzle from his position in 1913. His ideals and much of his program have been preserved, however, in the Labor Temple, founded by him in the East Side of New York in 1910. Situated in admittedly the most difficult religious field in America, and initiated as a venture of faith, this unique and splendid organization weathered both the adversities of location and the criticism of antagonistic superiors, and stands today as a monument to the courage and perseverance of its founder. Begun as an open forum, the Temple expanded into the institutional, settlement, and adult-education fields,[14] demonstrating Stelzle's faith in what the church could do "in building up the whole life of the people, with special emphasis upon their spiritual welfare."

10. *Proceedings* of the 118th General Assembly, p. 318.
11. See *The Gospel of Labor, Messages to Workingmen* (New York, 1906), and *Letters from a Workingman* (New York, 1908).
12. See *Christianity's Storm Center.*
13. See *American Social and Religious Conditions* (New York, 1912).
14. Edmund B. Chaffee, *The Protestant Churches and the Industrial Crisis* (New York, 1933), chap. x.

Both the General Convention of the Protestant Episcopal Church and the National Council of Congregational Churches took preliminary action leading toward official social-service programs at their meetings in 1901. By coincidence the resolutions were passed within a few hours of each other by bodies in session on opposite sides of the continent. During the Episcopal gathering in San Francisco a mass meeting sponsored by C.A. I.L. brought the aims of that society before the General Convention and a resolution was introduced by the Reverend Randolph McKim proposing that a standing commission be appointed to deal with the relations of capital and labor. Part of the divine mission of the church, he asserted, is to be "a mediator and peacemaker between those who are at strife"; the church "would be untrue to her Master—the Carpenter of Nazareth—if she were not the friend of the laboring man, and did not hold his welfare as dear to her heart as that of his employer." The commission was appointed and consisted of three bishops, three presbyters, and three laymen, whose duty it would be "to study carefully the aims and purposes of the Labor Organizations of our country," "to investigate the causes of industrial disturbances as these may arise," and "to hold themselves in readiness to act as arbitrators . . . with a view to bring about mutual conciliation and harmony in the spirit of the Prince of Peace."[15] Members of the Commission included Bishop Henry C. Potter, Dr. McKim, George Hodges, Seth Low, and Jacob Riis.

When the Commission reported to the next Convention in 1904 there had been no requests for arbitration. Causes of violence in various areas were described as "not so much economical as moral" in origin and due to an unfounded distrust and hostility that the church might well overcome by affording opportunity for conferences. The Commission had found widespread ignorance of the aims and spirit of labor organizations; it suggested ten books that would provide an introduction to the problem. It was convinced that "the organization of labor is essential to the well-being of the working people" and that the offenses committed by unions were as distinct from the cause of organized labor as was the Inquisition from the gospel.

15. Spencer Miller and Joseph F. Fletcher, *The Church and Industry* (New York, 1930), pp. 112–113. By permission of Longmans, Green & Co., publishers.

The Commission was continued. Its 1907 report, marked by a more mature viewpoint, held that both capital and labor had rights and urged them to submit all differences to arbitration if "friendly conference" failed. Child labor was scored as "a plain menace to the general welfare, and hostile to the spirit of the Christian religion." Communications had been received from the Christian Social Union, C.A.I.L., the Companions of the Holy Cross, the Eight-Hour League, and the Christian Socialist Fellowship. Summarizing these, the Commission proposed the coördination of various Episcopal groups interested in the labor problem, the promotion of sympathetic relations with labor organizations, and the use of the press to aid in increasing knowledge and interest on the part of church people.[16] This plan would require diocesan committees on social service and a central body authorized by the General Convention. As a result of these recommendations the Commission was made a permanent agency.

Its 1910 report included a wider range of social concerns than the problem of labor and capital; the Lambeth principles concerning property were endorsed; Labor Sunday was commended to the church; the appeal of the Federal Council of Churches in behalf of labor was accepted; and several statements made concerning the relations of the church to labor. In adopting this report the General Convention reconstituted the Commission as a "Joint Commission on Social Service" to consist of five bishops, five presbyters, and five laymen, whose task would include study, coördination, coöperation, and encouragement of "sympathetic relations between capital and labor"—a combination of functions necessary if the church was to face its social obligations squarely.

In October of the next year the Commission appointed the Reverend F. M. Crouch to the full-time position of field secretary, and an extensive educational program and correspondence were begun. By 1913 active social-service agencies had been set up in seventy-five dioceses and missionary districts, although during this time most of the Commission's work in industrial relations was being carried on by C.A.I.L. The General Convention of 1913 made the Joint Commission a permanent body, passed several resolutions on child labor, and declared that

16. *Op. cit.,* p. 115.

. . . The Church stands for the ideal of justice, and . . . demands the achievement of a social order in which the social cause of poverty and the gross human waste of the present order shall be eliminated; and in which every worker shall have just return for that which he produces, a free opportunity for self-development, and a fair share in all the gains of progress.[17]

Its activities now taken over by the Commission, the Christian Social Union, pioneer educational society founded in 1891, disbanded.[18]

The first official action toward a social-service program to be taken by the National Council of Congregational Churches was voted at the session of 1901 at Portland, Maine, when a memorial from the Committee on Labor Organizations of the Massachusetts General Association was presented by the Reverend Frank W. Merrick, requesting the formation of a commission on labor. As appointed, the Committee comprised Merrick, Washington Gladden, William Jewett Tucker, David N. Beach, and William A. Knight. A 15-page report was presented at the next triennial meeting.[19] The group had met several times, correspondence had been carried on with labor officials, bibliographies obtained from John Mitchell, Carroll D. Wright, and other specialists; one member had attended conventions of the American Federation of Labor and the Civic Federation, and two had studied and reported on specific industrial situations for the press.

The report first discussed "the function of a church labor committee," suggesting that the church limit its activities "primarily to the social and moral phases of the labor question"; its first service should be to itself—to get information and stimulate interest. The Committee had asked the state Congregational associations to appoint committees auxiliary to it, with the purpose of helping "toward a better knowledge of indus-

17. *Op. cit.*, p. 120.

18. C.A.I.L. formally disbanded and transferred its work to the Department of Christian Social Service in May, 1926, when the Department created the office of secretary of industrial relations. C.A.I.L. and the C.S.U. were described above in chap. ix.

19. National Council of Congregational Churches, *Eleventh Triennial Session, Portland, Maine, 1901* (Boston, 1901), p. 37, and *Twelfth . . . Session . . .* (Boston, 1904), p. 414.

trial conditions, and of the spirit of the churches"; to establish sympathetic relations with organized and unorganized labor, aiding workers' movements for physical, social, and moral betterment; to affiliate with other organizations having similar aims; and to keep the Labor Committee of the National Council informed as to conditions found and efforts made "to promote the well-being of the industrial part of the community."[20] Several state organizations had adopted these suggestions. In its discussion of the industrial situation the Committee emphasized its ethical aspects in words almost identical to those employed by the Episcopal reports just examined. Both trade unionists and employers were urged to exercise "the right use of power" and to cultivate a sense of responsibility that would "conserve social well-being for the present and the future." Attention was called to "the high social duty" of the church to emphasize good will, justice, and brotherhood, to teach restraint and patience, to embody the religious spirit in democratic form, and to uphold the highest ideals of personal and social life.

As specific recommendations the Committee urged the churches "to take a deeper interest in the labor question, and to get a more intelligent understanding of the aims of organized labor." This might be done by "fraternal personal contact" with workers, and through study. The report promised to publish bibliographies obtained from the American Institute of Social Service. It suggested that the Committee be continued, that state committees be formed, that these relate themselves to similar bodies within other denominations, and that they try to "get such expression from workingmen's and employers' organizations and leaders, as shall . . . best promote social welfare." In conclusion, two points were stressed: that the industrial question "has come to stay" and that nothing short of "justice to capital and labor alike" can touch its cause; and "only by the principles of the Gospel" can the ends properly sought by all employers and workers be attained.[21]

The report was accepted and the name of the group changed to "Industrial Committee"; Graham Taylor, Samuel G. Smith, and five others were added to it. The 1904 session at Des Moines gave considerable further attention to the industrial problem and attended in a body a meeting of the city Trades and Labor

20. *Twelfth Session*, pp. 415–416.   21. *Op. cit.*, pp. 415–420.

Assembly which was addressed by Taylor and by E. E. Clark, Grand Chief Conductor of the Order of Railway Conductors. The Triennial Council in 1907 heard five addresses on social problems as well as a ten-page report of the Industrial Committee. The latter had divided into five subcommittees that had concentrated on the problems of child labor, immigration, socialism, organized labor, and employers' unions. Upon their study of these issues the Committee based several recommendations: that regional commissions deal with the child-labor situation locally, that they give the problem of immigration their best thought, and that they exert themselves in behalf of improved employee-employer relations. The National Council was asked to memorialize Congress to establish a Children's Bureau and to regulate hours of work in the District of Columbia. It was proposed to make the Industrial Commission a permanent body, and in view of the usefulness of the Presbyterian Department of Church and Labor, the Committee asked the National Council to provide a paid secretary.[22]

Lack of funds prevented carrying out the last recommendation until 1910, when a much stronger demand was made by the Committee. That year regional commissions on industry were said to be at work in twelve states, and others were asked to fall in line. The National Council was asked to approve the social creed of the Federal Council of Churches and to coöperate with it. The Congregational Brotherhood of America was requested to become the executive agency for the churches in the program of social action. With the acceptance of this report and the calling of the Reverend Henry A. Atkinson to the industrial secretaryship, the Congregational Churches of the United States formally provided for an aggressive program of social action.

Atkinson carried on a great many activities, including "a correspondence course in social service studies" covering three years' reading in the literature of social Christianity. In 1913 the National Council rechristened the Industrial Committee as the "Commission on Social Service"—an indicative change. The work of the Brotherhood was committed to this group and a budget of $6,000 provided for the social-service program. It is hardly necessary to follow further developments of a well-established and effective policy.

22. *Thirteenth Triennial Session* . . . (Boston, 1907), pp. 319–320.

Social action was officially embraced by the Methodist Episcopal Church (North) largely as the result of the efforts of a voluntary organization that pushed the claims of social Christianity within Methodism much as C.A.I.L. and the Christian Social Union had done for the Episcopalians. The Methodist Federation for Social Service was organized in Washington, December 7, 1907, as the outcome of a year and a half of negotiation and study by five socially minded ministers: Elbert R. Zaring, Herbert Welch, Frank Mason North, Harry F. Ward, and Worth M. Tippy.[23] These men had proposed "the formation of a society to stimulate a wide study of social questions by the church, side by side with practical social service, and to bring the church into touch with neglected social groups." It would be "an effort to apply the sane and fervid spirit of Methodism to the social needs of our time." A program of propaganda, organization, and publication was decided upon as the means of realizing the Federation's purpose thus expressed in its constitution: "To deepen within the church the sense of social obligation and opportunity, to study social problems from the Christian point of view and to promote social service in the spirit of Jesus Christ."

The first means of propaganda utilized by the Federation was a series of pamphlets explaining its purpose and setting forth social-gospel principles. One of these asserted the "urgent necessity for the application of the Christian principles of righteousness and brotherhood," with the qualifying statement that the kingdom of God could not be supposed to have fully come while industrial peace, social justice, commercial morality, and political integrity "do not yet prevail." The Federation organized and carried out "study that is practical and will result in action, and a service that is effective because informed."[24] Local and regional organizations were planned and conferences on social action held annually. A significant meeting was that held in St. Louis in November, 1908, when a group of sociologists and religious leaders gathered for a three-day discussion of *The Socialized Church*, as the addresses were later entitled.

Social issues had first been brought to the attention of the General Conference of the Methodist Episcopal Church in

23. This account is based upon official records in the office of the Federation.
24. Methodist Federation for Social Service, *What is It?* (n.p., n.d.), p. 6.

1892, when a memorial "prepared with great care" and adopted without dissent by the New York East Conference had been presented to it. This was repeated in 1896. In 1904 a report covering certain phases of the social question had been presented, but at the Baltimore General Conference of 1908 four memorials were presented and acted upon. These requested the formation of a department of church and labor, a special secretary of immigration, a commission to investigate the relation of the church to social problems, and recognition of the Federation for Social Service.[25] The response to these requests was generous. One third of the Episcopal Address was devoted to social questions, the famous "Social Creed of Methodism" was adopted, and the Federation recognized and commissioned to study four phases of the relationship of Methodism to social action.[26]

The statement on "The Church and Social Problems" opened with the affirmation that the teachings of the New Testament contain "the ultimate solution of all the problems of our social order" and that the evils vexing civilization will disappear "when the spirit of Christ shall pervade the hearts of individuals, and when his law of love to God and man shall dominate human society." In view of the gravity of the social situation and the responsibility of the church, the Methodist statement welcomed every gesture toward "reconciliation, fraternity, and permanent coöperation." It commended employers who had "exhibited a fraternal spirit and a disposition to deal justly and humanely with their employees." "Fraternal interest in the aspirations of the laboring classes" was professed, and the fundamentally ethical purposes of the labor movement recognized. Gratification was expressed over the growth of the spirit of conciliation. It was hoped that the practice of conference and arbitration would increasingly supplant strikes, lockouts, boycotts, and black-listing. Members of the church were urged to "the fullest

25. Worth M. Tippy, ed., *The Socialized Church* (New York and Cincinnati, 1909), Appendix II.

26. The four "questions" were: what specific principles and measures of social reform demand the approval of the church? How can the agencies of this church best be utilized or altered so as best to promote those principles? How may we best coöperate with other denominations to this end? How can theological school curricula, and Conference studies, best be modified to better prepare our preachers "for efficiency in social reform"? Tippy, *op. cit.*, p. 281.

possible promotion of the principles of industrial peace and brotherhood"; the church in its own employment of labor should exemplify the principles set forth.

The "Social Creed" followed:

The Methodist Episcopal Church stands:

For equal rights and complete justice for all men in all stations of life.

For the principle of conciliation and arbitration in industrial dissensions.

For the protection of the worker from dangerous machinery, occupational diseases, injuries, and mortality.

For the abolition of child labor.

For such regulation of the conditions of labor for women as shall safeguard the physical and moral health of the community.

For the suppression of the "sweating system."

For the gradual and reasonable reduction of the hours of labor to the lowest practical point, with work for all; and for that degree of leisure for all which is the condition of the highest human life.

For a release from employment one day in seven.

For a living wage in every industry.

For the highest wage that each industry can afford, and for the most equitable division of the products of industry that can ultimately be devised.

For the recognition of the Golden Rule and the mind of Christ as the supreme law of society and the sure remedy for all social ills.

Further there was recognized the responsibility of the Christian church "for these great concerns of humanity." The organization of the Federation for Social Service was noted "with satisfaction" and its objects heartily approved. In conclusion the church was summoned "to continue and increase its works of social service" both in study and in preaching. Brotherhoods, Sunday Schools, and Epworth Leagues were commissioned "to awaken and direct the spirit of social responsibility"; every church agency was exhorted to "touch the people in their human relationships with healing and helpfulness." May "all 'the people called Methodist,' " concluded the charge, seek that "kingdom in which God's will shall be done on earth as it is in heaven."[27]

The General Conference of 1912 adopted the report of the Federation and declared it to be "the executive agency of the Church to rally the forces of the Church to the support of the principles and measures thus approved." Three bishops were appointed to its executive council, and that year the Reverend Harry F. Ward was called to be its secretary. The Federation was now able to carry out an expanded program along the lines it had already begun. Approved by the General Conference in 1916 and in 1924, the Federation was now the "authorized agency in the Methodist Episcopal Church for the purpose of raising before the church the question of the social implications of the gospel of Jesus."[28]

Official action leading to the development of a social-service agency was taken by the American Unitarian Association at its annual business session in 1908 when a resolution proposed by President Samuel A. Eliot was adopted:

Resolved, That the Association heartily approves the establishment of a department of Social and Public Service, to the end that our churches may be assisted, individually and collectively, to take part in all endeavors for civic reform, social regeneration, and economic justice.[29]

The Reverend Elmer S. Forbes was appointed secretary of the Department, the work of which consisted chiefly in preparation of literature and the development of social-service committees in churches. One of Forbes's first tasks was a survey of what Unitarian churches were doing in social-welfare work. His findings were published in the first of a long and distinguished se-

27. Methodist Episcopal Church (North), *Delegated General Conference Journals, 1908*, pp. 545–549. Also Daniel A. Goodsell, ed., *The Doctrines and Disciplines of the Methodist Episcopal Church, 1908* (Cincinnati and New York, 1908), pp. 479–481.

28. The Federation received no financial support from the Church. In 1912 the statement "The Church and Social Problems" was revised; see the *Discipline* for 1912, pp. 512–514.

29. This action was taken May 27, 1908. See *The Christian Register,* 87 (1908), 668. The words "economic justice" were amended to the original resolution after a motion put by the Rev. John Haynes Holmes.

ries of bulletins dealing with social problems. Five of these appeared in 1909, eight the next year; by 1915 there were thirty-six studies, dealing with such matters as boys' work, industrial warfare, child labor, housing, vocational guidance, the rural church, conservation of natural resources, and control of tuberculosis. Some of the contributors to the Unitarian Social Service Series were Mary E. Richmond, Thomas N. Carver, Luther M. Gulick, Paul M. Strayer, Charles F. Dole, and Francis G. Peabody.

The Unitarian Church, historically liberal and at this time frequently expressing itself on social issues of the day, refused to commit itself to anything resembling a social creed or formal statement. A characteristic sample of the activities of its Department of Social and Public Service was a conference held in Boston in 1913, at which the relation of the churches to various social problems was considered. Speakers included Peabody, Forbes, Anna Garlin Spencer, Frederic Almy, and a number of other Unitarian clergymen. They discussed the social function of the church, practical methods of social service, programs of action, the activities of certain outstanding churches, and the application of Christian ethics to business; the papers were published as *Social Ideals of a Free Church.* In fostering a social-service program that laid its primary stress upon education, Unitarians were continuing a policy that had long characterized this liberal denomination.[30]

The Northern Baptist Convention, founded in 1908, took official cognizance of the social gospel at its initial meeting. On the motion of Samuel Zane Batten a committee was appointed to investigate what Baptist churches were doing in the field of social service, to report its findings "from time to time to the churches through the religious press," and to bring in a report and recommendations to the convention of 1909.[31] A resolution was passed approving of "every movement to promote the social efficiency of the Church," and urging the ministry and churches "to emphasize the social significance of the Gospel, and to lend their aid to the united efforts of Christian men to arouse the civic conscience and to compel social righteousness in politics,

30. Cf. chap. iii, above.
31. Northern Baptist Convention, *Annual, . . . 1908* (St. Louis, 1908), p. 79.

commerce and finance."[32] Another resolution condemned child labor.

In 1909 this committee reported planning a "Social Service Series" of pamphlets to be written by "men of recognized standing and expert knowledge." Issued by the American Baptist Publication Society, these would be of permanent value and would deal with the relations of the church to the family, to the community, to wealth and industry, to politics, and with the general question of social waste. It had been found that Baptist churches were doing very little in the way of social service, although a sense of need for knowledge was apparent among pastors and churches.

The 1909 report was given largely to "the church and labor and industry." After reviewing industrial conditions in the light of the social principles of the gospel, the committee declared that a "most obvious duty" rested on the churches. It recommended that the "Social Creed" of the Federal Council be adopted by the Convention. Members of the churches were urged "to consider anew the great fundamental and social ideals of Christianity" through study of the ethics of the prophets and of Jesus and as contained in the kingdom of God ideal. It was proposed that "a systematic and comprehensive effort" be made to instruct the people in the social duties of the churches. The committee recommended that a commission "on moral and religious education" be created to coördinate the educational machinery of the denomination, and that social service be made an official department with a paid secretary. Save for the last item, the report was adopted.

The next year's report noted the progress of the Social Service Series and the issuance of a *Social Service Bulletin*. A course in social readings had been prepared for ministers and religious workers. The now official Commission had coöperated with state conventions in securing the creation of regional social-service commissions and had made suggestions for a year's schedule of study of social topics; its members had been active in many forms of social service. By the 1912 convention the Commission found itself "fully organized" and pursuing an aggressive program. The Social Service Series now numbered sixteen monographs, written by leaders like George W. Coleman, James Q.

32. *Op. cit.*, p. 101.

Dealey, Clinton R. Woodruff, Charles F. Thwing, Owen R. Lovejoy, and A. W. Wishart.[33] Specific problems were suggested for study during the ensuing year: dance halls, the social evil, parental oversight, conservation of life, safety of workers, workers' rest day, the right use of Sunday, prison reform, and socialism. A social-action program was outlined that dealt with the church, the family, civic betterment, and industrial progress. Recommendations were made for church instruction in "social duties from the Christian point of view" and for the adoption of "some means and plans whereby the devotion and effort of the people may become most effective in behalf of social righteousness and civic betterment." Correspondence courses in social service were proposed, as was an arrangement with the Publication Society for the promotion of the social-service program.[34]

The Commission's report to the 1913 convention described the full establishment of a social-service agency for Northern Baptists. During the year the American Baptist Publication Society had created a Department of Social Service and Brotherhood and had elected Samuel Zane Batten, then professor of social science in Des Moines College, as its secretary and head. In organizing for a "larger and more effective" program Batten divided his activities between the preparation of literature and field work. His educational program included a topic-a-month church study course covering the "social service year." Reading courses obtained from the Federal Council of Churches were recommended for pastors. Eight lines of study were available to adult classes and brotherhoods: the social ethics of the Old Testament or of Jesus, the social awakening, principles of social service, social institutions, duties, problems, or activity. These courses were based on the best materials, whether New Testament studies, sociology, social gospel, or Christian ethics. As "service" activities the Department outlined practical approaches to issues such as child labor, the social evil, industrial conditions, temperance work, and industrial brotherhood. In summary the report pointed out that the function of the church

33. For complete references see the writer's forthcoming *Bibliography of Social Christianity.*

34. Northern Baptist Convention, *Annual* for 1912 (Philadelphia, 1912), pp. 161–170.

in social action lay primarily in religious and ethical motivation rather than in specific effort; the desirability and need for provision of social training in colleges and theological schools were stressed; and the people were urged "to consider the relation of Christian principles to the acquisition and use of wealth."[35]

Thus did the denomination of Walter Rauschenbusch embrace the social gospel.

In 1912 it was said that eleven other denominations had pledged themselves to carry out social-service programs through their existing organizations.[36] However, the acceptance of the social gospel by the churches was most obviously demonstrated in the "Men and Religion Forward Movement," which was the most comprehensive evangelistic effort ever undertaken in the United States. Although it had not been planned to stress social messages disproportionately, the popularity of this phase of its program virtually converted the Movement into a social-gospel campaign, so that Rauschenbusch could well say that it had "probably done more than any other single agency to lodge the social gospel in the common mind of the Church," and that it had "made social Christianity orthodox."[37]

The Men and Religion Forward Movement was primarily a lay program that grew out of a conviction that the times were ripe for "a new and unusual consecration for service." The object of the Movement was declared to be "an effort to secure the personal acceptance of Jesus Christ by the individual manhood and boyhood of our times, and their permanent enlistment in the program of Jesus Christ as the world program of daily affairs." The Movement not only utilized methods of evangelism, but aimed "to increase the permanent contribution of the Church to the best life of the Continent, socially, politically, commercially and physically, and to emphasize the modern

35. *Idem,* 1913, pp. 123–139.

36. These denominations were: Free Baptist, Christian, Disciples of Christ, German Evangelical Synod of America, Mennonite Church, Reformed Church in America, Reformed Church in the United States, Society of Friends, Methodist Episcopal Church, South, United Brethren, and United Presbyterian—see R. F. Cutting, *The Church and Society* (New York, 1912), pp. 222–223.

37. Walter Rauschenbusch, *Christianizing the Social Order* (New York, 1912), p. 20.

message of the Church in social service and usefulness." Religious organizations were enlisted in "a worthy and workable plan of permanent specialized effort for men and boys."

The campaigns were handled by teams of experts who traveled widely. A total of over 9,000 addresses were given to audiences aggregating almost 1,500,000 persons. One of the six divisions of the program was social service. Charles Stelzle was dean of this team, the other members of which were I. J. Lansing, Raymond Robins, J. W. Magruder, and Graham Taylor. Meetings given to the presentation of the claims of social Christianity drew the largest attendance in practically every city. The social-action message was based upon a careful survey of seventy principal cities having a combined population of 20,-000,000. Data thus compiled concerned population, government, social influences, industrial life, the saloon, social-service agencies, public schools, libraries, recreation, juvenile delinquency, and religious conditions. On the basis of this information specific programs were outlined to meet local conditions, the recommendations being designed variously for the church, for social workers, for the municipality, and for the state, with general recommendations for the correlation of these programs.

The suggestions to the church proposed a thorough survey of local conditions, listing problems. Church members should be canvassed for specific social tasks, a social-service group developed in every church and such groups in various churches coördinated. Ministers should discuss social problems more frequently. Open forums were suggested, as were conferences of social-action groups, publicity campaigns, and social-service revivals. The exchange of fraternal delegates with central labor bodies, observance of Labor Sunday, and the employment of a social-service expert concluded this group of proposals.

Those for social workers were similar, including city-wide organization, surveys, study of problems, and development of scientific methods. Recommendations for the city included a bureau of research and efficiency, a vice commission, specific measures to remove the social evil, supervision of dance halls and motion-picture theaters, use of municipal buildings as social centers, establishment of juvenile courts, and many other city betterment projects. For the state, the social-service teams proposed the creation of a crime commission, renovation of county workhouses, passage of labor legislation, and similar remedial measures. Among their general recommendations, these speakers suggested regular month-by-month study and practice of specific measures in a completely correlated campaign. The mutually exclusive features of certain agencies were pointed out, in order that duplication and confusion might be avoided. Finally, the importance of enlisting "the citizens as a whole" in any reform program was pointed out.

At the final conference in New York the Movement's Social Service Commission presented a report in which the current widespread social discontent was recognized and "the Christian's God-given opportunity" declared to be in sympathy with and the spiritualization of it. It was held that the social teachings of Jesus needed to be set forth and men made to feel that God is behind those ideals "and that the Kingdom of Love has the backing of the universe." The social outlook is vitally connected with evangelism, missions, church unity and membership, continued the report, which went on to relate the kingdom of God to the economic life, to the family, recreation, civic life, relief, and correction. In conclusion the organization of the church for social action was discussed.[38]

In this manner the Men and Religion Forward Movement combined evangelistic fervor and method, interchurch coöperation, and the techniques of sociology. Its success was proof of the widespread acceptance of social Christianity throughout American Protestantism.

The penetration of the social gospel into all progressive religious communities was indicated, finally, by the development of a strong social emphasis and program in the Student Christian Movement. Student groups had long been interested in affairs outside their own immediate academic circles.[39] In the decade prior to 1912 at least four currents were moving them toward social commitments. Naturally, schools and colleges ab-

38. Men and Religion Forward Movement, *Messages,* II, *Social Service* (New York, 1912), pp. 1–108.

39. See, for example, Clarence P. Shedd, *Two Centuries of Student Christian Movements* (New York, 1934), pp. 100–102.

sorbed some of the social-gospel currents around them. Men like Rauschenbusch and Stelzle frequently lectured in the colleges.[40] Certain influences also came into the American student movement from British student circles.[41] Secondly, particular lines of study led naturally to social concerns. Bible study, in which fifty thousand students were engaged in 1907–8, turned enthusiastically to the social teachings of Jesus, with several hundred groups following Professor Jenks's course.[42] Summer conferences and techniques such as those developed by R. H. Edwards at the University of Wisconsin were stressing the social aspects of religion.[43] A third parallel influence was the development of various types of social service, especially in the older Eastern universities. Evangelistic deputation work expanded into boys' work and community service.[44] In the fourth place certain social-service programs of the parent Y.M.C.A. brought students into the teaching of English and other services to workers and immigrants.[45]

This emphasis on social service gradually pushed into the national policy and program of the movement. In 1908–9 and for several years thereafter, E. C. Carter devoted himself, as a member of the national staff of the Intercollegiate Y.M.C.A., to the spread and correlation of social-service activities. In 1909, W. D. Weatherford, another national staff member, originated a program of interracial study and conference, and himself prepared texts on the subject. This work soon assumed basic significance with the addition to the staff of A. M. Trawick. In 1912 R. H. Edwards was called from his university pastorate at Wisconsin to become the Movement's first "Director of Social Study and Service." Edwards set out at once to promote "the service programs throughout the country as a whole and

40. Presbyterian Church in the United States of America, *Proceedings* of the 122d General Assembly (Philadelphia, 1910), p. 360, and Charles W. Gilkey, "Some Work Done by the Movement in North America," in the *Report* of the World's Christian Student Federation Conference at Oxford, 1909, p. 92.

41. William H. Morgan, *Student Religion During Fifty Years* (New York, 1935), p. 87.

42. Gilkey, *op. cit.*, pp. 103–104. Jenks's book was typical of much of the literature described above in chap. xii.

43. See chap. xvi, above.

44. See, for example, Yale University Christian Association, *The Record,* 11 (June, 1901), 17.

45. See, for example, *op. cit.,* 18 (June, 1908), pp. 4–5.

to undergird them with an adequate philosophy."[46] His department aimed "to present to the students of its constituency insistent messages of balanced Christianity, and man by man to
enlist them in the service of the Kingdom."[47]

This growth cannot be followed in detail here (and there is
as yet no adequate study of it). Edwards carried his challenge
to college men and women beyond the actual social problems of
the day: "Nothing short of a life purpose and a life service is
demanded, for nothing less than the reconstruction of the social
order will suffice. The issues are stern issues and the best the
men and women of our generation have to give is barely adequate."[48] Full recognition of the place of the social gospel in
the American Student Christian Movement came in 1914 with
the calling by Dr. John R. Mott of a conference on social problems. This meeting, attended by the leaders of social Christianity as well as of the Movement, marked an epoch in the social
thinking of the student community. The conference came to believe it imperative that the discontent of the time be spiritualized, and it construed the Christian task as pointing out "specifically what the application of the spirit of Christ to existing
conditions would mean": "The great contribution that we as
religious people have to make is to preach the living God as behind the social transformation. Only as a man is dedicated to
the Kingdom is he in fellowship with God. Only as we confront
students with the social needs of to-day will they grow hungry
for God." But in the colleges, not in "the actual areas of social
injustice and neglect," lay "the most critical battlefield" of the
day.[49]

In its official phase social Christianity was, again, concerned
primarily with the labor problem, and the insistence upon social
justice was a strong note in the pronouncements of these church

46. Morgan, *op. cit.,* p. 91.

47. *Year Book of the Y.M.C.A.'s of North America, 1912–1913* (New York,
1913), p. 325. See also Edwards, *Volunteer Social Service by College Men* (New
York, 1914); Morgan, *op. cit.,* p. 91; and Edwards, "Glimpses and Some Principles of Service," *North American Student,* 2 (1913–14), 271.

48. (Edwards) *The Challenge of American Social Problems to College Men
and Women,* n.p., n.d. (published without signature).

49. Council of North American Student Movements, *The Social Needs of
Today and the Colleges of North America . . .* (New York, 1914), pp. 38–44.

bodies. They expressed strong sympathy with the workers and emphasized the ethical aims of the labor movement, at the same time appearing anxious to heal the breach between the churches and the working class. The interests of social-service commissions soon widened to include other aspects of the social scene, and in so doing took on a more melioristic and palliative tone, although they never shared the socialistic views expressed, for example, by Rauschenbusch. Methodological emphasis was placed principally upon education and considerable effort expended in obtaining the best sociological materials. But programs were not restricted to study; plans for church and community social action were developed, and stress laid upon the need for and value of federated efforts.

In a sense the recognition of the social gospel by the denominations and their provision for paid workers to cultivate the field represented the most concrete expression of the movement that can be chronicled in its first half century. Although another chapter is to be devoted to the social aspect of church federation as exemplified in the Federal Council, the denominational moves, inasmuch as they were closer home to the churches, doubtless represented more real gain for the rising social conscience of American Protestantism than did the loosely constituted Council in its early years.

CHAPTER XVIII

THE CHURCHES FEDERATE FOR
SOCIAL ACTION

> This Federal Council places upon record its profound belief that
> the complex problems of modern industry can be interpreted and
> solved only by the teachings of the New Testament, and that Jesus
> Christ is final authority in the social as in the individual life.[1]

THE climax of official recognition of social Christianity was
attained in the organization of the Federal Council of the
Churches of Christ in America in 1908. The significance of this
was twofold. Not only was the social gospel acknowledged in an
impressive manner by this most representative body in American Protestant history, but social action was itself one of the
important factors that brought the Federal Council into being.

The influence of the social gospel upon movements toward
the unity of the churches was an important aspect of the rise of
social Christianity. Efforts in behalf of church unity had been
initiated as early as the overtures of Samuel S. Schmucker in
1838, but not until the last few years of the nineteenth century
was any real progress made in this direction. Precipitated by
the rising threat of an irreligious civilization and given point
by the growing emphasis on the social aspects of Christianity,
the federative movements that came into being around the turn
of the century were based upon social-active impulses rather
than creedal or doctrinal agreement. The gradual emergence of
this new idea represented an implicit victory of the first magnitude for the social gospel. As Dr. Charles S. Macfarland has
said, the ideal of unity "came from men who were wrestling with
the practical tasks of the churches in what was becoming a hostile or increasingly unaccommodating social order." Although
the assumption that creedal uniformity was necessary played
some part in early negotiations looking toward federation, the

1. Federal Council of the Churches of Christ in America, Commission on the
Church and Social Service, *The Church and Modern Industry* (New York,
1908), p. 14.

search for "some simple basis of a common faith in Jesus Christ to do his work in the world together" finally produced the Federal Council.[2]

Religious groups had been learning to work together for a long while. The Young Men's and Young Women's Christian Associations, the United Society of Christian Endeavor, the various missionary movements, organizations such as the American Bible Society and the American Tract Society, the many temperance groups and other reform bodies, had all assumed a certain unity of purpose, such aims frequently being of a definitely social character. The earliest significant events that tended to bring Protestants together on essentially social grounds were the great Evangelical Alliance conferences of 1887, 1889, and 1893.[3] Following these widely attended gatherings the Alliance launched an aggressive campaign for the organization of local branches whose purpose was "to bring conscience to bear on the life of the nation; to close the chasm between the churches and working men; to gain the strength which comes from organization."

The first of many steps leading directly to the formation of the Federal Council was the founding in 1894 of the "Open and Institutional Church League," which numbered among its founders Charles L. Thompson, Frank Mason North, Charles A. Dickinson, Josiah Strong, John B. Devins, Leighton Williams, Gaylord S. White, and Elias B. Sanford—the last named its indefatigable secretary. The Platform of the League declared that the church should "take the leading part in every movement which has for its end the alleviation of human suffering, the elevation of man, and the betterment of the world." It should stand for "a ministry to all the community through educational, reformatory, and philanthropic channels." Sanford, in an address at the League's first annual conference in 1895, stated its philosophy in a few words. If organic union is not at present possible, he asserted, "Christian unity as a spiritual reality and as a practical factor, bringing the denominations into federative relations through which they can work out the problems of Christian service in city, country, and abroad without

2. Charles S. Macfarland, *Christian Unity in Practice and Prophecy* (New York, 1933), p. 53.
3. See chap. vi, above.

the present waste of forces" is surely coming and the League is destined to play an important part in bringing it.[4] Furthering its aims by means of an attractive journal, *The Open Church*, and the widespread promotional activities of Sanford, the League attained a strategic position by 1899.[5]

During these years parallel currents of local church federation were moving with broadening sweep. Many of the Evangelical Alliance branches ripened into bodies aiming less at a crusading type of reform than at an increasing emphasis upon such methods as were in use by the Federation of Churches and Christian Workers of New York City. In this atmosphere of rapidly crystallizing federative sentiment Sanford's activities were doubly effective. He was largely responsible for the founding in 1900 of the "National Federation of Churches and Christian Workers," a body viewed by its organizers as "the forerunner of an official Federation of Churches," to which they planned it should give place.[6] When the National Federation was officially organized in Philadelphia the following year, at a meeting attended by delegates of thirteen state or city federations, its constitution phrased the first of three objects as "cooperation among Churches and Christian Workers throughout the United States for the more effective promotion of the interests of the Kingdom of God."[7] At the conference of 1902 plans were made for the calling of a significant national meeting in 1905 and committees were appointed to carry out the work of securing official denominational representation at that time. As the result of three years of painstaking labor there met at Carnegie Hall, New York, November 15, 1905, "the most officially representative gathering of the Protestant forces of the United States up to that time."[8]

This "Inter-Church Conference on Federation" gave the unanimous approval of its five hundred delegates to a plan that, when adopted by the denominational bodies represented, would constitute the "Federal Council of the Churches of Christ in America." In contrast to the elaborate doctrinal proposals

4. Elias B. Sanford, *Origin and History of the Federal Council of the Churches of Christ in America* (Hartford, 1916), pp. 37 ff., 398–403.
5. The League was mentioned in chap. ix, above.
6. Sanford, *op. cit.*, p. 120.
7. *Federation Chronicle* (New York, 1901).
8. Macfarland, *op. cit.*, p. 54.

of Samuel Schmucker the plan and its preamble were "a mas-
terpiece of artlessness, and consequently of inclusiveness" and
the social note was strong throughout the document. The preamble recognized the timeliness of manifesting "the essential
oneness of the Christian Churches of America, in Jesus Christ
as their Divine Lord and Saviour, and to promote the spirit of
fellowship, service and coöperation among them." It was hoped,
among other objects,

To bring the Christian bodies of America into united service for
Christ and the world.

To secure a larger combined influence for the Churches of Christ
in all matters affecting the moral and social condition of the people, so as to promote the application of the law of Christ in every
relation of human life.[9]

Two sessions were devoted to social topics, such as labor and
capital, citizenship, family life, law and justice, discussed under
the general headings of "a united church and the social order"
and "a united church and the national life." Among the speakers
were William Jewett Tucker and Henry Van Dyke.

The conference adopted resolutions concerning the family,
the social order, and international affairs. With respect to society it declared that since in the divine order of things there
could be "no discord between labor and the accumulated results
of labor known as capital," that private capital ought to be administered as "a sacred trust for the common weal," "that each
party in the complex whole of society must patiently endeavor
to appreciate others and to coöperate with all in creating by
evolution the best social system and complete social harmony."
The resolutions saw "in the numerous revelations of 'graft' in
many high places of business and politics" the growing sanction
of "not only wicked, but criminal" usages, and urged that "all
unrighteous political and commercial customs of rich and poor
shall be brought to the bar of conscience by faithful preachers,
teachers and publicists." Especially should the pernicious doctrine that "corporations have no souls" be set aside for the Mil-
tonian doctrine that nations, parties, and associations are
"moral persons." The conference further went on record against

9. Inter-Church Conference on Federation, *Church Federation*, Elias B. Sanford, ed. (New York, 1906), pp. 33–34.

"the manifold and often disguised forms of popular gambling" and declared for "the enactment and enforcement of laws against impurity."

During the interim between the Inter-Church Conference and the first meeting of the Federal Council in December, 1908 —the "Plan of Federation" having been ratified by the requisite number of religious bodies considerably prior to that date —the continuing committee maintained an active interest in social problems. Its first report, issued in 1906, contained a statement by Charles Stelzle on "The Churches and Organized Labor";[10] in 1907 attention was given to temperance, the immigration problem, international arbitration, and child labor.[11]

When the Federal Council convened in Philadelphia in 1908 it comprised an officially delegated body representing thirty denominations.[12] That its power was only advisory perhaps added to the force of its pronouncements if not to their weight. Social interests to which attention was given were immigration, family life, international relations, and labor. A special theater meeting was held in the interests of the church and labor at which D. A. Hayes, fifth vice-president of the American Federation of Labor, Bishop E. R. Hendrix, president of the Federal Council, and Charles Stelzle spoke to an audience that Hayes described as the largest gathering of workingmen he had ever seen in Philadelphia.

The important action of the Council with which we are here concerned was the adoption of the committee report on "The Church and Modern Industry," presented and largely prepared by the Reverend Frank Mason North.[13] An 18-page statement, this epochal formulation opened with an acknowledgement of the headship of Christ and his absolute authority "in the individual heart and in the associated life of men." Christ's mission is not merely to reform society but to save it. He is more than the world's Re-adjuster; he is its Redeemer.

10. Inter-Church Conference on Federation, *Church Federation, First Annual Report* of the Executive Committee (New York, 1906), p. 47.

11. *Idem,* 1907; pp. 3–9, 19–20.

12. Federal Council of the Churches of Christ in America, *Report of the First Meeting . . . Philadelphia,* 1908, Elias B. Sanford, ed. (New York, 1909), p. 7.

13. *Op. cit.,* pp. 226–243. For a summary of North's career see a memorial entitled *Frank Mason North, December 3, 1850—December 17, 1935,* "Prepared and Published by Friends of Dr. Frank Mason North" (New York, 1936?), p. 6.

The new emphasis upon the coming of the kingdom on earth gets its meaning from the fact that there is a heaven in which that will is done; we must not forget that "the Church becomes worthless for its higher purpose when it deals with conditions and forgets character, relieves misery and ignores sin, pleads for justice and undervalues forgiveness." The church stands forever for the two-world theory of life, and in dealing with human conditions is bound to take the viewpoint of Christ which ever discerns "the world that now is and that which is to come."

With Christ's example before us it is impossible to accept a class gospel; his message comes to men as men, and is authoritative equally "at the council table and at the forge, . . . to the man who gives to a common enterprise his muscle and to him who gives to it his mind." The appeal of the gospel is based upon the inherent worth of every man in God's sight. Rich and poor are natural or artificial groups existing in society; they are not classifications made by the church of Christ. To the church there are but two kinds of men—those who follow Christ and those who do not; it must be a benefactor of all classes and must aim to establish a brotherhood as broad as human life and extending to the lowest depths of human want.

The church, continued the report, is not an end in itself. It is a conservator of the truth, but it is the truth that counts. The church is the representative of Christ—the ambassador, not the king or province. Through it is revealed the meaning of righteousness, justice, salvation, not for its own sake, but that sinners may be redeemed and "that these ideals may be worked into the lives of men and become the principles of the new social order." The kingdom, the establishment of which is the church's task, is coming to be seen more broadly. As the representatives of the churches of Christ in America, our primary endeavor is the building of his kingdom in these United States. It is the church of America "which must deal with the social and industrial problems of America." To this end the Federal Council hoped to find "some method for bringing the Protestant Christianity of America into relations of closer sympathy and more effective helpfulness with the toiling millions of our land."

Turning to a survey of social and industrial conditions the committee observed the estrangement between the church and the workers, the "separation between the rich and the cultured and the churches," and declared that the church had been taken unawares by industrial progress. The effects of the industrial revolution "have in a generation created a community life to which the thought of the Church has not rapidly adapted itself." Christianity has evolved a civilization which it is now its first task to inspire and direct; it has produced a social crisis in which its visions must concrete themselves into principles of action. The church does not stand for the present social order, but only for so much of it as accords with the principles laid down by Jesus Christ. Further, there are many phases of the present industrial conditions in the United States that cry aloud for immediate remedy. "Multitudes are deprived, by what are called economic laws, of that opportunity to which every man has a right." To impersonal causes of injustice and disaster "are added the cruelties of greed, the heartlessness of ambition and the cold indifference of corporate selfishness." The unemployed comprise an "army." Industrial and railroad accidents crowd our institutions and tenements with widows and orphans. Reckless competition drives women and children to labor, while the "homes" of wage earners in our great cities are an indictment of our civilization and their wages are meager without warrant of reason:

The helplessness of the individual worker, the swift changes in location of industrial centers, the constant introduction of labor-saving appliances, the exactions of landlords, add uncertainty to privation. The hazard of the mine, the monotony of the shop, the poverty of the home, the sickness of the family, the closing of the doors of higher opportunity react with dreadful precision upon temperament and mar character.[14]

That workers should organize for social and industrial betterment belongs to the natural order; their efforts toward improved conditions of work and larger possession of themselves "is welcome evidence of a Divine call within them to share in the higher experiences of the intellectual and spiritual life"; it is their right as it is the right of men everywhere, within the law, to combine for common ends—a natural right that "exists in the nature of things." Despite its errors organized labor is to

14. *Op. cit.*, p. 234.

be regarded as an influence not hostile to our institutions but potent in beneficence. When rightly guided trades unionism should be accepted not as the church's enemy, but as the ally of a church that believes in the gospel of Christ as a reality to be actualized by the furtherance of social justice and that intends to study and fully understand the situation. Not content to announce abstract principles it must work steadily toward the translation of these into conduct and it may well accept as its chief responsibility "the creation of that atmosphere of fairness, kindness and good will" in which employer and employee may find the common basis of understanding that will come to them from the inner sense of brotherhood rather than from outward pressure.

On the basis of this analysis the Committee on the Church and Modern Industry appealed to the Federal Council to "give utterance, by appropriate resolution, to its convictions touching the industrial conditions which concern the multitude to whom the churches are appointed to present and re-present our Lord." Further, it was recommended that without commitment to a specific program the Federal Council would "extend to all the toilers of our country and to those who seek to organize the workers of the land for the furtherance of industrial justice, social betterment and the brotherhood of man, the greetings of sympathy and confidence and the assurance of good will and cooperation." To this end a "Statement" and resolutions were presented.

The pronouncements of this Statement, in ten sections, were adopted and given wide currency by the Council. (1) At the outset it was asserted that the complex problems of modern industry can be interpreted and solved "only by the teachings of the New Testament, and that Jesus Christ is final authority in the social as in the individual life." The interest of the church in men is therefore neither recent nor artificial. But (2) Christian practice has not always harmonized with Christian principle; the organized church has not always spoken out, and its plea for righteousness has not always been uttered with boldness. Although the church has sometimes faltered it has nevertheless gone farther and suffered more in the mighty task of putting conscience and justice and love into our civilization than has any other organized force. (3) The church now confronts the most significant crisis and the greatest opportunity of its long career. Its ideals and principles have in part become the working basis of organizations for social and industrial betterment that do not accept its spiritual leadership and that are estranged from its fellowship. The church must not merely acquiesce in movements outside of it making for human welfare but must demonstrate by deeds its primacy "among all the forces which seek to lift the plane and better the conditions of human life."

Although it recognized (4) the complex nature of industrial and social relationships, the Federal Council would neither defend nor excuse "wrong doing in high places or in low, nor purpose to adapt the ethical standards of the Gospel to the exigencies of commerce or the codes of a confused industrial system." While (5) it asserted the right of capitalists and workingmen "to organize for common ends" such organization could not "make wrong right, or right wrong"; the church must meet social bewilderment by ethical lucidity and assert the gospel's prerogative to test "the rightness of both individual and collective conduct everywhere." (6) The "fraternal spirit and disposition to deal justly and humanely" exhibited by certain employers were regarded "with the greatest satisfaction," and labor organizations that had "raised the efficiency of service, set the example of calmness and self-restraint . . . and promoted the welfare not only of the men of their own craft but of the entire body of workingmen" were likewise commended. Such organizations (7) furnish proof that "the fundamental purposes of the labor movement are ethical" and highly beneficial to society. As omens of industrial peace and good will, the report noted (8) "the growth of a spirit of conciliation, and of the practice of conference and arbitration in settling trade disputes," expressing the hope that these methods would supplant the strike, lockout, boycott, and blacklist. "Lawlessness and violence on either side of labor controversies are an invasion of the rights of the people and must be condemned and resisted."

Paragraph (9) contained the formulation of social principles since known as the "Social Creed of the Churches," as it first appeared. This statement was taken almost verbatim from the Methodist pronouncement on "The Church and Social Problems"—which had also been written largely by Frank Mason North—except for two paragraphs declaring "the right of all men to the opportunity for self-maintenance" and "the right of workers to some protection against the hardships often result-ing from the swift crises of industrial change." The "creed" was considerably modified by the Council in 1912, in which form it then stood for twenty years. The Statement concluded with an address:

10. To the toilers of America and to those who by organized ef-fort are seeking to lift the crushing burdens of the poor, and to re-duce the hardships and uphold the dignity of labor, this Council sends the greeting of human brotherhood and the pledge of sym-pathy and of help in a cause which belongs to all who follow Christ.[15]

To its constituent bodies the Council recommended that the churches more fully recognize "the great work of social recon-struction" in progress, the character, extent, and ethical value of the labor movement, the responsibility of Christians for so-cial ideals, and the obligation of the churches to supply spir-itual motivation and standards to all movements for social bet-terment. In order that the study of social problems be stimu-lated it was proposed that "courses in economics, sociology and the social teachings of Jesus, supplemented, wherever possible, by investigation of concrete social facts" be established in all theological schools and as far as practicable in other schools and colleges, and that study classes and reading courses on so-cial questions be instituted in the churches. Closer relationships with workingmen, study of the meaning of trades unionism, and acceptance of the mediatorial function were urged upon churches and their members. The report further suggested that the church not only "aim to socialize its message" but that it also modify its equipment and procedure in the interest of more democratic administration and larger social activity, providing in its buildings for "the service of the community as well as for the public worship of God." The church must not fail either to emphasize its relation to the movements making for the better-ment of social and industrial conditions, or to call this relation-

15. *Op. cit.*, p. 239.

ship—both historical and present—to the attention of churches and workingmen alike.

In concluding its report, the committee recommended the organization of a "Commission on the Church and Social Service" that would be representative of the churches allied in the Federal Council. It would study social conditions, act for the Council, and "in general afford by its action and utterances an expression of the purpose of the Churches of Christ in the United States to recognize the import of present social movements and industrial conditions, and to co-operate in all practicable ways to promote in the churches the development of the spirit and practice of social service and especially to secure a better understanding and a more natural relationship between workingmen and the Church."[16]

The Commission on the Church and Social Service was duly constituted and under the voluntary secretaryship of Charles Stelzle initiated a program the subsequent development of which attained for it a position of genuine significance in the religious life of the nation. A wide correspondence was begun and conferences held with some of the leading social workers of the country. A large quantity of literature was distributed, particularly the "creed" just summarized, and a smaller pamphlet entitled *The Church's Appeal in Behalf of Labor*. Stelzle served as fraternal delegate to the American Federation of Labor each year and Labor Sunday was widely observed. By 1911 "the momentum of the work already accomplished and the wide and rapidly opening field" led to the establishment of the program on a budgetary basis and the Reverend Charles S. Macfarland was called as secretary of the Commission. Under Macfarland's direction an expanded program was put into operation. His office was planned as a national center for information, acquiring a library of over one thousand volumes by 1912, when the first quadrennial report was presented to the Federal Council in session at Chicago. This report described the Commission's plan of work as embracing educational and promotional activities, and fostering interdenominational coöperation, the cultivation of relationships with various social movements, support of the Men and Religion Forward Movement, industrial investigations, a program to aid the country church, agitation

16. *Op. cit.*, p. 242.

for the observance of Labor Sunday, and other specialized activities.[17]

Perhaps the most important operation carried out by the Commission during its early period was an investigation of the steel strike at South Bethlehem, Pennsylvania, in 1910. As an example of the Commission's methods the 21-page report of the special investigating committee consisting of Stelzle, Josiah Strong, and Paul U. Kellogg, may be cited in some detail. According to the report the strike had been precipitated when three machinists in the Bethlehem Steel Works were discharged "for daring to protest in behalf of their fellows against Sunday labor." As a result issues were raised that concerned not only the nine thousand men employed in the plants but "brought to the attention of the American public certain industrial problems which cannot be settled by capital and labor alone. The American people must assume a distinct share in the responsibility for their solution."

The special committee investigated the history of the strike, its basic causes, the action of the ministerial union in the community, the charges made by labor against the churches, and similar aspects of the problem. Labor organizers had declared that the churches had almost all, Protestant and Catholic alike, given "no aid to the men who were fighting for a great moral issue"; according to them the churches had collected funds through the corporation's office, and the Protestant ministerial association as a body had "practically championed the cause of the corporation." The committee found none of these charges true. The ministerial association had appointed a board that did serious work toward conciliation. No Protestant churches had ever used the company's collection offer, and the Catholics only on certain requests. The Federal Council's committee did find that the Bethlehem ministers' association implied that its sympathies were with the corporation when it administered a "sharp rebuke" to the men for attempting to embarrass and cripple the company, while at the same time it issued "no corresponding censure" of the corporation "for compelling un-

17. *Report* of the Commission on the Church and Social Service to the Federal Council of the Churches of Christ in America as adopted by the Council, December 9, 1912, in Quadrennial Session at Chicago. Also in *Christian Unity at Work,* Charles S. Macfarland, ed. (New York, 1913), pp. 161–194.

necessary and increasing Sunday work through a period of years." The committee found evidence that the ministers were sincerely desirous of serving the best interests of the workers, including the strikers, but their conduct in the crisis was positive proof "that they are too far aloof from the workingman to understand him and win his confidence":

Nothing could be more exasperating to the workingman than to assume that he desires to persuade his employer "to deal generously and magnanimously" with him. What he desires and demands is not generosity and magnanimity at the hands of his employer, but simple justice. Not until ministers get close enough to the workingman to gain his point of view can they hope to influence him to any extent. We deem it the duty of ministers not simply to record a formal protest against industrial evils, which may serve to pacify a partially awakened conscience, but to arouse a righteous indignation on the part of the Church and of the general public which will make the continuance of such ills impossible.[18]

The committee made two sets of recommendations. Those to the Federal Council and to the public declared the twelve-hour day and the seven-day week "alike a disgrace to civilization" and listed the industries operating on this schedule, declaring that there ought to be laws requiring three shifts in all industries operating twenty-four hours a day and that the churches should work for such laws. The churches should inaugurate a movement to place in the hands of the courts or other authoritative agencies the determination of when industrial operations are continuous. The Federal Government should purchase only materials made on a six-day basis, with three shifts instead of two for twenty-four-hour work. The churches and the Federal Council were urged to set aside a day at their conferences and conventions for the discussion of industrial conditions and the relation of the churches to them. The attention of the churches in all parts of the country should be called to the existence of the continuous processes in such industries as iron and steel, paper, railroads, street railways, telephones, mines, smelters, and glass, and ministers should be urged to visit such works in their localities in order to learn to what extent employees were

18. *Report* of the Special Committee of Investigation Concerning the Industrial Situation at South Bethlehem, Pa. . . . (New York, 1910), pp. 14–15.

obliged to work seven days a week. Federal and private studies on wages and hours of labor were recommended, as was their investigation by government bureaus. Some method should be provided whereby employee grievances could be aired. In summary, attention was called to the basic tenets of the "Social Creed" as the principles on which the Federal Council had previously asserted that the churches must stand.

To the ministers in Bethlehem the committee proposed that they collectively take a stand against the seven-day week in order that the people might know their position. In view of the contention that workers abuse their Sunday, a committee should be appointed to investigate "what opportunities for clean recreation are open to the working people of the Bethlehems; what opportunities a six-day, twelve-hour man has for enjoying any outdoor amusement except on Sunday; what opportunities the seven-day, twelve-hour man has at any time for enjoying them; what the mechanics and others who have Saturday half holiday do with it," and other specific points. A forum for fearless discussion might be organized; the churches could give over at least four meetings a year to social problems; the company might be asked for a report of the number of men working Sundays; and a committee could be appointed to investigate industrial accidents and other conditions having a bearing on the situation.[19]

This report, representative of the Commission's activities along concrete lines, describes one of its most important functions.[20] Of the wide range of its literature only an indication can be given. In 1912 twenty pamphlets dealing with such subjects as "A Plan of Social Work," reading lists, the reports we have summarized, "A Social Service Catechism," and "The Study of Social and Industrial Questions" had been prepared and distributed in large numbers. The first of a series of handbooks, *The Social Creed of the Churches*, edited by Harry F. Ward with Henry A. Atkinson and Samuel Zane Batten, ap-

19. For the results, see Macfarland, *Across the Years* (New York, 1936), pp. 224, 227.

20. The 1912 report noted the investigation of the industrial situation at Muscatine, Iowa, by a committee including Atkinson, Batten, Ward, and Graham Taylor. A more important inquiry was that into the Colorado situation in 1914. For a general discussion of these activities of the Commission, see Macfarland, *op. cit.*, pp. 218–231.

peared before 1912 and was followed by such volumes as Ward's *Year Book of the Church and Social Service in the United States* in 1914 and Macfarland's *The Churches of the Federal Council* in 1916. In addition to its own literature the Commission used and recommended materials gotten out by the various denominational agencies and their secretaries, including books like Batten's *The Christian State* and *The Social Task of Christianity*, Stelzle's various volumes on the relation of church and labor, Ward's *Social Ministry*, and Macfarland's *Spiritual Culture and Social Service*. All these as well as study courses and bibliographies were "in wide and constantly increasing demand."

These broadening contacts and a deepening realization of the nature of the social problem resulted in a maturing social thought that made certain important changes in the "Social Creed" when the Federal Council met in quadrennial session at Chicago in 1912. Social justice was given a new emphasis and "other matters than those strictly industrial" were included in the now classic document. Widely—almost universally—adopted by the Protestant denominations of America, the 1912 formulation of the fully-developed program of social Christianity—unmodified until 1932[21]—serves as a fitting close to our analysis of the rise of the social gospel:

The Churches must stand:

1. For equal rights and complete justice for all men in all stations of life.

2. For the protection of the family, by the single standard of purity, uniform divorce laws, proper regulation of marriage, and proper housing.

3. For the fullest possible development for every child, especially by the provision of proper education and recreation.

4. For the abolition of child labor.

5. For such regulation of the conditions of toil for women as shall safeguard the physical and moral health of the community.

6. For the abatement and prevention of poverty.

7. For the protection of the individual and society from the social, economic, and moral waste of the liquor traffic.

21. For the 1932 statement see Macfarland, *Christian Unity in Practice and Prophecy,* pp. 295–315.

8. For the conservation of health.

9. For the protection of the worker from dangerous machinery, occupational diseases, and mortality.

10. For the right of all men to the opportunity for self-maintenance, for safeguarding this right against encroachments of every kind, and for the protection of workers from the hardships of enforced unemployment.

11. For suitable provision for the old age of the workers, and for those incapacitated by injury.

12. For the right of employees and employers alike to organize for adequate means of conciliation and arbitration in industrial disputes.

13. For a release from employment one day in seven.

14. For the gradual and reasonable reduction of the hours of labor to the lowest practicable point, and for that degree of leisure for all which is a condition of the highest human life.

15. For a living wage as a minimum in every industry, and for the highest wage that each industry can afford.

16. For a new emphasis upon the application of Christian principles to the acquisition and use of property, and for the most equitable division of the product of industry that can ultimately be devised.[22]

And in conclusion the report declared: "The final message is redemption, the redemption of the individual in the world, and through him of the world itself, and there is no redemption of either without the redemption of the other":

The Gospel is outgrown, the Christian pulpit is superfluous, the Church of the living Christ goes out of existence when the truths of the gospel, the vocabulary of the preacher, and the constitution of the Church no longer contain the words, God, Sin, Judgment, and Redemption, and they are gigantic and capacious words, belonging to a vocabulary that can interpret the whole universe of right and wrong, both individual and social. They are applicable to every problem in God's world.[23]

22. *Report* of the Commission, 1912, pp. 20–21.
23. *Op. cit.*, p. 26. For the 1908 and 1912 statements see Macfarland, *op. cit.*, pp. 296–298. The Federal Council faced a long struggle against many obstacles before it developed into an effective force. This phase of its history is beyond the scope of the present study. See Macfarland, *Across the Years,* chaps. xii, xiii.

CONCLUSION

THE social gospel, as this study has surveyed its origins and development, may be regarded as American Protestantism's response to the challenge of modern industrial society. Although practically all denominational groups ultimately awoke to social issues, the movement took root and grew most vigorously among Unitarians, Congregationalists, and Episcopalians— three American religious bodies inheriting the state-church tradition of responsibility for public morals.

Other factors were even more significant. Both Unitarians and Congregationalists participated generously in the liberal theological trends of the nineteenth century. Roots of a social gospel of brotherhood are to be found in Channing's Baltimore sermon, while the "new theology" derived from Bushnell by Munger, Gladden, and other Congregationalists was itself inherently social. Episcopal clergymen, especially in New York City, were in reasonably close touch with the advanced social thought of certain of their Anglican brethren, and as leaders of a wealthy church carrying on an extensive city-mission program they were early brought into immediate contact with the problems of the new urban and industrial order as these were making a first appearance in acute form in the nation's largest city.

When, later, the social aspects of Christianity began to be stressed by leaders of Baptist, Methodist, and other bodies whose heritage was pietistic and separatist, the social gospel of this group was marked by an evangelical fervor and an ideology looking toward a kingdom of God raised on earth by consecrated groups of individuals, whereas the former tradition inclined to apply the "Christian law" of love to the transactions of society. This contrast was apparent between Gladden and Rauschenbusch, although the latter's fully developed gospel went far toward socialism.

The social situation produced by the industrial revolution in post-Civil War America was characterized by the rise of large-scale production units that drew together vast proletarian populations in hastily built, overcrowded cities. As clergymen looked at the consequent social maladjustment, their predominant concern was with the problem of industry, a question given added urgency by the strictures of socialism. From Gladden's pioneer addresses to *Working People and their Employers* to the Federal Council's statement on "The Church and Modern Industry," this was the crux of the social gospel. The religious and social needs of the cities received serious consideration, but these questions were usually traced back to their roots in the industrial revolution and the consequent conflict between capital and labor. Discussion of the ethics of wealth—property, corporations, monopoly—was likewise frequently carried on in this context. While social prophets were also concerned to some extent with such social facts as crime, the family, immigration, charity, the country church, saloons, church union, race, amusements, democracy, and housing, these were all of secondary importance. It may be said, therefore, that the social gospel was the reaction of Protestantism—markedly stimulated by socialism—to the ethics and practices of capitalism as brought to point in the industrial situation. In the large, social Christianity was not concerned with the problems of war, imperialism, race, democracy, or the use of force.

The religious social movement expressed itself in various concrete forms. The most obvious of these was the vast body of educational and propagandistic literature and activity: sermons, books, magazines, essays, conferences, study courses, theological school curricula, tracts, and evangelism. Several types of organization revealed the many-sided character of social Christianity: vaguely motivated groups such as the ephemeral Societies of Christian Socialists; definitely religious bodies with specific ideas as rallying points maintained a vigorous life over a long period—as the Brotherhood of the Kingdom; longest-lived of all was the Church Association for the Advancement of the Interests of Labor with its activistic program; and an equally effective society was the Christian Social Union, dedicated to a strictly educational policy yet embracing a wide range of interests. The most concrete organized product of the movement was the institutional church and the religious social settlement. A further addition to the permanent machinery of Protestantism was the official denominational social-action commission and the similar coördinating agency of the Federal

Council of the Churches of Christ in America. The development of the religious and social census and other sociological techniques represented still another contribution. Last, and not least, may be mentioned the supply of leaders furnished by the church to social work, the Socialist party, and the labor movement as a result of the social emphasis.

The social gospel rested upon a few dominant ideas that characterized the intellectual climate of opinion in which it grew. Its primary assumption was the immanence of God, a conception derived from the influence of science—Darwinian evolution in particular—upon Protestant theology. Belief in an indwelling God, working out his purposes in the world of men, naturally involved a solidaristic view of society—which was conveniently supplied by sociology. In an organic society with its interdependent relationships, as contrasted to the "sand-heap" theory of social organization, brotherhood might be genuinely realized among men who were equally the sons of their common Father. And to such a world the kingdom of heaven was brought down out of the skies to be realized progressively here and now. In addition to these more or less implicit foundations, the social gospel discovered for itself a Biblical and also autonomous basis in the social teachings of Jesus—an authority of equal weight to theist or humanist.

Turning now to the general characteristics of social Christianity, we note at the outset its dominant ethical strain and the emphasis placed upon the realization of the kingdom ideal in the present world. As compared with the older Protestant thought that it was gradually modifying, the contrast might be stated as implying a moralistic in place of a religious attitude, although in none of its leading thinkers did moralism ever assume the ascendancy. Considered as a corrective of and a reaction against an extreme otherworldly individualism, the ethicizing strain must be regarded as a healthful influence even though it afforded an opening for the entrance of humanism and moralism. The coming to earth of the kingdom of heaven necessarily implied an ethical ideal, as did the consequent notion of social salvation, which is meaningless apart from an ethical interpretation.

In the second place, sociology forced religion to a more realistic appraisal of its task. While Christianity's ideology re-

mained to a certain degree sentimental, lessons learned from social science gave the practical working program of the movement a new appreciation, for example, of the effects of environment, so that a conception such as social salvation, while naïve
in certain respects, nevertheless bespoke an appreciation of the
nature of the social controls. The realization that the individual
is saved in his social context rather than out of it, and therefore that the customs of society must be changed if he is to develop his full potentialities, was a far more realistic view than
the conservative attitude that had expected to perfect the individual soul in a celestial sphere while the present order was left
to decay.

But this interest in practical and ethical concerns did not
mean that the social gospel became irreligious. Its great
prophets were men of spiritual, even mystical, genius whose
message was characterized by a fundamentally religious and
evangelical fervor. Salvation, albeit social and taking place in
an earthly kingdom of God, was nevertheless the divine process
of redemption. Social salvation never became a mere program
of reforms. Herron, Rauschenbusch, and the Federal Council's
"Social Creed" of 1908 were conspicuous examples of this. Although much stress was laid upon collectivism and the effect of
external factors, the movement never lost sight of the basically
religious contention that the social crusade began in and existed
for the individual. While it is true that the social gospel, influenced as we have seen by evolution, conceived of God as immanent and as motivating the progressive development of his kingdom from within human society, and therefore tended to neglect the more pessimistic aspects of sin and judgment—natural
enough in the progressive era—this cannot be taken as evidence
that the movement was independent of a theistic center. "God,"
said Rauschenbusch, "is the common basis of all our life."

The social theology developed by the movement exemplified
several of these characteristics. It exerted a definitely ethical
influence upon the conceptions of God, man, sin, salvation, and
other doctrines. It proposed a new and realistic view of sin in
terms of the implications of a solidaristic society. This doctrine,
the crux of any theological system, took account of social facts
such as physical environment and the mores. In thus enlarging
the conception of sin from mere heresy or personal vice to in-

clude what Rauschenbusch called "the superpersonal forces of evil," while at the same time pointing out the responsibility of the members of society for its corporate sins, the social gospel produced a permanent revolution in the Protestant attitude toward this basic theological problem. It further provided the waning authority of theology with effective new sanctions to take the place of previously held logical abstractions.

One of the most obvious attributes of social Christianity was its belief in progress, which it absorbed naturally enough from the intellectual climate of the era, which was, as we have seen, under the influence of evolution. This was, however, the theological view of progress that regarded gradualism as God's method of bringing in the kingdom. "Progress," said Rauschenbusch, "is more than natural. It is divine." But it was not inevitable, and would be achieved only through sacrificial struggle against the entrenched forces of privilege and the common sanctions of custom. Nevertheless the social gospel shared the optimism of its age that in God's good time all desirable reforms would be brought to pass through the agency of an enlightened public conscience that would finally embrace the liberal program of progressivism, although the more radical prophets of social Christianity looked beyond this to a definitely socialistic goal. Progress, while regarded as ultimate, was not automatic.

A further characteristic of the social gospel was its note of crisis. From Josiah Strong's *Our Country* to Rauschenbusch's *Christianity and the Social Crisis* the prophets of the new faith cried out that "now is the accepted time." This sense of urgency gives added testimony to the religious character of the movement and also indicates its activistic nature. While the latter trait stood in marked contrast to quietism, it must be regarded as a later expression of definitely practical interests that had more or less characterized American Protestantism throughout the nineteenth century, rather than as a unique phenomenon somehow attributable to the social gospel itself. Social Christianity was the natural reaction of American *aktivismus*—always strongly missionary, and deeply involved in the slavery and temperance crusades—to the social conditions of the half century between the Civil War and the catastrophe of 1914–18.

The social philosophy of the movement was concerned more with criticism than with a constructive program of a practical nature. While its recipes remained mostly sentimental and utopian its diagnosis of modern society was its most realistic feature. The movement must at this point be regarded as both an implicit and explicit critique of capitalism. While the church rejected socialism as a methodology and most of those who embraced it left the fold, social prophets nevertheless appropriated its features that lent themselves to their purposes. Social Christianity therefore combined the strictures of religion and of socialism against a materialistic social order dedicated to the pursuit of profit regardless of ethical and spiritual values. The repudiation of the irreligious basis of socialism as well as its political program and emphasis upon the class struggle was the readily understandable rejection of elements naturally repugnant to Christianity. The doctrine of economic determinism was accepted with reservations and used to advantage in pointing out the real character of the social problem and the nature of effective remedies.

Such socialistic dogmas as public ownership or regulation, although rejected en bloc by the social gospel of the 1880's, came to be fully accepted by its later prophets, particularly Herron and Rauschenbusch. Religious fear of socialism was at first largely motivated by apprehension lest individual and spiritual values be lost in a collectivistic state and democracy be subordinated to bureaucracy. These objections were later reversed by leaders who saw the individual already the victim of a monopolistic capitalism that manipulated government for its own ends. It was believed that a Fabian socialism would produce a more equitable distribution of wealth, thus equipping the individual for the pursuit of the good life, and that it would bring a genuine realization of democracy in industry as well as in politics, in fact as well as in theory. These views may be cited as evidence of the realism in social-gospel analysis and the lack of it in a constructive program.

The critique of capitalism addressed itself to the basic assumptions of the established order. In the first place competition—"the law of tooth and nail"—was soundly condemned by writers from Edward Beecher to Henry C. Vedder, and no one castigated it more trenchantly than did Washington Gladden. Although proposed substitutes for it varied from vague forms of coöperation to state socialism, religious leaders agreed that unbridled competition was the absolute antithesis of the Christian ethic of love. While not all would have admitted that their criticisms struck at the heart of capitalism, these and related strictures nonetheless constituted a frank denunciation of the basic assumption of the extant order.

A similar attitude was taken with respect to freedom of contract. The rights of individuals could have found no stronger champions than the prophets of the new social-religious faith, but leaders of the social gospel were keenly aware of the "superpersonal" forces at work in the industrial world and of the rapidly vanishing freedom of the individual to bargain with giant corporations for his labor. Freedom of contract could exist only between equals. For this reason the social gospel openly avowed the right of workers to justice and to organize for collective bargaining and other constructive aims. Although many clergymen were slow to concede these viewpoints, the movement was nevertheless marked by a sincere effort to face this problem squarely, and at the height of its development reached a realistic view of the basic issues involved. Although appreciative of the need for and the ethical character of the trades union, social Christianity did not bestow upon it an unqualified blessing. The same attitude that prompted comparison of corporate authority to the rule of Louis XIV also cautioned the unions against abuse of power and privilege.

With respect to the profit motive the social gospel took the position that a moderate degree of such motivation may be necessary, but that profits must not be made at the cost of human welfare. The demand for economic justice rather than charity or paternalistic magnanimity indicated the attitude of social Christianity toward wealth. This viewpoint, however, was only attained after long experience and the strictures of socialism had indicated the inability of the traditional ethic of stewardship to control the power of wealth. Stewardship was then applied in a sense to the state, which, as the guardian of God's gifts to the people, should oversee their just distribution. While stewardship was still advocated as the proper attitude for the individual in regard to his own wealth, the essentially socialistic gospel of Rauschenbusch, for example, recognized the failure of an individualistic ethic. The problem was brought to point most effectively in the rise of corporate monopolies that in both practice and impersonal character were beyond the reach of any control but that of the state. The strongest denunciations of monopoly were those of Herron, whose mature gospel was socialism.

Criticism of the intellectual foundations of capitalism was epitomized in the reaction against *laissez faire* economics. It will be recalled that some of the earliest documents described in Part I took strong exception to the unchristian tenets of classical economic theory, while Professor R. T. Ely was giving popular expression to this viewpoint in the 1880's. Competition was declared to be the opposite of Christian love and coöperation, freedom to buy labor as a commodity in the cheapest market was condemned on religious grounds, and the practical materialism of the profit motive was branded as ethically subversive. Thus social prophets were from the beginning critical of the fundamental assumptions of capitalism, although their practical suggestions for change lacked the stamp of realism.

The methodology of social Christianity may be studied in two aspects. In the practical activities of the institutional churches, settlements, and federations utilizing sociological techniques, a concrete program was developed to meet the immediate needs of the community. The note of realism was less apparent in the philosophy of method, which was, in short, the application of the law of love to society. While such an ideal is in itself no more romantic than the related panaceas of other social philosophies—socialism, communism, anarchism—much social-gospel thinking at this point remained peculiarly naïve and sentimental. This was well illustrated in the proposals of Charles M. Sheldon's novels, the popularity of which was largely due to their utopian character.

However, the thought of social leaders underwent a distinct evolution in this regard. In the beginnings of the movement it was assumed that the ethic of stewardship would operate satisfactorily in the social situation as well as with individuals. When the course of events proved it inadequate, later thinkers were moved to propose a social application of the principle. This can hardly be regarded as a failure of the law of love, unless that law be interpreted in the narrow sense of stewardship. The real task of the social gospel—and one that it accomplished only in part—was the formulation of the law of love in terms equal to the demands of modern society. Herron gave this up as impossible, declaring that the ethics of Jesus were insufficient for the needs of the social revolution. But Rauschenbusch pointed out that certain significant areas of social life were already Christianized—that is, operating largely according to the law of love, and he enumerated the family, the church, and political life to the extent to which true democracy was being realized. He then declared that these areas must be extended into the unchristianized portions of society, and any practical method for the accomplishment of this end should be endorsed. Therefore he regarded efforts toward the establishment of industrial justice, economic democracy, wider distribution of wealth, and similar aims as fulfilling the law of love, though admittedly only imperfectly. Similarly those who proposed an "applied Christianity" aimed at this goal. Their understanding of the forces shaping society was shallow and they underestimated the stubbornness of the mores, but their intention was realistic, even though they did not succeed in stating an adequate Christian sociology.

From this discussion it is only too apparent that these leaders were very much the children of their age, drawing their ideology from the intellectual environment and rarely pausing to examine it or to follow basic assumptions to their logical conclusions. This was nowhere more obvious than in the question of the use of force. Could the law of love become operative through socialism without imposing its will upon a minority that clung to private ownership? The resolution of such problems was left to a later generation. These pioneers, evangelists of a broader and more ethical religion than the cramped individualism of the nineteenth century, were preachers of righteousness and of salvation to come, not careful sociologists or logicians.

Thus the social gospel was an indigenous American movement deriving its dynamics and its ideology from the social context in which it grew. It represented the unique American reaction to a social revolution that appeared in this country simultaneously with the development of the physical sciences, evolution, sociology, and Biblical criticism, all of which entered into its complex pattern. In this dynamic interplay of social forces and dominant ideas rather than in specific schools of thought or definite foreign influences the social gospel was wrought out—

the result of the impact of the industrial revolution and its concomitants upon American Protestantism.

When Walter Rauschenbusch stood on the platform of the Taylor Lectureship at Yale in 1917 to present his mature thought in its final formulation as *A Theology for the Social Gospel*, the drums of war were beginning to sound across the land. The great conflict brought an end to the era of optimism and progress in which social Christianity had developed. In the subsequent epoch that is yet in flux the American theological climate has been stirred by fresh currents that have tempered an overconfident and perhaps superficial social gospel with an augmented ecumenical consciousness and a deepened appreciation of the historical nature of Christianity. But the transfer of ideas has not all been in one direction. The permeation of the social viewpoint into the thinking of Christendom has been widespread and significant. This was dramatically illustrated in 1937 when the Oxford Conference on Church, Community and State embodied in its report on *The Church and the Economic Order* principles representative of the essential genius of the movement whose development has been chronicled in this volume. The social gospel has become an integral part of the thought and action of the Church, and one of the hopeful beacons in the present darkness that has descended upon mankind is the seriousness of effort and the genuine progress being made toward that persistently elusive goal—an adequate Christian Sociology.

INDEX

Figures in italics indicate important references or summaries.

Socialism, 181, 183; and teachings of Jesus, 207 ff.; in social settlements, 157; common to socialism and Christianity, 172; realized through socialism, 233; social effects of, 273; church must aim to establish, 307; realizable in an organic society, 320

Brotherhood of the Daily Life, 239

Brotherhood of the Kingdom, 20, 110, *131–134*, 182, 206, 228, 319

Brown, C. O., 71, 90

Brown, William T., 200

Bureaucracy, 73–74

Bushnell, Horace, theology of, 5, 61; influence on Gladden, 5, 28; influence on the social gospel, 318; *Christian Nurture*, 5

Business ethics, 49, 133, 250; criticism of, 45, 82, 101–102, 189, 305; of Reconstruction period, 11, 24, 32–34, 35; influenced by growth of wealth, 100; an unchristianized area of life, 222; illicit practices due to capitalism, 223; unregenerate nature of, 223; and the ethics of Christ, 255; study of, 266. *See* Capitalism; Christian Ethics; Socialism, etc.

CADMAN, Harry W., 95; quoted, 79; *The Christian Unity of Capital and Labor*, 88

C.A.I.L. *See* Protestant Episcopal Church

Calvin, Calvinism, 15, 26, 27, 125, 185

Capital, socialization of, 176, 180 (*see* Socialism, Socialization); must recognize rights of employees and public, 195

Capitalism, 121; criticism of, 27, 45, 145–146, 174, 180–181, 191, 236, 323–325; and industrial revolution, 11; contrary to Christian ethics, 172, 223; and communism, 196; religious basis of criticism of, 221; cause of competition, 223; frustrating trends toward coöperation, 225; religious life impossible under, 240; cause of poverty, 253; concern of social gospel with, 319. *See* Christian socialism; Socialism

Carr, Edward Ellis, 236, 237

Carter, E. C., 299

Casson, Herbert N., 86–87

Catholics, Catholic Church, 43, 103, 237

Census, socioreligious, 245, 251, 257, *275–278*, 320; early discussion of, 113; importance of, 274; first in the United States, 275; New Haven, 1880, 275; Hartford, 1889, 275; New York, 1897–, 276–278; by Men and Religion Forward Movement, 297

Census, United States, 277

Centralization, governmental, 73. *See* Socialism

Chalmers, Thomas, *The Application of Christianity to the Commercial and Ordinary Affairs of Life*, 6–7; *The Christian and Civic Economy of Large Towns*, 6

Channing, William Ellery, 318

Charity, 108, 137, 245, 275; scientific, 4, 104, 112, 253; in fiction, 148; concern of social gospel for, 319

Chautauqua, 163–164, 165, 263

Chicago Christian Socialist Center, 236

Chicago Civic Federation, 146, 159

Chicago Commons, 157, 169, 188

Chicago Theological Seminary, 138, 157, 167

Chicago, University of, 6, 115, 138, 167, 183, 267–268

Child Development, 316

Child Labor. *See* Labor, Child

Christian Citizenship, 161

The Christian City, 250

Christian Commonwealth Colony, Georgia, *195–197*, 237

Christian Endeavor, United Society of, 161, 263, 267, 303

Christian ethic in history, 3, *63–66*, 92, 273. *See* Apologetics

Christian ethics, 99; concerned with social life, 36; cure for labor problem, 88; solvent of industrial ills, 96; norm for social standards, 106; and the ethical character of religion, 129; definition, 130; versus competition, 138; application of, 139; and Nationalist Movement, 174; application to business, 293; churches urged to study, 294, 295. *See* Christian sociology; "Christian Law"; Golden Rule; Jesus Christ, Teachings of; Stewardship

Christian Labor Union, Boston, 42–49

right social order, 153, 164, 190; as basis of Christian Sociology, 169; and organic view of society, 173; and Christian Socialism, 180, 182; coming in America, 187; and crisis, 193–194; and election of 1896, 195; as practical communism, 196; eternal social ideal, 199; economics of, 199–200; interpretations, 1900–1915, 205; evolutionary nature of, 208; and labor movement, 226; inclusive ideal, 228; Jesus' view of, as fellowship of righteousness, 228; contains revolutionary force of Christianity, 229; divine, 229; teleological, 229; potential, 229–230; not limited to the church, 230–231; and individual salvation, 230; and for which the church exists, 230; humanity organized according to will of God, 230; epitomized in Christ, 230; as practical social program, 235; equated with economic perfection, with coöperative commonwealth, 243; and the socialized state, 254; subject of study, 271; coming of, dependent on social justice, 289; relation to social issues, 298; enlistment in service of, 300; receives meaning from kingdom in heaven, 307; widening concerns of, 307; ethical implications of, 320; progressive realization of, 320

Kingsley, Charles, 157; *Yeast, Alton Locke,* 7, 140

Kingsley House, Pittsburgh, 157

Knights of Labor, 69, *80,* 83, 95, 172, 173, 179

Kutter, Herman, *They Must (Sie Müssen),* 238

LABOR
Cautions to, obligations of, 29, 92, 95, 97, 151, 287, 310, 324

Child, 34, 42, 80, 108, 151, 222, 248, 270, 306; churches should work for betterment of, 247; subject of study, 262, 271, 288, 293, 295; hostile to spirit of Christianity, 285; resolutions on, 285; condemned, 294; church must stand for abolition of, 316

Hours of, 69, 80, 226, 270; less important than economic justice,

248; regulation of, 288; 6-day week, 291, 314–315; 12-hour day and 7-day week disgrace to civilization, 314; Sunday labor, 314; church must stand for 6-day week, 317; study recommended, 315; church must stand for gradual reduction of, 317

Labor Movement, 100, 164; moral nature of, 94, 226, 250–251, 286, 287, 290, 301, 310, 311, 324; forerunner of a Christian social order, 226; ethical and religious nature of, 246; embodies three great Christian principles, 250–251; purposes distinct from union offenses, 284; good outweighs errors, 308–309; ally of the church, 309; furnished leaders by social gospel, 320

Labor Problem, labor and capital, 40, 66, 116, 133, 136, 145, 225, 264, 305, 306; primary social-gospel concern, 24, 49, 54, 67, 78, 80, 117, 204, 256, 300–301, 319; in 1870's, 27–32, 35, 36–37, 38–39, 40–49; cure in Christian ethics, 31; workingmen's clubs, 39; attempts at reform, 40, 41–42, 58; Christian Labor Union, 42–49; Bible on, 44, 46–47; crux of modern problems, 49; *See* Strike of 1877; conditions, 1880–1900, 79–80; social gospel and, 79 ff.; *See* American Federation of Labor, *See* Knights of Labor; criticism of church, 83–86 (*See* Church and labor); church attendance, 84–86; Christian ethics the cure, 88; advances in 1890's, 150 ff.; mediation, 151–152; church organizations on, 150–152; sweatshops, 152; discussed at Chautauqua, 163; primarily an ethical problem, 222; importance, 1900–1915, 245 ff.; concern of denominations in setting up social action agencies: Baptist, 294, Congregational, 286–288, Methodist, 290–291, Presbyterian, 280–283, Protestant Episcopal, 284–286; concern of Federal Council, 306, 307–317

292; revealed through the church, 307; social and individual salvation inseparable, 317; as divine process of redemption, 321; indicated understanding of social controls, 321

Salvation Army, 155

Sanford, Elias B., 154, 303–304

Savage, Minot J., 73, 74, 75, 109–110

Schleiermacher, 220

Schmidt, Nathaniel, 131, 134

Schmucker, Samuel S., 302, 305

Schwab, Laurence H., *The Kingdom of God,* 128–129

Scott, J. E., 172

Scudder, Vida D., 177, 178, 181, 235, 244, 254; *A Listener in Babel,* 145

Security, 105, 225, 227, 311, 317. *See* Labor; Old age; Social justice

Seeley, John R., *Ecce Homo,* 22–23, 32

Sermon on the Mount, 45, 66, 83, 192, 213, 234

Sheldon, Charles M., 141–144; critique of writings, 148, 197, 325; *The Angel and the Demon,* 142; *Born to Serve,* 144; *The Crucifixion of Phillip Strong,* 142; *The Heart of the World,* 144; *In His Steps,* 140, *142–144,* 147, 148; *In His Steps Today,* 143; *Jesus Is Here,* 143; *The Reformer,* 144; *Richard Bruce,* 142; *Robert Hardy's Seven Days,* 142

Sheldon, Walter L., 58

Sin, doctrine of, 75, 220; and the organic view of society, 221; social interpretations of, 231, 269, 273–274, 321–322; and progress, 321

Single tax, 59, 60, 133, 152, 160, 161, 179; anticipated by Jesse H. Jones, 47; inadequacy of, 191–192; studied, 271. *See* Henry George; Land reform

Slavery, 92. *See* Antislavery

Slocum, A. Gaylord, 140

Slums, 145. *See* Cities; Tenements

Small, Albion W., 116, 176, 268

Smiley, James L., *Maud Muller's Ministry,* 145

Smith, G. B., coeditor, *Dictionary of Religion and Ethics,* 227

Smith, Samuel G., *Religion in the Making,* 271–272, 273, 287

Smyth, Newman, 61, 81, 82, 90, 117, 128, 130; *Christian Ethics,* 61, quoted,

128; "Sermons to Workingmen," 82

Social action, Social service, demand for, 139–140; popularized in fiction, 145; industrial, 261; religious social service as a career, 264; programs of, 152, 177, 204, 245, 246; development of techniques by churches, 257; study materials for, 263; programs as recognition of mature social gospel, 275; church as social agency, 278; regional programs, 294; development of denominational agencies, 280–301; Federal Council as, 311–317; programs evaluated, 319

Social Apostolate, 199–200

Social Christianity. *See* Social gospel

Social Creed of the Churches. *See* Federal Council of the Churches of Christ in America

Social Crusade, *199–200,* 235, 237

The Social Crusader, 199, 200

Social Engineering, 260–261

Social ethics, characteristic of liberal religion, 57; discussed at Chautauqua, 163; must be preached, 249; interest of sociologists in, 268 ff.; impotent without social science, 269. *See* Christian ethic in history; Christian ethics; Jesus Christ, Teaching of, etc.

Social Evil. *See* Vice

The Social Forum, 197, 236

Social gospel

  Characteristics: *318–327;* basic importance of labor problem and socialism to, 96–97, 98, 117, 171, 204, 244, 245, 256, 300–301, *318–319;* and the kingdom of God, 127; basis in teaching of Jesus, 205; religious character of, 207, 321; roots in doctrine of man, 213–214; theology for, 220; its contributions to theology, 229, 231, 322; as humanism, 243; importance of problems of cities, 256, 319 (*see* Cities); ally of sociology and reform, 257, 279; relations with social science, 257–279; importance of social scientists' view of religion as progressive force, 272, 274; social contributions, 279; insistence upon social justice, 300–301 (*see*